QUEEN ANNE

by the same author

BLENHEIM PALACE

GARDENER TO QUEEN ANNE

GRINLING GIBBONS

SARAH DUCHESS OF MARLBOROUGH

DAVID GREEN

QUEEN ANNE

CHARLES SCRIBNER'S SONS
NEW YORK

A—8.72(C)
Printed in the United States of America
Library of Congress Catalog Card Number 71–133575
SBN 684–10216–1 (cloth)
SBN 684–12970–1 (paper, SL)

Gratefully dedicated

to

THE TENTH DUKE OF MARLBOROUGH

I am deceived if in history there can be found any period more full of passages which the curious of another age would be glad to know the secret springs of.

Swift, writing of the age of Anne

Contents

Illustrations

Introduction

THIS was no ordinary woman. She might appear so. In fact she was strange as any Stuart and, at least towards the end of her reign, as unfathomable.

Her health was appalling. No other queen has had to be carried to her coronation. None has been less tutored in queenship, nor any more determined to serve well. She loved her country. She loved her Church. She had the strongest possible sense of duty. It was still not enough.

A queen needs to be infinitely wise. Should she not be so, she must rely on wise ministers and for better for worse stand by them. In this Anne failed, and perhaps for no culpable fault. She lacked perception and in spite of a stubborn will she was too easily imposed upon. She lacked too that royal detachment which would have spared her emotional strain; and on top of all this she took rebuffs too personally and was far too easily hurt.

In a queen 'as tough on her throne as Marlborough was on the battlefield', this may seem paradoxical. Yet beneath all those layers of robes and bandages, buried deep in that gross and gout-ridden form, there breathed a human being. In youth she had shown her feelings; as queen she learned to hide them. When at that baleful interview in 1710 she told Sarah 'That will be to myself' the door closed not only on Sarah but on the world. After that it became a guessing-game to discover what was in the Queen's heart; and she deliberately kept them guessing.

Sarah of course was prejudiced but she was not, like Abigail, sly. Little escapes her. Her witness is often the sole witness, and precious for that. When she goes, there is no one of comparable intimacy or comparable skill. Abigail is contemptible, the Duchess of Somerset lofty - and she keeps no journal. George of Denmark dies. Anne is left to confide in priests and doctors; and by a happy chance one of them, Sir David Hamilton, keeps a diary.

Where Sarah leaves off, Hamilton carries on. He is nothing like so good a writer but, if we may believe him, he is confided in; so that what he records is apt to be interesting and at times important. From him alone, for example, we learn that Anne came to regret her dismissal of Godolphin; and that just before she died she felt she must stifle her loathing for Hanover and have the Elector to stay with her in England. That is rich material, and the archives at Blenheim have furnished more. Many of Anne's letters have been published (Miss Curtis Brown's book is invaluable). Many have not and of these not a few are quoted.

Every biography is a jigsaw and for this one the pieces had been widely scattered. Some, in French, were in the Public Record Office; some were at Longleat; some in the British Museum; some in the 165 volumes published by the Historical Manuscripts Commission. Among the more curious were Harley's all but indecipherable memoranda – bundle upon bundle of them – scribbled to himself. Such a puzzle, after two and a half centuries, could never be perfectly reassembled, but it is to be hoped that the picture is now just a little more complete than it was.

Sir Winston Churchill would have Anne a great queen. Dr Johnson found her born for friendship, not for government. Certainly she was not fit to rule when she came to the throne, but she had the Marlboroughs and Godolphin to lean on – 'We four must never part' – and had she kept them her reign might well have been glorious to its end. But Sarah behaved rashly (she earned her dismissal twenty times over) and so made things easier for Harley and Abigail. Godolphin was dismissed. Marlborough was dismissed. Should they have been? No, but . . . Few could have withstood on the one hand that 'teasing' from her Groom of the Stole and on the other the wiles of Harley. Indeed what she found herself up against – pain and loneliness, faction, a heavy conscience – was surely more than enough to daunt most women. At the end – almost out of her mind with worry over the succession – time itself ran out and made nonsense of her decisions.

No, she was not a great queen; nor were all her actions noble. But she was so handicapped - so ill, so bullied, at the last so bewildered and desperate - one would need a heart of stone not to feel for her.

To look back at Anne now is to see that awkward phenomenon a queen of the transition, neither absolute nor powerless. We see her touching for Evil while doubting the Divine Right of Kings; mixing her ministry with Whigs and Tories - and appalled to see them fly at each other's throats.

Sir Winston Churchill sees Anne's reign as the supreme manifestation of British genius. His fine study of his ancestor - gloriously written, gloriously prejudiced - wears a nimbus of triumph with the banners of Britain streaming as never before. Indeed, so thoroughly and so well has he dealt with those campaigns that for a biographer of Anne to attempt to describe them again would be time-wasting futility.

Marlborough's genius Anne recognised, even though she was later to discard it. Swift she almost certainly regarded as a turbulent priest and writer of lampoons - no more; and since in her time he wrote the *Windsor Prophecy*, and *Gulliver* long after it, that is understandable.

Of the arts in Anne's reign it could be said that some of them at least shone well without her. She was no reader and, with a few exceptions, not much of a builder. Swift and Pope, Addison, Steele and Prior wrote without royal encouragement. As with building, so with education: the intention was there - 'The Queen being very ready', as Bolingbroke said in one of the last letters he wrote for her, 'to encourage learning and the compiling of useful histories' - but it seldom went further. Wren was finishing St Paul's; Vanbrugh and Hawksmoor designed great houses to be enriched with carving by Grinling Gibbons, frescoes by Verrio, clocks by Tompion and wainscot, furniture and silver of the same excellence. There never were finer craftsmen. Wherever one looks - at Blenheim, Chatsworth, Petworth, in churches and universities - the workmanship is superb. In Kneller, Dahl and Closterman as Court painters Anne, sandwiched between Van Dyck and Reynolds, was less fortunate; though she might have done worse. In music she shared Handel with Hanover and, at the risk of offending the Elector, she was given the lion's share.

Anne's nature was to choose the via media, to prefer the status quo.

She begged to be rescued from 'the merciless men of both parties', the extremists. The exuberance of these fanatics terrified her. It was beyond her to realise that the glory of her reign and of her country depended on the conviction and brilliance of a handful of eager men. Hers was not, as used to be supposed, petticoat government. She had considerable power; yet time and again she had to capitulate. Nor were her favourites the viceroys they were thought to be. At a time when Shrewsbury was saying that Abigail could if she chose make the Queen stand on her head, Abigail's letters to Harley were cries of frustration - she could not even get leave from Anne to see him.

Sarah might have had more power if she had shown more charity; and there surely lay her cardinal sin, in embittering one who might otherwise have seen out her reign as a benevolent queen and a warm-hearted woman. But patience wore thin (to the quick the slow can be unendurable), and then there was bullying and timidity and doubt - 'Maybe it is our brother' - Should she be there at all? The long nightmare of the succession followed: the quite impossible choice between Catholic stepbrother and the loathsome Lutheran at Hanover. This, with infirmity and pain, was too much for anyone to bear. Towards the end she seems reluctant to peer into her own conscience. Only her indomitable Stuart will and her faith can have kept her sane. She lacked resolution. One could not say she lacked courage.

Anne's outlook was insular. England was everything to her; as Queen she never travelled. She lived in small, stuffy closets. Europe? Marlborough's battleground. America? The place one sent missionaries to, and convicts; and useful for trade. She was told of other countries - of Spain, of Scotland and Ireland - as she was told about politics when she forced herself as she constantly did to attend Council; but she much preferred to hear the talk of the town. Today, as a goodhumoured woman she would probably have enjoyed pottering in her garden and giving (she liked giving) her neighbours plants. As it was she was not so much unintelligent as less brilliant than those about her. Compared with Somers, Shrewsbury and Godolphin she lacked personality, she lacked force. She was no wit but, as Sir Winston has said, she was remarkably English and she felt for her people.

Semper eadem - she was determined never to change and of course she did change. No one as ignorant and impressionable as she was in 1702 could have helped changing. Sarah nearly made a Whig of her. Harley switched her back to Tory. He went further and 'learned her to equivocate', so that the smokescreen about her, as about him, grew ever denser. Her contemporaries were, as they were meant to be, baffled; and now as one tries to penetrate it one finds glimmers flickering about ambiguities: nothing is black or white, only grey or camouflage. Speeches of course were written for her, but so were letters. Some of the very words she used - 'amuse', 'crazy', 'enthusiast', 'an ill man' - have changed their meanings and sometimes their spelling and pronunciation, e.g. 'You will find that her tiers were not very sinceare'.

But perhaps we search for truth when the answer lies in half-truth, for certainty in a world of doubt and compromise, of (as Lord Cowper said) 'trick and contradiction and shuffle'. A pious queen sets out with the highest ideals and then, gradually and inevitably, expediency sets in. Conscience gnaws, so does pain. Ministers and favourites tease and bully. It is all too much . . .

As a study in psychology - the queen with a conscience - Anne surely deserves a latter-day Shakespeare. For an ordinary writer to try to bring alive one so incontrovertibly dead is to ask for trouble; and indeed as Boyer says, 'How is it possible for an Impartial Analyst to escape the Lash of Prostituted Pens?' Even so there are moments when we seem to catch the ring of Anne's voice - 'Oh fie, there is no such thing. What, do they think I'm a child and to be imposed upon?' 'Why for God's sake must I who have no interest, no end, no thought but for the good of my country be made so miserable as to be brought into the power of one set of men?' - and at those times one can surely feel with her and for her, whoever it may have been, herself or her ministers, who finally let her down. One must not expect too much –

> Only a pure and virtuous soul
> Like season'd timber never gives,
> But though the whole world turn to coal
> Then chiefly lives.

Sarah in her musings on the Queen says interesting things. Anne, she told Lord Cowper, was 'neither good nor bad but as put into'. And again - 'Whether her memory will be celebrated by posterity with blessings or curses, time will show'. Even in Sarah's lifetime the curses (they were mostly her own) had died and she herself had mellowed. Today the blessings predominate.

CHAPTER ONE

AQUARIUS

1675 - 1680

'GENERALLY speaking', wrote Swift, 'the times which afford most plentiful matter for story are those wherein a man would least choose to live'.

Anne Stuart was born at St James's Palace in the year of the Plague, 1665, on February 6th (under the sign of Aquarius), at twenty-one minutes before midnight. Her father was James Duke of York, afterwards James II, her mother Anne Hyde. Anne was delicate. The chances against her surviving at all were eight to two: of the eight children eventually born to James and his first duchess, all but Anne and her sister Mary (three years older than Anne) languished and died. It was for those times the usual pattern. John Churchill had eleven brothers and sisters, five lived. With Anne herself as a mother the record would be still sadder.

Even so, with luck enough to survive birth and the Plague (which she escaped) and then to make some headway there were for Anne compensations. James, if his memoirs are to be believed, was an indulgent father. Anne's mother, though not beautiful, had wit; and in the background, besides sister and playmates, there was always some homely person like Mrs Danvers to act as rocker, comforter and protector, from the first breath and cry to the very last.

One cannot blame servants for not keeping diaries or journals. Occasionally one of them did; but not Danvers, who witnessed most of all. James briskly jotted down time and date of birth; and if we turn to his wife's diary we find that she left off keeping it when she was fifteen:

> I was born the 12th day of March in the year of our Lord 1637 at Cranbourne Lodge near Windsor and lived in my own country till I was 12 years old, having in that time seen the ruin both of church and state and the murthering of my King . . .[1]

After the Restoration of Charles II in 1660, on January 30th each year everyone in St James's Palace, children included, 'secluded themselves in mourning and sorrow', in memory of Charles I's execution in 1649. Much of the interregnum was spent by Anne Hyde with her family in Antwerp and Breda. She was appointed maid of honour to the Princess of Orange and was attending her on a visit to Paris in 1656 when she first met James. Three years later, at Breda, he made a contract to marry her; and on September 3rd 1660 in London, secretly and late at night he fulfilled that contract. He then begged his brother Charles II to be allowed to own the marriage publicly. Charles, then unmarried, consulted the bride's father, Sir Edward Hyde. The result was an explosion. Hyde pronounced his daughter a strumpet. She ought, he told Charles, to be sent to the Tower and he himself would vote for her execution... In a month or so the storm blew itself out. A boy was born on October 22nd and at Christmas the marriage was publicly owned. If the son had lived or if James had proved a tolerably good husband all might have been well; but the child died and James embarked on his dogged round of the maids of honour, his first favourite being John Churchill's sister Arabella. As Mrs Manley put it, after Churchill had become Duke of Marlborough, 'King James honoured his Grace's family so far as to mingle his own royal blood with it'. Of this liaison one excellent result was Arabella's son the Duke of Berwick who, in the fashion of the day, opposed Marlborough, his uncle, and remained his friend. Royal mistresses – James's, Charles's, Louis XIV's – were honoured. Anne Hyde, on the other hand, though 'of a certain innate grandeur', was regarded as a parvenue, damned less for herself than for her family who, though they might produce a Lord Chancellor, were not counted good enough to presume to marry a daughter to a prince of the blood royal.

In the Lely of Anne Hyde which still hangs in Kensington Palace one sees a large-featured young woman, her dark hair in ringlets, in a low-cut gown. The eyes are arresting. The bust is a Lely bust. But the hands and arms are beautiful; and these were inherited by Anne who, after looking at this portrait, told Sarah Churchill that, since her mother had died when she was six, she could not herself remember her features. In the Lely at Windsor (See page 25), completed by Gennari after the death of Anne Hyde, the pose of the Duchess is much the same; but here she caresses a strangely old-looking Anne, while Mary proffers a garland and James as Lord High Admiral (he had beaten the Dutch off Lowestoft in the year of Anne's birth) points with elegant hand to a globe.

As time went on, Windsor was to become the place Anne as Queen most liked to live at; though even there she preferred her Little House to the Castle. Wherever she was, at Windsor, Kensington or St James's, she chose small rooms and closets, preferring safety and stuffiness to the uneasiness and draughts of staterooms. Swift complained of the stifling atmosphere when closeted with the Mashams. Once within doors these were not people who liked fresh air. And indeed as one walks through St James's Palace today it is hard to imagine that those rooms were ever anything but gloomy. True, the building was much larger than it now is (thirty rooms were destroyed in the fire of 1809), but even in Anne's day far too many windows looked into courtyards and there was but one sunny range, on the south front.

There on that garden front, soon after the Restoration, the Yorks spruced up the rooms Charles had generously given them; and since Cromwell had used the palace as a barracks, much needed to be done. The Duchess's bedroom was enriched with carving and gilding and, next to it, her drawingroom was given new windows to allow her to step out on to a balcony. In a painting of 1690 (See page 24), misty though it is (the fog over St James's and Whitehall was constantly complained of), one plainly sees this balcony and, in a fair summer, a pleasant place it must have been. As one sat there the eye, ignoring the terrace-wall beyond the guard of honour of orange trees, dwelt on the strollers in the lime-avenue called the Mall, on Charles's canal and duck-decoys beyond it and so to a horizon of towers and rooftops: Westminster Hall and the Abbey and, east of those, the Tilt Yard, Cockpit, Holbein Gate, Banqueting House and the castellated parapets of the palace of Whitehall.

On a fine weekday at least a royal child might sit there without fear of mob-curiosity, since only 'persons of quality' then strolled in the park. On Sundays it was different, but then there was chapel, and after that one played in the garden, not the one in the painting but another, westward across the lane, where there were fountains and long walks between espalier fruit trees (See page 232). Beyond the espaliers (near what is now Trafalgar Square) there was a formal wilderness of yew and holly and there Anne and Mrs Danvers, sometimes with other children, could play for hours or just sit in the sun, tranquil and invisible.

Anne's infancy one would like to suppose happy, as most probably it was until a weakness in her eyes brought trouble. Her sister Mary suffered from 'sore eyes', but with Anne it took the form of a 'defluxion': her eyes watered and went on watering, and for this it was decided to consult an oculist in France. When she saw him she cannot have been more than four, since she stayed at Colombes near Paris with Charles I's widow Henrietta Maria, who died in August 1669. On the death of her grandmother Anne moved to her aunt's, the Duchess of Orleans. While there, an unknown artist painted her playing with a dog (See page 24), a pose which could not in fact have been held for more than two seconds. From this dark canvas still hanging at St James's Anne, with large, serious, light grey eyes (without sign of weakness) looks intelligently. She is of course babyish - fat-cheeked, fat-chinned, full-lipped - but there is too a hint of caution and of self-possession. She wears an embroidered robe and, on the back of fair-auburn curls, a beribboned bonnet. While she holds the dog, a King Charles spaniel, the painter not very successfully tries to do justice to her hands.

When Anne returned to England in 1670 her eyes were said to be very much better, but she was not cured. Every now and then throughout her life the trouble recurred as a serious handicap. It meant that by daylight or candle-light she was seldom able to read a book; while psychologically the defect made her self-conscious, and embarrassed her only less than blushing, a slight thing which caused her torment.

Anecdotes of children, royal or otherwise, bring yawns, and of the many that may once have been treasured about Anne and her sister mercifully but one survives and that, trivial in itself, gives the first helpful hint of the character that was to be Queen Anne's:

When they were children and walking in the park together they started a dispute between them whether something at a great distance was a man or a tree, her sister [Mary] being of the former opinion and she [Anne] of the latter. And when they came so near that both must be convinced it was a man, the late Queen [Mary] said, 'Now, sister, are you satisfied what it is?' But Lady Anne turned away after she saw what it was, persisting still in what she had once declared, and cried, 'No, sister, 'tis a tree!'[2]

At that age and at that seeming remoteness to the throne (with Charles, James, Mary and all their likely progeny before her) such manifestations of Stuart obstinacy were unimportant. Anne as a child was lovable and warmhearted, fond of her tall sister (if at times a little envious of her beauty), and of her parents; and then when she was six her mother, delivered of a child a month before, died of cancer. Anne Hyde had written the previous summer to her father (by then Earl of Clarendon) to tell him of her conversion to Rome; and now on her deathbed, in answer to an Anglican bishop who 'hoped she continued still in the truth' she said, 'What is truth? Truth . . . truth . . . truth . . .' and so died.

At Richmond the lease of what was left of the Tudor palace had been granted by Charles II to Colonel Edward Villiers and his wife Lady Frances who, as a reliable Protestant, had been chosen by Charles to be governess to his nieces. And so to Richmond they now went in the company of the six Villiers daughters and their brother Edward, who was to become Earl of Jersey; but of him they saw little. Except for clergymen theirs was a feminine world. The Villiers girls, though not popular with Anne, were lively and interesting. Barbara was to become Mrs Berkeley and later Lady Fitzharding; her sister Anne, Countess of Portland, and a third sister Elizabeth, Countess of Orkney. Another friend of Anne's who was often there, Miss Cornwallis, is said to have introduced her to Sarah Jennings. This first meeting is believed to have happened soon after Anne's return from France, when she was five and Sarah ten. 'We had used to play together when she was a child', Sarah remembered, 'and she even then expressed a particular fondness for me. This inclination increased with our years. I was often at Court and the Princess always honoured me with her conversation and confidence. In all her parties for amusement I was sure to be one'.[3] To which her descendant Sir Winston Churchill adds: 'There was a romantic, indeed perfervid element in Anne's love for Sarah, to which the elder girl responded warmly several years before she realised the worldly importance of such a relationship'.[4]

If as Sarah says a friend was what Anne most coveted (a friend wholly hers, for in this she could be possessive), here in Sarah Jennings was the very person she wanted, a friend with all the sparkle she lacked, cool-headed, quick-thinking, and with such radiant beauty that when she played with them even the Villiers children looked ordinary.

How Sarah's widowed mother, whose home was at St Albans, came by her Court lodgings at St James's has never been satisfactorily explained. There must surely have been some better reason than that they were 'to sanctuary her from debt'. Rightly or wrongly Mrs Jennings had the reputation of a sorceress and not a revered one. However it was, she stayed long enough at Court (before Sarah ousted her) to see two of her daughters, Frances and Sarah, maids of honour to the new Duchess of York, Mary Beatrice, whom James had married in 1673 (See page 40). James was then forty; and his bride fifteen. She came from Modena, where she had meant to become a nun. She was beautiful and chose her attendants for their beauty.

James had for some time given serious thought to a change of religion and on Jesuit advice had stopped communicating in the Church of England. This of course was noticed, and the marriage was regarded as one more step towards Roman Catholicism, to which Charles by the Treaty of Dover made with Louis XIV in 1670 was already secretly committed. 'I knew that King Charles and King James were with remarkable titles taking money of the King of France to betray their own honour and country', wrote Sarah to Mrs Godolphin, 'and the last of these kings sent a man into prison for saying that he was a Roman Catholic, who I saw go twice a day to mass'.[5] Years later Bolingbroke chose to blame it all on the exile of the royal family during the Commonwealth when, as he says, 'the two brothers Charles and James became infected with popery to such degrees as their different characters admitted of. Charles had parts and his good understanding served as an antidote to repel the poison.

James, the simplest man of his time, drank off the whole chalice and . . . drunk with superstitious and even enthusiastic zeal ran headlong into his own ruin whilst he endeavoured to precipitate ours'.[6] James denied this, saying that his first doubts were sown by an Anglican bishop who had sent him a tract to read in Flanders. The intention was to instil into him a healthy horror of Rome, but it had 'quite the contrary effect'.[7]

In 1673, the year of his second marriage, James found himself forced by the Test Act, which excluded Roman Catholics (and dissenters) from office under the Crown, to resign his office of Lord High Admiral; and as pressure increased it made James, as he put it, 'a sort of vagabond about the world'. The one ever predictable thing about religious persecution is that it automatically creates martyrs. Had James not made it for himself ad nauseam it would not be difficult to make at least a tolerably good case for his wearing a martyr's crown. After all, the opposing case was founded on nothing more substantial than terror, superstitious terror of sin and Hell fire, and of the long-dead fires of Smithfield, well stoked by Fox's Book of Martyrs which, with the Bible, had somehow found its way into every house. The main trouble with James was that, compared with Charles, he was a fool. Of Charles II it has been said that his profession was kingship. This could not have been said of James, he was too bigoted and he underestimated the skill needed for the job. England in any case was not constituted to function under a Roman Catholic monarch; but James, as Charles knew, was inadequate, and he was a bore. Years later his friends at St Germain were to find his escape-story soporific. 'As one listens to him', sighed Madame de Lafayette, 'one realises why he is here'.[8]

It was Charles's good understanding which made him insist on the Protestant upbringing of James's children; though his own attitude to all sects and creeds was languid. 'His natural laziness', wrote Buckingham, 'confirmed him in an equal mistrust of them all, for fear he should be troubled with examining which religion was best'.[9] No monarch was ever more relaxed; and yet at the same time he was not foolish enough to imagine that because he had had to beg from Louis, his posterity and the future of his country could forever be committed to that King and that religion. This was why Anne and Mary found themselves as children constantly in the company of Anglican bishops and chaplains whose business it was to see that both princesses were soundly saved. Nothing in Anne's youth was more important than this. When she came to the throne she would change in many ways but never in her devotion to the Church of England.

At every age Anne was impressionable and teachable, though by no means always tractable. Once a lesson was learned it was learned for life. In July 1675, with the backing of Lord Danby, Henry Compton then Bishop of Oxford was appointed Dean of the Chapels Royal and Preceptor to the Princesses Mary and Anne. By December he was Bishop of London and it was then that he bravely told James that his elder daughter Mary was ready for confirmation. James was displeased. His daughters' Protestant upbringing, he said, was much against his will. 'The reason why he had not endeavoured to have them instructed in his own religion was because he knew if he should have attempted it they would have immediately been quite taken from him'.[10] He referred Compton to the King, who forthwith commanded the Bishop to confirm Mary. Anne is said to have been confirmed on the same day as her sister (January 23rd 1676), but in view of their chaplain's (Dr Lake's)* statement that Anne made her first Communion on Easter Day (March 31st) 1678, this seems most unlikely. 'Her Highness', he adds, 'was not (through negligence) instructed how much of the wine to drink, but drank of it twice or thrice, whereat I was much concerned lest the Duke should have notice of it'.[11] Sarah may have been right in her poor opinion of Anne's instructors. Compton, a strong anti-Catholic, had his eye on the see of Canterbury and was lastingly hurt when the archbishopric was given to Sancroft on December 30th 1677. It was he who banished from Court Anne's intimate friend and kinswoman Cicely Cornwallis, the same who had introduced Sarah. Miss Cornwallis was a Roman Catholic. Sarah mockingly calls her Anne's first favourite; 'and the fondness of the young lady to her was very great and passionate but . . . the Duchess of York accidentally finding upon her daughter's table a letter to her favourite, unsealed up, read it and

* Edward Lake DD (1641–1704), appointed chaplain and tutor to Anne and Mary c. 1670. Wrote *Officium Eucharisticum: A Preparatory Service To a Devout and Worthy Reception of the Lord's Supper* (1673).

The Princess Anne of Denmark aged four painted in France by an unknown artist

St. James's Palace *c.* 1690, the garden front

Lely and Gennari: James Duke of York, Anne Hyde Duchess of York, The Princesses Mary and Anne

was very much displeased at the passionate expressions with which it was filled'. She was forgotten, adds Sarah, within a fortnight and years later reluctantly granted a small pension. 'Thus ended', she says, 'a great friendship of three or four years' standing, in which time Lady Anne had written, it was believed, above a thousand letters full of the most violent professions of everlasting kindness'. But these friendships of Anne's, she says, were no more than entertainments to pass the time. 'She still kept her heart untouched and unpossessed by anyone but herself'.[12]

This is unkind and almost certainly exaggerated. In the art of writing passionate letters to friends, whether as an antidote to boredom or for some better reason, Anne compared with her elder sister was a plodder. This is clearly brought out in their childish letters to Frances Apsley,* who was nine years older than Mary and twelve years older than Anne. In those charmingly ridiculous letters they play at husbands and wives and continue to do so after Mary and Frances have both been married. They are extraordinary letters but it would be rash to make too much of them. As a doctor has put it, 'Unless and until we all turn Freudian in our views, we shall continue to recognise that close associations and intimacies are possible between women without implying any homosexual basis at all . . . and I think this was so in the case of Anne'.[13] Her letters to Frances Apsley (signed 'Ziphares', Frances is 'Semandra'), though fervent, are not to be compared with her later and longer batch to Sarah.

Long days in female company, long, candle-lit evenings at cards in stuffy closets could be boring. There was music, there was dancing – 'She had an excellent ear, which qualified her for a true dancer and gave her a great relish for music, insomuch that she was accounted one of the best performers on the guitar'.[14] There were lessons in French and lessons in elocution (these last, by the King's command, given by an actress, Mrs Barry) and lessons in divinity; but no lessons in history, no lessons in life, nor ever the least attempt to train a princess in how to rule as a queen.

'I never yet saw a lady that was the better for her learning', Arthur

* Frances Apsley, primarily Mary's friend, was the daughter of Sir Allen Apsley, Treasurer of the Household to Charles II and James II. She married Sir Benjamin Bathurst.

Maynwaring told Sarah, 'and very seldom a man'.[15] Yet some felt differently and of those Bishop Burnet* held the strongest possible views. After blaming 'the irregularities of the gentry' on 'the ill methods of schools and colleges' he continued, 'The breeding young women to vanity, dressing and a false appearance of wit and behaviour, without proper work or a due measure of knowledge and a serious sense of religion is the source of the corruption of that sex. Something like monasteries [sic] without vows would be a glorious design and might be so set on foot as to be the honour of a Queen on the throne; but', he wisely concludes, 'I will pursue this no further'.[16]

Burnet was then writing when Anne was Queen, but while she was a princess the same applied; and indeed the nest of young queens in which she found herself must often have seemed like a convent without vows. It was no wonder at all that they took to playing endless games of cards. 'Gaming', declared Burnet, 'is a waste of time, that rises out of idleness and is kept up by covetousness. Those who can think, read or write to any purpose and those who understand what conversation and friendship are will not want such a help to wear out the day'.[17] But that – how to redeem the time – was the problem; and as Anne herself once wrote, with characteristic spelling, 'I am soe tyerd with this long day'. If she had been good at cards that would have been something, but whether it were whist or ombre or basset Anne frequently lost (James paid her debts); and certainly it is no wonder that ombre, in which one needs to look three moves ahead, never became her favourite game.

'Your Majesty', Sarah told her bluntly, many years later, 'has had the misfortune to be misinformed in general things even from twelve years old'.[18] It may have been so; and to try to correct it, intensive cramming from Sarah followed. Anne is said to have lacked depth, but she was no fool. She was not intellectual, not well read, not far-sighted. As Queen, surrounded by men with first-class brains – Somers, Marlborough, Godolphin . . . – her own intelligence, which was average and on occasion above it, looked duller than it was.

When Anne was twelve her chaplain wrote in his diary:

* Burnet, Gilbert (1643–1715), Bishop of Salisbury, wrote the *History of his own Time*.

> 1677, November 4. This week hath produced four memorable things: the Lady Mary and the Prince of Orange were married on the Sunday; the Duchess was brought to bed of the Duke of Cambridge on the Wednesday; the Archbishop of Canterbury [Sheldon] died on the Friday, and on the same day Lady Anne appeared to have the smallpox.[19]

Of these events perhaps the saddest was the birth of yet another shortlived baby (he died next month of smallpox) to Mary of Modena, who looked as though she was going to be no luckier in childbirth – she is known to have miscarried four times – than had been Anne Hyde.

The William and Mary match (William was twenty-seven, Mary fifteen) had been planned and rushed through by Charles II and Danby. Lake records that when, a fortnight before the wedding, James broke the news to Mary she wept all that afternoon and the following day. Compton married them in Mary's bedroom at nine in the evening on William's birthday, November 4th. The bridegroom's present was £40,000's worth of jewels. Louis XIV, says Burnet, received the news of the wedding 'as he would have done the loss of an army'.[20] As for James, he could hardly have been expected to welcome for son-in-law a Dutch Calvinist; but one had to be realistic and he made the best of it, 'assuring them that however he was represented abroad he did herein and would in all his actions aim at the security and peace of the kingdom and would never hinder but that his children should be educated in the religion of the Church of England; which caused general joy in the Council'.[21]

Anne was too ill to go to her sister's wedding. Dr Lake, forbidden to attend her in case of spreading the infection, told Compton that Anne's nurse was 'a very busy zealous Roman Catholic' who might upset her if left in sole charge. Lake was then allowed in. Here is his entry for November 12th:

> The spots appeared very many and her Highness somewhat giddy and very much disordered. She requested me not to leave her but come often to her; recommended me to her foster sister, that I would take care to instruct her in the Protestant religion . . . (November 13 and 14). Her Highness continued very ill.[22]

It was not for some days, when Anne was out of danger, that she was allowed to know that Mary had left for Holland with William. Smallpox was so common, it was considered lucky for a child to have it in mild form and, as Anne did, to throw it off with her face unmarked. The one tragic thing about it was that her governess, Lady Frances Villiers, caught the disease and died of it just as Anne was recovering.

The new governess, Anne's aunt Lady Clarendon, was not popular. She 'looked like a madwoman and talked like a scholar, which the Princess thought agreed very well together. She was very passionate, but they called her a good woman, I suppose', says Sarah, 'because her lord made a great rout with prayers; but she never did anything in her office that looked as if she had common sense'.[23] In time she could be got rid of, but that was not to be hurried.

As Anne entered her teens she began to travel; and from then on this – to Holland and what is now Belgium, and later to Scotland – would, apart from short trips in England, be all the travelling she would ever do. England was to be her world. In September 1678 Titus Oates with his Popish Plot was so successful in stirring up anti-Catholic feeling that thirty-four Roman Catholics were executed and suspicion began to drift towards the Yorks. In October Anne was taken by her stepmother to see Mary in Holland. This was a brief visit. Their travels began in earnest the following March when Charles made it clear to James that he would do well to go abroad. They would all then have embarked for the Hague, but at the last minute Charles forbade Anne to go; so she stayed behind with her half-sister Isabella. At the end of August they were allowed to join their parents in Brussels and from there Anne wrote to Frances Apsley:

> . . . The park here is very pretty but not so fine as ours at St James's . . . All the fine churches and monastries you know I must not see . . . but those things which I must needs see, as their images which are in every shop and corner of the street, the more I see of those fooleries and the more I hear of that religion the more I dislike it.[24]

Compton and Lake had kindled the Protestant fire. Now Shaftesbury (who backed Monmouth), Oates and others blew up the coals. Oates was soon found to be a liar. Far more substantial and disturbing was the discovery that Coleman, James's secretary, had written to Louis XIV's confessor, giving him cause to hope for the imminent conversion to Roman Catholicism of the three kingdoms. Suspicion centred upon James and there was talk of excluding him from the throne of England. He was to be banished 500 miles from Britain; his daughter Mary was to be made Regent during his life and if she died childless or left children under age, Anne was to be Regent. Any son of James would be raised as a Protestant . . .[25] and so on. The Exclusion Bill eventually came to nothing (in 1680 it passed the Commons but not the Lords). In the meantime Charles forestalled the possibility of his brother's enforced exile by sending him, in October 1679, to Scotland as Lord High Commissioner. Anne set out as though to go with him, but at Hatfield turned back.

At St James's the absence of her father and stepmother could not trouble Anne, provided she might often count upon the company of Sarah. Their religion was not hers and she had begun to mistrust the influence of Mary of Modena on James. Sarah of course was as down-to-earth about religion as she was about everything else. 'I believe', Anne told Mary, 'there is nobody in the world has better notions of religion than she has. It is true she is not so strict as some are, nor does not keep such a bustle with religion; which I confess I think is never the worse, for one sees so many saints turn devils, that if one be a good Christian, the less show one makes it is the better'.[26]

Sarah Jennings was now Sarah Churchill. Candid about some things, reticent about others, Sarah never reveals the date of her secret wedding, now believed to have been late in 1678 or early in 1679. John Churchill, says Boyer, was 'a youth of most beautiful form and graceful aspect, and being one of the pages of honour to the Duke of York, early attracted the eyes of the whole Court, kindled the wishes of even the most insensible of the fair sex and even rivalled King Charles II in his tenderest affection'.[27] His theft of the Duchess of Cleveland from Charles was indeed a measure of his charm and audacity. The affair lasted three years and was so notorious (after all, she was a Villiers) that, understandably, Sarah was in no haste to capitulate when Churchill, ten years her senior, turned to court her. Nor did it help him that his sister Arabella was one of the mistresses of James II. Sarah, moving warily through the Court of

Charles II, had surprisingly puritanical views. But the charm of the man only faintly comes through to us. Kneller and Closterman painted him (See page 40), others sculpted him in lead and in marble: the fire is missing. The features, good and symmetrical as the wig, tell us nothing, which perhaps is what the sitter intended. Even Sarah as his wife says little more than that he was handsome as an angel and carelessly dressed. With perhaps one exception it is all on the surface. That is when Bishop Hare, who had been his army-chaplain, reminds his widow of that 'inimitable sweetness' in his behaviour, 'not only easy to himself and delightful to others but what he abundantly found his account in'.[28]

Anne dreaded change, but she felt absolutely certain – and that was the main thing – that nothing in the world could ever change her friendship with Sarah. Always provided that, as she begged, she could count on the second place in Sarah's heart, she could never be the last. She would content herself with that 'little corner' still unoccupied, as she hoped, by Sarah's husband.[29]

CHAPTER TWO

REVOLUTION

1680 - 1688

IN the National Portrait Gallery a contemporary engraving of the Princess Anne shows her as seen or imagined by an unknown Frenchman (See page 56). Seated on a sofa, legs crossed beneath a very full skirt, she is dressed *au dernier cri*, from high headdress to painfully pointed shoes. There is lace and a froufrou of satin and rich embroidery, and from the low-cut bosom a cascade of bows. At the neck, pigeon's-egg pearls and on the back of the head a lace cap – the *tour* or *cornette* – with a foot of wired lace towering above the kiss-curled forehead.* The waist is smaller, the face prettier than in fact they were. High on her cheek she sports, as she often did, a patch. She looks pleased and pleasing. Indeed only that gesture, as with a long-gloved hand she raises a closed fan to her mouth, might seem to portend grimmer moments. 'When her fan went up to her mouth', says Sir Keith Feiling, writing of her as Queen, 'her mind had closed with a snap'.[1]

The two Mary's – Anne's sister and Mary of Modena – had both married at fifteen. By 1680 rumour had married off Anne several times – to the Duke of Florence, to the Dauphin of France – and now at Christmas to George Electoral Prince of Hanover. 'There was some discourse', recalls Coke, 'that he came on purpose to see the Lady Anne, but that not liking her person he left the kingdom without making any motion to the King or Duke of York for their consent to marry her . . . and though many affirmed that the lady to her dying day had an aversion to him, in particular for the supposed slight put upon her, perhaps there was nothing at all in this courting story, seeing [that] that prince tarried in England

*'There is not so variable a thing in nature as a lady's head-dress . . . About ten years ago it shot up to a very great height, insomuch that the female part of our species were much taller than the men'. Addison: *Spectator*, 22 June 1711.

from the 16th of December to the 11th of March following'.[2]

It made things no better when the grounds of the slight were alleged to be the ignoble lineage of the Hydes. Anne was easily and lastingly offended; although in this instance had she lived to see George's mistresses, she might not have taken it quite so deeply to heart. She would not, as his Queen was, have been imprisoned for adultery; but she still might not have left an heir.

In March, when George of Hanover left England, Anne's half-sister Isabella, in her fifth year, died. James and Mary were still in Scotland and there in July, after a five-day journey, Anne joined them. There she rode every day, often with her young stepmother. She wrote to Semandra (Frances Apsley) and asked for the Gazette. John Churchill was in attendance on James while Sarah stayed in London in the Jermyn Street lodgings. Their first child Harriet, who did not live, was born in October 1679; their second, Henrietta (also called Harriet) on July 19th, 1681.

In March 1682 James, sailing to Scotland to bring his household home, was shipwrecked in the *Gloucester:*

> . . . at least a hundred were lost . . . but his Royal Highness, as soon as they despaired of saving the frigate, got into his shallop & from thence went aboard the yacht; on which occasion such was the modesty & respect of those who attended him, many whereof were persons of quality as the Earls of Perth, Middleton etc., that no one whatever offered to go into it but whom his Highness pleased to call himself, which was only Mr Churchill & one or two more; but other boats coming to their rescue, most of the persons of quality & his Royal Highness's servants got off also.[3]

After a short stay James returned to London with Mary Beatrice, who was pregnant, and Anne. They travelled, very uncomfortably, by sea. In December Churchill was made Baron Churchill of Aymouth (a Scots peerage, to be anglicised to 'of Sandridge' on James's accession). No further excitement happened till the following summer when Lord Mulgrave* made what was called a brisk attempt

* John Sheffield 3rd Earl of Mulgrave (1648–1721), Groom of the Bedchamber to Charles II, became Marquis of Normanby and in 1703 Duke of Buckingham. His third wife ('the Princess') was the daughter of James II's mistress Catherine Sedley.

on the Princess Anne. Some said he had sent songs and letters, others that he had bribed Anne's governess; and some again, according to John Verney, would have 'his crime only ogling'.[4] Mulgrave himself denied that he had even written, but he was not believed. James had him dismissed the Court and sent to Tangier. Anne did not forget him. She could be lastingly hurt, and lastingly charmed. He would have his reward.

From Newmarket the following March Anne wrote to Frances Apsley, now Lady Bathurst: 'This place affords no news but of races and cockmatches, which you don't care for . . . I shall now be very quickly with you for the Duchess intends to go tomorrow sevenight. I can say no more at this time to my dear Semandra but that she shall ever find me the same I ever was'.[5] Had they kept to this plan, Charles and James and perhaps others with them were, it was said, to have been killed by the Rye House plotters. As it was, a fire which destroyed much of Newmarket caused them to set out for London three days earlier. Not everyone even then believed in the plot (informers were too common), but trials followed, Lord Russell was executed, Monmouth pardoned, and the Earl of Essex cut his own throat in the Tower.

No time could better have suited Sunderland* for secretly contriving Anne's marriage. The first thing was to make sure that no violent objection would be made to it by Louis XIV. Protests from James or from William could be overruled or ignored. After that the Danish envoy might be encouraged to make proposals to Charles II. In April 1683 he did. They were accepted and in May the engagement was announced. And so it was that 'a match that could have been of the greatest dynastic significance was huddled through in the most underhand manner'.[6]

On June 4th, before Prince George's arrival, Anne wrote reassuringly to Frances Bathurst, '. . . do not have so ill opinions of your Ziphares, for though he changes his condition yet nothing shall ever alter him from being the same to his dear Semandra that he ever was'.[7]

'He is a very comely person', wrote someone who saw Prince George arrive at Whitehall, 'fair hair, a few pock holes in his visage,

* Robert 2nd Earl of Sunderland (1641–1702).

but of very decent & graceful behaviour. The King & the Duke are very much pleased with him . . . Tomorrow Walcot, Rowse & Hone, three of the traitors that conspired the King's death, are to be hung, drawn & quartered, and the next day my Lord Russell is to be beheaded in Lincolns Inn Fields'.[8]

'Those that are resolved to like nothing the Court does', adds the Duke of Ormonde, 'give out that it is a French match & contrived to carry on that interest . . . None of them can deny but that it is time the lady should be married & that it is fit she should have a Protestant, and where to find one so readily they that mislike this match cannot tell'.[9]

Protestant princes were indeed hard to come by. William was a Calvinist, George a Lutheran. He was thirty, blond, presentable, 'a simple, normal man without envy or ambition and disposed by remarkable appetite and thirst for all the pleasures of the table . . . He had homely virtues and unfailing good humour . . . Anne accepted with complacency what fortune brought her'.[10] What more was to be expected? His 'good mien and behaviour', we are told, 'made such an impression on the Princess and on the whole Court that on July 28 he was solemnly married to her in the Chapel Royal at St James's by Henry Compton Bishop of London, in the presence of the King & Queen, the Duke & Duchess of York and the chiefest of the nobility'.[11]

Anne was showered with pearls and diamonds, while the bridegroom's £15,000-a-year from Denmark was made up by Charles and James to a more princely £40,000; and for good measure Charles threw in for Anne one of the less venerable parts of Whitehall Palace, known as the Cockpit. This was not the cockpit itself (octagonal, with a conical roof and lantern), which had been converted into a Court theatre, but the range next to it, which stood close to the site of 10 Downing Street and its garden and looked westward on to St James's Park and the canal.

'You may believe 'twas no small joy to me to hear she liked him', wrote Mary to Frances Bathurst on August 25th, 'and I hope she will do so every day more & more for else I am sure she can't love him & without that 'tis impossible to be happy, which I wish her with all my heart, as you may easily imagine knowing how much I love her'.[12]

Both Mary and Anne did their utmost to love the husbands chosen for them and both succeeded, although in Mary's case her love was not returned. Anne indeed from the outset seems to have seen George as a hero or at least as material out of which she could easily make one. Excitement and change were not at all what she wanted. Her days might seem humdrum. To her this was the happiest part of her life. To excuse a long silence she wrote to Semandra:

> . . . the Prince stays with me every day from dinner to prayers & by the time I come from prayers 'tis half an hour after four & on my playing days from that time I am always in expectation of company. On those days that I do not play I commonly go to Whitehall at six, so that that hour & a half which I have from prayers till I go to the Duchess I am glad sometimes to get a little of it alone, it being the only time I have to myself, and for the other part of it the Prince either comes to me or I go to him & we stay with one another till I go out . . . I am the same I ever was & ever will be to the last moment of my life.[13]

George too was finding life a whirl:

> We talk here of going to tea, of going to Winchester, and everything else except sitting still all summer, which was the height of my ambition. God send me a quiet life somewhere, for I shall not be long able to bear this perpetual motion. All my hopes are in the Italian players whom we expect here about the 20th of this month . . .[14]

With a modicum of ambition, with a dash of resolution and character he could have changed history, possibly for the better. He had no wish to. His natural role was inactivity, his place was the background and there, except for the occasional outing, it would have been wise and indeed kind to leave him. At Winchester that summer they hunted hares and looked at the palace Wren was building for Charles II. Then back to the Cockpit and those interminable games of cards. 'Sure there cannot be anything more disagreeable than to have company to entertain that will neither speak nor play at cards', Anne complained to Sarah, 'and that was my fate all the afternoon'.[15] George enjoyed riding and hunting and so did Anne, but now that the first of her seventeen pregnancies had begun, though she rode when she could, hunting had to be abandoned. In April she gave birth to a dead child.

Anne's life, as has truly been said, will never be justly judged if its sufferings are left out of the account.[16] Again and again there was to be disappointment after childbirth and quite soon she was to be racked, off and on for life, with what was called gout. For all this pain, except for laudanum, there was nothing, not even an aspirin, and there were no anaesthetics. For most of her short life, whether fighting faction at Council or nursing an asthmatic husband through the long stifling night, the thing forced to the front of her mind was pain. She tried to ignore it. She told her bedchamber-woman Abigail not to mention it, but it was there.

If only doctors could have owned their ignorance and left their patients alone! But no, they had to justify themselves with bleedings and cuppings and blisterings; and they were never more busy than in February 1685 at the painful death of Charles II. Secretly Extreme Unction was given by a Roman Catholic: the time for pretence was over; and James, more frank, less wise, was for throwing the mask off altogether. 'If he had not come after King Charles', wrote Burnet, 'James would have passed for a prince of a sweet temper and easy of access'.[17] As it was, after choosing his officers of state – Rochester Lord Treasurer, Clarendon Lord Privy Seal, Halifax Lord President, Sunderland and Middleton Secretaries of State, Godolphin Lord Chamberlain to the Queen – he urged Wren to build as quickly as possible a large new Roman Catholic chapel at Whitehall and in the meantime he and the Queen went openly to mass.

Anne's religion was not yet interfered with. Tracts might be left about and oblique approaches made by Sarah's sister Frances who had married a Roman Catholic, Lord Tyrconnel; but otherwise Anne was gently used. When James had a priest say grace at table, Anne contrived to be talking or looking the other way. She was now allowed to choose her own Court or 'family'. Lady Clarendon, grown 'more and more nauseous' – was packed off to Ireland and, with the Yorks' consent, Sarah was made first lady of Anne's bedchamber. It was never easy to get Anne to exert herself, but this at least, in Sarah's view, meant one madwoman the less. Even so Anne's

Court was still 'so oddly composed that', as Sarah said, 'I think it would be making myself no great compliment if I should say her choosing to spend so much of her time with me did no discredit to her taste'.[18]

Of Anne's other ladies-in-waiting Barbara Villiers, later to be Lady Fitzharding, was Sarah's favourite, (See page 136) while Lady Frescheville was her detestation. Mary, for no given reason, disliked her too. But Anne was, at least at this stage, fairminded and with her staff apt to stay stubbornly loyal. 'Never having heard no ill of this woman', she wrote to her sister in Holland, 'I thought I could not have a better'.[19] Sarah was assured however that no additions to the household would be made without her consent.

The perfect friendship, once made, had to be cemented. Anne, Sarah remembered, 'grew uneasy to be treated by me with the ceremony due to her rank and with the sound of words that implied superiority. It was this turn of mind which made her one day propose to me that whenever I should happen to be absent from her we might in all our letters write ourselves by feigned names such as would import nothing of distinction of rank between us. Morley and Freeman were the names her fancy hit upon & she left me to choose by which of them I would be called. My frank open temper naturally led me to pitch upon Freeman, and so the Princess took the other; and from this time Mrs Morley and Mrs Freeman* began to converse as equals, made so by affection & friendship'.[20] And if Mrs Morley's discourse 'had nothing of brightness or wit' but rather, 'an insipid heaviness . . . turning chiefly upon fashions & rules of precedence or observations upon the weather',[21] what did that matter? Mrs Freeman had more than enough brightness and wit for two.

Anne owned she was morose and needed to be entertained, yet one wonders if she was always as dull as Sarah chose to paint her. 'Lady Howard and Mrs Griffith have been with me today', Anne in one of her many undated notes tells Sarah. 'The first goes out of town tomorrow and says she loves the country mightily but yet looks very melancholy when she speaks of it. My other visitor at

* 'Mrs' at this date usually stood for 'Mistress'; as when Boyer notes, under the date February, 1711: 'Mrs Elizabeth Lock, a maiden aged 106, was interred at St Paul's, Covent Garden'.

my request mimicked you and several others. Lady Frescheville she does much the best, but for yourself she does overact you'.[22] Before and after her many pregnancies, most of them disastrous, Anne obviously needed cheering. On June 2nd, 1685, her daughter Mary was born. She lived nearly two years.

That first summer of James's reign was not propitious. On June 11th Monmouth landed at Lyme. On the 18th James assured Parliament that he had 'a true English heart . . . jealous of the honour of the nation'. With July came Sedgemoor and on the 15th Monmouth's execution. Without Charles to check or season it James's vengeance drove Judge Jeffreys to the West Country to conduct the Bloody Assize. At Exeter alone 243 prisoners, urged to plead guilty in expectation of mercy, were by one corporate sentence condemned to death. 'A black brand', asserts Coke, 'is set upon the reigns of those princes who shed much blood; nor do we read in any story such a sea of blood flowed from justice as it did in less than eight months after this King began his reign'.[23]

Sarah was surprised when these mass-executions seemed to leave Anne unmoved. The notions infused into her from infancy, she says, had stifled and suppressed her natural compassion. Like Prince George, all Anne then wanted was to be left alone. 'During her father's reign she kept her Court as private as could be consistent with her station', but 'when the designs of that bigoted unhappy prince came to be barefaced, no wonder there were attempts made to draw his daughter into the measures of that Court'.[24]

In October Louis XIV revoked the Edict of Nantes, with the result that thousands of French Protestant refugees were soon testifying here as to what it could mean to be persecuted under a tyrannical Roman Catholic rule; and those who listened to them wondered if their own King, egged on by Sunderland and Father Petre, had not himself become a fanatic. When the following June Anne had another daughter (Anne Sophia. She lived nine months), James visited her on the day of the christening, with a Jesuit priest. Anne burst into tears and the priest was sent away. That summer she found her own preceptor, Dr Compton Bishop of London,* suspended for disobeying James's command to suspend John Sharp, Rector of St

* Henry Compton, Bishop of London (1632–1713).

Giles, for using 'reflecting expressions' on the King and his Government; and before the year's end the Pope was pressing James to concentrate on winning her over to Rome. It was unthinkable. 'The Church of Rome is wicked & dangerous', Anne wrote to Mary, 'and . . . their ceremonies – most of them – plain downright idolatry . . . I do count it a very great blessing that I am of the Church of England & as great a misfortune that the King is not. I pray God his eyes may be opened . . . I will rather beg my bread than ever change'.[25]

When at this time (December 1686) Anne writes of John Churchill, she shows surprisingly shrewd foresight:

> . . . for though he is a very faithful servant to the King and . . . the King is very kind to him, and I believe he will always obey the King in all things that are consistent with religion, yet rather than change that I dare say he will lose all his places & all that he has.[26]

The year ended with the dismissal of Anne's maternal uncles, Rochester and Clarendon, for not turning Papist.

For Anne 1687 began tragically. In January she miscarried. This was due, she believed, to dancing, with a great deal of jumping, a new French dance called the rigadoon. In February, within a week of each other, she lost both her infant daughters, Anne Sophia and Mary. 'The good Princess has taken her chastisement heavily', wrote Lady Russell. 'The first relief of that sorrow proceeded from calming of a greater, the Prince being so ill of a fever. I never heard any relation more moving than that of seeing them together. Sometimes they wept, sometimes they mourned in words, but hand in hand, he sick in his bed, she the carefullest nurse to him that can be imagined. As soon as he was able they went to Richmond Palace . . .'[27]

In March Anne's proposed visit to Mary in Holland was cancelled by James. She was forbidden even to mention it. This she blamed on Lord Sunderland, 'a very ill man . . . working with all his might to bring in popery . . . I believe in a little while no Protestant will be able to live here . . . His Lady [Sunderland] is a flattering, dissembling, false woman . . . If either of you should come', she tells Mary, 'I should be very glad to see you . . . no tongue can ever express how much my heart is yours'.[28]

The secret, solemn correspondence is lightened only when Mary seeks her young sister's advice on a point of etiquette. There Anne is on favourite ground.

To the question you ask about lords' daughters, I kiss them all, but as to their sitting in the closet, it is what I can't give you a positive answer about, but I believe they should not, for the Queen has told me that when one dines with ladies in form, lords' daughters should not sit at the same table, nor that they should not go in one's coach & methinks since they are not to do either of these things, they should not sit in the closet in chapel neither . . . Ever since the late King died I have sat in the closet that was his in the chapel and there the great chair stands just as if the King were to come hither, and I sit on a stool on the left hand of the chair and . . . no ladies sit there but just my own.[29]

Anne was only too conscious that her Church was in danger. On March 25th John Sharp, the same who had been suspended for sedition, boldly preached before Anne at Whitehall.[30]

To another question of Mary's – how does she spend her day? – Anne answered:

We keep very good hours, for we have dined for the most part by a quarter after one, and from that time till four o'clock the Prince stays with me, except he goes out a-horseback at four o'clock. If I have no company I go to prayers & if I have company then we play at comet or insertin [?] & after everybody is gone I go to prayers before supper & I have supped every night by nine o'clock & so I am abed at eleven at latest & sometimes before.[31]

Anne as Queen would not have dreamed of dining so early. In 1703, for example, on the occasion of Charles III's visit to Windsor, they dined at three; but as the reign progressed it became fashionable to dine at four or even at five. Anne, to the disgust of Burnet, preferred dining in private and always did so after the death of Prince George in 1708. Food was apt to be wholesome rather than interesting. Venison helped to vary the royal diet, but potatoes, though long since introduced, were not eaten. Claret, Burgundy and Champagne (then a still wine) were drunk by the rich, but after 1703, when the wines of Portugal were far less heavily taxed than those from France, a great many took to port.

Wissing: Mary of Modena

Kneller: John Churchill, First Duke of Marlborough

Kneller: Sidney First Earl of Godolphin

Queen Anne (artist unknown)

A recurring worry voiced in Anne's letters to Mary was whether James would insist on her changing her religion. Up till now (June 1687), she tells her sister, she has been spared, but George is in Denmark until August and, as usual, she fears the worst. As for the Queen, she is 'a very great bigot' who inflames the King. 'She pretends to have a great deal of kindness' to her stepdaughter, 'but I doubt it is not real, for I never see proofs of it but rather the contrary'. Behind some of these suspicions and hatreds – of the Hydes (Rochester and Clarendon), of the Sunderlands, of Mary Beatrice of Modena – one senses the influence of Sarah Churchill; for though she might, as Anne told Mary, have 'a true sense of the doctrine of our Church', she was too often to be found wanting in Christian charity. Surprisingly however, albeit many years later, Sarah found something to be said for James – 'a good manager for the public without breaking any law but what proceeded from his weakness of having a mind that everybody should attend him in heaven, by establishing popery here'.[32]

In the summer of 1687, when the Papal Nuncio had been received in audience at Windsor, the Duke of Somerset had refused to conduct him to the King and had been dismissed. But now in the autumn James headed for the precipice. Having upset both universities, he seemed eager to alienate the Church. Perhaps it was his bluntness which appealed to Sarah. As Burnet put it, what Charles acted in masquerade, James did barefaced. 'Had James kept his head he might have kept his crown';[33] but the cool head and tact of a Churchill were two things he lacked. He underestimated the strength of the Church of England. The English moreover had sense enough to realise that just as in Elizabeth's reign there had been danger of England's becoming part of the Catholic empire of Spain, so now it might too easily be absorbed into that of France.

In October Anne again miscarried. In November Mary Beatrice, back at Whitehall after staying with James at Bath, found that she was pregnant. 'It is strange to see', wrote Clarendon in his diary the following January, 'how the Queen's great belly is everywhere ridiculed, as if scarce anybody believed it to be true. Good God help us'.[34] No Protestant wanted it to be true. To suffer James was hard enough; to see his line stretch out to the crack of doom, unthinkable.

And so begins that part of the Anne and Mary correspondence which throws doubt on their stepmother's pregnancy and so on her veracity. 'The tone of Anne's letters', notes their editor, 'turns from smug resignation to open vindictiveness. There is no reason to suppose that this is wholly due to her fear of losing a throne. The possibility of a protracted Catholic tyranny under a line of male Stuarts was as terrifying to her as it was to the rest of the nation. But these letters in which, egged on by Mary, she vilifies the Queen and eagerly searches for foul play do her no credit'.[35]

To quote one of them (from Anne to Mary, 20 March 1688) will be enough:

I hope you will instruct Bentley what you would have your friends to do if any alteration should come, as it is to be feared there will, especially if Mansell [James] has a son, which I conclude he will, there being so much reason to believe it is a false belly. For methinks if it were not, there having been so many stories & jests made about it, she should to convince the world make either me or some of my friends feel her belly; but quite contrary, whenever one talks of her being with child she looks as if she were afraid one would touch her. And whenever I happen to be in the room as she has been undressing she has always gone into the next room to put on her smock. These things give me so much cause for suspicion that I believe when she is brought to bed nobody will be convinced it is her child except it prove a daughter. For my part I declare I shall not except I see the child and she parted . . .[36]

No one reading that harsh letter would suppose the writer herself constantly pregnant: Anne had yet another miscarriage the following month. Boyer quotes a current report that the Queen, finding Anne too inquisitive at her toilet, threw a glove at her.[37]

Writing of James at this time Professor Plumb refers to his 'outright onslaught on the very basis of political power which, if successful, would have made the Stuarts as absolute as their French or Spanish cousins'.[38] But at last he received a check. His command that in May and June his Declaration of Indulgence be read in all churches throughout the kingdom was rejected by Sancroft, Ken, Trelawney and four other bishops. They were sent to the Tower.

On May 12th Anne 'designed for the Bath suddenly'. It seemed a strange time to go. 'I much wonder', wrote Bridget Noel to Lady

Rutland, 'the Princess of Denmark would not compliment the Queen and see her safely delivered before she went to the Bath'.[39] But she pleaded pregnancy and James, self-styled 'the most affectionate father upon earth', who had been begging her to stay, gave in to her and to her doctors and agreed to her going. Directly Anne had left, or so it was said, Mary Beatrice 'altered her form of reckoning and instead of dating it from meeting the King at Windsor in the beginning of October 1687 she began from her meeting him at the Bath about a month before'. She changed her mind too as to the place of birth and moved into St James's Palace.

On June 9th news reached London that Anne would be returning in three or four days. Next morning 'when most if not all the Protestant ladies were at church'[40] James Francis Edward, later to be known as the Old Pretender, was born. The birth room, at the east end of the south front, was thronged with Roman Catholics and a few others including Sidney Godolphin, the Queen's Chamberlain, who characteristically stood by the fireplace where he could hear everything but see nothing. Anne, the most essential witness of all, was 'industriously absent'.[41] On June 18th she wrote to her sister:

> . . . I shall never now be satisfied whether the child be true or false. It may be it is our brother, but God only knows, for she never took care to satisfy the world or give people any demonstration of it . . . After all this 'tis possible it may be her child, but where one believes it a thousand do not. For my part, except they do give very plain demonstrations, which is almost impossible now, I shall ever be of the number of unbelievers . . . One cannot help having a thousand fears & melancholy thoughts, but whatever changes may happen you shall ever find me firm to my religion and faithfully yours'.[42]

Paternity, in this case perhaps surprisingly unquestioned, is notoriously hard to prove; but how often has maternity been called in question? Rumour was never busier; a warmingpan was invented and a map painstakingly drawn to show the secret route taken with the 'supposititious babe' within it. Jokes were exchanged, few of them good ones. James and Mary Beatrice, most understandably, were shocked and appalled. The baby, taken ill, was for better air sent to Richmond. James and Mary followed but paused before crossing the Thames, fearing that they were about to see yet another little corpse in its cradle. But the child survived and his father lost no time in setting himself to gather statements from all the witnesses – 'above forty persons, most of them of the first quality' (including Lady Sunderland who had signalled to the King that the child was a boy) – prepared to testify that James Francis Edward was his mother's son: 'so many witnesses of unquestionable credit as if it seemed the particular care of heaven to disappoint so wicked and unparalleled an attempt'.[43] When all was ready James called a Council and invited Anne. But no, she was pregnant, she said, and could not attend; and when the evidence was sent to her she declined to read it: 'For I have so much duty to the King that his word must be more to me than those depositions'.[44]

Clarendon, calling on his niece next morning while she was dressing, found her in a different frame of mind:

> She presently fell to talk of the examinations taken yesterday & told me I had heard a great deal of fine discourse at Council, and made herself very merry with that whole affair. She was dressing & all her women about her, many of whom put in their jests. I was amazed at this behaviour and . . . whispered to her Royal Highness that she would give me leave to speak with her in private. She said it grew late & she must make haste to be ready for prayers . . .[45]

It was typical of Anne's excuses when he tried, and he tried often, to corner her about James. It was for her, he suggested, to reason with her father. To which she answered 'very drily' that she knew nothing but what her husband told her; she never spoke to the King on business. The more he pressed her the more reserved she became and said she must dress herself, it was almost prayer time. She could not be moved.[46] The one thing she may have learned from these embarrassing interviews was the value of silence, particularly when one is feeble at argument and one's case is a weak one. It would stand her in good stead.

Mary now sent Anne from Holland a questionnaire about the Pretender's birth, plus what has been called scabrous gynaecological chitchat. From it one picks out one unintentionally tender passage, where the Queen in labour begs James to hide her face with his head and wig (he did), 'for all the Council stood close at the bed's feet, and Lord Chancellor upon the step'.[47]

Louis XIV had sent James his congratulations not only on the birth of an heir but on having committed the recalcitrant bishops to the Tower. However, they were soon released, and when the verdict of not guilty was given in Westminster Hall there was 'a most wonderful shout, that one would have thought the Hall had cracked'.[48] On the same day an invitation, signed by Danby, Compton Bishop of London, the Earl of Shrewsbury and three other Whig lords, was sent to William in Holland. Acceptance meant invasion and risking his life; but if James was fanatical about religion, William was equally so about the conquest of France and for that, as Trevelyan said, he needed England as much as England needed him. With a small army of Dutchmen and a mixed entourage including his chaplain, Gilbert Burnet, he landed at Torbay on November 5th.

With an admirable economy of words, polished and repolished by a succession of helpers, Sarah in her *Conduct* describes the upheaval which followed William's invasion of 1688:

Upon the landing of the Prince of Orange in 1688 the King went down to Salisbury to his army and the Prince of Denmark with him; but the news quickly came from thence that the Prince of Denmark had left the King and was gone over to the Prince of Orange and that the King was coming back to London. This put the Princess [Anne] into a great fright. She sent for me, told me her distress and declared that rather than see her father she would jump out at the window. This was her very expression.

A little before, a note had been left with me to inform me where I might find the Bishop of London (who in that critical time absconded) if her Royal Highness should have occasion for a friend. The Princess on this alarm immediately sent me to the Bishop. I acquainted him with her resolution to leave the Court and to put herself under his care. It was hereupon agreed that he should come about midnight to the neighbourhood of the Cockpit and convey the Princess to some place where she might be safe.

The Princess went to bed at her usual time to prevent suspicion. I came to her soon after; and by the back stairs which went down from her closet her Royal Highness, my Lady Fitzharding and I, with one servant, walked to the coach, where we found the Bishop and the Earl of Dorset. They conducted us that night to the Bishop's house in the City and the next day to my Lord Dorset's at Copthall. From thence we went to the Earl of Northampton's and from thence to Nottingham, where the country gathered about the Princess; nor did she think herself safe till she saw that she was surrounded by the Prince of Orange's friends.

As this flight of the Princess to Nottingham has by some been ignorantly, not to say maliciously imputed to my policy and premeditated contrivance, I thought it necessary to give this short but exact relation of it. It was a thing sudden and unconcerted; nor had I any share in it farther than obeying my mistress's orders in the particulars I have mentioned; though indeed I had reason enough on my own account to get out of the way Lord Churchill having likewise at that time left the King and gone over to the other party.

Quickly after this time the King fled into France. The throne was hereupon declared vacant and presently filled with the Prince and Princess of Orange. The Parliament thought proper to settle the Crown on King William for life, and the Princess of Denmark gave her consent to it . . .[49]

It is history as one might wish to write and to read it: a logical progression of events, neatly and clearly recorded; but far too much has been glossed over or omitted.

Desertion from the army began with Clarendon's heir Lord Cornbury; and from the navy one of the first deserters was Churchill's brother George. It was very soon obvious that every step of the elaborate scheme had been most carefully planned and concerted: that Prince George and Churchill should join William, to be followed immediately by the flight of their wives from London. In fact there must have been some delay, since both husbands, separately, expressed surprise that Anne and Sarah had not left London sooner. The idea that they acted on sudden impulse is further ridiculed by Lediard's assertion that the back stairs by which they fled had recently been put in for that very purpose.[50] 'No indeed, it was not so much a piece of chance-medley-work as it has been represented'.

In Sarah's account something of Anne's terror (she was naturally timorous) and the breathlessness of the escape comes through; but for the scene next morning one turns to Pepys and learns that Sir

Benjamin Bathurst, who had married Frances Apsley and was now Treasurer of the Household, heard 'a sudden outcry of women, which upon his running out to satisfy himself in the occasion of found it to be a universal cry among the ladies that some or other had carried away the Princess . . . Mrs Danvers going into her Highness's chamber to call her and receiving no answer to her call, she opened the bed and found the Princess gone and the bed cold, with all her yesterday's clothes even to her stockings and shoes left behind . . .'[51]

Bishop Compton, a keen botanist, brought his gardener, George London, and the Earl of Dorset, who was his nephew. Not without reason he had been accused by James of talking more like a colonel than a bishop (he had been a cornet of dragoons), and as the flight went on, Compton became more and more militant. At Leicester he called for an association to punish Catholics should William come to harm. (Anne was said to be angry with those who refused to sign it). And for the entry into Oxford, where George was to be reunited with Anne, he rode 'at the head of a noble troop of gentlemen . . . in a purple cloak, martial habit, pistols before him and his sword drawn'.[52]

Both George and Anne had left farewell letters for the King and Queen. The first was unimportant (James said the loss of one good trooper had been of more consequence), and as for the latter, to quote James's *Memoirs*, 'No such letter was found or at least delivered to her [the Queen]; that would have spoiled the contrivance of having it believed she [Anne] was murthered'. And when it was published, its 'pretence of preserving the King by rising up in arms against him was counted but a scurvy doctrine even in common subjects during the late Rebellion, but what term to give it in children is hard to say'.[53]

Anne's letter was dated November 25 – the day Clarendon, at Court, found 'great crowds in the galleries and consternation in all men's looks',[54] and exactly a week after she wrote to wish William success in' so just an undertaking'.[55] The handwriting is hers but the style is not. After an apology, which makes no mention of the difference she is said to have had with the Queen the evening before, Anne explains frankly [sic]:

I am gone to absent myself to avoid the King's displeasures which I am not able to bear either against the Prince or myself... not to return before I hear the happy news of a reconcilement; and as I am confident the Prince did not leave the King with any other design than to use all possible means for his preservation so I hope you will do me the justice to believe that I am uncapable of following him for any other end. Never was anyone in such an unhappy condition, so divided between duty and affection to a father and a husband and therefore I know not what I must do but to follow one to preserve the other'.

After touching on religion she ends by begging the Queen 'to continue the same favourable opinion that you have hitherto had of your most obedient daughter & servant'.[56]

But if Anne was in a quandary (and she had the Churchills to resolve it for her), what of James and his Queen? 'The Stuarts?' exclaimed Louis XVI many years later, 'an unlucky family. I wish to hear no more of them'. James II was unlucky not only in large things but in small ones, as when at Salisbury his nose bled and went on bleeding and could not be stopped. 'Everybody in this hurly-burly', Dr Clarke remembered, 'was thinking of himself and nobody minded the King, who came up to Dr Radcliffe and asked him what was good for the bleeding of his nose. It was the last time that I ever saw him'.[57]

Forsaken at Salisbury James returned to London, only to find Anne gone. That is the moment, with both daughters against him, that he seems most like Lear; and whatever his shortcomings, one can but feel sorry for him. Enemies were to be expected, but 'to see those he had favoured, cherished and exalted, nay his own children rise thus in opposition against him, this was what required a more than natural force to support'.[58]

Among the favoured, cherished and exalted none of course was more prominent than Churchill. This, wrote his descendant and apologist, was the most poignant and challengeable action of his life.[59] Even in the cause of religion, which certainly meant more to him than it did to his wife, the betrayal of James was hard to justify; for however one viewed it the fact remained that here was the King's most trusted commander deserting to the King's enemy. 'The King', said James scathingly, 'must be abandoned and destroyed or else these good people's consciences could never be at rest'. Jacobite lampoonists enjoyed themselves:

> Ungrateful toadstool, despicable thing,
> Thus to desert thy master and thy King!
> Nay and thy maker too, who from the dust
> Raised thee, though to every man's disgust.
> For nothing sure can e'er redeem thy crime
> But the same treacherous act a second time.[60]

If Burnet is to be believed, Churchill had undertaken before the invasion to see that Anne and her husband should join William 'as soon as was possible'; while Clarendon, Anne's uncle, deliberately kept in the dark, ran between the two camps. On November 15th, appalled at the defection of his son, he flung himself at James's feet, but on December 3rd we find him with William, who tells him Cornbury's coming over was a seasonable service he would always remember. Two days later Clarendon sees Prince George, who amazes him by saying that Anne is not pregnant. She was. 'I then told him', he adds, 'with what tenderness the King spake of her when he returned and how much trouble he expressed to find she had left him; to which he said not one word'.[61]

'In a tempestuous night with the Prince not six months old' Mary of Modena, on December 9th, fled to France. James's exit, contrived some days later, was no less perilous; and it was said that while in a rainstorm his open boat was swept down the Thames, Anne and Sarah, both flaunting orange ribbons, 'went triumphant to the play-house'.[62] That is almost certainly untrue. James took to the Thames on the 18th and, according to Luttrell, the Denmarks did not reach London till the following day. Yet Anne did admit to Clarendon that on hearing of her father's flight she called for cards, 'because she was used to play and never loved to do anything that looked like an affected constraint . . . I was afraid', adds her uncle, 'such behaviour rendered her much less in the opinion of the world, even with her father's enemies, than she ought to be'. He told her so but found her 'not one jot moved'.[63]

The incredible had happened, 'a thing unseen, unheard of and unrecorded in history, that a king in peaceful possession of his realm, with an army of 30,000 fighting men and 40 ships of war, should quit his kingdom without firing a pistol . . . It looks as if heaven and earth had conspired against us'.[64] Thus wrote a Jesuit, but he was not alone. 'And now the throne being declared vacant', wrote Clarendon on February 6th (Anne's twenty-fourth birthday), 'the next business was to fill it & to that end it was proposed that the Prince & Princess of Orange might be declared King & Queen . . . I think this was the most dismal day I ever saw in my life. God help us. We are certainly a miserable, undone people'.[65]

It would take time to label the revolution glorious but at least, with one minor exception, it had been bloodless and as things quieted, several evils, it was found, had been bundled away, not the least of them Judge Jeffreys who, disguised as a sailor, was seized at Wapping. 'Treating him with that want of mercy which he had shown to others', runs the account, 'they carried him in his blue jacket and with his hat flapped down upon his face before the Lord Mayor, who as soon as the hat was lifted up and he beheld that countenance which was in use to strike terror wherever it appeared, fell into a faint with the shock of the surprise and died next day'.[66] Jeffreys was sent to prison, there to die the following April.

CHAPTER THREE

WILLIAM AND MARY

1689 - 1695

'YOU will find the Prince of Orange', warned James, 'a worse man than Cromwell'. It seemed very likely. In 1679 Bishop Ken had dared to remonstrate with him for his coldness to Mary, who was devoted to him. Ten years later Burnet lost favour by presuming to tread the same perilous path. 'I was set on by many', he says, 'to speak to him to change his cold way, but he cut me off when I entered upon a freedom with him, so that I could not go through with it . . . I wrote him a very plain letter . . . This offended him'.[1]

In exchange for a Roman Catholic the Church found itself landed with a stern Calvinist who was contemptuous of the Anglican liturgy and for part of the service kept his hat on. He might be, as indeed he was, a statesman of the first order and a brave king, dedicated to the destruction of France; but with few exceptions, one of them being his titular mistress Elizabeth Villiers and another her brother, Jersey, the English were nothing to him. Most of his favourites were Dutchmen. His asthma was so severe it was often hard to hear him, for coughing. Whitehall with its fogs had soon to be all but abandoned in favour of Hampton Court and the clear air and gravel soil of Kensington, where William bought and enlarged Nottingham House.

As strategist and statesman William in any impartial history must stand high. Anne saw him differently. To her he was the Dutchman who had married her sister and, albeit with her connivance, exiled her father. This showed no doubt a narrow and insular outlook but, as Mr Kenyon has remarked, all Anne's politics hinged on personalities.[2] This was feminine and fundamental and could never be changed.

When early in February Mary landed, she 'came into Whitehall', says John Evelyn, 'jolly as to a wedding'. Towering above William and in startling purple and orange robes she shocked Sarah by rummaging in closets and 'turning up the quilts upon the bed as people do when they come into an inn'; and all this with an air of delight when, as Sarah thought, she might at least have looked grave or even pensively sad.[3] But that was not the part she had been given by William to play. Forced to leave Holland, which she had grown fond of, and forced to bring with her Elizabeth Villiers, she was on arrival, though with many misgivings, forced to appear gay. Burnet found her a paragon. She was unquestionably devout and until now, like Mary of Modena, had lived the life of a nun with prayers four times a day. All she sought was 'a retired quiet life'. 'While I put the best face on', she writes in her sad journal, 'my heart suffered a great deal'.[4]

And now, was the throne vacant and had James abdicated? Many denied it. Indeed debate might have lasted forever had not William presented Parliament with an ultimatum. He was so made, says Burnet, that he could not think of holding anything by apron-strings. He would be neither regent nor consort. He and Mary would reign as King and Queen or they would return to Holland. Mary herself 'had been only for a regency and wished for nothing else',[5] but it was not to be. James, it was at last decided, had broken his contract with the nation and had left the throne vacant. William, in the names of himself and Mary, might exercise regal power for life, 'in prejudice of the Princess of Denmark's title', if he survived Mary. If Mary, who had had two miscarriages, had a child, that child would reign before any offspring of Anne's; though Anne's children would have precedence over any William might have by a second wife. 'Thus', runs the account in James's *Memoirs*, 'did they mangle the succession, chopping and changing it at pleasure, inverting the order among the Protestant heirs and totally excluding the Catholic ones till they had fixed a series of elective monarchs, and under a notion of preserving the laws unhinged them all at a stroke, even Magna Carta itself'.[6] As a blow to the succession and to the divine right of kings, if not to the constitution itself, it was second only to the execution of Charles I.

Anne, again pregnant, wavered. She would never, she told Clarendon in January, consent to anything to the prejudice of herself or her children. She knew very well, she added, what the Commonwealth party (Whigs) were up to, but she hoped the honest party (Tories) would not allow her to suffer wrong. Yet in March, after the reshuffle, Anne wished it to be known that she was extremely pleased with what had been done.[7] On April 11th she attended the double coronation. The story that while robing she sent for Mrs Dawson, who had attended Mary of Modena and Anne Hyde, as midwife, and asked if she could testify to the Pretender's being her brother (she said she could) is probably apocryphal,[8] as is almost certainly that of her receiving at this time her father's curse. News that James had landed in Ireland reaching William and Mary just before Compton crowned them 'put a scurvy damp upon their joys'. Anne's seeming inconsistency is accounted for by Sarah:

> And as to giving King William the crown for life, at first I did not see any necessity for such a measure, and I thought it so unreasonable that I took a great deal of pains (which I believe the King & Queen never forgot) to promote my mistress's pretensions. But I quickly found that all endeavours of that kind would be ineffectual . . . and that the settlement would be carried in Parliament whether the Princess consented to it or not.[9]

To William and Mary it must have been clear from the start that Anne, if not as Burnet described her a blind and passive tool of Lady Churchill's ambition, would do nothing without Churchill approval; and as one crisis succeeded another – over Anne's allowance, over her lodgings, over Sarah herself – this meant friction and bickering and at last total rupture. With insecurity in the air, and with so little humour, perhaps this was inevitable. But however it was, the decline of friendship between the two once devoted sisters was steady and miserable. Mary was garrulous, says Sarah, while Anne had nothing to say. Mary was insensitive; Anne too easily hurt.

The first row, about the Duchess of Portsmouth's lodgings which Anne wanted, was too trivial for comment. Suffice it to say that among the more obvious bones to be picked at Court, jobs and lodgings nearly always took priority. Anne was told no, and again no when she asked for Richmond Palace. The question of a fixed allowance was more serious, involving as it did the choice between being by William's favour a royal pensioner or having a reasonable allowance, as was certainly Anne's right, granted by Parliament. William's charity was apt to operate on the Robin Hood pattern: he granted his favourites £22,000 a year from James's estates in Ireland. Nearer home he was less dependable. When Anne, taken to task by Mary, admitted that 'her friends had a mind to make her some settlement', she was asked 'with a very imperious air, "Pray what friends have you but the King and me?" '[10] Anne was hurt and indignant. Lady Fitzharding, a favourite of Mary's, was asked to persuade Sarah, for her own good and Anne's, to desist from pressing for a parliament-sanctioned grant. When this failed, Shrewsbury brought a promise from William that he would allow Anne £50,000 a year; but Anne still preferred to have it voted by Parliament.

Prince George, now naturalised, was made Duke of Cumberland and sat in the Lords. Churchill was made Earl of Marlborough and a lord of the bedchamber to William.

On July 24th at Hampton Court Anne gave birth to a son. At his christening by Compton William stood godfather (the child was, rather surprisingly, named after him) and created him Duke of Gloucester. The following month the baby had convulsions but recovered and was declared 'a brave livelylike boy'. Throughout his eleven years he was in fact a pathetic creature, usually referred to in Anne's letters as 'my poor boy'; and to add to the irony he found his Boswell in a manservant called Jenkin Lewis. From him we learn of a presence-room packed with wet-nurses (Prince George, passing through, picked Mrs Pack, a Quakeress, to 'go to bed to the young prince, who mended that night'), and of the coach drawn by dog-size ponies presented by the Duchess of Ormonde. Gloucester loved horses and drums. At two he was shouting 'Dub-a-dub!' at the sentries and a year or two later playing soldiers with twenty-two Kensington boys, who taught him to swear. Kensington with its gravel-pits had an almost magical name for health, and so it was there that Anne took him, renting first a house of Lord Craven's and later Campden House* on Campden Hill. His governess was Lady Fitzharding, whom Lewis calls 'as witty and pleasant a lady

* Campden House: a drawing in the South Kensington Library is reproduced facing page 60 of *Queen Anne's Son* by Hester Chapman.

as any in England'; his governor, in infancy, Lord Fitzharding, who was already Master of the Horse to Prince George.

At the time of Gloucester's birth Burnet was trying to get the House of Hanover included in the Declaration of Right as a contingency in the succession to the crown of England. With Gloucester on the scene however it was felt that Hanover might safely be forgotten. As far as the public knew, Anne's heir was normal and likely to succeed her.

Gloucester's doctor was Radcliffe,* a brilliant eccentric who seemed to understand him. It was only when the child grew old enough to walk that it became obvious that there was something seriously wrong. Gloucester's head was too big for him (it may have been hydrocephalus) and although in time he learned to run on level ground and could make an elegant bow, he was apt to totter, stairs were too much for him and if he fell he could not get up without help. For this his father, who was not brutal but stupid, was prepared to beat him, while his mother sat by in a perspiration of fear. Marlborough's heir Lord Churchill (later Lord Blandford), three years older than Gloucester, was made Lieutenant-General of the schoolboy-army and on fitting occasions saluted with seven guns. When playing at war Gloucester would be entirely carried away and once when interrupted was heard to sigh, 'Who would be a prince?'[11]

This was Anne's seventh pregnancy. She was to have ten more, none of them successful and all more or less painful, dangerous and harmful to her constitution. She soon lost her figure.† Sarah, with a son and three daughters living, was luckier, but she too knew how it felt to bear a child and lose it. She must have sensed Anne's fears for Gloucester and the awkwardness of keeping him from public view. Nine days before his birth Sarah's daughters Henrietta and Anne had been joined by a third, Mary; and a second son, Charles, would complete the family the following August. Anne was at the

* Radcliffe, John (1650–1714), appointed 1686 first physician to Princess Anne. In 1691 Queen Mary granted him 1,000 guineas for his services to the Duke of Gloucester; but soon after Mary's death in 1694 he offended Anne and lost her favour.

† The narrow-waisted figure in Kneller's portrait dated 1689, at Blenheim, (p. 192), need not be taken too literally.

Cockpit, Sarah at Holywell, the riverside house Marlborough had built at St Albans. Whenever possible the two young mothers were together, exchanging notes on babies and remedies, while their husbands were at the Irish war; a campaign from which Marlborough would return triumphant but George less so, having been snubbed by William and denied the privilege of riding in his coach. Nothing however could shake Anne's confidence in her husband; nor could anything change her devotion to Sarah, who remembered

> . . . they were shut up together for many hours daily. Every moment of absence she counted a sort of a tedious lifeless state. To see the Duchess* was a constant joy and to part with her for never so short a time a constant uneasiness, as the Princess's own frequent expressions were. This worked even to the jealousy of a lover. She used to say she desired to possess her wholly & could hardly bear that she should ever escape from this confinement into any other company. All who knew the tempers of them both knew it to be a confinement indeed for one who had a very great sprightliness & cheerfulness of nature joined with a true taste of conversation, to be perpetually chained as it were to a person whose other accomplishments had not cured the sullenness of her temper nor wholly freed her conversation from an insipid heaviness . . . The Duchess had too great a sense of her favour not to submit to all such inconveniencies to oblige one who she saw loved her to excess . . . But though there was this passionate love on the one side and as I verily believe the sincerest friendship on the other, yet their tempers were not more different than their principles & notions on many occasions plainly appeared to be.[12]

The thing to do, Anne decided, was to bind Sarah to her by every possible means, including of course money. The cornucopia painted by Verrio and Kneller in the foreground of their portraits of Anne as Queen was not yet hers; but such store as she then had the Churchills should share; and charming was her manner of giving. 'I have had something to say to you a great while', she writes to Sarah, 'and I did not know how to go about it. I have designed ever since my revenue was settled to desire you would accept of a thousand pounds a year. I beg you would only look upon it as an earnest of my goodwill, but never mention anything of it to me, for I shall be ashamed

* Sarah, then Countess of Marlborough.

The Princess Anne of Denmark (French artist unknown)

William III

Queen Mary II

Prince George of Denmark and Dr George Clarke

to have any notice taken of such a thing from one who deserves more than I shall be ever able to return'.[13]

Before accepting, Sarah sought the advice of Sidney Godolphin, who saw no reason in the world for refusing. Godolphin, one of Charles II's 'chits' (that coterie of brilliant young men which had included Sunderland and Rochester), had been Chamberlain to Mary of Modena and was now 'thought necessary for the Treasury, since all the rest were strangers to the revenue which he understood well'.[14] Short and of a forbidding countenance, (See page 40) he was the widower of Margaret Blagge who had died in 1678 giving birth to their son Francis. He enjoyed gaming and horse-racing (the famous Arabian took his name) and was said to be still in love with Mary Beatrice to whom in France, with William's permission, he sent presents. To the world at large he was Bacon Face but to Anne Mr Montgomery, whom she liked and trusted.

Queen Mary's favourite was Shrewsbury, the dynamic young Secretary of State (See page 233). He was blind in one eye and was nicknamed the King of Hearts. Burnet calls him the best beloved of all the ministry and says he deserved to be so. Mary trembled with emotion whenever he appeared.[15] Her dread was that the Marlboroughs should in opposition to William set up a pro-Anne faction. As it was she had trouble enough with the supporters of James. 'Another thing vexed me at this time', she noted, 'was to see Lord Clarendon engaged in a party for my father, which was discovered by a letter that was intercepted writ all with his own hand'. Clarendon, who had refused to take the oath of allegiance to William and Mary, was now sent to the Tower. His brother Rochester, though he had taken the oath, at first lost favour because, like Godolphin, he voted for a regency. Later however he regained favour with Mary, even though that meant losing it with Sarah and with his niece Anne.

Mary was thoroughly miserable. Her sister, she said, 'affected to find fault with everything that was done, especially to laugh at afternoon sermons'. Anne's form of service was not 'high', but Mary's could hardly be lower. Mary felt so ill at this time she longed for death. 'My sore throat', she says, 'increased & with it my satisfaction . . . I had often wished to die of a consumption, but now I thought this yet better, for I thought I should see myself die & have my senses, which I imagined to be the happiest death that could be'.[16] It must have seemed to her an ill omen when Anne's baby of October 1690, hurriedly christened Mary, lived but two hours; but in every calamity Mary piously perceived the hand of God. The fire which the following Spring destroyed her rooms in Whitehall Palace 'heartily frighted' her, 'but blessed be God', she adds, 'it was stopped and all went over'. After another fire, at Kensington, Mary wrote, 'This has truly I hope weaned me from the vanities I was most fond of, that is ease & good lodgings'. God was given credit for preserving William and keeping him at a safe distance from James, 'though He began to humble us a little by the news from Ireland of a loss they had made of some pieces of artillery'.[17]

No less ridiculous was the thwarting of Prince George's Design of Going to Sea. It seemed innocent enough. All he wanted was to join the navy, without rank, but William ordered Mary to dissuade him and if necessary to forbid it. This upset everyone including Anne who, smouldering, withdrew with George to the spa at Tunbridge. Before leaving, Anne wrote to Sarah:

> . . . We have all our failings more or less & one of mine I must own is being a little hot sometimes, which I hope you will pardon when you consider how much real kindness Mrs Morley has for Mrs Freeman. I have at last got my dear Lady Marlborough's picture home & am so mightily pleased with it I would not part with it for anything . . .[18]

The portrait (Kneller inspired by Sarah in her prime. (See page 72)) is not disappointing. The turn of the head, the slanting look, the tip-tilted nose, the fair hair curling down to the bare shoulder – these, with the cherubic lips, give us at least some notion of the looks that appealed to Anne. 'I hope you don't believe your picture can make me think of you more than I did before', she told her, 'for that is impossible, but 'tis a pleasing thing to look upon when I can't see the original'.[19]

In Kneller's less well known portrait of Anne as Princess (at Blenheim (See page 72)), there are similarities of pose – the low-cut gown, with hair curling on to shoulder – but in expression there is all the difference in the world; for where Sarah hints at archness, Anne is dignity and calm. Anne's eyes and brow are fine, as are her hands; and indeed the figure as a whole, as she toys with orange-blossom,* has presence and charm. She looks sensible and trustworthy. Standing before it at Blenheim one can believe, as Sir Winston says, that Anne was a very real person who would have faced death for the sake of her friends. When they were attacked or, as the Churchills now were, disgraced, her loyalty was unshakable. Right or wrong, she would share their misfortune.

The cause of Marlborough's fall in January 1692, when he was suddenly dismissed, is still not absolutely certain. Most historians however are prepared to believe Burnet when he says that William 'had very good reason to believe that he (Marlborough) had made his peace with King James and was engaged in a correspondence with France. It is certain', Burnet adds, 'he was doing all he could to set on a faction in the army & nation against the Dutch & to lessen the King'; while Sarah had become 'so absolute a favourite with the Princess that she seemed to be the mistress of her whole heart & thoughts'.[20]

Foremost among the Jacobite letters fathered on Marlborough was that 'most penitential & dutiful' one said to have been sent on December 1st to the exiled James from Anne. It may have been intercepted. At all events it took five months to reach him at La Hogue, which, considering that a letter could then reach America in six months, was a long time. Like Anne's last letter to her stepmother, this to her father is not typical of her style. The sentences are long and involved. There is only one short one – 'If wishes could recall what is past I had long since redeemed my fault' – and that certainly might well have been Anne's. James, when at last he did get the letter, is said to have remarked to Captain Lloyd, who brought it him on board, that Anne was surely better than her sister Mary; whereupon Lloyd 'put his head round the door and with a rough seaman's oath and rude canine comparison' declared both were bitches.[21]

On January 9th the quarrel between Mary and Anne burst into

* In this portrait, dated 1689, Anne stands beside an orange-tree growing in a vast urn. A little later the pro-Orange symbolism would not have been so stressed.

flames. The Queen sent for her sister, who was pregnant, and taxed her with her grant to Sarah of a thousand a year. It was outrageous. Sarah must be dismissed. Anne, knowing her weakness in argument, said little, but from what she did say it was obvious that nothing on earth was going to make her obey. At this Mary lost her temper and threatened to have Anne's allowance reduced. Anne then flared up and the scene ended in fury and dismay.[22] Marlborough's disgrace came twelve days later, and a fortnight after that Anne took Sarah to Court. The audacity of it – to flaunt her barefaced in the enemy's camp – was worthy of Marlborough himself. Nor could Anne who loved etiquette possibly not know that the wife of a disgraced officer never appeared. The whole Court including Mary were as dumbfounded as they were meant to be.

By a letter next day from Mary Anne was again told that Sarah must go. 'It is very unfit Lady Marlborough should stay with you, since that gives her husband so just a pretence of being where he ought not'. Bringing her to Court had been the strangest thing that ever was done. It had worsened their quarrel and made it public. Still it was not too late. 'I love you as my sister', Mary assured her, 'and nothing but yourself can make me do otherwise . . . It shall never be my fault if we do not live kindly together, nor will I ever be other by choice but your truly loving and affectionate sister'.[23]

It was a kind and reasonable letter, but the notion of having to part with Sarah struck Anne to the heart. In an agitated hand she wrote at once to her:

> I have just now received such an arbitrary letter from the Queen as I am sure she nor the King durst not have writ to any other of their subjects & which if I had any inclination to part with dear Mrs Freeman would make me keep her in spite of their teeth & which by the grace of God I will & go to the utmost verge of the earth rather than live with such monsters. I beg I may speak with you as soon as you can possible [sic].[24]

Anne then asked her uncle Rochester to carry a letter to Mary, and when he refused she sent it by a servant:

> . . . A command from you to part with her must be the greatest mortification in the world to me and indeed of such a nature as I might well have hoped your kindness to me would have always prevented . . . Your

care of my present condition is extremely obliging, and if you would be pleased to add to it so far as upon my account to recall your severe command (as I must beg leave to call it in a matter so tender to me & so little reasonable, as I think, to be imposed upon me that you would scarce require it from the meanest of your subjects), I should ever acknowledge it as a very agreeable mark of your kindness to me . . . There is no misery that I cannot readily resolve to suffer rather than the thoughts of parting with her . . .[25]

'In all this', wrote Mary in her diary, 'I see the hand of God and look on our disagreeing as a punishment upon us for the irregularity by us committed upon the Revolution'.[26] The surprising thing was that she never mentioned the Devil. One thing was certain: whether for good or bad reasons Stuart blood was up, and thanks to Stuart obstinacy reconciliation looked all but impossible. Already the breach was the subject of Court gossip. Anne received an anonymous letter:

. . . have a care of what you say before Lady Fitzharding, remember she's Lord Portland's & Betty Villiers's sister. You may depend upon't that these two are not ignorant of what is said & done in your lodgings . . . The King & Queen have been told that there has not passed a day since Lord Marlborough's being out that you have not shed tears. If I durst I could soon convince you that his misfortune comes from your own family. If it ended in his turning out he might leave it with patience, but if resolutions hold he will be confined as soon as the Parliament is up, & if you do not part with his Lady of yourself you will be obliged to [do] it. Would you but enquire where Lady Fitzharding was the week before he had his dismissal, you would find that her tears were not very sincere . . Upon the whole matter he's the luckiest gentleman in England* whose sister governs the King & his wife the Queen & is the entire confident of poor deluded Lady Marlborough. If you slight this advice I wish you may not have cause to repent it.[27]

Whoever the writer was, he or she was well informed; for Sarah

* Probably referring to Edward Villiers first Earl of Jersey (1656–1711), brother of Lady Fitzharding, Betty Villiers (afterwards Countess of Orkney) and Anne Countess of Portland married to William's Dutch favourite Hans Bentinck Earl of Portland. They were all children of Anne's late governess Lady Frances Villiers. Lady Jersey and Lady Fitzharding were close friends of Queen Mary's.

was now ordered by the Lord Chamberlain to leave the Cockpit, and in May Marlborough would be sent to the Tower. But Anne was not to be daunted. If Sarah must quit the Cockpit, though it was Anne's by her marriage settlement, she would leave it too. She sent for the Somersets and asked to borrow their Thames-side house, Syon. 'As soon as this was known', wrote Sarah, 'the King did all he could to dissuade the Duke from letting the Princess have the house, but his Grace had too much greatness of mind to go back from his promise, so there was an end of that matter'.*[28]

At Syon Anne lived 'in an obscure retirement, more like a private person under disgrace than the presumptive heir to the crown'.[29] Pettiness ensued. By royal command Anne's guards were removed (she was robbed on the way to Twickenham); at St James's Church she was no longer to have the text put on her cushion; and when, later, she took George to Bath, the mayor was instructed to do her no honour. The Court was forbidden to call. As persecution it was pitiful and missed its mark. 'I think', wrote Anne to Sarah, "tis a thing to be laughed at'. Precisely so.

On April 17th Anne gave birth to a boy who lived only a few minutes. She was seriously ill. Mary, arriving at Syon with Lady Derby and Lady Scarbrough, found no servant to conduct them and had to make her way to Anne's bedside by the back stairs. What was worse, she 'could hardly get an answer' from Anne.[30] But was that really so surprising? According to Sarah the Queen never asked Anne how she did nor expressed the least concern for her nor so much as took her by the hand. All Mary could find to say was, 'I have made the first step by coming to you and I now expect you should make the next by removing my Lady Marlborough'. To which Anne answered that she had never disobeyed her except in this, which she hoped one day would appear as unreasonable to her as it did to herself. Mary then rose and left. She could hardly have shown less feeling; although afterwards she owned she was sorry she

* Sarah's *Conduct*, begun in 1710 but not published until 1742, has in draft, at Blenheim and at Althorp, many amendments. This applies particularly to Charles Seymour Duke of Somerset, whose stock with Sarah fell heavily in 1710, when he conspired with Harley, to rise again later when, after the death of Marlborough, he sought her hand in marriage.

had reopened the subject of Sarah: she had noticed Anne tremble and turn as white as the sheets.[31]

On May 5th Marlborough was arrested for high treason and sent to the Tower. 'A dreadful plot broke out', Sarah explains, 'which was said to have been hid somewhere, I don't know where, in a flower-pot; and my Lord Marlborough was sent to the Tower'. As an informer Young, who had manufactured the plot, was even more transparent than Titus Oates; and the letter he had forged was so well hidden it could not be found. From William's standpoint it was a pity Young had had to interfere. His own secret service was efficient and one of his regular spies, John Macky, boasted that he had 'made such discoveries as rendered King William entirely master of the Jacobite correspondence and pointed out every person concerned'.[32] Marlborough stayed in the Tower for some weeks after Admiral Russell had scotched the invader at La Hogue. Anne sent encouraging letters to Sarah

> . . . for methinks it is a dismal thing to have one's friends sent to that place . . . I am just told by pretty good hands that as soon as the wind turns westerly there will be a guard set upon the Prince & me . . . But let them do what they please, nothing shall ever vex me so I can have the satisfaction of seeing dear Mrs Freeman; and I swear I would live on bread & water between four walls with her without repining; for as long as you continue kind nothing can ever be a real mortification to your faithful Mrs Morley, who wishes she may never enjoy a moment's happiness in this world or the next if ever she proves false to you.[33]

Never for a moment must Sarah dream of leaving her. 'I beg it again', she insisted, 'for Christ Jesus's sake that you would never name it any more to me, for be assured if you should ever do so cruel a thing as to leave me, from that moment I shall never enjoy one quiet hour. And should you do it without asking my consent (which if I ever give you, may I never see the face of heaven), I will shut myself up & never see the world more, but live where I may be forgotten by human kind'.[34]

There was, then, to be no reconciliation with Mary. Anne on recovery made some attempts at one, only to be told it was deeds that were wanted and not words. 'Sure never anybody was used so by a sister', she exclaimed to Sarah; and no doubt Mary was saying or thinking much the same. When Rochester in an obsequious letter offered himself to Anne as peacemaker, she told him she would have been much better pleased if she had thought him sincere. As it was she suspected that his influence with Mary had caused much of the trouble. Even after this, Rochester dropped a hint that if only Anne would dismiss Sarah now, Mary might allow her to return later. The temptation to tease proved irresistible. Lady Fitzharding was sent to Mary with a disingenuous message so phrased as to incense her. It did. 'Upon the delivery of this message', wrote Sarah, 'the Queen fell into a great passion & said her sister had not mistaken her for she never would see her upon any other terms than parting with me, not for a time but forever, adding that she was a Queen & would be obeyed'. This she repeated several times and with so much vehemence that even Lady Fitzharding was appalled.[35] After this the most Mary could bring herself to do was to send rattles and toys to the Duke of Gloucester; and on one occasion, when he paid her a birthday visit and was saluted at her gates, he told her his mama had once had guards too but now she had none.

On Marlborough's release there was little rejoicing. He was still out of favour; and during his absence his younger son Charles had died, leaving him with one male heir, Lord Churchill. Anne offered to create a place for Marlborough in her household, but that was declined.

Gloucester was often ill with what was called an ague, for which Radcliffe prescribed the Jesuits' bark or powder (quinine), which he loathed and was apt to vomit. 'My poor boy has vomited this afternoon', Anne writes to Sarah, 'whether it will prove anything or no God knows. However 'tis impossible to help being alarmed at every little thing . . .' And then, more cheerfully, 'I have been knotting all this day, in order to be a good workwoman against you employ me. I wish you saw me work for I'm sure it would make you laugh . . .'[36] She plans an informal visit to St Albans without attendants – 'it would be very impertinent to give you the trouble of entertaining any of my mob' – and vows that for one glimpse of Mrs Freeman she would gladly drive to Jerusalem.[37]

Anne's letters to Sarah are not, one would say, the products of a dull mind. Certain themes (notably devotion and constancy) recur, but she can be and often is outspoken – too often in fact for Sarah's comfort. Knowing how frequently letters were intercepted, Sarah cautioned Anne against referring to William as Caliban or the Dutch abortion; and when she persisted, though she kept the letters as she kept everything, she scratched the expletives out.

Anne wrote:

I know you hate writing and so do I, and to people that are indifferent to me I have been three hours writing a dozen lines, but methinks when one's heart goes along with one's pen 'tis no difficult matter to write half that number; and so when I receive one kind word or two from dear Mrs Freeman I am more pleased than with a volume on any other subject, for indeed to what purpose should you and I tell one another yesterday it rained and today it shined? As for news you will have it from those that are more intelligible & when it has been all over the nation it will at last come to Campden House, which is time enough to anyone that is not more inquisitive after things of that kind than I am. I will not pretend to find fault with your expressions, but the more freely you write the more welcome your letters are to your faithful Morley, who has more satisfaction in reading what her dear dear Mrs Freeman calls nonsense than all the eloquence in the world can express.[38]

Without Sarah's replies, which she insisted on being burned, ('I kissed your dear kind letter over & over', Anne once told her, 'and burnt it much against my will'),[39] it is still obvious that Mrs Freeman, usually though not always, wrote less freely than Mrs Morley and altogether less warmly than Mrs Morley would have liked. Anne moved from Syon to Campden House, Kensington and then to Berkeley House, on the site of Devonshire House in Piccadilly; and wherever she went, if Sarah was absent, she expected to hear from her by every post. When she did not, or when Sarah wrote of resigning, Anne was thrown into agitation. George, she told Sarah, agreed with her. The notion of obeying the monster's command was unthinkable. 'No, my dear Mrs Freeman, never believe your faithful Morley will ever submit. She can wait with patience for a sunshine day and if she does not live to see it yet she hopes England will flourish again. Once more let me beg you would be so kind never to speak of parting more, for let what will happen, that is the only thing can make [me] miserable'.[40]

For by no means the last time one admires her resilience and spirit. She continued to miscarry, in March 1693 and in the following January, and must often have felt alarmingly ill. On one such occasion, in 1694, she sent twice to Dr Radcliffe who told the second messenger, 'Her Highness's distemper was nothing but the vapours and she was in as good a state of health as any woman breathing could she but give in to the belief of it'.[41] Not surprisingly, though he had done much for Gloucester, he was dismissed and never reinstated.

When that December Radcliffe was called in by William to attend Mary, he found her smallpox beyond any doctor's cure. Burnet, whose idol she was, blamed Radcliffe – 'a professed Jacobite' – for her death, but that was nonsense. William collapsed at the bedside and was himself thought to be dying. When he could speak he said he had never known her have one fault. Her death in her thirty-third year left him in despair.

Anne had once told Sarah, 'If she [Mary] should die at my feet I could not love her more than I do';[42] and while she was dying she sent messages from her couch (she was trying to prevent a miscarriage) and offered to go to her. The note from Lady Derby, a lady-in-waiting, declining her offer, was brief and formal, but the postscript – 'Pray, Madam, present my humble duty to the Princess' – convinced Sarah that Mary's disease was mortal. Anne indeed made desperate efforts at a last-minute reconciliation (Lady Fitzharding 'broke in, whether they would or not'), but the evidence for any response from Mary is slight. According to Lewis Jenkins Anne felt her death deeply and this, with her miscarriages, undermined her health and (she was only thirty) aged her prematurely.

It was now obviously in William's interest to become reconciled to Anne, for unless he married again and had children, he must at his death leave the crown to her. Sunderland, whose enemy Mary had been, was chief peacemaker. Sarah in her memoirs blows hot and cold about him, as she later did with his son. He changed his religion twice within six months, she reminds us and, for James, prosecuted the bishops before betraying him to William. On the other hand on behalf of Anne, who could never endure him, 'he had upon all occasions shown himself a man of sense and breeding' and now, having overcome Portland's objections, he arranged a meeting at Kensington Palace. Anne in a sedan-chair was carried to William's presence and on arrival Jenkin Lewis opened the chaise door. William came forward to greet her, but both were too moved to speak. Anne had loved her sister. William on her deathbed found he had loved his wife. One may still see at Kensington the 'mourning frame', meant for Mary's portrait, which William commissioned Grinling Gibbons to carve. It has smiling and weeping *putti* and in the centrepiece two doves, not billing and cooing but turning away their heads.

Anne's guard was restored and she was given most of Mary's jewels (some were still in Holland). George continued to be snubbed, but on March 29th Marlborough was summoned to an audience with William and kissed hands.

Almost everyone now agreed that Mary had been a saint, altogether too good to live. Only a Jacobite dared to say, 'She was too bad a daughter and too good a wife'.[43] James mourned in private and asked that there should be no Court mourning in France. Mary, he said bitterly, was being canonised for 'a sort of parricide' and for having got the better of her duty to her parents; while as for Anne, 'notwithstanding her late pretence of repentance', she now seemed better contented to let William usurp her right rather than that her father, 'who had always cherished her beyond expression, should be restored to the possession of his; so that all the King got by it was an additional affliction'.[44]

Mary's death had encouraged the Jacobites, and before she was buried Shrewsbury received an anonymous letter which began: 'My husband is drawn in I doubt to plot against the King . . . The Princess would not accept of the Crown if the King was dead except it was to bring in her father, for she is now ready to bite her nails for giving away her right . . .'[45] This was as unlikely as the letter she was supposed to have written to James, seeking his sanction for her acceptance of the crown should William die.[46]

In the autumn of 1695 James sent Berwick, his son by Marlborough's sister Arabella, to England with a view to planning an insurrection. He stayed in disguise for some months and then, having done his duty and in the course of it discovered a plot to assassinate William as he returned from hunting, thought it time to leave. The attempt, planned for February 15th, he thought 'difficult to execute' and he was right. When the time came, forty armed conspirators were mustered, but the two who were traitors had told Portland, who persuaded William to stay at home; and so it was that by denying himself a day's hunting William, who had never been popular, became for a short while a martyr.

Trials and executions of nameless desperadoes followed, but national bloodlust demanded a scapegoat of standing. Sir John Fenwick, son-in-law of the Earl of Carlisle and a noted rebel, though not present at the attempt, would have been ideal had he not, in his confession, charged Marlborough, Godolphin and Shrewsbury with treasonable correspondence with James's Court at St Germain. This was no news to William, but to have it shouted in Parliament had not been part of his plan. He still wished to ignore it, but the hunt was up and Shrewsbury, called by his contemporaries timorous, found the strain too much and retired to the country broken, at least temporarily, in health. William, who liked him, refused for the time being to accept his resignation. He did however accept Godolphin's, much to his dismay.

In November the Denmarks were offered St James's Palace, which they accepted, but returned to Campden House while the new place was being got ready. William, as usual, was abroad and Anne was not named regent in his absence, but at least she was not persecuted and now the Court, headed by sycophants and place-seekers, began to drift towards her. Sarah could control them. It was the halfwitted Carnarvon who at an evening reception blurted out to Anne, 'I hope your Highness will remember that I came to wait upon you when none of this company did'.[47] Everybody laughed.

CHAPTER FOUR

WILLIAM

1695 - 1702

As heir-presumptive to the throne of three kingdoms Anne at thirty, uneducated and untrained, found herself entirely dependent upon her advisers. 'She would not go to take the air', wrote Sarah, 'unless somebody advised her to it'.[1] She was strong willed and determined to do her duty, but in William's reign she was allowed no share in state business and learned of events by hearsay. As Burnet remembered, 'She was not made acquainted with public affairs. She was not encouraged to recommend any to posts of trust and advantage, nor had the Ministry orders to inform her how matters went nor to oblige those about her'.[2]

Her impressions of people and of politics were bound to be coloured by the views of those who had access to her: the Churchills and Godolphin and to a lesser degree John Sharp Archbishop of York, who was soon to become Anne's favourite churchman. One wonders how much or how little, at this stage, what Marlborough was to call the detested names of Whig and Tory meant to her. She seems quite early to have realised that 'a wise and good prince may unite his subjects and be himself the centre of their union'.[3] She feared extremes, her own nature was that of moderation; yet she feared too anything tainted, as she judged the Whig party to be, with republicanism. She must and would always support the Church, and what she knew as the Church party was the Tory party. Perhaps, she must have thought, once the crown was hers she could put an end to the whole factious system. It was ridiculous to expect anything but weakness from a country divided against itself. She would be Queen of all her subjects and would, as she said, have all the parties and distinctions of former reigns buried in hers.[4]

It seemed unanswerably sensible and logical – the notion of governing with the best talent available, regardless of party – and it appealed not only to Anne but to Marlborough and Godolphin, and later to Robert Harley; but the awkward fact remained, as it still does, that for one reason and another a coalition government in England has never for long been made to work, 'so hard a thing it is, in such divided times, to resolve to be of no parties'.[5]

At this very time, the leaders of the Whig faction whom Anne was most to dread – to be called the Junto – were, with Shrewsbury as their go-between with William, gathering strength. They were Tom Wharton, 'bluff, blasphemous and randy',[6] who boasted of having sung James II out of three kingdoms with his nonsense-song *Lilliburlero*; John Somers the Lord Chancellor, who had defended the seven bishops and of whom Bolingbroke was to say 'There was never a wiser or a better man'; Charles Montagu (later Lord Halifax) Chancellor of the Exchequer and founder in 1694 of the Bank of England; and Admiral Edward Russell (later Earl of Orford), who had signed the invitation to William and was the victor at Cape La Hogue. Joined later by the younger Sunderland they would form the most formidable team in the history of English politics. They would be the bane of Anne's life, but for the moment she could ignore them.

Sarah, herself a Whig, though Marlborough and Godolphin were at this stage labelled Tory, of course knew all about them; and later, on this whole vital question of politics, she would need to sound Anne to the depths and if need be convert her. But for the time being the thing was to approach queenhood in general terms, to appeal to her sense of duty and justice and to say nothing that might frighten her or run counter to what had been schooled into her by the Church.

'I used to pass many hours in a day with her', she recalled, 'and always endeavour to give her notions of loving her country, of justice and governing by the laws & making herself be beloved rather than feared, and I always showed her how easy that was to do when she had [it] so much in her power to do good; and I ever told her that nothing was so great & honourable as to govern upon the conditions that a crown was taken, nor no way so certain as that to keep it as long as she lived'.[7]

Belated and superficial though it was, she could (insofar as it went) have had worse schooling; and it might well have been better for both if Sarah had gone no farther. Here were two women of integrity, goodwill and commonsense. Anne as a figurehead – the Pious Queen – would have done very well. She had perfect confidence in her friends. Why should they not undertake for her without tormenting her with party politics, for which she had no taste? Sarah was shocked when Anne's talk turned to gossip. Certainly she should have been better prepared to reign; yet life was hazardous. Everyone had expected Mary to outlive William but she had not. Anne, who in 1696 miscarried twice, might too easily die in childbirth or, medicine being what it was, in a hundred other ways. She was not, like Sarah, forever wishing she had been a man. On the contrary, her interests were feminine; why pretend they were otherwise? When not in pain she liked to dwell on friends and family, on cards and clothes or on the talk of the town. And she liked to be amused. She told Sarah:

> Lady Fretchville [sic] gave me an account today of Mrs Lowther's having been robbed, which was entertaining enough as she told it, but I doubt it will not be so much so in a letter, because it will want the addition of her airs in telling it.
>
> Yesterday Mrs Lowther went somewhere out of town to see a sister of hers & coming home was set upon by highwaymen. One of them came up to her with a pistol & bid her deliver or she was a dead woman. She desired him to take away his pistol & promised to give him what she had. She put her hand into her pocket to take out her money, which was not above twenty shillings. He took her by the hand & giving her a great squeeze bid her not be afraid, only kiss him. She had a relation with her in the coach, who cried out to her, 'Kiss him! Kiss him, cousin!' which Mrs Lowther did, & the gentleman was so civil that he told her if she had had a necklace of never so much value about her neck he would not have took it, but went away & would not suffer any of his comrades to come to her coach . . .[8]

But Sarah soon wearied of such prattle, as she did of Anne's doting and importunate letters. She had drawersful of them, she said, in all her houses, and what did they amount to? 'Her letters were very indifferent', she later remembered, 'both in sense and spelling, unless that they were generally enlivened with a few passionate expressions, sometimes pretty enough but repeated over & over again without the mixture of anything either of diversion or instruction'.[9]

True, her spelling – 'wellcum', 'paypour', 'Wensday' – was as wayward as everyone else's including Sarah's; but for the rest Sarah's verdict is churlish and less than fair. Allowing for everything one can think of, Anne's letters to Sarah were still very remarkable. Whether she liked it or not, they were, at this stage (and it lasted for years), love letters; not instructive, not very diverting, they were not meant to be, but real, loving, at times passionate and poured from a full heart.

This of course to a woman like Sarah, happily married and of an exceedingly dry and commonsensical turn of mind, could be embarrassing; yet no biography of Anne could be honest were this longlasting infatuation overlooked.

There are now three main themes: devotion, constancy and death. Those might seem usual enough. Vehemency is the surprising thing. At times, so great is Anne's effort at emphasis, at attempts to bare her soul on paper, she seems about to hurl herself bodily on to the page. Sarah was or said she was shocked. As Arthur Maynwaring remarked, Anne's passion meant nothing to her; and so these 'expressions' of Anne's, 'backed with vows which strike one with a sort of horror at what happened afterwards' missed their mark, as did the oaths that went with them: 'imprecations of God's displeasure upon herself if any consideration ever made her consent to part with' Sarah.[10] That of course was in the time of Mary, when Anne vowed that Mrs Morley would never part with Mrs Freeman till she was fast locked in her coffin. And when the guards had failed to salute Prince George ('I can't believe it was their Dutch breeding alone without Dutch orders that made them do it'), Anne added, 'but nothing great or small can ever trouble me as long as dear Mrs Freeman's kindness continues to Mrs Morley, which I don't in the least question can ever alter, and nothing but death can ever change her'.[11] Later letters ended: '. . . and give me leave once more to assure you I am nor never will change and for Jesus' sake do not doubt what I say'; or '. . . and beg for Christ Jesus' sake you would never think of being anywhere but with me as long as I am above ground';[12] 'My dear dear Mrs Freeman goodnight. I shall think it an

Hampton Court: The East Front looking onto the Great Fountain Garden

The Royal Palace of Kensington c. 1702

Sarah Duchess of Marlborough

Kneller: Princess Anne of Denmark with an orange flower (1689)

Playing cards printed in the reign of Queen Anne

age till I see you again & once more be assured I am as unchangeable as fate';[13] 'I will live and die most passionately my dear Mrs Freeman's'.[14]

The long affair had its jealousies and misunderstandings. 'I know I have a great many rivals', wrote Anne, 'which makes me sometimes fear losing what I so much value'.[15] One of her rivals, as she supposed, was Lady Sunderland: 'You have often told me that I had no reason to be jealous of her & therefore I will not complain any more till I see more reasons for it, but I assure you I have been a little troubled at it'. Anne warned Sarah particularly against Lady Fitzharding: 'Remember none of that family were ever good for anything';[16] while Sarah counters with her own suspicions, which Anne hastens to quell. Mrs Morley has, she insists, 'a constant heart, loves you tenderly, passionately and sincerely and knows the world too well (if she were of a fickle temper) ever to be charmed with anybody but your dear self who deserves more from me than ever any friend did from another . . . I hope', she concludes, 'I shall get a moment or two to be with my dear Mrs Freeman that I may have one dear embrace which I long for more than I can express'.[17]

On the whole tempestuous business the husbands remain silent; Marlborough as always deliberately so. (He had a 'tenderness' for the Queen as queen, we know little more); while George of course scarcely ever emerges as more than a lay figure and a mildly comic one at that. He 'had not spirit enough to help himself', says Dartmouth.[18] He was perfectly content with his 'extraordinarily tender and affectionate'[19] wife; and in broken English he was eager to approve whatever she chose to do or say. If she wanted to keep Sarah as her first lady-in-waiting of course she must keep her; and when in her absence Anne wrote long letters, he was happy to stand, glass in hand, staring down through a window at the passers-by. Asthma troubled him and so did gout, but over a bottle or two with Marlborough's brother George he could forget both. It was Mulgrave who unkindly suggested he was forced to breathe hard in case people took him for dead and buried him; 'at which some of the gods smiled and said it were well for the good of mankind if all other princes were as quiet as he was'.[20]

In July '96, on his seventh birthday, Gloucester was installed a

Knight of the Garter at Windsor. Closterman's portrait (See page 137) is of a sad, sensitive boy weighed down with giant tassels and robes. With too exquisite hand he gestures in what looks like despair. At Windsor he stood the ceremony well, but had to leave afterwards in the middle of dinner: his diet ordinarily was extremely dull and plain. However, he was soon well enough to hunt deer in the park, where he was blooded by Mr Masham, a page to Prince George.[21] 'My boy continues yet very well', Anne reported to Sarah, 'and looks better, I think, than ever he did in his life; I mean more healthy, for though I love him very well, I can't brag of his beauty'.[22]

The King his godfather had given him an onyx and diamond George to hang on his Garter chain; yet as Burnet records, William's attitude towards Anne still went not much farther than what civility and decency required. Anne for her part was willing to do what she could. Perhaps, she thought, if she made much of his birthday it might speed the thaw. Sarah would know what to do. On October 20th Anne wrote to her from Windsor:

I writ yesterday to ask your opinion what must be done on the birthday, being unwilling to depend on my own in anything, especially at this time, being much more inclined to have a play, but I doubt that will not be so well liked, because a ball is reckoned a thing of more respect & I think I have heard the King does not care for plays. One very good pretence there is for a play, which is the shortness of the time for people's learning to dance . . . Without doubt there are people that will find fault with mantoes,* for one must expect every new thing will be disliked at first, the generality of the world disapproving of every fashion they do not bring up themselves. I did not think my Lady Fitzharding would have been of the number of those that did not approve of mantoes, not being at all formal herself, but she speaks of it with an air as if she did not think it respect enough. She thinks people can't be so fine as in gowns, and since mantoes are to be worn, that a play would be best, for mantoes cannot be worn at a ball. I told her since they were the dress, it was as much respect to be in them as gowns and that I might certainly be as fine in them; but she did not seem wholly to approve of what I said. She came hither yesterday, which I wondered at, not expecting to have seen her till we came to London.

* Manto (anglicised *manteau*): a cloak or tunic, left open to show the petticoat, the latter often hooped and embroidered.

I think it will be better not to say anything to the lady ['Bathurst' has been added in Sarah's hand] about her husband's faults, for it will do no good, and since there is nobody perfect but dear Mrs Freeman I must have patience with the rest of the world and look as much into all my affairs as I can. If I were not satisfied with you I should be the greatest monster that ever breathed, for as I have often said, I do really believe there never was nor will be such a friend as dear Mrs Freeman . . .

When I have tried the manto you intend for the birthday I will tell you my thoughts of it, but before I see it I dare say it will be better than what any other body can choose, at least it will be so in my opinion. I shall want you mightily when I am dressed, there being nobody that will take that care to see all my things in order as you will do; but do not think I say this to desire you to come a minute sooner than you have a mind to. Since you think the ways will not give me leave to make you a visit as I had a mind to, I will give over that pleasing thought, but shall wish the birthday past that I may have the satisfaction again of telling my dear Mrs Freeman myself that I am most faithfully hers.[23]

It had to be a ball. On September 20th Anne had suffered a miscarriage of twins: a son of seven months, the other 'of two or three months'.[24] She still felt a cripple (she spells it 'creeple') 'and inclined so much to vaypours'. She dreaded extra fatigue. Yet on November 4th she gamely led the dance and danced admirably. As far as William was concerned she might have spared herself the effort. 'His Majesty was extremely out of humour'.[25]

The Bathurst affair was even more troublesome. Anne's Treasurer of the Household, Sir Benjamin Bathurst, Frances Apsley's husband, had according to Sarah been caught in the act of trying to cheat Anne and George in the matter of revalued guineas. Clipped coins had been recalled for recoining and in the process the value of guineas was called down from thirty shillings to twenty or twenty-one. Bathurst, says Sarah, 'imposed so much on the Princess as to cheat her of the third part of all she had'.[26] This almost certainly was exaggerated. From letters of Anne's at Blenheim, however, and particularly one in which she writes of 'a much greater abhorrence of him [Bathurst] than ever',[27] it looks as though he followed long-established custom in taking bribes from tradesmen and from place-seekers, whether he succeeded in placing them or not. His wife, who had been Mary's favourite, was now nicknamed by Anne and Sarah the Nag's Head.

Anne had 'convulsion fits' in December, but was well enough by her birthday to enjoy *Love For Love*, and a second ball in the sour King's honour the same evening. One wonders what she made of Congreve. Four weeks later Luttrell notes:

> Several new plays having been lately acted contrary to good manners, the Lord Chamberlain has given orders that none be acted hereafter till his secretary has perused them.[28]

In June and July Anne and George took the waters at Tunbridge. On their way back to Windsor in August they dined with the Earl of Dorset at Knole. It sounds a tranquil time, not appreciably disturbed by those prophets of doom who have always been with us. One of them, a Mr Beverley, who had written a book to prove that Christ's coming to judge the world would be on August 23rd, made on August 28th public recantation. He had he owned, been mistaken in the time 'but believed 'twas not far off'.[29]

In October William and Louis XIV signed the Peace of Ryswick, a treaty in which the interests of the exiled Stuarts were not forgotten. Mary of Modena, William agreed, was to have £50,000 a year. But according to Dalrymple a far more important clause had been omitted. William, it was said, had offered to have James Francis Edward educated in England as his Protestant successor, but James II had declined. He 'could not support the thought of making his own child a complice to his unjust dethronement', nor of his changing his religion.[30] This may have been a myth; for while it might not be difficult to imagine William riding roughshod over Anne, it would have meant too trampling down young Gloucester, and that, unless he saw his condition as hopeless, must surely have given him pause. However, Sir Winston Churchill was not alone in believing these Jacobite records one of the mare's-nests of history.

Early in December Anne had her ninth miscarriage. She was unable to attend the opening of the chancel of St Paul's. Compton, bishop and botanist, sat in his stall between oak columns enriched by Gibbons with lilies and tuberoses; but everyone was impatient to have the whole building finished, so much so that the previous

March Wren's £200 a year had been halved, to make him, as they hoped, more expeditious.

On January 4th, 1698, a fire caused, it was thought, by the carelessness of a servant who put charcoal ashes into a closet, destroyed Whitehall Palace, including the 'Protestant and Popish chapels'. Thanks to Wren and others who fought the flames Inigo Jones's Banqueting House ('the first truly classical building in England')[31] survived. The rest was in ruins. William, standing among the ashes, said if God would give him leave he would rebuild it much finer than before; but that was not to be, and in the meantime, to Anne's discomfort, the King commandeered the Chapel Royal at St James's while the Banqueting House was being 'fitted up for a chapel'.[32]

In March Henrietta Churchill, the eldest of Sarah's daughters, married Francis, the only son of Godolphin and the late Margaret Blagge. Henrietta (or Harriet) was strong-willed and handsome, her husband good and dull, not stupid like George of Denmark, but tedious. Anne in her diffident way begged that her 'poor mite' of a wedding-present (£10,000) might be accepted, 'being offered from a heart without any reserve, with more passion and sincerity my dear Mrs Freeman than any other can be capable of'. Sarah accepted £5,000. 'The Princess having but £50,000 a year', she explains, 'I thought the offer too large for her income'.[33] Anne gave another £5,000 to her god-daughter Anne (the second daughter) when in the first week of 1700 she married Sunderland's heir Lord Spencer.*

With William's promise that spring of a separate establishment for Gloucester, Anne's hopes had begun to rise. It was high time for him to leave Lady Fitzharding and 'to be put into men's hands'. But it would be a costly business. What with this and Mary of Modena's allowance, William told Parliament he would need an additional £100,000 a year. It was granted. 'Yet', says Sarah, 'he never paid one shilling to the Queen; and as to the Duke, the King not only kept him in women's hands a good while . . . but when his Highness's family was settled, would give him no more than £15,000 a year.

* Charles Spencer (1675–1722), on the death of his father in 1702, succeeded as 3rd Earl of Sunderland. From him by this second marriage to Anne Churchill descend the Spencer (Earl Spencer) and the Spencer-Churchill (Duke of Marlborough) lines.

Nay, of this small allowance he refused to advance one quarter, though it was absolutely wanted to buy plate and furniture, so that the Princess was forced to be at that expense herself.

'But this was not all. The King (influenced I suppose in this particular by my Lord Sunderland) sent the Princess word that though he intended to put in all the preceptors, he would leave it to her to choose the rest of the servants except one . . . This message was so humane & of so different an air from anything the Princess had been used to that it gave her an extreme pleasure and she immediately set herself to provide proper persons . . . for the several places . . .

A little before he left England to make the campaign the King told my Lord Marlborough (who was now restored to the army and was to be Governor to the Duke of Gloucester) that he would send a list from abroad of the servants he would have in the Duke's family, not in the least regarding the former message he had sent to the Princess; which my Lord observing, took the liberty to put his Majesty in mind of it, adding that the Princess, upon the credit of that message, had engaged her promises to several persons and that not to be able to perform those promises would be so great a mortification as he hoped his Majesty would not give her at a time when anything of trouble might do her prejudice, she being then with child. Hereupon the King fell into a great passion and said she should not be Queen before her time and he would make the list of what servants the Duke should have.[34]

One can only suppose that the servants approved by the Marlboroughs were disapproved of by the King. Sarah spares no pains to make William look boorish. Perhaps he was; but one wonders if Anne's names for him – Caliban and the rest – were her own or if from the first he had been damned by someone else.

It was something, indeed it was much that Marlborough was to be Gloucester's governor. (Shrewsbury was offered the job and declined it). Less pleasing was the appointment of Burnet, now Bishop of Salisbury, as his preceptor. He would be conscientious, nobody doubted that, but he was known to be a busybody and he was not liked by Anne. She said herself she considered his appointment the greatest hardship imposed by the King, who well knew her aversion. Burnet knew it too and tried to back out, but William was insistent and so the Whig bishop gave in. 'I saw all that Court except Lord Marlborough and his Lady were against me', he wrote. 'I lived very well with them and I thought that was enough'. John Macky found him 'a large, bold-looked man, of great learning but neither of prudence nor temper'.[35] Dartmouth is merciless and to Burnet's boast of having 'had the honour to be admitted to much free conversation with five of our sovereigns' adds, 'He was the standing jest of the Court in every one of them for his confident intrusions and saucy, rude behaviour'.[36] He was a gossip, he was inquisitive and indiscreet, but he was no fool and everyone studying that period owes a debt to him. The main loser in the deal was Gloucester himself, crammed day after day at Windsor with jurisprudence, Greek and Roman history, the Gothic constitution and the beneficiary and feudal laws. A Board of four Privy Counsellors set themselves to examine him once a quarter.

Throughout the summer of '98 Anne had been unwell. On September 17th she miscarried, and four days before that Luttrell noted: 'The Princess of Denmark is ill of the gout'. Gout has never been common in women, but at that embryonic stage of medical knowledge doctors when in doubt diagnosed either gout or 'the ague'. This is the first of countless references to Anne's 'gout', which, beginning in knee and foot, recurred, spread and steadily worsened. Few women can have been more plagued by pain and illness. In January 1700 her long series of miscarriages ended, but by then 'gout' had become established. From one cause or another (see Appendix I) she was soon having to call herself a perfect cripple.

From time to time we hear news of Gloucester – that he has been given a regiment of Dutch guards (but they had to return to Holland); that he fired a salute on Queen Elizabeth's birthday; that he was to have 'the late Queen's lodgings at Kensington, that the King may have him under his protection' . . .[37] But he was still at Windsor on July 24th when his eleventh birthday was celebrated and he danced. He became heated and fatigued (there is mention of 'a surfeit') and next day was obviously ill. Radcliffe came reluctantly, diagnosed scarlet fever (they had thought it was smallpox) and was appalled to learn that the child had been bled. 'Then', said he, 'you have destroyed him and you may finish him, for I will not prescribe'.

On the 30th he died. The body, which quickly 'turned green and yellow', went by royal barge to lie in state in the House of Lords (no one to be admitted unless in mourning) before burial in the Abbey. Anne, dry-eyed, seemed 'occupied with high and awful thoughts'. According to Jenkin Lewis (but he had left her household three years before), 'Her afflicted husband beheld with silent astonishment the pious fortitude of his beloved Princess'. She appeared to be stunned with grief and then, as she began to revive a little at Windsor, she was 'daily carried in her chair to the garden, to divert her melancholy thoughts'.[38]

These thoughts, Miss Strickland would have us believe, were 'wholly and solely fixed on her father. All she felt as a parent reminded her of her crimes towards him'. And so, after 'meditating on the retributive justice of God', Anne wrote to James, 'pouring out her whole heart in penitence and declaring her conviction that her bereavement was sent as a visible punishment from Heaven for her cruelty to him'. The least she could do in reparation was to use her utmost power to restore her brother, if ever she came to the throne . . .[39] It is the attitude any pious Victorian would have liked her to adopt, but it is in fact founded on nothing more reliable than Macpherson's Stuart Papers;[40] and as Miss Strickland admits, Anne's letter to her father 'has not yet come to light'. James of course was told of the death. The French Court mourned for a fortnight; and that was all.

It was no mawkish age. This (found among anonymous doggerel at Longleat) was typical:

> For Gloucester's death, which sadly we deplore,
> Tho' Fate's accus'd, we should commend the more,
> Lest he with Burnet's faith should be imbu'd
> And learn of Churchill truth and gratitude;
> Lest two such masters should their rules instil
> And his young soul with pois'nous precepts fill.
> Untimely force Heav'n kindly did employ
> And to preserve the man destroy'd the boy.[41]

Anne directed that July 30th was always to be kept by her household as a day of mourning; and for the rest of their friendship, in her letters to Sarah, Anne called herself 'your poor unfortunate faithful Morley', a play on the Churchill motto adopted by Marlborough's father: faithful but unfortunate. She still hoped for an heir but, mercifully for her, the eighteenth pregnancy (and disappointment) was never to be. For a time she stayed on at Windsor and there, between castle and forest, she bought from Godolphin the house where her mother had been born, Cranbourne Lodge. She liked the setting of Windsor Castle but, after Gloucester's death, the place seemed sad and cavernous. As Queen she much preferred her Little House, sometimes called the Garden House.*

Burnet, writing of Anne in 1700, says 'her Court was very thin; she lived in a due abstraction from business so that she neither gave jealousy nor encouraged faction'.[42] 'It was an unhappiness to the Queen', Coke adds, 'that she was not much acquainted with our English history & the reigns & actions of her predecessors, she beginning to apply herself to it but a little while before King William died'.[43] Of more recent history she may have known no more than Sarah told her. The fall of the Junto the previous year and the emergence of Robert Harley as Tory leader in the Commons will have meant little to her; nor was she to know that now, while she recuperated with the Marlboroughs at Holywell, William at Loo was discussing the succession to the English throne with Sophia Electress of Hanover.

Sophia is called by her biographer a woman worthy to mount a royal throne. She undoubtedly was. A warmhearted extrovert, she was richly endowed with common sense. She had too a sound sense of loyalty and justice. At the risk of offending William she told him she lamented the fall of James, who had honoured her with his friendship. As for his son the Pretender, 'so young and so eager to recover what his father had thrown away', when she heard that he was to be declared a rebel, she told Leibniz, whom she consulted in everything, that his personal merit deserved a better fate.[44] Sophia was a widow. She spoke six languages. As a granddaughter of James I

* Not to be confused with the present Garden House. Mr Mackworth-Young finds that Queen Anne's Little House lay just south of the upper ward of the Castle. Bought for the Denmarks in 1690 it was enlarged for George III and demolished by George IV. It is shown in a Kip engraving in *Britannia Illustrata* (1707).

and a Protestant (believed to be a Calvinist, though her family were Lutherans), she was now, since the death of Gloucester, the most likely-looking candidate for the English crown. She was quite the most sensible. The only drawback was age: she was seventy. Even in 1689 when she was not quite sixty she had told Burnet, 'Je ne suis plus d'une age à penser à d'autre royaume que celui des cieux'. As time went on however and the thing looked more probable it began to appeal to her, if not for herself, then for her Lutheran son George and his posterity. She was not so philosophical, she said, as to scorn all talk of a crown. In the meantime she would like officially to be known as the Hereditary Princess. She was a calm person and meant to remain so. If the call came she would answer it. Otherwise she would be content where she was. 'The legend of her having often declared that she would die content if *Sophia Queen of Great Britain* could be inscribed on her tomb is', wrote A. W. Ward, 'irreconcilable with the whole tenor of her known private thoughts, as well as of her public acts'.[45]

At this meeting with William in the autumn of 1700 she is said to have coaxed him to repeat his offer to James to adopt the Pretender. Nothing came of it; and in the following March, by the Act of Settlement, Parliament settled the reversion of the crown, after Anne's death (in default of her issue), upon Sophia and her descendants. Although William had been partly responsible for this Act himself, he cannot have found some of its clauses palatable. No foreigner on the throne of England was without Parliament's consent to leave the country (William had been abroad every summer except one), nor to make war for the defence of territory not belonging to England; nor was any MP to hold an office of state. Little of this could, in the event, be enforced, but at the time the invidious points were resented. The Act was shepherded through the Commons by Robert Harley, elected Speaker a month before.

Harley from the first had been surrounded by an aura of sanctity. His father, Sir Edward Harley MP, was a country squire of Puritan stock with estates in Herefordshire and across the Welsh border. At the age of nine Robert was sent to a Dissenters' academy at Shilton near Burford (two of his friends there, Harcourt and Trevor, became Lord Chancellor and Lord Chief Justice). His upbringing was in fact unexceptionable, leading as it did to a lifelong belief in divine indulgence. 'To the end of his life', writes his biographer, 'Harley laced his letters to relatives with pious phrases'.[46] Writing to his father in June 1700 he says, 'I pray God direct and keep a poor worm sensible of his weakness and supported by the power and wisdom which is from above . . .' and a few days later, 'I look up to Heaven for direction'.[47] It was what Sir Edward wanted to hear.

In the time of Cromwell it might have done very well, but now to attempt the role of Praise-God Barebone was to risk ridicule from such godless opponents as Tom Wharton who, it was said, had committed gross sacrilege and was beyond salvation. To Anne, brought up to mistrust Dissenters and Catholics alike, the name Harley must at this stage have meant little. As a manipulator of the Commons he was unparalleled and as Speaker (nominally neutral but in practice, at this time, not so) he now had every chance to use that gift. Swift testifies to his skill 'both of lengthening out and of perplexing debates'; although, as Lady Hamilton now adds, his own debating style was nebulous and vague. Perplexity was the keynote. In politics a moderate, he had succeeded his neighbour and friend Paul Foley as leader of the Country Whigs. Like Marlborough he professed to be of no party and like him he found himself called a Tory. With his Dissenter background he would naturally, as the Whigs did, tolerate Dissenters; but at all times he chose to be noncommittal, tortuous and secret.

'The business of party is so confounded', wrote Lord Strafford to the Electress Sophia, 'that even a native of our country can hardly distinguish them'. Tories and Whigs were less manifestly different than Royalists and Puritans, yet they were just as bitterly opposed. 'I am sure you know', Strafford continued, 'what is called Tory are those which are for the Church of England, which is all or almost all the clergy of England, a great majority in the Parliament and nation and almost all the landed men in the kingdom'.[48] It sounded simple but needed qualifying; for while it was true that Anne knew the Tories as the Church Party, the bishops' benches in the Lords were, thanks to Calvinist William, packed with Low Church bishops such as Bishop Burnet. On the other hand not a few of the greatest and most influential landowners, like the Duke of Newcastle, were

Whig. Recently some of them had got together with such wits as Congreve, Prior and Vanbrugh to help Tonson the publisher establish the Kit-Cat club, to which Marlborough and Godolphin would later belong.

But Whig and Tory outlooks were opposed in other matters. As instigators of the Revolution in '88 the Whigs, in Anne's eyes, were, if not republicans, at least non-believers in the divine right of kings; and although in her own case she might not wish her right to be called divine, she was extremely sensitive on the question of royal prerogative and of the succession. Tories, as Sarah chose to see them, were Jacobites to a man; which of course was nonsense; but any party risks being judged by its extremists. In wartime the rift was still more marked, many Tories being for a restricted war, with reliance on the navy; Whigs opting for total involvement in Europe, for bold and vast operations for which they were prepared to vote vast supplies. That in fact was the chief reason for Marlborough's becoming, like his wife, a Whig, for had he remained a Tory he could not have counted on money (much of it raised by the Land Tax) for his campaigns. The City, a Whig stronghold, had no illusions about trade and what would happen to it if France won a monopoly. There were also minor issues; and the party-system was further complicated by the Court party of office-holders who usually though not always voted with the party in power.

Some years ago the theory was put forward that, in Anne's day, family-ramifications were more powerful than party and had more influence on voting both in Lords and Commons. This has since been controverted. Nevertheless the influence was there and in some cases (e.g. the Duke of Newcastle alone controlled ten seats) could be important. The House of Lords had great power and could if so inclined jettison any Act passed by the Commons. Bishops were voters of weight who to the detriment of flock and pocket had to spend months within call of Westminster. The Cabinet system was in its infancy and would often have Whig and Tory members; while at the head of it all a monarch of limited yet still very considerable power might, regardless of party, choose and dismiss her ministers at will.

The Tories might, as Strafford told Sophia, have a great majority in Parliament and nation, but the Whigs were much better organised. As Professor Plumb puts it, 'The Whig Junto realised they were a minority and this imposed on them a unity . . . Their main strength lay in their territorial magnificence enabling them to influence elections, out of proportion to their numbers'.[49]

William, so often absent, had devised a system of managers to act as go-between with himself and Parliament. It worked well enough to be continued in the reign of Anne, her managers then being Marlborough and Godolphin, with Harley shepherding the Commons and attending to much else. Dr Snyder finds that Godolphin and Harley began to work together regularly in the Tory ministry of 1701;[50] although it was not until the summer of 1702 that Harley began formally to visit Queen Anne.

Today the violence of faction in the early 1700's is hard to imagine. The Whigs were out to destroy the Tories, and the Tories the Whigs; to 'hurt those who stood in opposition to us', as Bolingbroke admits, and 'to break the body of the Whigs'.[51] It was in this vicious frame of mind that in 1701 Somers, Halifax, Orford and Portland were impeached for their parts in the first Partition Treaty of 1699, 'whereby large territories of the King of Spain's dominions were to be delivered over to France'. When the charges failed, Halifax wrote to Shrewsbury, who by then had retired abroad ('Better a cobbler', he told Somers, 'than a statesman'): 'I think our escape has proved that our vessels were pretty tight and not so full of leaks as our enemies maliciously pretended and our friends ridiculously believed'.[52] The treaty had been an attempt by William and Louis to settle the succession of the Spanish Empire, which then included Belgium and large tracts of America, so as to maintain the balance of power without recourse to war. Unluckily, no sooner had the treaty been signed than the heir agreed on – Joseph Ferdinand of Bavaria – died; so all was to do again.

By the second Partition Treaty, called by Trevelyan a masterpiece of William's diplomatic skill, the chief beneficiary was to be Austria, but France was to be compensated with Naples, Sicily and Lorraine. The Emperor of Austria blindly refused to sign unless his younger son were promised the Spanish Empire intact. Charles II of Spain then signed a will in which he named as his successor Louis XIV's grandson Philip of Anjou, and in November 1700 Charles of Spain died. It meant then that unless Louis backed the will, the whole of the Spanish Empire would go to the Austrian, Charles. He did back it; and so France and England again moved towards war.

Trevelyan adds:

The great war was made inevitable not by the acceptance of the will but by the interpretation Louis put upon it in the following months by seizing the Dutch Barrier, by showing that he regarded the Spanish Netherlands (now Belgium) as French territory, by excluding the English merchants from the American trade and by treating the Spanish Empire as a prize for French commercial exploitation and a field of manoeuvre for French armies. By these measures he converted the English Tories to the need of war before ever he crowned the edifice of pride and folly by proclaiming the Pretender as King of England. Against these errors, which were to prove so fatal to France, Louis received fair and full warning. His Ambassador in England was Marshal Tallard . . . The English people, he said, want peace, but only if security be given.[53]

James II died on September 6th, 1701. When at his bedside Louis promised to recognise James Francis Edward as King of England, 'all that were present, as well French as English, burst into tears, not being able any other way to express that mixture of joy and grief with which they were so surprisingly seized'.[54]

When the news reached London, William was still abroad. Luttrell notes (for September 11): 'The Princess of Denmark admits of no visits and on Sunday goes into mourning'. And for September 18: ''tis reported his Majesty has sent orders to forbid the Court going into mourning for the late King James by reason that [Court] of St Germain did not go into mourning for our Queen . . . The Pope has ordered several thousands of masses'.[55] According to Miss Strickland, Anne 'went through all the pageantry of sable like a modern Cordelia' and appeared thus in chapel; but for her St James's lodgings she was in a quandary, at first putting them into mourning and then having it all removed. From Windsor she wrote to Godolphin:

I cannot let your servant go back without returning my thanks for the letter he brought me and assuring you it is a very great satisfaction to me to find you agree with Mrs Morley concerning the ill-natured, cruel proceedings of Mr Caliban, which vexes me more than you can imagine, and I am out of all patience when I think I must do so monstrous a thing as not to put my lodgings in mourning for my father. I hope if you can get a copy of the will Lord Manchester says he will send over you will be so kind as to let me see it, and ever believe me your faithful servant.[56]

On William's return he gave orders for mourning 'as for a relation: persons of quality not to put their liveries into mourning'. The muddle, whether intended or not, was to prove Anne's last wound from that quarter.

To his son the Pretender, James on his deathbed is said to have said,

> Never put the crown of England in competition with your eternal salvation . . . Remember kings are not made for themselves but for the good of all the people . . .
>
> Honour your mother, that your days may be long, and be always a kind brother to your dear sister, that you may reap the blessings of concord and unity'.[57]

Anne is said to have been greatly touched by 'an affecting letter written to her by her father before his death, in which he recommended his family to her'.[58] No such letter has survived, although it may have been burned at her death. What is more certain is that her stepmother wrote as follows:

> . . . Some few days before his death he bid me find means to let you know that he forgave you all that is past from the bottom of his heart and prayed to God to do so too; that he gave you his last blessing and prayed to God to convert your heart and confirm you in the resolution of repairing to his son the wrongs done to himself. To which I shall only add that I join my prayers to his with all my heart, and that I shall make it my business to inspire into the young man who is left to my care the sentiments of his father, for better no man can have.[59]

Anne may well have been moved. 'It may be it is our brother . . .' But if heart should rule head to enthrone that young Roman Catholic, would that not brand her a traitor to the Church and might not civil war follow? In herself she was neither bold nor self-seekingly ambitious, yet infirm as she was and anxious, she would do her duty and she would keep the faith. War and stratagem were not of her choosing, but if she found them at her throne when she came to it, she would play her part.

Luttrell ends the year (1701) with a mixture of jottings:

November 11. Mr Godolphin has resigned as Privy Counsellor and First Commissioner of the Treasury.

November 18. His Majesty designs speedily for Windsor to visit the Princess, who is extremely afflicted with the gout. One Mr Maynwaring is made a commissioner of Customs, the salary £1200 per annum.

November 20. An information is brought in the King's Bench against twelve of the players, Mrs Bracegirdle, Mr Vanbruggen [sic] etc., for using indecent expressions in some late plays, particularly *The Provok'd Wife*, and are to be tried the latter end of term.

December 11. Yesterday morning most of the nobility went to St James's to compliment their Royal Highnesses the Princess & Prince of Denmark upon their return thither from Windsor.

December 23. The Duke of Shrewsbury is arrived at Rome to divert himself with the curiosities of that city.[60]

On February 20th, 1702 William rode for the last time in the park near Hampton Court. No assassin lay in wait for him, nothing deadlier than a molehill, upon which his horse Sorrel is thought to have stumbled. The collarbone that broke was set and with his arm in a sling he joggled by coach to Kensington. Pneumonia set in. On the 28th he sent a message to the Lords to tell them of his 'earnest desire that they would consider of a union between England and Scotland'.

On March 7th an Abjuration Bill was passed, repudiating the Pretender and making it high treason to compass Anne's death. William was too weak to sign it but was just able to apply his stamp. He sent for Portland (Bentinck), 'but though his Lordship placed his ear as near his Majesty's mouth as he could and though his Majesty's lips were seen to move, yet was he not able to hear any distinct words'.[61] As a matter of form he was dosed with Sir Walter Raleigh's Cordial and quinine. On March 8th he died. 'It is very rare', ran the post-mortem report, 'to find a body with so little blood as was seen in this'.[62] The will directed burial without pomp, beside his Queen.

Sarah was surprised at not feeling more satisfaction, 'so little is it in my nature', she explains, 'to retain resentment against any mortal (how unjust soever he may have been) in whom the will to injure is no more'.[63]

King William was dead. Bishop Burnet hurried to tell Queen Anne.

CHAPTER FIVE

SEMPER EADEM

1702

BURNET threw himself at Anne's feet, 'full of joy and duty'. Might he be the first to congratulate the new Queen? He was as usual exceeding his brief and, says Dartmouth, was 'universally laughed at for his officiousness'.[1] A more welcome caller was John Sheffield, now Marquess of Normanby, who as Lord Mulgrave had made his brisk attempt on Anne twenty years before. Anne, now in deep mourning for her father, remarked that it was a very fine day. 'Your Majesty must allow me to declare', said Normanby, 'that it is the most glorious day I ever saw'.[2]

For weeks the sky had been overcast, but 'This day' (so runs Boyer's entry for March 8th) 'afforded a remarkable mixture of sorrow and joy, but the latter as it was more general so it seemed to be justified by heaven itself, the sky having never been more serene nor the sun shone more bright & glorious'.[3]

Because Dutch William was dead and an Englishwoman had succeeded, the surge of loyalty was sincere. When she was proclaimed that Sunday afternoon and met Parliament, the cheers were so deafening that her reply to the Speaker's address could not be heard. No matter. She 'was pleased to order it him in her own handwriting'.[4]

'Persons of quality' swarmed to St James's in such numbers that by the evening Anne was too exhausted to receive more. Among those not admitted was her uncle the Earl of Clarendon who, unlike Rochester his brother, still declined to take the oaths. He now wrote to Anne:

Having endeavoured all the ways I could to be admitted to the honour of waiting upon your Majesty, I hope you will not be offended that I presume by this once more to approach your royal person as near as I can that I may have the happiness, at least this way, to present my duty to your Majesty upon your accession to the Crown & to assure your Majesty that no subject you have can have more duty for your sacred person and authority than I have, nor can wish you greater nor more lasting peace and prosperity. May your reign be long and glorious, may you be victorious over all your enemies, may you be forever fixed in the hearts of your people and may all the blessings of heaven and earth continually attend you . . .[5]

Though he was her mother's brother, it was impossible for Anne to receive him while he remained a non-juror.* Others were luckier. 'She received all that came to her in so gracious a manner', says Burnet, 'that they went from her highly satisfied with her goodness and her obliging deportment, for she hearkened with attention to everything that was said to her'.[6] She was not, as her sister Mary had been, garrulous, but when she did speak everyone was charmed with her voice, a soft contralto. There was moreover 'a sweetness in the pronunciation that added much life to all she spoke'.[7] Dartmouth was captivated. 'It was a real pleasure to hear her', he wrote, 'though she had a bashfulness that made it very uneasy for herself to say much in public'. Even that however, when for the first time (March 11) she drove in state to the Lords and addressed her Parliament, could stand her in good stead, for 'happening to blush very much when she spoke her speech from the throne, some compared her to the sign of the Rose & Crown'.[8] Others were pleased to say that they 'never saw an audience more affected: it was a sort of charm'.[9]

In double mourning (black for James, purple for William), after touching on the importance of a union with Scotland and of supporting our allies against France, she said, 'As I know my own heart to be entirely English I can very sincerely assure you there is not anything you can expect or desire from me which I shall not be ready to do for the happiness & prosperity of England, and you shall always find me a strict & religious observer of my word'. What more could be said? 'If she acts as she speaks', said the dying Sunderland, 'she will be safe, happy and adored'. Only afterwards was Burnet sour enough to point out that 'both these expressions had

* Non-juror: one who had refused to take the oaths of loyalty to the Crown.

been in her father's first speech, how little soever they were afterwards minded by him'.[10] But the general impression was good.

Sir Robert Southwell three days later wrote:

We are now in a new world, and after so great a thunder-clap surely never was there so quick a calm, for within eight hours after the King's death Queen Anne was fixed in the throne. This blessing was due to a sitting Parliament which had power of continuance, for had there been a dissolution by the King's death things had been at large & perhaps uncertain. Her Majesty charmed both Houses on Wednesday last, for never any woman spoke more audibly or with better grace. And her pressing to support our alliances abroad will commute for what the Dutch may take amiss in that emphasis which her Majesty laid on her English heart. But it did very well at home and raised a hum from all that heard her . . . There will no doubts remain but that the true interest of England will have preference to any other . . .'[11]

It was not simply that Anne was English. She was devoted to England and to the English people, and this they quickly realised. From the first there was enormous goodwill on their side and on hers. In her health she was weak, but her spirit was something to be reckoned with. Sir Winston Churchill pronounces her 'one of the strongest personalities that have reigned in these islands . . . as tough on her throne as Marlborough was on the battlefield'. As one would expect it was this toughness – her 'marvellous tenacity of willpower, right or wrong' – which most appealed to him. 'Her intellect', he owns, 'was limited, but her faith, her conscience, her principles and her prejudices were for ten years a factor in the life of England and in the fortunes of Europe, which held its own with the growing power of Parliament and the victories of Marlborough'. Her interests were the Church, Marlborough 'her faithful servant, guide and champion, and Sarah, her dear bosom friend from childhood onward. Besides these she cared intensely about the glory of England, which mattered a great deal, and about her husband Prince George, who mattered very little except to her'.[12]

On this question of Anne's character and capacity historians have been by no means of the same mind. Ralph, a contemporary, gave her 'as much good sense as most women and more than most monarchs'.[13] Trevelyan went further: 'For all her simplicity, the wisest and most triumphant of her race'. More recently she has been called the quintessence of ordinariness; yet was any Stuart ordinary; and even if she had been, would not the spectacle of an ordinary woman thrust upon the English throne be extraordinary and her dilemma of extraordinary interest?

At her accession, if Sarah is to be believed, Anne was the most ignorant and helpless creature living, entirely dependent upon the Marlboroughs and Godolphin, who acted 'like Mentor in *Telemachus*'. 'Godolphin', adds Burnet, 'was the man of the clearest head, the calmest temper and the most incorrupt of all the ministers of state I have ever known . . . He served the Queen with such a particular affection & zeal that he studied to possess all people with great personal esteem for her'.[14]* He was shrewd and sensible, though apt to be cautious when he needed to be bold. Through the reigns of Charles, James and William he had adapted himself to a violently changing world without like Sunderland losing his virtue. With the wretched James he had gone, as Sarah put it, to the seaside. William had made him head of the Treasury; and now Anne was to lean heavily upon him for eight years. Though he had married a saint, now dead, he was anything but sanctimonious. He did not, like Harley, make 'a clutter' of his religion. His passion was horse-racing, his haunt Newmarket. Macky remembered his 'slow speech' and 'awful, serious deportment' and added: 'does more than he promises'. In 1702 he was fifty-seven. On the accession day he wrote to Harley:

> You were pleased to tell me today in the House of Commons that what the Queen was to speak from the Throne was to be to the same purpose with what she said at Council . . . I wish you could have time to make a draft of it yourself & appoint us to come to your house tomorrow night to see it. I think her speaking can't be deferred longer than Tuesday . . . She is very unwieldy & lame. Must she come in person to the House of Lords or may she send for the two Houses to come to her?

And the following day: 'I suppose the Queen will come to the House, but I doubt whether she has any robes'.[15]

What to say? What to wear? Unready in mind and body, though

* In a letter to Anne, Godolphin assures her: 'I serve you with an affection equal to my duty.'

not in spirit, Anne leant on Godolphin and Marlborough and they on Harley, and no one was disappointed.

Anne's first action was to appoint Prince George Generalissimo and Lord High Admiral. She would have liked him to be King Consort and, in Holland, Stadtholder and Captain-General, but those appointments were tactfully prevented. Marlborough was made Captain-General of the Queen's armies at home and abroad and Master-General of the Ordnance. On March 13th he was awarded the Garter Anne had vainly begged for him from William ten years before.

In the foreground of Verrio's Apotheosis of Queen Anne (See page 137), still to be seen at Hampton Court, a tumbled cornucopia spills coins and coronets. Anne delighted to give, to scatter largesse upon the nation and – joyfully and shamelessly – upon her personal friends. Thus it was that (to quote Sir Winston Churchill) 'romance received a belated dividend with compound interest' when Normanby (once Mulgrave) found himself, to the general amazement, Lord Privy Seal and, later, Duke of Buckingham. Tom Wharton on the other hand, frowned on for riotous living, was made to surrender his staff of office, as Comptroller of the Household, in the presence of the Queen.

On March 30th Anne, voted the same annual revenue as William (£700,000), told the Lords she would surrender a seventh of it to be applied to the public service, even if it meant straitening herself in her own expenses. It was munificent, it was generously meant, but ought it to be afforded?* The Civil List ran into rough water towards the end of the reign; and Hanover grumbled that but for this benevolence a grant might have been voted to the presumptive heir.

While St James's was hung with mourning Anne and George had been staying at Windsor, but two days after the funeral (at midnight on April 12, George being chief mourner. Burnet thought it 'scarce decent') they moved into Kensington Palace (See page 72). Anne had always liked Kensington and although the gardens were Dutch and stuffed with box (she disliked the smell), she would soon have

* 'The late Earl of Godolphin often said that, from accidents in the customs and not straining things to hardships, the revenue did not come to, one year with another, more than £500,000'. *The Opinions of Sarah Duchess of Marlborough*, p. 5.

them changed. The most urgent task was the appointment of her 'family' or household before the coronation on St George's Day, April 23rd. The Duke of Devonshire was made Lord Steward, the Earl of Jersey Lord Chamberlain, Sir Edward Seymour Comptroller and Peregrine Bertie Vice-Chamberlain.

Sarah was appointed Groom of the Stole,* Keeper of the Privy Purse and Mistress of the Robes. The other ladies of the bedchamber were the Duchess of Ormonde, the Marchioness of Hartington, the Countesses of Burlington, Scarbrough and Abingdon, Lady Charlotte Beverwort, Sarah's daughters Lady Harriet Godolphin and Lady Anne Spencer; Lady Frescheville and the Earl of Rochester's daughter Lady Hyde. A few months later they would be joined by the Duchess of Somerset.

The office of Groom of the Stole was a sinecure, but as Mistress of the Robes Sarah, at least at the beginning of the reign, took her duties seriously. Naturally she would see that the proper robes were worn, but she would not be frivolous or extravagant. 'Some people', she remembered, 'to be revenged of me for not letting them cheat have said she was not fine enough for a queen, but it would have been ridiculous with her person and [one] of her age to have been otherwise dressed. Besides, her limbs were so weakened with the gout for many years that she could not endure heavy clothes, and she really had everything that was handsome and proper for her'.[16]

Nothing, for that time, could be more businesslike than the large bound volume of Sarah's accounts, as Mistress of the Robes, still preserved at Blenheim. From it we learn that for making the coronation petticoat Mrs Banks charged thirty shillings, and that Mrs Ducaila, the tirewoman, 'for dressing her Majesty's head on the Coronation Day' received £10 15s. Mrs Ducaila at the same time charged for 'a head of hair with long locks & puffs' (£12) and 'for a pair of favourites† to her Majesty's head of hair' (2s. 6d.) Evidently for state occasions (and very likely for portraits too) Anne sported a wig; though how she disposed of the twenty-four yards of gold

* The stole was a narrow vest lined with crimson sarcenet, embroidered with roses, fleurs de lys and crowns.

† Favourite: a curl or lock of hair hanging loose upon the temple, worn in the 17th and 18th centuries. *O.E.D.*

ribbon, from the same tirewoman, 'for her Majesty's head', is not known.[17]

Anne was thirty-seven. Since the birth of Gloucester she had grown corpulent and now, as the pageant with heralds, train-bearers and a strewer of herbs began to assemble, she found she had gout in knee and foot and could not walk. There would be nothing for it but to let yeomen of the guard carry her, under a canopy, in an open chair of state with a low back so that the six-yard train might flow over it to the Duchess of Somerset and her train-bearers behind.

Jewels for the crown, hired for Mary of Modena, were again hired for Anne. As Celia Fiennes saw her the Queen appeared in crimson* velvet, 'her robe under was of gold tissue, very rich embroidery of jewels about it, her petticoat the same of gold tissue with gold and silver lace between rows of diamonds embroidered, her linen fine . . . her head as well dressed with diamonds which brilled & flamed'. At the Recognition the Queen was seen to turn to the four sides of the Abbey. 'Then last of all, the Archbishops held the crown over her head, which crown was made on purpose for this ceremony, vastly rich in diamonds, the borders & the globe part very thick set with vast diamonds, the cross on the top with all diamonds which flamed at the least motion'.[18]

She was crowned Queen of England, Scotland, Ireland and France; the last, in Miss Strickland's view, an absurd fiction of national pride. By the Queen's command, John Sharp Archbishop of York, though suffering from the stone, preached the coronation sermon from the odd text Anne had chosen from Isaiah: Kings shall be thy nursing fathers and queens thy nursing mothers. This was followed by the other Archbishop (Tenison, who for the rest of his life retired to the wings) expressing the hope that Anne would 'leave a numerous posterity to rule these kingdoms after you by succession in all ages'. For a queen afraid of blushing it must have been a difficult time. Between bishops she staggered to the altar for Communion and was anointed. The Bible was presented, bishops were kissed, gold medals scattered. The peers, led by Prince George, did homage . . . The motto on the coronation favours was: God has sent our hearts content.

* Boyer says it was purple.

'He must begin to govern', writes Bolingbroke of his Patriot King, 'as soon as he begins to reign'. There was to be no pause for breath; and Anne from the first was determined to be no cypher. Health permitting, she would never spare herself, she would attend every Cabinet meeting,* read every petition, appoint bishops and ministers, see ambassadors and envoys, address Parliament, write letters to princes and do a thousand other things . . . Looking back on this time, nine years later, she said that at her coming to the Crown she had found a war prepared for her, and that was true. William with his Partition Treaties had done all that was possible to prevent it, but at the same time he had cemented the Grand Alliance to make sure of strong allies should war prove, as it had proved since, inevitable.

On May 4th 1702 England declared war against France and Spain, our allies then being Austria and Holland, our expressed aims to curb the exorbitant ambitions of France and to restore the balance of power in Europe. But a great deal more was involved.†

At home Anne began to form her first ministry, predominantly Tory. Some appointments she had already approved – Nottingham and Hedges as Secretaries of State, Pembroke as Lord President, Harley's friend Boyle as Chancellor of the Exchequer, and his schoolfellow Harcourt as Solicitor-General, Jersey as Lord Chamberlain, Wright as Lord Keeper, Seymour as Comptroller of the Household, Somerset as Master of the Horse – but the most important post

* 'It is a surprising fact that Anne attended more Cabinet meetings than any other monarch in our history; indeed, no meeting was a Cabinet without her, and she averaged over one a week for her entire reign – usually these were on a Sunday and lasted for several hours . . . Anne's reliance on a large Cabinet Council was a major factor in political instability. Every Cabinet from 1689 to 1714 rapidly disintegrated into faction; their composition rarely remained stable for over a year'. Plumb: *The Growth of Political Stability in England*, 105–6.

† The Foreign Policy of William and of Anne (until 1710): 'to prevent the hegemony of Louis XIV and to restore a balance of power in Europe between the dynastic Houses of Bourbon and Habsburg . . . to secure the Protestant line and the Protestant religion in England . . . to protect the frontier of the United Provinces (Holland) by means of a Barrier and . . . to recover for the maritime powers their former trade with Spanish Territories in the Old and New Worlds'. Holmes & Speck: *The Divided Society*, 88.

of all, that of Lord Treasurer (equivalent to Prime Minister and sometimes called so), was left to the last. Rochester, her uncle, expected to be chosen and was disgusted at being fobbed off with the Lord-Lieutenantship of Ireland. Marlborough pressed for the appointment of Godolphin and was successful.

When all the major and most of the minor jobs and sinecures had been filled it became obvious that the Marlboroughs and their connections were to be quite astonishingly well represented. This, whether or not they deserved it, was bound to cause trouble from those 'jealous of the great power lodged in one family'; for as Boyer points out, 'The Duke of Marlborough had the absolute command of the army, his brother Admiral George Churchill had the chief management of the navy under an indolent High Admiral [Prince George]. All the Court favours were dispensed by his Duchess; and the Treasury in the hands of the father to his son-in-law. So that the disposal of all offices civil and military and of the wealth of the kingdom seemed to depend on one single person'.[19]

It must indeed have seemed so, though in fact the monopoly was not quite so sweeping and comprehensive. Sarah's influence in her offices was considerable, but if she attempted trespass she was resisted. Naturally she had tried her utmost to people her world at Court with her own relations (this was common form); and to see that her own daughters should be ladies of the bedchamber had been simple enough. Bedchamberwomen were different, for though they did not have to be daughters of earls, their pedigrees still needed to be good. Luckily for Sarah's poor relations the Hills, when she first heard of them Anne was a princess and her entourage not too closely vetted. Sarah as an act of charity wanted to smuggle in her two cousins Abigail and Alice Hill and if possible the two ragged waifs that were their brothers too. Boys in fact were not difficult: Godolphin found a job for one, while the other, known to his drinking companions as Honest Jack, was absorbed into the family of Prince George. Abigail needed instant rescue: she had smallpox. Sarah, fearless and competent, dosed her with ass's milk and in one way or another probably saved her life. Then the job . . . One of Anne's bedchamberwomen had just died, but Sarah hesitated to push Abigail, because she had been a domestic servant in the household of Lady Rivers, a flaw which would normally have ruled her out. But Sarah's friends were reassuring. Have no fear, they said, 'for if she had not been a gentlewoman, there was none in the Princess's family at that time that were gentlewomen except Mrs Danvers, who had in some measure lost the advantage of her birth by having married a tradesman. So', Sarah continues, 'upon these encouragements I spoke to the Princess for Mrs Hill and she was pleased to admit of her for a bedchamberwoman. And as soon as the Duke of Gloucester's family was settled, the Duke of Marlborough being his governor, it was in his power to make the younger sister his laundress, which he did'.[20] The children's mother was grateful and told her benefactress that although Mr Harley stood in the same relationship to her indigent husband as she did to Sarah, he had done nothing for them. So that was that. Sarah had gone out of her way to help them; they must now fend for themselves. They did.

Anne was delighted with the conscience Sarah showed in all her duties, for it tallied with her own. The robes were as they should be, the accounts were strictly kept (no more cheating, no more poundage for tradesmen); and now orders were given that places in the royal household were no longer to be sold nor bribes taken for getting them.

Swift would have us believe that no sooner was Anne on the throne than her love for Sarah cooled. He says:

> That lady had long preserved an ascendant over her mistress while she was princess, which her Majesty when she came to the crown had neither patience to bear nor spirit to subdue. This princess was so exact an observer of forms that she seemed to have made it her study and would often descend so low as to observe in her domestics of either sex who came into her presence whether a ruffle, a periwig or the lining of a coat were unsuitable at certain times. The Duchess, on the other side, who had been used to great familiarities, could not take it into her head that any change of station should put her upon changing her behaviour, the continuance of which was the more offensive to her Majesty, whose other servants of the greatest quality did then treat her with the utmost respect.[21]

Some of this was true. Sarah was neither well bred enough nor sufficiently tactful to appreciate that while Anne's other ladies were treating her with the deference due to an anointed Queen, for Sarah to turn her back and chat with someone else meant embarrassment for everybody. It was by no means a straightforward situation. Sarah had had to ask Anne to take less notice of her in public; and her own casual attitude, deliberate though it was, may not have been deliberately offensive. Whatever the plan was, Anne put up with it, and neither bad manners nor political nagging (proselytising for the Whigs) had at this stage any effect on her love. If it had, neither her speech nor her letters showed it.

Anne tells Sarah in May:

> . . . Lord and Lady Portland took their leave of me this morning. She I thought looked a little grave, but he was in one of his gracious ways and I fancy is fool enougn to think his unreasonable demands will some time or other be complied with, but if they were never so just and that I had money to throw away I think he should be one of the last to be considered. Mentioning this worthy person puts me in mind of asking dear Mrs Freeman a question – if you would not have the lodge for your life: 'for all her days", which I pray to God may be many and as truly happy as this world can make you . . . I went to Kensington to walk in the garden which would be a very pretty place if it were well kept, but nothing can be worse. It is a great deal of pity and indeed a great shame that there should be no better use made of so great an allowance, for I have been told the King allowed £400 a year for that one garden . . . Your poor unfortunate faithful Morley is with the tenderest passion imaginable yours.[22]

Long after Anne's death Sarah would be finding Windsor Lodge 'a thousand times more agreeable than Blenheim'. Even Swift was enthusiastic, pronouncing the lodge and its setting 'the finest places for Nature & plantations; and the finest riding upon artificial roads made on purpose for the Queen'.[23]

Portland, who had managed or mismanaged the royal parks and gardens for William, was ousted, and by the first summer of Anne's reign very nearly all of them were in the competent hands of Henry Wise. This diligent person was in partnership with George London at the Brompton Park nurseries (the Victoria & Albert Museum stands on part of the site): so handy for Kensington Palace and for housing in winter the royal and tender 'greens', (e.g. orange-trees and myrtles).

George London, 'of a healthy, strong constitution', had stood by his master Bishop Compton in Anne's flight from the Cockpit in '88. Since then he had set up on his own account, riding on horseback up and down the country, to advise noblemen on their planting, while Wise tended the 'magazine of cut greens' at Brompton; and it was Wise, the younger partner, who was pitched upon, liked and trusted by Queen Anne, whose 'love to gardening', says Switzer, 'was not a little . . . Her first works', he adds, 'were the rooting up the box and giving an English model to the old-made gardens at Kensington',[24] but that was only a beginning. She had resolved, she said, to restrain the expense of the gardens; but enthusiasm soon ran away with her, and by 1706 she had for this one hobby run through £26,000.

Wise's kingdom was vast. His nominal masters had to be noblemen with sinecures (at Windsor Sir Edward Seymour succeeded Portland as Ranger, while Normanby (Buckingham) took over the rangership in St James's Park, where only he was allowed to drive a coach and only Wise to ride on horseback); but Wise was directly responsible and did most of the work. Not for nothing was his motto 'Be ye wise as serpents and harmless as doves'. At Hampton Court alone acres of lime-bordered canals and elaborate parterres (the Great Fountain Garden had thirteen fountains) needed to be kept just so; while for Kensington and Windsor Wise's draughtsman (probably Bridgman) made ambitious designs, some of them on a Versailles scale.

Not the least of Wise's responsibilities were what were known as her Majesty's chaise ridings; and with William's fate in mind, these were a responsibility indeed. Wise, looking back later, remembered how the Queen had commanded him 'to choose a person to catch the moles in both parks at Windsor, and Treasurer Godolphin directed me to contract with a person for same at £30 per annum'.[25] After that the ridings – not straight but twisting among trees – were levelled, 'that the Queen may pass well to the upper & dry parts of the park at any season of the year'. Swift's amused admiration of Anne out hunting – 'in a chaise with one horse . . . drives furiously like Jehu and is a mighty hunter like Nimrod' – is often quoted. At Windsor, Miss Strickland adds, she used as Princess to mount her horse under what was afterwards called Queen Anne's oak, 'but after the birth of the Duke of Gloucester her enormous size precluded this and she followed the chase in a light one-horse chair constructed to hold only herself and built with enormously high wheels. In this extraordinary and dangerous hunting equipage she was known to drive her fine strong hackney forty or fifty miles on a summer's afternoon'.[26] It is a dashing picture (she wore a dark cloak and hood), marred only a little by thoughts of gout and, towards the end, leading-strings too apt, unless the equerries were nimble, to become entangled in trees.

The wonder was that she ever found time for it. She told Sharp she scarcely had time to say her prayers. On the other hand, as she once remarked to Sarah, (offering a lame excuse for not having written): people could usually make time for what they most wanted to do, and in Anne's case at this stage it was hunting. And so that summer, after everything had been seen to in London – Sophia ordered to be prayed for as heir-presumptive, Marlborough sent to Holland, William's strongbox opened (Had he tried to will the crown away from Anne? No such evidence was found), and Harley, for his first private audience, led by Godolphin up the Queen's back stairs[27] – Anne took George to Windsor. From there it was easy to drive to Hampton Court for Council meetings, returning the same day to Windsor, 'where she takes the divertisement of hunting almost every day in an open calash in the forest'.

This was to be the pattern throughout the reign: Windsor and Hampton Court for the summer, Kensington and St James's for the winter. She never as Queen revisited Scotland. She never saw Ireland. She never (with a war lasting until 1713) again went abroad. Travelling even to an English spa could be agony and royal progresses were rare. Such a progress however was inevitable now. Bottled water from Bath was delivered at Windsor three times a week; but George's asthma had worsened and, in the doctors' opinion, cried out for Bath itself. Gone were the days when the mayor could be commanded not to do Anne honour nor to accompany her to church. It had now to be a state visit, and they chose to go via Oxford. As the coach swayed and joggled by rutted tracks Anne had to forget her gout and George his asthma. But nothing they looked at was ugly. Buildings merged with their backgrounds. Crops flourished without poison (harvests at the beginning of Anne's reign were remarkably good); so did woods and commons, hedges and wasteland, there was room for them all. Fish swam in clear rivers. The air was unpolluted by fumes or noise. Above the trotting of horses birds could be heard to sing. All in all the journey might have been pleasant or at least tolerable but for the end of it when, within half a mile of Bath, a sort of mobile guard of honour rode out to meet them. Men dressed as grenadiers were well enough, but with them were two hundred virgins 'richly attired like Amazons with bows and arrows', and 'all of them with a set of dancers who danced by the side of her Majesty's coach and waited upon her Majesty to the West Gate of the city, where they were received by the Mayor and corporation in their formalities'.[28] Not surprisingly George's asthma became 'very violent', but after rest and much drinking of waters he improved. Bath was very small and very crowded (Sarah found it 'noisy and stinking' and Abigail made trouble about her lodgings), but the waters were judged a panacea, not only for invalids, but for women wanting children. Mary of Modena had set an example others had followed; and as Macky remarked, after one visit to Bath they 'often proved with child even in their husbands' absence'.[29]

'I intend tomorrow (an it please God)', Anne tells Sarah, 'to take physic in order to drink the spa [spelt 'spaw'] waters, which my doctors have advised me to & I have a great inclination for them myself, hoping they make my Lady Charlotte come to me, for unless I can compass that it is to be feared my vapours will rather grow upon me than decrease & I can never have any manner of hopes of the unexpressible blessing of another child, for though I do not flatter myself with the thoughts of it, I would leave no reasonable thing undone that might be a means towards it . . .'[30]

It might be thought that Anne's ambiguous references to Lady Charlotte were to her lady of the bedchamber Lady Charlotte Beverwort,* whom she seems to have regarded as something of a

* Lady Charlotte Beverwort (or Beverwaert) died in December, 1702. According to Sarah she was particularly good in sitting up all night with Anne when she was ill.

joke; but this jest is different, being nothing more than Anne's code (to Sarah) for menstruation:

. . . I have not yet seen Lady Charlotte, which I wonder very much at, for I used to be very regular & I cannot fancy she has taken her leave for nine months, because since my three first children I have never bred so soon . . .[31]

. . . Lady Charlotte made her appearance a-Saturday & yesterday but is quite gone again today & this visit was so very cold I am apt to think 'tis a confirmation of the apprehensions I told Mrs Freeman in my last I was in . . . I hope you will never be weary of being told by your faithful Morley that as her days increase so does her kindness for her dear dear Mrs Freeman.[23]

Little less than a miracle was needed now for Anne to conceive a healthy heir. But there it was. If it could work for Mary Beatrice it could work for her. The alternatives were daunting: James Francis Edward R.C. or Hanover. She knew not which was the more distasteful. 'At heart', Sir Winston found, 'she was a Protestant-Jacobite. While in her person and in her policy she barred the return of the rightful heir, she embodied the claims of blood and affirmed the Divine Right of Kings. She reverenced the principles the overthrow of which had brought her the crown. She desired to have it, to keep it and to transmit it to an heir of her own body. There was therefore an innate discordance in the bosom of this virtuous and pious woman'.[33]

There was as she hoped this one natural way to solve the dilemma, but it was not to be. 'God sent a worm to madden his handiwork'. Some fault, some never-to-be-acknowledged flaw scotched or killed what Anne wanted more than anything on earth. She must indeed have been strongminded for this innate discordance not to have torn her apart. Even on the question of Divine Right she was in two minds. For herself no, she had no wish to pretend that she was in any sense divine. When in 1710 the Duke of Shrewsbury read her an address from the City of London Anne 'immediately took exception to the expression that her right was divine, and this morning told me that having thought often of it she could by no means like it and thought it so unfit to be given to anybody that she wished it might be left out'.[34]

Yet here she was at Bath touching thirty poor people for the King's Evil! What then, if anything, did 'the Lord's anointed' mean? Perhaps so far as the sufferers were concerned it was not really of such consequence since, as Macaulay said, 'Nothing is so credulous as misery'; and better too to be touched by a Queen who believed in God than by a King like Charles II who seemed more confident of his Divine Right than of the Lord's existence.

In England, touching for scrofula, which affected the glands, particularly in the neck and throat, went back to Edward the Confessor. Elizabeth touched 'boldly and without disgust . . . handling them to health . . . herself worn with fatigue'. Charles II, whose healings were 'very uncertain', touched in the Banqueting House at Whitehall, which Anne preferred as it was airy. James II touched in England and later in France, where he found himself competing with Louis XIV. In 1709 an informer, Anne Bubb, claimed to have heard a Jacobite neighbour say that the Prince of Wales (James Francis Edward) could make a firmer cure of the King's Evil than the Queen.[35] William had mocked at the whole business as popish superstition. Anne's reviving it is unlikely to have been her own notion; it may have been Sharp's. However it was, according to Oldmixon she was 'induced to resume touching by way of asserting her hereditary right to the Crown'.

When in 1707 the Book of Common Prayer was reprinted, the Service of Healing remained substantially the same. The mystery was not in words but in 'those secret rays of divinity that do attend kings and queens'. Anne was the last English monarch to practise it.

While still at Bath Anne held a Cabinet Council on a Sunday evening (September 5). The outlook, she was told, was good. In Flanders Marlborough was besieging fortresses along the Meuse; while at home, thanks to the decisive elections of July, the Church Party (Tories) seemed firmly in the saddle.

'As near as I can guess by the elections', Harley wrote to Godolphin, 'though there are many violent Whigs left out, yet those who come in their places will be for moderation & safe counsels unless deceived by the artifice of some few hot men, whom I hope the Government will take care to prevent by applying proper antidotes . . . It will be of great service to have some discreet writer of the Government side, if it were only to state facts right, for the generality err for want of knowledge & being imposed upon by the stories raised by ill-designing men'.[36]

Hardly a momentous letter and yet here was Harley or a great deal of him in a nutshell: moderation (no extremes, no extremists) and medicine, his prescription for an antidote against hot men's poison being subtle propaganda. Add secrecy and intelligence (with a small 'i' and with a capital) and an ingratiating and sometimes sanctimonious manner and, for most of the reign, you have him. (See page 232) In some ways years in advance of his time, it was he alone who fully appreciated the potential value of propaganda in politics. Defoe and Swift were still in the background. The hack for the time being, and not a bad one, was Charles Davenant, who in October told Godolphin:

> What I have been doing these last two months . . . is to recommend moderation as the interest of both sides . . . What I lay down is by no means intended to those who rule but is addressed to the great & little vulgar & is offered as a cure & to heal the divisions that are among us.[37]

Moderation as a cure for faction was, like coalition, in theory common sense, and in practice as surely doomed to failure as was Sir Walter Raleigh's Cordial for the cure of virulent smallpox. If every man had been a moderate it could in a tepid sort of way have worked, but in an age producing Whigs like Wharton and young Sunderland and Tories like Rochester, Nottingham and Seymour, there could only be war. To Anne this was acutely distressing. She saw a house divided against itself, 'a kind of conspiracy against the rest of the nation', and so throughout her reign, repeatedly and vainly, she begged for it to end. She and her managers must be above party and must act as peacemakers. Surely it should not be difficult to make those 'few hot men' see reason? As for herself, she would tackle the job in hand, however trivial. Here for example was a question of etiquette:

'We are a little puzzled', wrote Secretary Hedges to Nottingham,' about an instruction to the Earl of Winchilsea, and the question is whether he should kiss the Electress of Hanover's hand. The Queen thinks it should not be & in my humble opinion her Majesty is in the right; but then she is told it has been done before & that makes the difficulty. I find some are for leaving of it to my Lord without any direction & that I think will be a hardship upon him, and therefore should be glad to know your Lordship's thoughts upon this point'.[38]

Winchilsea, who was Nottingham's cousin, would kiss or not kiss at Hanover only upon royal command. 'It is', he objected, 'too nice for me to decide of myself or to act in without a positive command one way or the other . . . I am informed 'tis true most of the English have done it and some of character, which doubtless will make my reception the colder if I omit it'.[39] Hedges was in a quandary: 'On the one hand it is doing too much, and the other denying her a respect paid by others'. He took a fortnight to find courage enough to return to the Queen at Bath. At last, on September 27th, he wrote to Winchilsea:

'The Queen being informed that the respect of kissing the Electress of Hanover's hand has been usually observed . . . and that it would be a downright affront for an Englishman not to do it, her Majesty has been pleased to direct that your Lordship do observe that ceremony if you find it be expected when you come there'.[40]

In the first week of October the Queen and her Consort, (See page 136) both feeling restored, returned to London. On the 20th Anne opened Parliament. Harley had been re-elected Speaker, and five days later he had a long private audience with the Queen. 'She was graciously pleased', he said, 'to use most gracious expressions towards me beyond my deserts'.[41] Knowing as she did from Godolphin of Harley's skill with the Commons, this was the moment to charm him, to make certain of his goodwill, and she did.

Anne was intent on securing a princely allowance for George. Should he survive her he was to have £100,000 a year. It was patently ridiculous and at the same time not to be questioned without offending the Queen. The Commons passed it but when it reached the Lords they found mischievously tacked to it a clause which might have precluded George as a naturalised subject from holding office under a Hanoverian king. This few would have minded, but the procedure of tacking the clause to a money bill infuriated the lords and many opposed it. As for Anne, she had counted on the Bill and now pressed for it 'with the greatest earnestness she had yet showed in anything whatsoever'. Marlborough and Godolphin joined with Rochester and Nottingham to force the thing through as it stood. It passed with the narrowest majority; the Queen showing grave displeasure with those who had opposed it, 'among whom', adds Burnet ruefully, 'I had my share'.[42] But Anne's lasting anger was reserved for Marlborough's son-in-law Sunderland who, having recently succeeded to the earldom, made it his first step to speak against the Bill. Sarah, gently wooing Anne for the Whigs, was distracted, for now the Queen would have some reason for believing, as she was said to, that all Whigs had cloven hooves. It would take days and weeks of coaxing to induce a less rigid frame of mind.

The next thing to be faced, early in November, was the Occasional Conformity Bill, devised by the Tories to put an end to the Dissenters' practice of dodging the Test Act (whereby all holders of public office had to be Church of England communicants) by paying occasional lip-service to the Anglican sacrament before returning to regular worship in their chapels and tabernacles. As Sir Winston Churchill remarks, one can hardly conceive an issue better adapted to make a quarrel; for it involved the full range of belief and unbelief, from deep faith to cynical expediency. Again Prince George, who had his private Lutheran chapel and took the Anglican sacrament once a year, was in an awkward position. 'Now though the Prince has no scruple of receiving the sacrament in our church', wrote Godolphin to Harley, 'yet I thought the Queen seemed almost equally unwilling either that he should be forced to do it or that he should need any clause to exempt him from doing it'.[43] The Bill, passed by the Commons, did not reach the Lords until January. Anne, who took her monthly Communion very seriously, felt bound to send George to vote for the Bill, along with Marlborough and Godolphin. In the event however it was amended out of existence and dropped.

On November 12th the Queen drove to St Paul's for the Vigo thanksgiving. The heroes of Vigo Bay were the Duke of Ormonde, the Tory grandee in command of the land forces, and Admiral Sir George Rooke who, half-crippled with gout, had to forego the thanksgiving. The Queen in a coach and eight, with Sarah and her daughter Anne Sunderland, headed a long procession which was cheered from St James's to the City. The Tower guns fired salvoes while within the cathedral the *Te Deum* was sung. Marlborough was still abroad and Godolphin had had alone to solve the nice problem of seating. 'I hope the House of Lords will take the expedient of sitting as a House', he told Harley, 'it was the best I could think of for the easing of that difficulty'.[44] Given the choice of turning his back on the High Altar or on the Queen who sat facing it in the chancel, no loyal peer could hesitate, though the clergy, in their immediate presence, had to be content with a faceless congregation. (See front endpaper.) As the first thanksgiving of the reign it had glamour and novelty. The guns, the gilded coaches and fine clothes, and nodding wigs, the beribboned horses all made for colour and excitement.

> As threat'ning Spain did to Eliza bow,
> So France and Spain shall do to Anna now;
> France that protects false claims to another's throne
> Shall find enough to do to keep her own.

Only later in the reign, when one *Te Deum* soon succeeded another – and some were sung in Notre Dame – did the pomp and propaganda wear thin and the whole performance degenerate into what Sarah called a poppitt-show.

But Anne, towards the close of 1702, was neither simpleton nor cynic. As a devout Anglican and as Supreme Governor of the Church she had a strong conscience and meant to obey it. The Archbishop of Canterbury, Tenison, like Burnet and Compton, she found too latitudinarian. John Sharp was the man. He would advise her and help to allay faction; and Sharp could rely on Harley,* whose background of dissent might conveniently be forgotten. Anne's immediate wish was to make Sharp her Almoner, and in this Providence helped her by tripping the incumbent. Lloyd Bishop of Worcester, then Almoner, seemed a harmless old soothsayer, but he was said to have interfered in the election of Sir John Packington.[45] Lloyd denied it, but before his plea had been heard he was dismissed as Almoner, leaving the way clear for Archbishop Sharp. At this there were murmurs in the Lords, but the Queen told them tartly that it was her undoubted right to continue or displace any servant attending her, when thought proper.[46] It was the first rebuff.

And now came the question of rewarding Marlborough. His conquests in Flanders, though as nothing compared with victories to come, justified in Anne's view some special bounty and in October she had told Sarah she meant to make him a Duke. When Sarah received her letter – its 'every sentence poised to enhance the gift'[47] – she let it drop from her hand as though she had heard of the death of a friend. She felt that in no way at that time could a dukedom be afforded. Marlborough however was pleased and grateful. Heinsius, Grand Pensionary of Holland, agreed that he must accept, if only for prestige with the Grand Alliance. But Anne went still further. She asked Parliament to agree to a grant, to support the dukedom, of £5,000 a year; being herself unable to perpetuate it beyond her lifetime. There was a pause. Marlborough was known to have £10,000 a year from the Dutch; nor was Sarah's income from her offices inconsiderable. Remembering William's wild grants to his favourites, what was Parliament to say to 'such exuberance of rewards'? With 'unexpressible grief' they said no; and the Queen, says Coke, 'was not pleased with this balk'. Very well, if Parliament declined to be generous, she had herself more ways of giving. She wrote Sarah a letter which could not have been more characteristic:

* 'At the end of 1702 Godolphin committed the Ministry's ecclesiastical management to Harley, who as Speaker already handled management in the House of Commons'. G. V. Bennett: *Robert Harley, the Godolphin Ministry & the Bishoprics Crisis of 1707* (E.H.R. Oct. 1967).

December 16

I cannot be satisfied with myself without doing something towards making up what has been so maliciously hindered in the Parliament, & therefore I desire my dear Mrs Freeman & Mr Freeman would be so kind as to accept of two thousand a year out of the privy purse, besides the grant of the five. This can draw no envy for nobody need know it. Not that I would disown what I give to people that deserve, especially where it is impossible to reward the deserts, but you may keep it a secret or not, as you please. I beg my dear Mrs Freeman would never any way give me an answer to this, only comply with the desires of your poor unfortunate faithful Morley that loves you most tenderly & is with the sincerest passion imaginable yours.[48]

Sarah declined the offer; although nine years later, after her dismissal, she claimed it with arrears. That however, at the end of Anne's coronation year, was impossible to imagine. Re-reading her letter and especially the close of it, Swift's contention that 'upon her first coming to the throne, Lady Marlborough had lost all favour with her'[49] surely must be rejected. As long as Sarah's kindness continued Anne for her part would be as unchangeable as fate. She kept saying so and she meant it. She may have been too emotional for a queen. She may, as Dr Johnson said, have seemed better fitted for friendship than for government, but to her friends, if they would let her, she was determined to be loyal.

Two days before Christmas Anne adopted a motto. 'It was' (so ran the announcement) 'her Majesty's pleasure that whenever there was occasion to embroider, depict, engrave, carve or paint her Majesty's arms, these words SEMPER EADEM should be used for a motto, it being the same that had been used by her predecessor Queen Elizabeth of glorious memory'.[50]

In religion Anne would be a rock – 'I will choose to live on alms', she had said, 'rather than change' – and the same went for friendship, perhaps even for life. As a self-confessed pessimist she dreaded change (too often for the worse) as she dreaded extremes and the clash of extremists. If there had to be parties and party tyranny 'rendering the Government like a door which turns both ways upon its hinges',[51] she would remain above it, the one constant, impartial power all might appeal to.

'The Queen is resolved', wrote Sir John Leveson-Gower on December 26th, 'not to follow the example of her predecessor in making use of a few of her subjects to oppress the rest. She will be Queen of all her subjects and would have all the parties and distinctions of former reigns ended and buried in hers and in order to it expects that those whom she employs shall give the first example. Her Majesty's intentions and resolutions are great and for the common good'.[52]

What more could be asked of her?

CHAPTER SIX

BLENHEIM

1703 - 1704

For Sarah, and so for Anne, the year 1703 would be flawed by tragedy; yet it began promisingly enough. Anne's birthday was celebrated with 'extraordinary rejoicings throughout the kingdom . . . There had not been such a magnificent appearance at Court for twenty years'.[1] Three days later Sarah's third daughter Elizabeth married the heir to the Earl of Bridgwater.

Lord Blandford, Sarah's only son, now seventeen, 'of a comely, beautiful form, affable temper and excellent parts',[2] had gone to stay with his godfather Godolphin at Newmarket to avoid smallpox, which was raging at Cambridge. It was too late. Anne wished the doctors she sent could fly with their medicines. 'Your poor unfortunate faithful Morley is on the rack for you', she wrote to Sarah, 'and begging you would have a care of your dear dear self'.[3] Next day she wrote again:

> I pray God he may do well & support you, and give me leave once more to beg you for Christ Jesus' sake to have a care of your dear precious self & believe me with all the tenderest passion imaginable your poor unfortunate faithful Morley.[4]

When Blandford died, the doctors feared for his mother's reason. She was forty-three. She haunted the cloisters of Westminster Abbey or shut herself up alone at Holywell. 'We hear the Duchess of Marlborough bears not her affliction like her mistress', wrote Lady Pye to Abigail Harley, 'if report be true that it hath near touched her head'.[5] Marlborough, after making a new will in favour of Francis Godolphin, had to leave for Flanders. From there he wrote to his wife solemnly and movingly, begging her to follow whatever her doctors prescribed. Anne, it was said, looked as though she had lost another son. She wrote again now:

It would have been a great satisfaction to your poor unfortunate faithful Morley if you would have given me leave to have come to St Albans, for the unfortunate ought to come to the unfortunate, but since you will not have me, I must content myself as well as I can till I have the happiness of seeing you here . . . God Almighty bless & comfort my dear Mrs Freeman & be assured I will live & die sincerely yours.[6]

Had she been snubbed? It would have been kind to let her come. But Sarah wished to see no one except Marlborough and that was impossible. How cold, one wonders, was her letter to Anne? She dutifully burned it.

Neither Queen nor Duchess now had a male heir. For Sarah Anne would in time arrange for the title to descend through the female line.* For herself she would often contemplate death but she would not face up to the grim choice for the Succession. Harley told her that in Amsterdam they were saying she had accepted the crown only as trustee for her stepbrother. Sarah thought the report mischievous and on her return to Court tried to counteract it with practical common sense:

I remember one day I told the Queen, when she was easy with me, that I thought there was nothing in the world so good for her as well as for England as to desire of her own accord to have the young Prince of Hanover and breed him as her own son, which would in the first place secure her own line against the Roman Catholics and make the young man acquainted with the laws and customs of a country that one day (though I hoped it was a long way off) he would govern; to which she answered, not being very well pleased, that she believed nobody of her age and who might have children would do that; which was a very vain thought and I believe proceeded more from her pride or fear of having anybody here to be courted than that she really could expect children, though she was not forty, because she had had before seventeen dead ones.[7]

It was cold hard sense and it had not the least appeal for Anne. Her

* Henrietta Godolphin, Sarah's eldest daughter, became on Marlborough's death in 1722 Duchess of Marlborough in her own right. She outlived her son and died in 1733. The dukedom then descended to Charles Spencer, son of Marlborough's second daughter Anne and the 3rd Earl of Sunderland, from whom the Dukes of Marlborough are directly descended.

reign might be long; her stepbrother might turn Protestant; smallpox could demolish a dynasty; almost anything might happen. She would close her mind to it and attend to more pressing affairs. Now the wretched Rochester, her uncle, had refused to go to Ireland as Lord Lieutenant. She had dismissed him and would send Ormonde. She had made four Tory peers and, at Sarah's insistence, added a Whig, Lord Hervey. In her speech to the Lords at the end of February she reminded them of the great hazards she had run for the Church of England. She approved a proclamation, inspired by Sharp, against profaneness and immorality. She intervened for condemned prisoners. She encouraged the building of a church and school on 'a little farm adjoining to the town of New York'.[8] She would have touched for the Evil, but gout was in her hands, so she postponed it until April (100 touched) and May (200 in St James's Palace courtyard). On April 17th she made time to knight 'an eminent man midwife' called David Hamilton, who had yet (though not as midwife) to play his part.

Things great and small clamoured for her nod. One day it would be the Methuen Treaty with Portugal (good wine, a troublesome ally and committal to the dangerous policy of No Peace Without Spain); the next a bundle of oddments:

> The Queen reads the petition of Sir Godfrey Kneller, praying payment of £570 due to him for drawing several pictures of her Majesty and the late King. (The Queen's answer is her Majesty does not care for the picture of £350. The others are to be paid for).
>
> The Queen reads the petition of Thomas Tompion, praying payment of £564 15s due to him for clocks, watches etc., presented by the late King to the Duke of Florence. (The Queen's reply is her Majesty has no occasion for his clocks and watches).
>
> The Queen reads Mr Wise's estimate of £1800 for works in St James's Park. (The Queen takes the estimate away with her).[9]

Alterations in park and palace, at St James's and Kensington, were to be made while Anne was at Windsor, where the Court moved on May 20th. In St James's Park Wise was transplanting large limes and widening the canal by twelve feet; while for Kensington he planned a sunk garden made from a gravel-pit and a mount to 'answer' it, on the ground just taken in on the northern side. There was talk of a banqueting-house . . .

At Windsor Anne would have the southern slope planted with fruit trees, which must be limed to protect them from deer. It was pleasant there even when one could not hunt. George had been ill but was better and could be left with his ship-models while she attended Council at Hampton Court. There she heard of a Mr De Fooe [sic] who, for his *Shortest Way with Dissenters*, was to stand in the pillory three times and to be gaoled.

The brain of Daniel Defoe teemed with ideas, some of them good ones. Those he tried out for himself – as merchant-adventurer or as pamphleteer – often led him to shipwreck. Yet for others, whether as economist, promoter or journalist, he could be brilliant and invaluable. With his bold plans for improving credit, or again for colonisation, he had been respectfully listened to by King William. It was even said he had had a hand in founding the Bank of England and in the recoinage. As a creative thinker he deserved to be rewarded; but on the contrary he found himself, now the father of a large family, bankrupt and in gaol. From Newgate he wrote to his friend William Paterson: 'Like old Tyrell who shot at a stag and killed the King, I engaged a party & embroiled myself with the Government'.[10] His pamphlet, meant ironically, had misfired. Paterson told Harley and Harley told Godolphin, who replied:

> I thank you for the hints about Scotland. De Foe would be the properest person in the world for that transaction, but I doubt the rigour of his punishment t'other day will have made it seem practicable to engage him. If you can have any means of sounding him I wish you would try it . . .[11]

Harley obtained his release in November and began to train him as a spy.

At Windsor Anne was informed that someone of mischievous mind had had George elected High Steward of Colchester: 'a mighty proper employment for the Queen's husband', as Sarah said. It was a joke Anne failed to appreciate, 'an ugly foolish thing' ill-disposed persons would make the most of. But Sarah would see to it as she saw to everything. Anne, thanking her, ended her letter: '. . . being now in great haste to be dressed, this being my company day, though the weather is so bad I fancy nobody will come. However I will be in a readiness to receive anybody that will give themselves that trouble. Therefore for this time, my dear dear Mrs Freeman, farewell'.[12]

It was hardly to be wondered at that with two chronic invalids at the head of it Anne's Court was dull. Even Mary of Modena at St Germain now knew that Anne had to have a cleverly designed chair to lift her bodily into her coach,* and it was rumoured that an even more elaborate affair with pulleys, once used by Henry VIII at Windsor, was being refurbished to carry the Queen from floor to floor. No wonder she preferred her Little House to the Castle. No wonder the company she dressed for stayed away.

'Queen Anne', wrote Burnet, 'is easy of access & hears everything very gently, but opens herself to so few & is so cold & general in her answers that people soon find that the chief application is to be made to her ministers & favourites, who in their turns have an entire credit & full power with her. She has laid down the splendour of a Court too much & eats privately, so that except on Sundays & a few hours twice or thrice a week at night in the drawingroom, she appears so little that her Court is as it were abandoned'.[13]

The few who went complained that access to the Queen was blocked by Sarah. Sometimes, when the petition was trifling or Anne had gout, this was necessary; sometimes not. On her own ill-chosen ground of politics Sarah herself had begun to find resistance. While Anne was Princess it had seemed natural and of no immediate consequence that she was wedded to the Church or Tory Party. Now it mattered a great deal and Sarah was trying to change it. The Tories – Nottingham, Rochester, Seymour – were not prepared to serve under Anne's managers, the duumvirs Marlborough and Godolphin, and to back them in a full-scale war; while the Whigs, and in particular the Whig Junto, insisted on more power if their votes were to be counted on for ever-increasing supplies of money. Godolphin and Sarah found themselves between two fires, and even

* 'A chair made so well that it is lifted with her in it into the coach, and then she moves herself to the seat and the chair (is) taken away'.

Lady Rachel Russell to her daughter Lady Granby, 30 Oct. 1703. (HMC XII, App. 5, 176).

less to be envied was Marlborough who, on top of all this, was maddened and frustrated by the Dutch. Their troops were excellent, but their War Office had notions quite their own. Field Deputies with power of veto were sent to the front with Marlborough and if the battle he had planned seemed too risky they said no, their troops were not to be engaged. Marlborough was a master of tact as well as of tactics; but even a third-rate general could hardly have been expected to put up with much of this. Both Marlborough and Godolphin began to liken themselves to galley-slaves. Both threatened to resign; and Sarah of course would have thrown in her lot with them. Anne answered from Windsor:

The thoughts that both my dear Mrs Freeman and Mr Freeman seem to have of retiring gives me no small uneasiness & therefore I must say something on that subject. It is no wonder at all that people in your posts should be weary of the world, who are so continually troubled with all the hurry & impertinences of it; but give me leave to say you should a little consider your faithful friends & poor country, which must be ruined if ever you should put your melancholy thoughts in execution. As for your poor unfortunate faithful Morley, she could not bear it, for if ever you should forsake me, I would have nothing more to do with the world but make another abdication, for what is a crown when the support of it is gone? I never will forsake your dear self, Mr Freeman, nor Mr Montgomery, but always be your constant faithful servant; and we four must never part till death mows us down with his impartial hand.[14]

In Sir Winston's view it is a letter which ranks Anne with Elizabeth. Certainly the idea of mass-resignation and abdication, if taken seriously, is momentous and the whole letter typical: pure Anne before her pen was guided by Harley. The close is fascinating: once again the obsession with death, and the tight quorum – Anne, the Marlboroughs and Godolphin – which excluded Prince George and Harley. With three shrewd and intimate friends Anne felt she could run the country. Without them she would be helpless and lost; and indeed when she needed to be carried everywhere, this feeling of helpless dependence must have been driven home.

In August Anne and George were again in Bath, where they dined in public to the music of oboes and trumpets, and 'such a crowd of country-people came in, there was no stirring'. For the mob it was a rare chance. Not much is recorded of them – the 'great and little vulgar' of the age of Anne – nor was much heard from them then. They might gaze, they might cheer, they might occasionally demonstrate; among themselves they might argue politics; individually they had no say. Any sort of appeal to them was, for a man of breeding, bad form. Only an outsider like Sacheverell would dream of such a thing, 'so dangerous it is to let loose a giddy, unthinking multitude'.[15] Except in towns and cities like London and Bath they were not thick on the ground, the total population (under six million) being almost exactly two million less than that of Greater London today.

With room to breathe and move, tolerably well fed on dull wholesome food (bread, cheese, fish, poultry, soup, not much meat and no potatoes), relatively untouched by war, ignorant of Court conspiracy, often illiterate, on the whole they were content. Life was short. They lived in jeopardy and knew it. Smallpox could carry them off. Babies died. Men rotted in debtors' gaols. Robbers were branded, women hanged. Surgery of any kind, even for a tooth, was a nightmare, pain had to be endured. Roads were impossible in winter, footpads prospered, letters were intercepted, bathrooms all but unheard of, lavatories primitive, entertainments usually crude and few. Yet in spite of all this one could be healthy and happy, as many were.

Returning from Bath in September Anne still could not set foot to ground; and she soon found herself faced with a load of other troubles, not the least of them protests against mismanagement at the Admiralty. This was partly political (there had been murmurs in William's time), but nevertheless, as Godolphin told Harley, it 'must needs be very disagreeable to the Queen & particularly uneasy to the Prince',[16] who was too easily imposed upon. There was also the ridiculous business of Clarendon's *Rebellion*.

'I suppose you know', Henry St John wrote to Harley, 'that the second part of a very famous history is ready to be published. Before it is a very long & polite epistle to the Queen, full of temper & the calmest counsels . . .'[17]

The history, finished in France, had been edited by Clarendon's son Rochester, who had dedicated the second volume to Anne. She hardly knew what to make of it. 'This history', she read in the dedication, 'may lie upon your table unenvied and your Majesty may pass hours & days in the perusal of it, when possibly they who shall be the most useful in your service may be reflected on for aiming too much at influencing your actions & engrossing your time . . .' There followed warnings against separating Church from state (i.e. the Tories must govern) and other 'appearances of hazard'; the conviction that 'Your real happiness will very much depend upon yourself and your choosing to honour with your service such persons as are honest, stout and wise'; and finally the injunction: 'For God's sake, Madam, and your own be pleased to read Him with attention & serious & frequent reflections & from thence in conjunction with your own heart prescribe to yourself the methods of true & lasting greatness and the solid maxims of a sovereign truly English'.

The delivery of a large and heavy volume could hardly have been worse timed.

'When I shall be able to walk again', Anne wrote to Sarah, 'God knows, for last night . . . I got a pain in my knee, which continues still but I thank God is not very bad . . . Sir Benjamin Bathurst sent me Lord Clarendon's history last week, but having not quite made an end of the first part, I did not unpack it, but I shall have the curiosity now to see this extraordinary dedication, which I should never have looked for in the second part of a book and methinks it is very wonderful that people that don't want sense in some things should be so ridiculous as to show their vanity . . . I beg my dear Mrs Freeman would be so kind as not to say anything to anybody that I have a pain again in my knee, for else when people come from London [to Kensington] I shall be tormented with a thousand questions about it. I have yet kept it to myself & hope I shall be able to do so till it is quite well again'.[18]

Anne would still make time to write to Sarah, when hours and days for the perusal of Clarendon were out of the question. As for 'such persons as are honest, stout and wise', these of course were the very ones she had chosen. If they were envied, if Hydes and Churchills hated each other, that was no fault of hers, nor perhaps of theirs. One could not love everyone. She had some dislikes herself. 'It was also observed', notes Burnet, 'that our Court kept too cold civilities with the House of Hanover and did nothing that was tender or cordial-looking that way; nor were any employed who had expressed a particular zeal for their interests. These things gave great jealousy'.[19]

Now Sophia was asking for Anne's portrait. 'A good copy will be as good as an original',[20] Marlborough told Sarah. That was the attitude: no need to put oneself out or spend much money. Sarah went to Kneller's studio, bought 'a very ill copy' and had it sent to Hanover. She was stunned at the response. Sophia, vowing she valued the portrait more than the whole universe, sent Sarah the universe worked in tapestry (then valued at £3,000), plus some £3,000 in cash for silver sconces and so on for the room in which the tapestry was to be hung. These last, Sarah thought, might prove useless and troublesome. Instead she ordered plain gold plates, bearing the Electress's arms. Sadly but one survives today at Blenheim to remind her posterity of what she called 'that bounty which I had so cheap'.[21]

In the intricate jigsaw of the reign of Anne – and 'no reign was ever more memorable than this for important events'[22] – this was a very small piece. Only a handful at Court would hear of it. But in November the whole nation was shocked by the most violent storm that had ever been known, and no one then alive would ever forget it. Beginning at one a.m. on the 27th it raged until seven, 'rolling up great quantities of lead like scrolls of parchment & blowing them off the churches, halls & houses . . . At sea abundance of brave men irrecoverably lost'.[23] The Bishop of Bath and Wells (Kidder) and his wife were killed in bed by the fall of a chimneystack. At London Bridge the Thames was blocked by wrecked shipping. Anne at St James's Palace was alarmed. Chimneys and battlements fell, the park was ravaged. That the storm should make nonsense of Wise's transplanting was not surprising – limes, acacias and a hundred elms had gone – but it had even toppled Wolsey's oaks. Anne collected herself and issued a proclamation for a general fast, 'imploring Almighty God that he would avoid sending such high winds in the future', and 'that it would please Him to pardon the crying sins of this nation which had drawn down this sad judgment'.[24]

Little advance had in some ways been made since the Middle Ages.

If it had been a fire, blame could have been laid upon Roman Catholics, but in an act of God His people must take their share. Dissenters too were heretics, and the Occasional Conformity Bill, revived between storm and fast, might harry them. Anne herself saw 'nothing like persecution in this Bill', but agreed that her Lutheran Consort should abstain from voting. Again it passed the Commons and again, though Marlborough and Godolphin felt obliged to vote for it, it was shipwrecked in the Lords: 'a triumph of methodical, energetic organisation' on the part of the Whigs.[25] Faction was in the air; Anne's appeals for concord were useless. Even the dogs in the streets and the cats on the roofs, Swift told Stella, were more quarrelsome than usual; 'but why should we wonder at that when the very ladies are split asunder into high church and low and out of zeal for religion have hardly time to say their prayers?'[26]

Anne loathed controversy. It split the nation, and now it was beginning to affect her friendship with Sarah. 'I resolved from the beginning of the Queen's reign', wrote Sarah afterwards, 'to try whether I could not by degrees make impressions in her mind more favourable to the Whigs'. It might seem hopeless, it might seem folly, but if Marlborough was to be supported it was necessary. Certainly it was far from easy, since Anne had been taught to expect from them 'the same usage that her grandfather King Charles I had from such sort of people; and her own inclination being to be fond of the Tories – being very ignorant, very fearful, with very little judgment – it is easy to be seen she might mean well, being surrounded with so many artful people who at last compassed their designs to her dishonour'.[28] Sarah in fact found herself up against conviction linked with obstinacy. To Anne the very name of Whig was anathema. Very well, as 'the honest party' the pill could be sugared; but no, the good work proceeded but by slow degrees. Something still retarded it and made it go very heavy.

'I cannot help being extremely concerned you are so partial to the Whigs', Anne told Sarah, 'because I would not have you & your faithful Morley differ in opinion in the least thing'.[29] And now again she begged 'dear Mrs Freeman . . . she would never let difference of opinion hinder us from living together as we used to do. Nothing', she ended her letter, 'shall ever alter your poor unfortunate faithful

Morley, who will live & die with all truth & tenderness yours'.[30] If tenderness had ever existed on Sarah's side, it was giving way now to exasperation, to her 'Lord, Madam, it must be so'. She owns herself that she 'argued frequently with the Queen and sometimes not without a warmth natural to sincerity, which yet hitherto did not appear to leave any uneasiness behind it'.[31] Anne vowed she was unchangeable, and so was Sarah. When tact and tenderness might have triumphed she relied on cold reason. It was impossible, she thought, for her to offend the Queen. Sooner or later sense must triumph, it always did. But for Anne it was saddening: 'for what is a crown when the support of it is gone?' She was too vulnerable. Crippled and tormented, she looked to Sarah as she had always looked for encouragement and love. To be badgered instead was intolerable.

Even now, Anne told Parliament, her enemies could not be more industrious in contriving to ruin the kingdom. She had 'unquestionable information' of a plot in Scotland, promoted by France; and while that was being scotched she had to prepare herself for the state visit of the Archduke Charles of Austria, hopefully styled King Charles III of Spain and now on his way to occupy his kingdom.

Contemporaries make of him a fairytale figure, 'a very pretty gentleman about nineteen years old, tall and slender,' 'a melancholy look, very good eyes, very white teeth and a very becoming smile ... his voice something inward, pronounces his words slow'.[32] He spoke little (in French) and smiled less, but his fragile looks were deceptive. One who had watched him dine at sea said he had eaten enough at one meal to keep a Lazarus six months. Prince George, sent to meet him at Petworth (Somerset's Sussex house, then unfinished), was fourteen hours in his coach, which overturned, without eating. The last nine miles took six hours.

Next day at Windsor the Queen received the young King at the head of the stairs. He touched the hem of her petticoat before they embraced and kissed both cheeks. Anne then led him in and introduced him to 'about forty ladies of the first quality', all to be saluted with a kiss. In the finer points of etiquette Charles, it was noticed, was just as punctilious as Anne herself. 'He supped that night with the Queen, who gave his Majesty the right hand at table, which he with great difficulty admitted. The next day his Majesty having notice that the Queen was coming to make him a visit he met her at her drawingroom door, endeavouring to prevent her, but her Majesty went on to his apartment, from whence he led her Majesty to dinner'. His table manners were quite new and much wondered at. When he liked the look of a dish – candied orange-flowers it might be – he pointed at it with a fork. Bread, on the other hand, was treated sacramentally, broken into 'small mammocks', laid upon a plate covered with a napkin and placed on his left hand, 'from whence he takes it bit by bit but keeps it always covered'.[33] This was strange enough; but his best performance was saved until after supper when with many a flourish and protestation he made Sarah give him the napkin for the Queen's hands. Then, after going through the motions of washing the tips of Anne's fingers, he returned the napkin folded about the diamond ring he had been wearing, 'as a mark of his great esteem for her Grace'. It was nobody's fault that Lady Frescheville had coveted it and was so contemptuous of her own present – a cross of five brilliant diamonds, 'the prettiest set in the world' – that she gave it away.[34]

Charles returned to Petworth before embarking for Spain, with high hopes of reigning there; but Spain was to reject him. One day he would be an emperor, but that day was years ahead. For his visit to Windsor Anne had disguised her gout, but directly he had left, it again became severe. In January her first physician, Sir Thomas Millington, died. Contemporary accounts of her health (See also Appendix I) are not always helpful, e.g.:

'1704 January 5. The Queen is perfectly recovered and the better for having now a sharp fit of the gout in both hands.'[35]

On her birthday she confirmed the bounty (£16,500) she had promised for the support of the poorer clergy, whose contributions to monarchs (firstfruits and tenths of benefices) had been helping towards the upkeep of select pensioners including Nell Gwynne's son the Duke of St Albans. William had been importuned by Burnet to divert this bounty into more needy and perhaps more deserving channels. Only now however, with the help of Sharp, Godolphin and possibly Harley, was the good work carried through. 'Your Majesty has in this surprising instance of your kindness for the

Church', Sharp assured her, 'outdone all your predecessors since the Reformation'. He doubted not, he added, but that glorious rewards were laid up for her in the heavenly kingdom.[36] The gift was necessary and did much good, for some livings were not then worth £10 a year and few exceeded £50. 'Her memory', Boyer predicted, 'will be blessed in all succeeding generations'.

The birthday was further celebrated with a performance of Dryden's *All For Love*, followed two days later by *Hamlet*, 'out of compliment to Prince George'.[37] *Lear* might have proved too painful. Command-performances at Court might be well enough, but if Anne was to believe what she had heard of Drury Lane and of Lincoln's Inn Fields, the public theatre was a scandal. On January 18th she gave 'particular orders that no plays be acted contrary to religion & good manners, upon pain of high displeasure & of being silenced from further acting'. No member of the audience was to mount the stage or go behind the scenes and no woman was to presume to wear a vizard-mask in either of the theatres.[38] As with the theatre, so with masks: in public masks were worn by prostitutes; at a Court ball a mask could be worn by the Queen herself. In Sarah's neat accounts of the robes two entries (for 1704 and 1708) refer to 'a mask with glass eyes', the second bought for the Queen by a Mr Nightingale. It cost four shillings and sixpence.

For one sovereign or another the Court was so often in mourning that Anne wore coloured clothes whenever she decently could:

> A silver tissue manto, flowered with blue & lined with pale blue . . . A cherry-coloured pink & white flowered silk nightgown lined with lutestring . . . A striped snail hood . . . A fine French-laced tippet . . . A scarlet velvet under-petticoat with lace . . . A Parliament robe of crimson Genoa velvet lined with white mantua, the old ermine cleaned & put in again & a new velvet cope with a great gold & crimson cord & large silk tassels . . . A rich fox muff . . . A morning-gown in willow-green satin . . . A sky-blue manto & petticoat embroidered with gold & peacock's feathers . . . A fine lace head & ruffles . . . Six ivory & tortoiseshell fans . . . A fine Turkey hankercher embroidered with gold . . . Amber powder & a paper of patches . . .[39]

All this and much more Sarah noted as Mistress of the Robes, for these were personal to the Queen. The robing of her household (except for her ladies-in-waiting and maids of honour) was the concern of the Great Wardrobe, the Master of which was the Earl of Montagu. If as Lord Delawarr remarked an office in the royal household was a blessing far more valuable than life itself this, the Mastership of the Great Wardrobe, was above every other blessing, for not only was it a well-paid sinecure (£2,000 a year plus £200 for a deputy), but it was held for life. Sarah's problem was this. She had secured Montagu's son as husband for her youngest daughter Mary. She now wanted to make certain that the job would stay in the family. Unfortunately, in March 1703 the decree had gone out: the Queen grants no reversions. Sarah was not deterred. It took time, but on March 16, 1704 she was able to tell the Earl (soon to be Duke), 'I have done all I could to procure it as I hope you will like, the Queen having at last consented that your son shall have the reversion of the Master of the Great Wardrobe for life, with the same appointments your Lordship now has'.[40] They might all breathe again. Place-hunting for relatives was as it had always been common practice, but with the Marlboroughs it threatened to become a monopoly. Anne liked giving and resented pressure. The initiative should come from herself.

For the beginning of 1704 Luttrell gives a fair picture of surface-events:

February 29. This being the Prince of Denmark's birthday, 'twas celebrated at St James's and the Court very gay upon the occasion.

March 9. The Infanta of Portugal, whom the King of Spain was to have married, is dead of the smallpox.

March 21. The Duke of Berwick is made a grandee of Spain.

March 28. The Earl of Carlisle Earl Marshall of England hath made Mr Vanbruggen [Vanbrugh] Clarenceux King of Arms.

April 18. The Queen touched several persons for the Evil at St James's. Her Majesty designs for the Bath at the latter end of May.

But behind all this much was happening of which Anne knew little or nothing. She may have known of Godolphin's reliance on Harley – 'It is necessary', he had told him, 'that the Duke of Marlborough &

you & I should meet regularly at least twice a week if not oftener to advise upon everything that shall occur',[41] – but she may barely have heard of Harley's rescue from prison of Defoe, now blessing him for his benevolence not only to himself but to 'a virtuous and excellent mother to seven beautiful & hopeful children, a woman whose fortunes I have ruined'.[42] Harley would be recompensed, Defoe promised, by 'the foundation of such an intelligence [service] as never was in England . . . a correspondence effectually settled with every part of England & all the world beside & yet the very clerks employed do not know what they are doing';[43] a prediction which, thanks to Harley's strange methods, became almost too literally true.

Of Harley it can safely be said that he loved secrecy for its own sake, even though in his own office that might mean entrusting security to underpaid clerks. With Marlborough the case was different. His international intelligence-service was efficient and well paid. The secret of his long march to the Danube was against all odds kept a secret until he chose to reveal it. In February he had written to Sarah, 'I have no other hopes than that some lucky accident may enable me to do good'[44] – and that from the man whose motto was Faithful But Unfortunate! She was not expected to believe it. Holland had to be persuaded to part with troops, Austria had to be rescued, France and Bavaria beaten. 'He had', says Churchill, 'to measure the potential movements of his allies with as much care as those of the enemy, or his own marches and the supply of his own troops'.[45] His capacity as general is obvious enough, but the size of his mind can be under-estimated. It was that that made him, in the eyes of his contemporaries, 'the great cement' of the Grand Alliance and 'the first man of the age'.

Anne of course had to know and to authorise at least part of the Danube plan: 'It may be taken as certain that she knew that her army was to be sent very far into Europe to save the Empire, and that she meant that it should go, and desired to bear the consequences whatever they might be'.[46]

The battle of Blenheim was not fought until August, but by April 8, when Marlborough embarked at Harwich, his plans will have been far advanced. With most of Europe on his shoulders he might well seem to have had enough to contend with, but no. This was the moment for Sarah to accuse him of infidelity (her long narrative of complaint was handed him on the quay; but luckily she forgave him by letter a few days later). He had also to deal, at a distance, with the political crisis promoted by Nottingham. This champion of the Tories (Marlborough wrote to Godolphin from Harwich) was threatening resignation unless he could get such alterations made in the Cabinet Council as he thought essential for the safety of the Church. He was 'very positive that the Queen could not govern but by one party or the other' and that party must be his. The Queen, he was sure, would back him. It was only Marlborough and Godolphin who stood in the way . . . But he was wrong. Anne certainly was for the Church, she always had been, but never for extremists and decidedly not for those who would try to browbeat her for the sake of party. She dismissed his two lieutenants – Lord Jersey and Sir Edward Seymour – and a few days later, albeit with much show of reluctance, accepted Nottingham's resignation. In a cryptic note to Sarah Anne called her to witness that she had 'never had any partiality to any of those persons'.

One side-effect was amusing, another momentous. Of the first, Boyer notes: 'The Earl of Jersey dismissed & his staff (as Lord Chamberlain) given upon a very weighty consideration to the Earl of Kent'. And in the margin: 'It was then reported & very generally believed that he lost designedly a vast sum of money at cards to a certain Duchess'.[47] If Sarah was as competent at cards as she was in most things she cannot have found it taxing to beat the Bug, as Kent, a standing jest of the Court, was called. A moderate Whig, he was harmless enough: one of the sort described by Bolingbroke as 'too low to be much regarded and too high to be quite neglected, the lumber of every administration, the furniture of every Court'.[48]

The momentous appointment was Harley's as Secretary of State, in place of Nottingham. He was appointed, says Boyer, 'as one that had not yet made himself obnoxious to either party'. A more recent historian has called it 'an untidy accident, a stop-gap measure, almost a panic move'. Harley himself resisted it until the middle of May. As Speaker of the House of Commons he knew how to use his power without showing his hand. As Secretary he would be committed and with a huge extra load of responsibility and work. Devious as he was he did in fact continue for a while to walk the tightrope 'in such an unprecedented manner', as a friend assured him, 'that both sides believe at a proper time and occasion you will show yourself entirely in their distinct interests . . . The Duke, the Treasurer & yourself', he added, 'are called the Triumvirate & reckoned the spring of all public affairs; and that your interests & counsels are so united & linked together that they cannot be broken nor in any danger of it during this reign . . .' A pity perhaps that the writer should also find need to tell him, 'I have heard of people's talk that you fall in with this Ministry not for any particular value or esteem for the persons but as what the Court had resolved upon to be the Ministry . . . and that your aim is in time to be the Prime Minister yourself'.[51]

Second in importance only to that of Harley was the appointment of Henry St John (See page 232) to be Secretary at War. 'We came to Court', he wrote later, 'in the same dispositions as all parties have done, that the principal springs of our actions was to have the government of the state in our hands';[52] but the time to declare it was by no means yet. The thing was to keep people guessing, whether one were Marlborough, Harley or St John or, as she became more wary, the Queen herself.

It was the business of spies to penetrate smokescreens; and so as Marlborough nears Blenheim we find Nathaniel Hooke* reporting to Louis XIV's minister de Torcy that Marlborough's enemies in England are preparing to censure him for taking the army so far, but he is sure of the Queen, who is completely dominated by his wife ('un empire absolu sur elle'). Godolphin, he adds, is Sarah's creature and never acts except in concert with her. As for Marlborough himself, he has been shrewd enough to oust Nottingham and to put in his place the Speaker, thus by one stroke making certain of both Queen and Parliament.[53]

Marlborough, it has been said, could not afford to lose and so he

* Nathaniel Hooke (1664–1738), Irish Jacobite and Roman Catholic convert, was loyal to James II. Naturalised French in 1706 he fought at Ramillies and Malplaquet. Spied for Jacobites in Scotland. Helped Sarah in her old age to re-write her *Conduct*, but she did not appreciate his trying to convert her to Roman Catholicism. Q.A.

never did lose. Certainly if he had lost this his greatest gamble, at Blenheim, he would have been ruined, nor could Sarah's influence with Anne have saved him from the fury of the Tories and of the Dutch. As it was, 'Never did any age' (so ran the *Newsletter* account) 'produce a more glorious victory'. Marlborough's hastily pencilled note, telling of Tallard bundled into his coach; the dusty horseman bringing that note to Anne, as she sat in the gallery above the terrace at Windsor; the bells and bonfires . . . all these are familiar; and something of Anne's relief is reflected in the thousand guineas she gave the messenger, Colonel Parke, with her miniature; but the full meaning could not be grasped at once. Only later was it realised that 'for the first time in modern history an absolutist regime had been beaten to its knees by a limited monarchy' and that 'the charge at Blenheim would open to Britain the gateways of the modern world'.[55]

'So glorious a victory', wrote Anne to Marlborough, 'will not only humble our enemies abroad, but contribute very much to the putting a stop to the ill designs of those at home'.[56] Vienna had been saved by a hairsbreadth, and so in a sense had Marlborough. Even those Tories who, groaning beneath a heavy Land Tax to pay for the war, had been baying for his blood, now cheerfully owned he had paid a dividend. The Whigs of course went further. At Blenheim, declared Lord Hervey, Marlborough had 'acquired to himself the immortal honour of having secured the liberties & peace of Europe from being in our days at least endangered through the voracious, restless spirit of that common disturber of the quiet of mankind, *Louis le Monstre*'.[57] The Dutch monster was dead, and now this French one – well equipped to chastise us with scorpions – had, it was hoped, been irretrievably crushed.

Even so there were still as there always are, critics and carpers. Should not Prince Eugene, they protested, be given more credit? And what of Gibraltar? In all the excitement about Blenheim, Sir George Rooke's conquest seemed in some quarters to have been overlooked. In their congratulations the Lords, Shrewsbury was told, had ignored it (though the Commons had 'hooked it in'), 'for my Lord Marlborough's friends thought that and Blenheim ought not to be mentioned on a day'.[58] But Harley at once saw Gibraltar for what it was: 'the greatest thoroughfare of trade in the world'.[59] Rooke, Defoe told him, was now the darling of the Tory extremists. 'The victory at sea they look upon as their victory over the Moderate party & his health is now drunk by those here [Bury St Edmunds] who won't drink the Queen's nor yours. I am obliged with patience to hear you damned & he praised, he exalted & her Majesty slighted & the sea victory set up against the land victory'.[60] For the factious there was never a shortage of bones to pick or rattles to squabble over.

For the Blenheim thanksgiving on September 7th, however, 'the rejoicings were suitable to the great occasion and her Majesty's subjects gave all the demonstrations imaginable of their affection to her Majesty's person & zeal for her government'.[61] According to Luttrell, Anne's coach-and-eight (the horses 'curiously decked with white & red ribbons made up like roses') carried not only herself and Sarah but Prince George and Lady Frescheville; but John Evelyn differs. 'None with her', he says, 'but the Duchess of Marlborough in a very plain garment, the Queen full of jewels'.[62] Whether or not the contrast was deliberate, there could be no contest in looks.

At St Paul's Anne was carried from coach to throne, where she joined in the *Te Deum* and heard the Dean preach from one of the most savage texts in the Psalms (58, verse 10): The righteous shall rejoice when he seeth the vengeance: he shall wash his feet in the blood of the wicked. 'Verily', adds the psalmist, 'there is a reward for the righteous, verily he is a God that judgeth in the earth'. As Anne had told Sarah, next to God Almighty, the victory had been 'wholly owing to dear Mr Freeman'; but how attempt to reward him? She had made him a duke. The Emperor, with her sanction, had made him a Prince of the Holy Roman Empire. What else was left to give?

The day before the thanksgiving, Evelyn noted, had been wet and stormy, but the day itself was 'one of the most serene and calm days that had been all the year'. If only such sunshine days would last! *Semper eadem* – let her people take it to heart and labour as she unswervingly did for the common good. 'My inclinations', she told Parliament that autumn, 'are to be kind and indulgent to you all. I hope . . . there will be no contention among you but who shall most promote the public welfare . . . This would make me a happy Queen, whose utmost endeavours shall never be wanting to make you a happy and flourishing people'.[63]

No contention? Nothing could be more desirable and nothing, in the circumstances, more unlikely.

CHAPTER SEVEN

'THIS BOILING NATION'

1704 - 1706

ANNE as Queen never visited Scotland. Its people puzzled her. 'These strange people', she called them, and again, 'These unreasonable Scotsmen'. Nothing came to her from that quarter but petitions, varied at times by such extraordinary questions as 'Can a native of Scotland be a Governor of any of her Majesty's Plantations in America and remain in England?'[1] It appeared that he could.* In loyalty as well as in religion they were divided, the Highlands a hive of plotting Jacobites, many of them fonder of France than of England. Officially the Scots acknowledged Anne's sovereignty, while resisting union with England and refusing to look to Hanover for a successor.

Godolphin in 1704 hoped by getting rid of Queensberry, the unpopular Royal Commissioner, and promising office to the Country Party, to win Scotland over to the project of the Hanoverian Seccession. Instead, Scotland presented him with an Act of Security which stipulated that in the event of Anne's death without issue, the same person was not to succeed to both kingdoms unless free trade were in the meantime extended to Scotland. Other provisions pointed towards a Scots Commonwealth with 'no shadow of power left with the [English] Crown'.[2] Unless the Queen sanctioned that Act, no supplies would be voted. At first Anne flatly refused – it was 'a downright submission' – but a few days before the battle of Blenheim Godolphin persuaded her to sign. In Swift's view it bore the seeds of separation and left no alternative but union or the risk of civil war.

After Blenheim, submission to Scotland looked nonsensical and Godolphin was heavily blamed for his pusillanimity. 'We have got the Treasurer into a cleft stick', boasted Wharton, 'let him leave us

* The Earl of Orkney, appointed Governor of Virginia in December, 1709, was still colonel of a guards regiment in England in 1714.

now if he dares'.[3] Nevertheless it was Wharton and the rest of the Whig Junto who eventually rescued him with the Aliens Act, a counter-ultimatum devised by Somers, to make all Scots aliens (their exports to England rejected) unless they approved the Union and acknowledged the succession as approved by England. But before this had happened Anne witnessed stormy scenes in the Lords where Godolphin was attacked for leading England into danger. The Queen, says Burnet, knew that he was aimed at 'and she diverted the storm by her endeavours, as well as she restrained it by her presence'.[4]

In the Lords she sat at first on the throne, but feeling cold moved, as Charles II used, to a bench beside the fire where, with Sarah and Lady Frescheville, she stayed for three hours. No doubt her presence 'prevented some heats' but not all of them. When a scathing reference was made to William, 'Lord Somers rose up and said it was unbecoming a member of that House to sully the memory of so great a prince & he doubted not but a man who could reflect on King William before his successor would do the same by her present Majesty when she was gone'.[5]

When it came to faction, as it did for the rest of the reign, there was little to choose between England and Scotland. In the Lords Anne watched Whig savage Tory; while from Scotland another of Harley's spies, William Greg, was reporting on 'this boiling nation, which all their extraordinary pretences to sanctity & reformation above their neighbours could not hinder from hugging an airy phantom [the Pretender] which if ever realised must needs prove their ruin'.[6] In Scotland, he said, they were drinking the Pretender's health as openly as one drank the Queen's in England. Yet for England's sake they had to be humoured. 'I love your nation', wrote Harley to the Earl of Leven, 'You will please to forgive the overflowing of my zeal and affection to the noble Scots nation whose ruin, if Heaven be not more merciful, will be upon their own heads'.[7] There was still just a chance of their proving an asset.

If Scotland could cause heat in the Lords, that was nothing to the high fever perennially and deliberately engendered by the Occasional Conformity Bill. This time, at Nottingham's instigation, it was to be tacked to the Land Tax – 'a most desperate attempt of an angry squadron' – and so foisted, in the face of all acceptable usage, on Parliament. Thanks however to what Marlborough called Harley's prudent management, it was defeated in the Commons by 251 votes to 134; and in the following month (December) it was thrown out of the Lords. Sarah was elated. She sent a scathing note on vote-catching to the Queen.[8] But the whole operation was to prove a goad to Providence. In the view of a modern historian, 'By driving the High Church party leaders into opposition, Marlborough and Godolphin began that long train of events which resulted in their own humiliation and the return of the Tories in 1710'.[9]

Marlborough in Hanover had been well out of the worst of this imbroglio. On all counts indeed he was more usefully employed, captivating Sophia and her unlovable son the Elector, who in ten years' time was to succeed to the British throne. No one then alive could be more suave, more winning, more persuasive: Marlborough epitomised success. Years later when at the same Court his rivals set themselves to undermine him they failed to touch the foundations; they had begun too late.

On December 14th Anne welcomed Marlborough at St James's and gave him a diamond sword. She then went to Windsor, where Godolphin was installed as a Knight of the Garter. By January 3rd she was back at St James's Palace to watch from Lady Fitzharding's window the captured colours from Blenheim carried from the Tower to Westminster Hall, saluted as they went by forty guns in the park. On January 18th, after pondering alternatives such as statues (one of the Queen and the other of Marlborough), Anne decided to make over to Marlborough and his posterity the royal estate at Woodstock, consisting of a manor house battered by Cromwell and several villages encircling a wild park, known in all as the Hundred of Wootton. The park had first been enclosed by Henry I. Henry II had built a Trianon there, on a Sicilian model, for Rosamund Clifford. Elizabeth I had been imprisoned in the manor's gatehouse for two years. Even James II had managed to lodge there for hunting, though his courtiers complained that the place was uninhabitable.

When, 'under the auspices of a munificent sovereign' (as a Blenheim inscription reads), the princely gift was given (See page 328) it was generally understood that, as part of Marlborough's reward, the house that was to be built for him there (then known as the Castle of Blenheim) would be paid for by the Queen and nation, the only proviso being that on every anniversary of the victory at Blenheim a replica of the captured royal standard of France should as quitrent be delivered at Windsor to the reigning sovereign. It was a charming idea and very typical of Anne.

Boyer,* writing in the year of Marlborough's death (1722), went so far as to say that in 1705 Anne ordered the Comptroller of her Works (Vanbrugh) to build in Woodstock Park a most stately palace or castle, 'which would indeed have proved a worthy monument of the Duke of Marlborough's immortal actions if the skill and genius of the architect had been equal to the Queen's liberality'.[10]

Today Vanbrugh's skill and genius (plus those of Hawksmoor, who partnered him) are widely acknowledged to have been more than equal both to Anne's bounty and to the all but impossible challenge of designing a national monument in which generations of dukes and their households might comfortably live. The long, sad, complex tale has been told elsewhere. Anne, after viewing with George at Kensington Vanbrugh's model of the place and approving it, lost interest. At least she never went near the building, far from finished as it was when she died. Whether or not it was folly on Anne's part to give so lavishly, it might fairly be said, as she once excused Abigail to Sarah, that 'it was very natural and she was very much in the right'; even though it left nothing for the rebuilding of Whitehall or the palace at Winchester. As for Marlborough, he set his heart upon it and that, in Sarah's opinion at least, was folly too. 'Great is the man and great have been his actions', wrote a contemporary, 'but all these favours create enemies'. From beneath his sarcophagus at Blenheim there half-emerges a dragon intended as Envy. It had been roused by Marlborough's appointments. It was roused again by Blenheim: 'a finer palace than the Queen's'.

In old age Sarah gave it in Anne's favour that she 'made no foolish buildings'. She built churches, patched and added to her palaces,

* Abel Boyer (1667-1729), a Huguenot, settled in England in 1689. Wrote two accounts of the reign of Anne. Taught Anne's son, the Duke of Gloucester, French.

Kneller: Sarah Duchess of Marlborough at cards with Lady Fitzharding

Boit: Miniature of Queen Anne and Prince George of Denmark

losterman: William Duke of Gloucester in Garter Robes

Verrio: Queen Anne as Justice on the Drawing Room ceiling at Hampton Court (detail)

spent much on gardens and gave orders for the rebuilding of the house at Newmarket but, perhaps luckily, never attempted anything so ambitious as the rebuilding of the Tudor parts of Hampton Court. It was a time for good buildings great and small (one has only to look at Queen Anne's Gate), and for superb craftsmanship, but royal taste is not always to be trusted. However, it seems fitting that Anne as a patron of the arts (a role she was not strong in) should, for architecture, be remembered by, on the larger scale, the Gibbs, Archer and Hawksmoor churches and on the smaller by the orangery or banqueting-house Vanbrugh designed for her at Kensington.* It was finished in 1705. 'After the Queen had built her Green House at Kensington Palace', wrote Defoe, 'she was pleased to make it her summer supper room'.[11] Originally three rooms – drawingroom, music room and ballroom – and neighboured by Wise's mount and sunk garden with myrtles and orange-trees, it must have been a delightful place for Anne to be carried to in her chair of a summer's evening. It was not large (she shared Sarah's distaste for grandeur) and she invited only those few she had a mind to. The round, apse-rooms at each end were just the size she liked. Even today, by a miracle, the white interior with carving by Gibbons remains unspoiled; although outside, Wise's works have gone and a football-pitch has been substituted for his orange-tree terraces.

Now in 1705 began those long absences of Sarah's which brought sadness to Anne. As Princess of Mindelheim she was said to despise the duties of her office; but if there was any truth in that, which is doubtful, it was but a minor reason. Holywell and Windsor Lodge were far more to her liking than St James's and Kensington, while Anne's company, as she afterwards owned, she found less and less entertaining. She left three deputies: her daughters Harriet and Anne and, at a lower level, Abigail Hill. Surely that was enough . . .

'I am in so dull a way', Anne wrote to Sarah from Kensington, 'I came hither to dinner & hoped to pass this day with Mr Morley

* Kensington Orangery, previously attributed to the triumvirate: Vanbrugh, Wren and Hawksmoor, now, thanks to Mr Howard Colvin's researches, proves to have been designed by Vanbrugh alone. Another orangery – but far more conventional – was added for Anne to the south-western range at Hampton Court.

without being troubled with impertinences I can't avoid at London, but for all I came in my chariot, vermine* followed me & has not left me a minute till now. Between her company & Lady Charlotte's, who came to me today, I am so oppressed that I have hardly life or soul left in me, which I hope will excuse me for saying no more but that Mrs Morley doats on her dear Mrs Freeman & I am with all my heart & soul yours'.[12]

Into these intimate notes, which Anne made a point of not signing or dating, there now crept a note of pathos, mounting almost to despair as the bleak months dragged on. With a dull Court and a duller husband, herself sick and naturally morose, she longed for Sarah to cheer her. Instead, when Sarah wrote, the page was peppered with 'Majesty', a trick she well knew saddened and sickened the desolate Queen:

> I must disobey my dear Mrs Freeman and answer her letter in writing, because I can't help being uneasy that you call me twice Majesty & not once mention your poor unfortunate faithful Morley; and therefore I beg if it is not very troublesome that you would write two words before you go to bed to let me know if you are either angry with me or take anything ill, that I may justify myself if you have any hard thoughts of me . . . and be so just to your poor unfortunate faithful Morley as to believe I ever did, do now and ever will love my dear Mrs Freeman beyond all expression.[13]

Anne's next letter is singed, as though someone had begun to burn it and then changed her mind:

> I am very sorry to find Majesty twice in so short a letter as I received tonight from my dear Mrs Freeman, that being always a sign of your having unkind thoughts of your poor unfortunate faithful Morley, who is more yours than it is possible to express, and for God's sake tell me why I should say so if 'twere not true. I never did deceive you nor never will & it is not in my nature to say I am tenderly fond of you (which is as true as Gospel) if I were not so. I was once so happy as to be believed by my dear Mrs Freeman. Oh do not let me lose your credit, which I cannot be conscious to myself I have ever forfeited, but believe me what I really am, unalterably yours. As to the living you write about, you may easily enough imagine I will do anything you desire, but intending to be always

* A nickname for someone not now identifiable.

very careful in disposing of anything of this nature, I hope you will not take it ill if I desire you would enquire where this gentleman lives . . . that I may get the Archbishop of York to inform himself if he be proper for it, and if he finds him to be so, he shall be sure to have it; and give me leave once more to assure you I am nor never will change and for Jesus' sake do not doubt what I say.[14]

Sarah afterwards boasted of having stacks of such letters. They made no impression on her. She endorsed one: 'Letter when the Queen was fond of Mrs Hill, but not known'; and the other: 'I believe when this letter was writ she was fond of Mrs Hill and was a long time fearful that it should be known'. But that was written with hindsight. Not until after Abigail Hill's marriage in 1707 did Sarah discover that 'fondness'. In 1705 she merely sensed that Anne had changed. Anne still wrote or seemed to write from the heart, without reserve, even without dignity. Yet when duty to the Church came in, she paused. Sarah went blindly on, asking and not giving and at the same time failing to see that loss of credit on her side – not the Queen's – could cost her everything. They were already at cross-purposes, Sarah begging for a bishopric, Anne for Sarah's love. If Marlborough had been in England he would almost certainly have made Sarah if not less cold in her letters, at least more attentive to Anne and more diplomatic. But that was impossible and sooner or later favour with nothing to feed on was bound to decline. Few but Sarah herself would say that her fall, when it came, was not in some ways deserved, but for Marlborough – 'faithful but unfortunate' – it was monstrous bad luck that he too should have to be dragged down.

There was then, as there appears to be still, much to be said for being on the losing side. While Marlborough was fighting not with an elusive enemy but against faction and recalcitrant allies, Marshal Tallard, whom he had conquered at Blenheim, though now a prisoner, had the liberty of Nottingham and its countryside for ten miles around. While he hunted with the Duke of Newcastle or stayed at Chatsworth (they sent him champagne), Wise was laying out for him a miniature parterre, designed to centre upon Louis XIV's emblem of a sunflower. As French Ambassador in William's day he had been known and liked by everyone including Anne. Now he could resume these friendships and by one means or another secretly send over his impressions to France. Godolphin, he told de Torcy in January 1705, wanted peace, and if Marlborough were not so headstrong he would be of like mind, for without another success 'this campaign' he would be ruined. A few days later Marlborough told Tallard he respected Louis and so did Anne. They wanted peace, but Parliament would not hear of a Frenchman on the throne of Spain.

Three months afterwards, de Torcy assured Tallard that everyone in France was counting on him to arrange a peace. What were the chances of bribing Marlborough? After all, the cost of two or three months' war might be better spent as a reward for his bringing about the peace. Would Godolphin and Sarah be likely to help? Tallard's reply was cautious. Godolphin and Marlborough were so deep, to approach them one must go armed with a sounding-line, and even then very slowly . . . He had learned not to underestimate them.[15]

By the summer Marlborough was writing to Godolphin, 'I am weary of my life . . . If you could know all I suffer here abroad you would agree with me in begging of the Queen that I might never more go out of England'. And to Sarah, 'But really my spirit is so broke that whenever I can get from this employment I must live quietly or die'.[16]

For Anne the year 1705, after a dreary start, was proving more tolerable, being enlivened with two progresses, the first to Cambridge and Newmarket, the second to Winchester. Her reception at Cambridge in April had been particularly heartening, for besides the usual manifestations of joy and loyalty – bells, conduits awash with wine, her way strewn with flowers, and three hundred Ladies and Gentlewomen admitted to kiss her hand – the scholars of St John's had made 'loud & uninterrupted acclamations of *Vivat Regina*! on their knees through all the courts in thickset numbers as the Queen passed forward & backward';[17] while at Trinity she had sat upon a throne to dine with the Chancellor (the Duke of Somerset) and the Master (Dr Bentley). While there she knighted its most celebrated Fellow Isaac Newton. The University, in return, could hardly do less than scatter its degrees among her attendants: Sunderland, Orford, Albemarle, even Tom Wharton and the Bug (Kent) suddenly found themselves Doctors of Literature.[18] It was of course routine.

The same could be said of Anne's dining a day or two later at the house of the High Steward, the Earl of Orford, but since he happened to be one of the Whig Junto, it caused much speculation. At Newmarket there were no such complications. She ordered her house there to be rebuilt, gave a thousand guineas for a horse and presented it to George and watched the races.

The Winchester progress in late summer was almost as successful. The Queen, says Coke, was 'extremely reverenced and caressed wherever she came'. At the Hampshire county-boundary she was greeted by the High Sheriff and ninety javelin-men who, like the Amazons of Bath, escorted her the rest of the way. She had it in mind to finish Charles II's palace and make it over to George. He could live there if he survived her. Flamsteed the Astronomer Royal reported in August: 'Sir Christopher Wren is going down to Winchester to view the buildings there which the Queen has a mind to finish . . . He is a very honest man, I find him so, and perhaps the only honest person I have to deal with'.[19] Wren reckoned the finishing would cost £18,000; but the plan came to nothing. For Anne and George, as for Charles, Wren was never to lead it; and for that England is the poorer.

Between the two progresses the Whigs openly and Harley secretly gained ground. Whig gains in the general election in May made the parties roughly equal in the Commons, with some seventy Court supporters to hold the balance. The Whig grandee Newcastle, a friend of Harley's, had displaced Tory Buckingham (once Mulgrave) from the post of Lord Privy Seal. Marlborough and Godolphin realised that they could not much longer count on Whig support for the war (and for the Union with Scotland) unless the Whig leaders were given more power. But to fall into the hands of the Whig Junto would not in the least have suited Harley. For him it was 'Let there be moderation in all things'.

In June, while Blenheim Palace was being founded, Harley put out feelers in various directions, to Newcastle, to Cowper . . . He wrote to the Queen; and though there could as yet be no question of his being as closely accepted as Mr Montgomery or Mr Freeman, yet she had begun to sign her replies to him 'Your very affectionett freind'. Something of this must have reached the ears of Godolphin, something that suggested a drifting away from the Triumvirate, even perhaps an attempt to set up on his own. Protesting innocence, he was brought to heel.

Harley was upset. The situation as he saw it called for oil and at the same time for much caution. Not for nothing was Godolphin called Volpone. The letter Harley had now to send him was not going to be easy to write. Should he begin by saying 'The greatest concern I have is that I cannot serve the Queen as I wish', or 'It is my greatest trouble that I cannot serve the Queen so well as I should or as she deserves', or 'Though I serve the Queen with zeal & affection, yet I cannot live without trouble lest her service should suffer in my hand?' He finally chose 'I am justly conscious to myself that the utmost service I can perform to her Majesty falls infinitely short of what the Queen deserves, nor can it bear any proportion to the reverence & affection I have for your Lordship & the Duke of Marlborough, by whose indulgence & too kind recommendation I have those marks I now enjoy of the Queen's favour . . .' So far so good, but what of his inner self? Could one offer 'nakedly to open my soul to your Lordship?' Perhaps not. He discarded 'nakedly' and wrote of his 'very soul' being united with Godolphin's, 'I have no other views, no other passions', he ended, 'than to be subservient to your Lordship; if I go astray it shall be only for want of your direction . . . I know my own heart & I can die a martyr for the Queen's service, and I am as sure that nothing can tear me from being your servant'.[20] The draft at Longleat bears plainly the marks of uncertainty and agitation.[21] Even when re-written and polished the letter was not a good one. It can hardly have fooled Godolphin, let alone Sarah, who had seen from the first that the man was out for himself. However for the time being a calm set in and by September Harley was writing to Godolphin collectedly:

> I shall always submit myself to your direction. I take it for granted that no party in the House can carry it for themselves without the Queen's servants join with them; that the foundation is, persons or parties are to come in to the Queen & not the Queen to them; that the Queen hath chosen rightly which party she will take in . . . If the gentlemen of England are made sensible that the Queen is the Head and not a Party, everything will be easy & the Queen will be courted & not a Party; but if otherwise . . . [22]

But of course the Queen must be above party. The danger was, as Mr Holmes points out, that once a party had too big a majority, it could dictate terms to the Queen's managers and so in effect to the Queen.

'The real foundation of difference between the two parties is removed', wrote St John, echoing his 'Dear Master' (Harley), 'and the Queen seems to throw herself on the gentlemen of England, who had much better have her at the head of 'em than any ringleaders of fashion . . .'[23]

Provided the gentlemen of England lived up to their name, all might yet be well. At least they seemed on the whole more loyal and more intelligible than the gentlemen of Scotland. 'The nobility of Scotland', Defoe told Harley, 'are an odd kind of people, to say no more of them'.[24] Anne was displeased to find Queensberry, who had deserted to the opposition, reinstated in the Scots Ministry as Lord Privy Seal. Even though it was largely through his influence that that ministry, headed by Argyll, carried through an Act appointing Commissioners to treat for a Union with England, Anne could not forgive him. To Godolphin she referred to Queensberry's 'tricking behaviour' which had made him odious to her. 'It grates my soul', she wrote, 'to take a man into my service that has not only betrayed me but tricked me several times'. Against her own better judgment, as she thought, she agreed to his appointment: 'I will do myself the violence these unreasonable Scotsmen desire, and indeed it is an unexpressible one'. Queensberry, Argyll, Hamilton, she trusted none of them but, to get the succession and Union settled, she knew she must use them. As for the Church, 'Episcopal ministers everywhere', Hooke reported to de Torcy, 'never mention Queen Anne in their prayers and several are bold enough to pray for the King of England'.[25] Isaac Watts might compose flattering odes –

> The vengeance of thy rod, with general joy,
> Shall scourge rebellion and the rival boy . . .

but if reports were true, far too many Scotsmen preferred the rival boy to his stepsister and were prepared to welcome him.

Nearer home some mischievous person had published a 'false, scandalous & traiterous libel' called *A Memorial of the Church of*

England, containing 'most injurious reflections on her Majesty for displacing some Ministers'.[26] Easy enough to have it burned by the public hangman, but who was the author? Very few were in the know but Harley was among them and Cowper had his suspicions.

From a pack of more or less corrupt politicians Sir William (afterwards Lord) Cowper stands out as unique in his acceptance by both parties as an honest man. Even Godolphin, whose integrity was beyond question, was thought too timorous and too easily browbeaten by Sarah and the Junto. Cowper, an eminent lawyer and orator, charming, modest and fairminded, a practising Christian, in politics a moderate Whig, was now put forward as Lord Keeper, in place of the Tory nonentity Sir Nathan Wright. Sarah, as advance-agent for the Whigs, made it her business to run down Wright and to praise Cowper, and this she did with such fervour that she nearly defeated her object. Anne, highly suspicious, wrote Sarah what the latter described as her first peevish letter. Anne was not to be fooled, this was Whig versus Tory. 'I know both their principles very well', she wrote, 'and when I know myself to be in the right, nothing can make me alter mine'.[27] Nor could anything touch her more nearly than the appointment of her Lord Keeper, the very guardian of her conscience and adviser on Church patronage. To remove Sir Nathan, 'a warm stickler for the Church', to make way for a Whig, must surely be folly.

From Windsor Anne sent Godolphin a *cri du coeur*, hoping that a moderate Tory might be appointed. A few more favours for the Whigs must put her in their power. 'I know my dear unkind friend', she added (meaning of course Sarah), 'has so good an opinion of all that party that to be sure she will use all her endeavour to get you to prevail with me to put one of them into this great post . . . But I hope in God you will never think that reasonable, for that would be an unexpressible uneasiness & mortification to me. There is nobody I can rely upon but yourself to bring me out of all my difficulties & I do put an entire confidence in you, not doubting but you will do all you can to keep me out of the power of the merciless men of both parties & to that end make choice of one for Lord Keeper that will be the likeliest to prevent that danger'.[28]

Yet in time she gave way and signed Cowper's appointment;

nor did she ever find cause to regret it. It had made no difference, she said later, to her friendship with Sarah; but she was not one to forget when her will had been overruled. As it was, she made a proviso that the disposal of certain benefices in the universities was to remain in the hands of Harley.[29] Already the Junto had pushed their candidate Wake into the bishopric of Lincoln in the face of Sharp's nominee, Sir William Dawes. Obviously things were drifting the wrong way.

To allow more time for his duties as Secretary of State Harley had surrendered the Speakership; and now in October his successor was to be Bromley (a Tory) or Smith (a Whig). 'The good or little success of this Parliament', everyone agreed, 'must depend upon the choice of a Speaker'. Anne begged Lady Bathurst to insist on her son's voting for Smith and was offended when he voted instead for his friend Bromley. Prince George's secretary, Dr George Clarke, was dismissed on the election day for refusing to promise his vote for Smith when urged by his master to do so.[30] Eleven other Tory placeholders similarly lost their jobs. 'The contest was very great and the Court engaged warmly for Mr Smith', who was voted in.*

November brought the important and provocative proposal, made by Lord Haversham in the House of Lords, that in order to guarantee the Protestant Succession in the House of Hanover, the Electress Sophia should be invited to live in England. It was provocative because it was calculated to embarrass the ministry and the Queen. It was important because as things turned out it alienated Anne from the Tories. It was, as Mr Holmes says, a squalid manoeuvre, and with no other purpose than to damage the standing of Marlborough, Godolphin and the Whig chiefs, either with the Queen if they supported the invitation or with Hanover and the rank and file Whigs if they opposed it. However, the trap was dodged. Thanks to the brilliance of Somers a Whig counter-attack was staged which culminated in the Regency Act, piloted through the Commons by Harley.[31] Anne, again in the Lords, was appalled to hear Lord Haversham ask, 'Is there any man, my Lords, who doubts that if

* Smith stood as 'a Court candidate with Whig support rather than as the party nominee endorsed by the Court.' Speck: *The Choice of a Speaker in 1705*: IHR Bulletin 37 (1964).

the Duke of Gloucester* had been alive, her Majesty had not been more secure than she is?' And worse was to come. Buckingham of all people added that 'the Queen might live till she did not know what she did and be like a child in the hands of others'. It needed only a gibe from Wharton (and that was always forthcoming) to make the debate ludicrous. When the Queen called for concord among her subjects, he said, there must have been a divinity about her, for now by a miracle all were in favour of the Protestant Succession. He would not, he could not, he ought not to suspect the sincerity of those who moved for inviting the next successor over. The jest was not to her humour; but then what better was to be expected of a Junto lord? What wounded her most were those shafts from the Tories, for these – Buckingham and Nottingham – were the very men who had warned her against inviting a successor. Should she do so, they had said, she would thenceforward reign by their courtesy only.[32] For a Queen to have such flagrant turncoats about her was insufferable. Why should she stomach them?

'I am sensible of the services those people have done me that you have a good opinion of', she told Sarah, 'and will countenance them and am thoroughly convinced of the malice & insolence of them that you have always been speaking against'.[33] She had no intention of throwing herself into the arms of the Junto. Even so, to Sarah it must have looked as though she had won more than half the battle.

If Anne had known Sophia of Hanover (in Burnet's view the most knowing and the most entertaining woman of the age), she might well have felt differently. Sophia for her part, by writing to the Archbishop of Canterbury, let it be known that she would with Anne's approval be willing to come over. She was never to be invited. Anne could not forget the insult of being turned down by Sophia's son on account of Anne Hyde. 'The Duke of Hanover', Hooke told de Torcy, 'once refused to marry the Princess Anne because of the humble birth (*peu de naissance*) of her mother, and the Queen remains deeply resentful of that refusal . . . Several who were then at Court have confirmed this. I don't know if this resentment

* According to Boyer, 'The Queen was so touched with the sound of that dear name that she went out of the House to dissipate her grief'. (*Annals*: 1705, 196). If she did, she returned in time to hear Buckingham.

alone will suffice to make the Queen break the Hanoverian Succession, but it would appear to be a big help to those whose interest it is to revoke it'.[34]

For a monarch to be swayed by emotion must seem deplorable; yet there can be no doubt that Anne did take these things personally and lastingly. Over the Hanover debate in November she is said to have wept for three days and nights.[35] She had barely recovered when Rochester took it upon himself to raise the old battle-cry 'The Church is in danger!' It never failed. Amazing as it seems, this too she took personally. How dared they suggest it when she, God's Vicegerent, was there to champion the Church! It was bait she would always rise to: 'that darling phantom', as Sarah called it, 'which the Tories were ever presenting to her imagination & employing a will in the whisp to bewilder her mind & entice her (as she at last unhappily experienced) to the destruction of her quiet and glory'.[36]

From all the turmoil the one good thing to emerge was the Regency Act, which provided for regents to govern in the hazardous gap that might occur between the death of Anne and the arrival of her successor, who would be proclaimed by order of the Privy Council. Seven officers of state would act as regents in collaboration with others to be nominated by Hanover. Sophia and her issue were, at Burnet's instigation, naturalised, and Sophia herself was pacified by Marlborough.

In the tail of 1705 mischiefmakers were still to find scope. On December 20th Charles Caesar referred in the Commons to a noble lord, 'without whose advice the Queen does nothing, who in the late reign was known to keep a constant correspondence with the Court of St Germains'. Godolphin's *tendre* for Mary of Modena was of course common knowledge; to mention it was in the worst possible taste. Caesar was sent to the Tower. On the same day the Lords debated the question of a reward for the discovery of the author or authors of *The Memorial of the Church of England.* Godolphin and Cowper had privately suggested £500, but Harley 'laboured mightily to have it but £200 and so it was, nobody caring to speak after him (at Cabinet Council), the Queen having been wearied before with too much on such a subject; from whence', adds Cowper, 'I guess the Secretary knew or conjectured who were the authors & had no mind they should be discovered'.[37]

On Christmas Day the Queen held another Council. She had gout in her knee, but she had a new doctor whom she liked. His name (no one could spell or pronounce it) was Arbuthnot, a Scotsman.* He had, as the nearest doctor at hand, 'performed good and successful services' when Prince George had suddenly been taken ill at Epsom. In October, by Anne's express command, he had joined her household as Physician Extraordinary. There was little he could do for her gout, but she liked his company. He was sincere and witty.

Seventeen hundred and six began with Marlborough's arrival from Holland with the Duke and Duchess of Shrewsbury. For Marlborough 1705 had been a frustrating year. There had been no second Blenheim. The laurels had been gathered in Spain by Peterborough, the hero of Barcelona. 'It is in keeping with the fantastic character of Peterborough's career', comments Trevelyan, 'that his one great achievement as a soldier probably did more harm than good to his country and to the world. Had he failed in the attempt on Barcelona the Allies must have abandoned all serious intention of placing Charles III on the Spanish throne . . . Peace might have been arranged years earlier on terms at least as good as those of Utrecht'.[38] Marlborough's greatest victories – at Blenheim, Ramillies and Oudenarde – were to go by alternate years.

The Court was agog to see the Duchess of Shrewsbury. Rumour said she had pursued the King of Hearts from Rome to Augsburg whence, at the start of the honeymoon, he had written to Harley:

> . . . Yesterday morning I was married to a widow lady I was acquainted with at Rome who, though an Italian, I am thoroughly persuaded will be not only a good wife but a good Protestant, she having to my knowledge made her change to our religion upon arguments well grounded as to the next world, as she entirely satisfied the Protestant minister who examined

* John Arbuthnot, FRS (1667–1735), 'the Queen's favourite physician' (Swift, 1709), author of *The History of John Bull*, *The Art of Political Lying* and various political pamphlets. Swift found his humanity equal to his wit. Other friends were Pope, Prior, Congreve and Peterborough. In November 1709 he became Physician-in-Ordinary, succeeding Dr Hannes. A Tory with Jacobite leanings. Fond of cards and music.

her before he would join us in marriage yesterday. However, as to the sincerity of this act, time & her behaviour will be the best proof & I wish people would be contented not to judge till they might do it upon grounds that were reasonable . . .[39]

He had quite forgotten the English Court. 'Sure, my Lord', wrote St John to his kinsman Lord Cutts, "tis a matter of great merit to make an ancient Roman beauty a convert at the expense of making her a wife'.[40] The women were even more venomous. Lady Cowper said all the world knew that the Duchess's brother had forced Shrewsbury to marry her, but what a match for a man who might once have had the Duchess of Somerset! This Italian 'with all her prate and noise' was 'the most cunning, designing woman alive'. True, she could be entertaining. She could even make the Queen laugh. But at times she exceeded the bounds of decency.[41] Sarah mistrusted her, but that applied to almost everybody. She thought she saw Shrewsbury eyeing her gold key. Shrewsbury himself was angled for by Whigs and Tories, but for the time being he declined to take office.*

The Court had scarcely got its breath before Buckingham, *en troisième noces*, married Lady Anglesea, the natural daughter of James II and Lady Dorchester. This new duchess also, as The Princess, became a Court jest, to be regarded with her Duke as natural champions for the Jacobites.

In January, after Anne, laid up with gout, had received the Council in her bedchamber, Marlborough and Godolphin secretly conferred with the Junto lords and made a pact with them about ecclesiastical appointments.[42] Where bishops meant votes it was no longer enough to leave their nominations to Harley and Sharp. Sooner or later Harley must know of the new arrangement. In the meantime he asked Marlborough and Godolphin to dinner with Somers and Halifax, St John and Sunderland, Cowper and Boyle, and in Tokay

* On 29 January 1706 a French spy (Le Vasseur) reported to Gaultier: 'Shrewsbury will be Lord Chamberlain & her Majesty will give Kent the money ('10,000 pieces') he gave the Duchess of Marlborough when she procured him this place'. (PRO Baschet transcr. 3/31/193).

Shrewsbury became Lord Chamberlain in 1710.

toasted love and friendship and everlasting union. The health had been better drunk, Cowper suggested, in clear white Lisbon; by which he was understood to refer to 'that humour of his [Harley's], which was never to deal clearly or openly but always with reserve if not dissimulation or rather simulation & to love tricks even where not necessary but from an inward satisfaction he took in applauding his own cunning. If any man was ever born under a necessity of being a knave', added Cowper, 'he was'.[43]

This was damning enough; but if there was to be a battle of wits, Harley would welcome it. He too would have secret meetings. He knew the way now by the Queen's back stairs. He befriended the bedchamberwomen (Abigail and her sister were his kinswomen). He befriended Samuel Masham, equerry to Prince George. He befriended Arbuthnot. For weeks at a time Anne was now bedridden and so, for those who had access, she was a captive audience, of which Harley was to take more advantage than Sarah, who often preferred to write.

For her birthday Anne, still with the gout, was treated to 'a fine ode sung in concert'. Next morning George was much indisposed. In March he spat blood and by the end of April was pronounced dangerously ill. However, he recovered. Ailing though she herself was, Anne sat up with him at night, in a vast four-poster hung with red curtains, and helped him fight for breath. To an optimist the outlook must have seemed gloomy, and Anne was not that. 'I am', she told Marlborough, 'of a temper always to fear the worst'. Yet in the face of all this she resolved in May to touch for the Evil as many poor people as she could 'before hot weather . . . I do that business now', she told Sarah, 'in the Banqueting House, which I like very well, that being a very cool room, and the doing of it there keeps my own house sweet & free from crowds'.[44]

Sarah, seldom now in London, found herself pleading by letter for the rector of Sutton, a Mr Stephens, who in a pamphlet had libelled Harley and criticised Marlborough's conduct in his last campaign. He had been fined and ordered to stand twice in the pillory, with a paper pinned to his hat. He was in fact taken to the pillory and shown it before being told of the reprieve, most reluctantly granted.

'I have, upon my dear Mrs Freeman's pressing letter about Mr

Stephens', wrote Anne, 'ordered Mr Secretary Harley to put a stop to his standing in the pillory, till farther orders, which is in the effect the same thing as if he was pardoned. Nothing but your desire could have inclined me to it, for in my opinion it is not right. My reason I will tell you when I have the happiness of seeing you. Till then, my dear Mrs Freeman, farewell'.[45]

What with gout and George's asthma and these endless petitions, Anne was 'over head & ears in the spleen'. It was May and the fruit trees Wise had planted at Windsor had shot to admiration; but she needed something more to cheer her. 'The best medicine for a Prince', wrote Peterborough, 'is news of a victory'; and now, when things seemed at their worst, came the news of Marlborough's triumph at Ramillies. 'No battle in the eighteenth century', writes Churchill, 'produced comparable direct results. The fortress-barrier was for a while shorn away like grass before the scythe. As Blenheim saved Vienna, so Ramillies conquered the Netherlands'.[46]

For the thanksgiving on June 27th 'a greater number of the nobility attended than ever was known upon such an occasion; the Duchess of Marlborough & the Countess of Burlington in the coach with her Majesty, the Prince not there, being unable to endure the fatigue'.[47] The service in St Paul's lasted from 1.30 to 4.15. The Queen joined in the *Te Deum* ('after the composition of the late famous Mr Purcell') while the guns of the Tower were discharged.

Ramillies had nearly cost Marlborough his life. (Bringfield was beheaded by a cannonball while helping him to remount). The victory, he hoped, would mean giving the Queen 'the glory of making an honourable and safe peace; for', he piously added, 'the blessing of God is certainly with us'. [48]The Emperor offered to make him Governor of the Low Countries (£64,000 a year), as vice-regent for Charles of Spain, but the Dutch opposed it and so he had to decline.

Success was going to the allies' heads. In Spain Galway and the Portuguese had advanced on Madrid and expected Charles to mount his throne there. In northern Italy Eugene had repulsed the French and linked up with the Duke of Savoy to take Turin. Louis XIV made a tempting peace-proposal to Holland, reluctantly rejected. Victorious as we were and committed to ejecting Philip from Spain, we would not hear of it.

'I am sorry to find the French party have still so much power in Holland as to fill the States with such jealousy', Anne wrote to Sarah from Windsor on July 4th. 'If they knew my temper they would be very easy, I having no ambition after the King of Spain is settled on his throne but to see an honourable peace, that whenever it pleases God I shall die I may have the satisfaction of leaving my poor country and all my friends in peace and quiet. I can't help being in pain for this accident, but I hope as you do the Duke of Marlborough may find out a proper expedient to compose it. I am very glad all the difficulties in the Union are at end here and wish with all my heart it may meet with none in Scotland'.[49]

Thanks to Peterborough who, instead of conducting Charles III to his throne, fell out with him and let him linger for months in Catalonia, before himself absconding to Genoa, the allies' biggest chance in Spain was thrown away. Sunderland's remonstrance – that he return forthwith to explain his extraordinary manner of leaving Spain – was useless, as were Peterborough's scurrilous reflections upon his former friend the King.[50]

As for the Union with Scotland – 'for putting the two nations on one bottom to all posterity' – the Commissioners had drawn up a treaty, but in Scotland there was still fierce resistance. 'Certainly', wrote Defoe to Harley from Edinburgh, 'a Scots rabble is the worst of its kind . . . I heard a great noise & looking out saw a terrible multitude come up the High Street with a drum at the head of them, shouting & swearing & crying out all Scotland would stand together, 'No Union!' 'No Union!' 'English dogs!' and the like . . . The guards were insulted & stoned as they stood'.[51] At Glasgow things were no better, the mob 'so audacious as to hang in effigy one of the Lords Commissioners with the articles about his neck.'[52]

But they had underestimated the Commissioners, who included Somers and the Junto. In October Halifax assured Robethon in Hanover:

I can now tell you very confidently that the Union will be agreed to in Scotland . . . They proposed a general fast, which would have taken up three weeks, but that was waived because the Assembly of the Kirk had not asked it and when it was moved there it was rejected, and the Assembly has directed the ministers to offer up prayers for the success of the

Union, and now the clergy have made this step it cannot fail of succeeding.[53]

'We shall esteem it', said Anne, 'the greatest glory of our reign to have it now perfected'. But ought it to be left to the prayers of the Scots clergy? 'The parsons here', wrote Defoe again from Edinburgh, 'are unaccountable people, humorous, jealous, partial, censorious, haughty, insolent and above all monstrously ignorant'.[54] As intercessors perhaps they were best ignored. Much work would still need to be done and much pressure exerted before the Union could be sealed and confirmed. At times it still looked impracticable but, says Boyer, 'by a surprising chain of success Heaven had prepared the way for the accomplishment of that great work in order to crown her Majesty's unexcelled piety by completing the happiness of all her subjects'.[55]

It was a stirring thought.

CHAPTER EIGHT

THE ARBITRESS

1706 - 1707

IN paint and in ink there is no paucity of portraits of Queen Anne. Kneller (at his best better than likely) painted her again and again. His least flattering picture, which still hangs in her closet at Kensington, (See page 41) gives her that 'small tincture of sourness' occasioned by the 'defluxion' in her eyes and by more or less constant pain.

For pen-portraits we have Sarah's, in many lively versions, all to some extent prejudiced.* And we have too, for this time, the stark account of one of the Scots Commissioners, Sir John Clerk. Some people, in their memoirs, come through to the reader as truthful and likeable and this is one of them. When his father was sick he nursed him and cured him; and when he himself took ill he set out from Penicuik to ride to Bath and after some hours in the saddle found he was cured. Every minute he spent in London was begrudged for he longed to be tending his plantations at home; and in his kindly descriptions of Anne – the 'poor mean-like mortal' with her 'nasty bandages' – one catches a soft accent and sympathetic tone:

> I was frequently at Kensington with my patron the Duke of Queensberry, where the Queen kept her Court, and I twice saw her in her closet . . . One day I had occasion to observe the calamities which attend human nature even in the greatest dignities of life. Her Majesty was labouring under a fit of the gout and in extreme pain & agony, and on this occasion everything about her was much in the same disorder as about the meanest of her subjects. Her face, which was red & spotted, was rendered something frightful by her negligent dress, and the foot affected was tied up

* e.g. 'Queen Anne had a person and appearance not at all ungraceful, till she grew exceeding gross and corpulent. There was something of majesty in her look, but mixed with a sullen and constant frown that plainly betrayed a gloominess of soul and a cloudyness of disposition within'. (*Corresp.* II, 119).

with a poultice & some nasty bandages. I was much affected at this sight & the more when she had occasion to mention her people of Scotland, which she did frequently to the Duke. What are you, poor mean-like mortal, thought I, who talks in the style of a sovereign? Nature seems to be inverted when a poor infirm woman becomes one of the rulers of the world; but as Tacitus observes, it is not the first time that women have governed in Britain, and indeed they have sometimes done this to better purpose than the men . . .[1]

Surely, one might think, she deserved an easier passage. Yet her people of Scotland (especially the Jacobites headed by the Duke of Hamilton, soon to prove turncoat) had resistance in them yet: the Act of Union was not to be passed until the following March. Ireland too called for a firm hand: 'She understood they had a mind to be independent', as Anne told Lord Cowper, 'but they should not'.[2]

England pressed hardest of all. The Junto had made it clear to Godolphin that, in return for their efforts to effect the Union, they must have more power or they would not continue to vote supplies for the war or to support his ministry. The man they had named to represent them in the Cabinet was Marlborough's son-in-law Sunderland. He was to be put in as Secretary of State for the southern division, in place of a Tory nonentity, Sir Charles Hedges; Harley remaining as Secretary of State for the north. Sunderland, as an extreme Whig, obnoxious to Anne as his parents had been, was far from ideal, but in Junto parlance he was the nail that would go and they knew they could count on his mother-in-law to drive that nail home. To Sarah this was no more than cold logic to which even Stuart obstinacy must in time give way. All it called for was persistence and courage, and those she had. Anne's cosy political notion of moderation – picking and choosing the men she most liked and trusted – she saw as primitive and parochial and dangerously old-fashioned. It was all (or could easily be) so simple. Marlborough had more than proved his worth at Blenheim and again at Ramillies. With solid support at home, Europe would be laid at the Queen's feet; not otherwise. For Sarah, whose goddess was reason, it was beyond words frustrating that Anne could not or would not see things as she did. There was far too much sentiment and self-pity.

There was 'nothing great or firm or regal', there was no vision, nothing of the impartial arbitress the Queen was supposed to be. It was deplorable. However, if Marlborough and Godolphin could be won over to the Whigs, then so could Anne. Through the summer and autumn of 1706 Sarah campaigned as vigorously for Sunderland as Marlborough did for the allies and for the Queen. Anne was never more stubborn. She showed 'immense powers of willpower, resistance and manoeuvre . . . She would not have Sunderland – she could not bear him. He was, she felt, a brazen freethinker and at heart a Republican'.[3]

As August wore on, Sarah drew deeply on her small store of patience. ''Tis certain that your Government', she explained, 'can't be carried on with a part of the Tories, and the Whigs disobliged . . . Your security & the nation's is my chief wish & I beg of God Almighty as sincerely as I shall do for His pardon at my last hour that Mr and Mrs Morley may see their errors as to this notion before it is too late. But considering how little impression anything makes that comes from your faithful Freeman, I have troubled you too much & I beg your pardon for it'.[4]

By invoking the Almighty she had tried to speak Anne's language, but it was by no means a success. Anne read the word 'notion' as 'nation' (in the version at Blenheim it does look like 'nation') and was offended; and even Sarah was appalled to find her letter ignored. When with Godolphin's help there had been an *éclaircissement*, Sarah remained in truculent mood. After referring to Anne's 'great indifference and contempt in taking no notice' of her last letter, and touching on the plight of Godolphin driven to the verge of resignation, she repeated unabashed (though without 'notion' or 'nation') what she had said before. In Anne's soft answer she showed sympathy for Godolphin – 'His leaving my service is a thought I cannot bear & I hope in God he will put all such out of his own mind' – and ended, 'I hope you will not go to Woodstock without giving me one look, for whatever hard thoughts you may have of me I am sure I do not deserve them, and I will not be uneasy if you come to me, for though you are never so unkind I will ever preserve a most sincere & tender passion for my dear Mrs Freeman'.[5]

Sarah's endorsement of this letter is interesting:

She was under the witchcraft of Mrs Hill, however she says she does not deserve the hard thoughts which I may have of her & desires that I would give her one look before I go to Woodstock. What she means by that I don't know, for I am sure I never was at Windsor without waiting upon her. She adds that she would not be uneasy if I would come to her & calls me unkind, but nobody of common sense can believe that I did not do all that was possible to be well with her, it was my interest to do so. And though I had all the gratitude imaginable for the kindness she had expressed to me for so many years, I could have no passion for her that could blind me so much as to make me do anything that was extravagant. But it was not possible for me to go to her as often as I had done in private, for let her write what she will, she never was free with me after she was fond of Mrs Hill, and whoever reads her letters will find a great difference in the style of them when she really loved me from those where she only pretended to do so.

The long endorsement ends with a recapitulation of the 'notion' and 'nation' incident, which had lead to Anne's 'pretended kind letter. But', concludes Sarah, 'if her heart had been the same as it was when she writes that she would go upon her knees to serve me,* I am apt to think she would not have been displeased at the shape of any of my fine letters'.[6]

Even so, Sarah might have done better not to send as she did another captious reply. But there it was. She lacked Marlborough's patience and she lacked his finesse. He himself was uneasy about the Sunderland project and still more concerned if it meant friction with Anne who, as he said, needed no advice to help her to be very firm and positive. He could not yet feel about her as his wife did. On the contrary, if he had a thousand lives he would, he vowed, still venture them all for the Queen.

Godolphin, badgered beyond endurance, bore the brunt of it all: the importunity of the Junto, the anguish of Marlborough, the bitterness of Sarah, the obstinacy and dismay of the Queen. 'I cannot struggle against all the difficulties of your Majesty's business', he told her bluntly, 'and yourself at the same time'. He must resign. 'I have

* In 1692, when Sarah's mother was dying at St Albans, Anne had written: 'I hope in Christ your mother will do well and . . . I beg my dear Mrs Freeman would always be so just as to believe I would go round the world upon my bare knees to do her or hers the least service'. (Blenheim E 12).

worn out my health & almost my life', he wrote, 'in the service of the Crown'. Might he not spend the small remainder of his days in liberty and quiet?[7] It was a pitiful letter, but Anne would not give in. A little later in the struggle Anne begged Sarah not to push on Marlborough and Godolphin to the point of resignation; but might it not be that Anne herself was being pushed on or at least strongly supported by unseen hands?

Anne now began writing Godolphin magnificent letters, letters worthy of a great and clever queen, but were they her own? The theme – the folly of throwing herself into the hands of a party – is no new one, but as Dr Bennett observes, it is now presented with surprising force and clarity. 'All I desire', she writes, 'is my liberty in encouraging & employing all those that concur faithfully in my service, whether they are called Whigs or Tories, not to be tied to one or the other; for if I should be so unfortunate as to fall into the hands of either, I shall look upon myself, though I have the name of Queen, to be in reality their slave; which as it will be my personal ruin, so it will be the destroying of all Government, for instead of putting an end to faction, it will lay a lasting foundation for it . . .' And then the great outburst – 'Why, for God's sake, must I who have no interest, no end, no thought but for the good of my country be made so miserable as to be brought into the power of one set of men and why may I not be trusted since I mean nothing but what is equally for the good of all my subjects?' After adding a further doubt – that she could ever get on with Sunderland as Secretary ('finding by experience my humour & those that are of a warmer will often have misunderstandings') – she ends by begging Godolphin: 'Never leave my service, for Jesus Christ's sake, for . . . that is a blow I could not bear'.[8]*

In September Anne attempted a compromise – to make Sunderland a minister without portfolio – and again begged Godolphin not to resign or she would be 'lost and undone'. Godolphin, like Marlborough, had a tenderness for the Queen while at the same time

* And again: 'For God Almighty's sake make me easy, which I can never be if you leave me. Do but consider how you could by such a cruel action expose me to the violent humour of all parties and disturb the affairs of all Europe.'.

finding her exasperating. He now told Sarah, 'You are much better natured in effect than you sometimes appear to be, and then you chide me for being touched with the condition in which I saw 83 [Anne]. You would have been so too if you had seen the same sight I did. But what troubles me most in all this affair is that one can't yet find any way of making Mrs Morley sensible of 83's mistakes, for I am very sure she thinks 83 entirely in the right'.[9] All he could do was to warn Anne that the coming winter was likely to prove the most critical of her reign. Her 'future quiet and happiness' were at stake.

In October Sarah sent Anne a long and candid letter in which she went so far as to bid her reflect whether she had never heard that the greatest misfortunes ever to have befallen her family had not been occasioned by bad advice and 'an obstinacy in their tempers'.[10] In her own case it might too easily force Marlborough and Godolphin to resign and if they did, then indeed would she find herself in the hands of a violent party, of men who, she was sure, would show her very little mercy or humanity . . . Sarah could be right. In the event she was. But as Churchill comments, 'What patience could survive such endless intimate assaults, what love such endless candour?' Her lectures to Anne (page after page of spiky writing) went 'far beyond the province of a woman subject'.[11]

Altercation and argument might have gone on for months had not Marlborough returned in November and put an end to it. On December 3rd Sunderland, to Anne's grief and humiliation, was made Secretary of State. At the cost of favour and friendship the long battle had been lost and won.

It was Harley of course who had lent the Queen secret strength. Like himself his hand is hard to decipher. In the British Museum, on loan from the Duke of Portland, there are bundles and bundles of the cryptic memoranda Harley wrote to himself. For an audience with Anne about Sunderland, for example, he would jot down: 'If so much pressed now to take him in, when most think him unfit, will it be possible to part with him when he appears to be so?'[12] And again: 'Can you stop the Whigs that they will not possess themselves of your authority if you stand not here?'[13] Obviously Sarah's suspicions of Harley's influence with Anne at this date were well founded; yet nothing could look more innocent than the kind of note Harley was then receiving from the Queen:

> I forgot when you were here to ask you whether you had writ to the Bishop of London [Compton] about the French Minister he recommended. I spoke with him myself when I was at Kensington & he promised me to take care the book that is called my life should not be printed, but I dare not trust to the Bishop in this matter & therefore desire you would give yourself the trouble to enquire after this book & take care it may not be printed, for it would vex me very much to have such a ridiculous thing as this appear in the world.[14]

The only hint of intimacy is her signing herself (as was now her habit with him) 'Your very affectionett freind'. In September she sent him from Waltham Forest a fat stag, and told him to take care to have his letters handed to the page-in-waiting at the back stairs.

There can be no doubt that if Sarah had been at her post the back stairs would have been better guarded. Soon she would be regarding Abigail as a sort of two-faced watchdog, and indeed there was something in it, for was she not related to Harley as well as to Sarah? Godolphin had his suspicions and in October Harley again found himself accused of disloyalty. His line of injured innocence plus devotion was much the same as before: 'I know myself too well to be fond of any notions of my own. I have no other views but the Queen's service, with that attachment to your Lordship and my Lord Marlborough which I shall always preserve . . . I have no measures nor will have any but what shall be submitted to the test of your better judgment . . .'[15] and so on. He might have to crawl for years before his plans had matured and he could throw off the mask. For the time being his policy must be one of quiet obstruction. It was the kind of thing he was good at and seemed to enjoy.

Marlborough, though not one to underestimate an enemy, was still sure he might count upon the Queen. Harley might be disloyal but he was in a lower category. Anne's heart had long since been engaged elsewhere: no one could ever mean as much to her as the Freemans and Mr Montgomery. As for himself, his mind was full of the descent upon Toulon. Godolphin and Sunderland (now

Harley's opposite number), and of course Sarah, must attend to the home front; his hands were full.

Painted by Laguerre on the walls of the Saloon at Blenheim are spies with big ears. This was their heyday, with everyone watching and informing on everyone else. Queens of course are and ever have been watched all the time. No one had watched her more narrowly than Sarah; now it was Abigail's turn. Godolphin watched Harley. Sarah, though too often now at a distance, watched the world. There were always so many things to attend to, some of them quite small. For Windsor she gave Grinling Gibbons a strange commission. He had carved game and fish there for Charles II. Now he was to carve 'a cock's head for the Duchess of Marlborough's sideboard and a snake's head for the basin at the Queen's back stairs'.[16] It was an age of symbolism, whether veiled or manifest. Dr Arbuthnot, whose crest was a peacock, thought of changing it to a cock's head bearing the legend *Vigilando*.[17]

Marlborough was as usual being observed by French spies. 'Who shall say but that he awaits a good offer from France to make peace?' suggested Le Vasseur to Gaultier in December, 'I would like to put it to the test'; and then, with disingenuous mischief, 'If Marlborough won't take a bribe, you had better try conquering him in the field'.[18] What an excellent plan! But how inscrutable he was. Just now he seemed to have taken his cue from Harley, for he was enlisting rogues. A certain Abbé de la Bourlie, now calling himself the Marquis de Guiscard, had had an audience with the Queen at Windsor, although she had been warned that he carried poison and was still in the pay of France. There was some thought of his heading a company of Huguenots. Now he had left for Holland and no one would mind if he never returned . . .[19] So ran Le Vasseur's report. He then turned his attention to the Queen. When she came to the throne, he said, she was unquestionably Tory, and to show she would never change she had soon afterwards adopted the motto *SEMPER EADEM*. Now however she had seen fit to break her vow and embrace the Whig interest. Whigs now governed and had all the best places with the exception of the Lord-Lieutenantship of Ireland, still held by Marlborough's enemy Ormonde, *le plus grand seigneur d'Angleterre*, as popular in Ireland as he was in England. Crossed, he could cause revolution. If he would but devote himself more to Mars and less to Bacchus and Venus he would be perfect.[20]

Seventeen hundred and six ended with small rewards all round and with another thanksgiving, at which Burnet preached. The £5,000-a-year-forever, denied Marlborough in 1702, was now granted, and provision made for his title to descend by the female line. Godolphin and Wharton were created earls; Cowper was made a baron. Sophia's grandson (George II-to-be) was made Duke of Cambridge. 'The Duke of Cambridge's patent being passed', wrote Godolphin to Harley, 'should not a messenger be sent with it by the next packetboat to Mr Howe [in Hanover]?'[21] The memorandum seemed innocent enough; and Godolphin would be dead before the crisis over that patent happened.

And what too could be more innocuous than a queen's new-year enquiry after the health of her Secretary of State? Nevertheless as a gauge of Harley's progress and favour this was deemed significant. 'When I waited on the Queen yesterday', St John told him, 'she enquired after your health and expressed her concern for your illness in such terms as I am sure came from the bottom of her heart. She said so much of your having prejudiced your health in her service & showed so much trouble that I thought it was proper for me to tell you particularly of it'.[22] Most proper of course and most gratifying; for in this field too (wearing out one's health in the Queen's service) there was the keenest competition. Throughout the whole of 1707 and not without reason Godolphin and Marlborough, from their respective galleys, continued to groan; Marlborough especially, as he told Harley, longing for 'a happy end to this troublesome war of which your humble servant is very weary'.[23]

It was true enough that they were all wearing themselves out, yet none would prove so shortlived as the Queen; and even then the wonder was (so say doctors today) that she lasted as long as she did. Medicine was all but useless if not dangerous: no antiseptics, no anaesthetics, no painkillers; and she was sufficiently strongminded (says Sarah) not to take to drink. What, then, sustained her, what propped her mind? Faith in God, Church and nation, and a stubborn conviction that she was doing her duty. Her love for her people was real and extraordinary and they knew it. The Scots were puzzling, but if they would let her take them under her wing, why so she would.

'I desire and expect from all my subjects of both nations', she declared, when at long last, in March, the Act of Union had been ratified, 'that from henceforth they act with all possible respect and kindness to one another, that so it may appear to all the world they have hearts disposed to become one people. This will be a great pleasure to me'.

The Union with Scotland, Anne said later, was the happiness of her reign. Certainly it was her best and most lasting monument, although at the time, in both countries, fears and hard thoughts remained. 'All the Scots will pour in upon us next week',* Godolphin warned Harley in April, 'I wish before they come we could pour out the English and that I might go Monday to Newmarket'.[24]

To the Union thanksgiving at St Paul's on May 1st Anne rode with the Duchesses of Marlborough and Somerset, but without Prince George, who had been prescribed the air of Hampton Court. The sermon was preached by Dr Talbot Bishop of Oxford, whose promotion Sarah took credit for but later regretted. London made a brave show of acclamation and goodwill. Only the Scots absented themselves in numbers from their own thanksgiving and had the Queen's proclamation publicly burned.[25]

'The Scots are prepared to declare unanimously for King James', Louis XIV was told, 'provided he will never agree to the Union'. Obviously it was in his interest while at war with England to make trouble in Scotland, even though a complete restoration might not have suited his book. In the meantime, for our defeat at Almanza in April, it was his turn to command a *Te Deum* in Notre Dame. It has been said that Marlborough, whose nephew Berwick made this great conquest, underestimated its importance and hoped to compensate by the taking of Toulon.[26] The blow to the allies was in fact so disastrous as to be irrecoverable. After that, 'No peace without Spain!' rang forlornly. 'All is lost in Spain', Gaultier was assured by his spy in London, 'The British can't get over Almanza, and blame it on King Charles'.[27]

* At Westminster Scotland was to be represented by 16 lords and, in the Commons, by 45 Members of Parliament. Wren was ordered to build new galleries for them.

But for Anne trouble abroad was more than matched by trouble at home. In the Almanza month of April she had found Convocation so rebellious that she had written to the Archbishop of Canterbury of 'a plain invasion of Our Royal Supremacy' and had threatened proceedings.[28] Moreover, for the appointment of two bishops she had ignored her ministers and had taken matters into her own hands. The vacant bishoprics were at Chester and Exeter. There was also the Regius Professorship of Divinity at Oxford, which Anne promised to Smalridge, a protégé of Harley's. Under protest she yielded to Marlborough and gave his candidate Potter the professorial chair. She insisted however on appointing Blackall, an anti-Whig controversialist, Bishop of Exeter, and another Tory, Sir William Dawes, Bishop of Chester. She had committed herself and, as Godolphin told Marlborough, had become entangled in a promise that was extremely inconvenient. 'The candidates', notes Dr Bennett, 'were Sharp's, but the principle of exercising her prerogative was Harley's'.[29]

Godolphin begged her to think again. It was useless. She wrote:

It is a greater trouble to me than can be expressed to find you think it necessary to put so much stress upon a thing that is so very uneasy to me . . . I have been considering ever since I saw you about the two bishops and of the single point concerning Dr Blackall, and the more I think of these things the more I am confirmed in what I said a-Wednesday night that I could not answer it neither to God Almighty nor myself, my consience and honour being too far engaged in that matter for me to alter my intentions and therefore I hope you will not insist upon it.

Whoever of the Whigs thinks I am to be hectored or frightened into a compliance, though I am a woman, are mightily mistaken in me. I thank God I have a soul above that and am too much concerned for my reputation to do anything to forfeit it as this would and I cannot see any just reflections that can be made upon my refusing it.

Nothing grieves me so much as that you have still a notion in your thoughts that you cannot serve. Give me [leave] to tell you freely it is very possible [?] and that you have all the obligations in consience and honour to continue in business, for if you do not, all things must fall into confusion and you do not only exopse me to ruin but betray your country & your friends & for no reason but because I will not consent to do a thing that is a breach of my word & will expose me to the contempt of all mankind. Therefore let me conjure you to consider & weigh well what I say, for God's sake, for your own & for her sake who I am sure is more sincerely your friend than those who torment you to press me to so unreasonable a thing. And do not think any more of that cruel request you mention in your letter, for I can never consent to it, and if you should put it in practice I really believe it will be my death, for the concern I have been in ever since Wednesday is not to be imagined by any but me that have felt it.

To which she adds the postscript: 'I beg you would not let this be seen by anybody, no not by my unkind friend'.[30]

In the last few lines, reminiscent as they are of her pleas to Sarah in the time of William and Mary, her hand shakes with emotion.

The Junto were furious: Godolphin and Marlborough had broken their agreement. Wharton in a rage told Godolphin 'it was one of my Lord Marlborough's and his tricks and he would make them both repent it'.[31] An ultimatum was issued: if the Junto were not given their way with Church appointments, they would go into opposition with the Tories and lead an attack on the Admiralty which, mismanaged as it was, looked like making the biggest scandal of the reign. It was blackmail of course but of a kind then accepted as common political practice. It often worked. However, an attack on Prince George as Lord High Admiral was for Anne, as they well knew, as unthinkable as the unfrocking of bishops; and so for the future she undertook to toe the party line.

The bishops appointed stayed* and the wrangle continued. The Junto blamed Godolphin and the Marlboroughs and they of course tried to take Anne to task for submitting to Harley; but that was not easy. 'I believe you have been told, as I have', Anne wrote to Marlborough, 'that these two persons were recommended to me by Mr Harley, which is so far from being true that he knew nothing of it till it was the talk of the town. I do assure you these two men were my own choice. They are certainly very fit for the station I design them . . .' She who disliked writing now filled page after page with cool argument and refutation. 'I find Lady Marlborough has said

* Their appointments however were not officially confirmed until January, 1708, when Trimnell (a Whig) was made Bishop of Norwich.

that I had an entire confidence in Mr Harley. I know so much of my own inclination that I am sure I have a very good opinion of Mr Harley & will never change it without I see cause, but I wonder how Lady Marlborough could say such a thing when she has been often assured from me that I relied entirely on none but Mr Freeman and Mr Montgomery . . .'[32]

Provided his loyalty might be relied on by her ministers, nothing of course could have been more proper than Anne's confidence in her Secretary of State. Unfortunately, as Sarah says, 'the Ministry began to be assured of the secret practices of Mr Harley against them' and she herself 'discovered the base returns made by Mrs Masham,' upon whom she had 'heaped the greatest obligations'.[33] Her belated discovery, in the summer of 1707, was of Abigail Hill's marriage to Samuel Masham, which had occurred some months before.* Secret weddings were by no means uncommon. Sarah's own had been so private that its date is still not known. That Sarah had never been told at all of Abigail's marriage did take some stomaching but even that she was prepared to put down to 'bashfulness and want of breeding' and, with an effort, to overlook.

'I embraced her with my usual tenderness', Sarah goes on, 'and very heartily wished her joy'. She would break it to the Queen – or did she already know? Abigail, who 'had by this time learnt the art of dissimulation pretty well, answered with an air of unconcernedness that the bedchamberwomen had already acquainted the Queen with it'. Interesting. Sarah went straight to Anne and asked why she had not been told. Anne unwisely said, 'I have a hundred times bid Mrs Masham tell it you and she would not'. The very idea of a hundred such closetings with a bedchamberwoman was disturbing. There was a mystery and Sarah would solve it. She did. In less than a week she discovered that her once downtrodden cousin had become 'an absolute favourite; that the Queen herself was present at her marriage in Dr Arbuthnot's lodgings, at which time her Majesty had called for a round sum out of the Privy Purse; that Mrs Masham

* Lady Pye, writing to Abigail Harley on 12th May, 1707, refers to the match and says she has heard Abigail Masham greatly commended for a sober woman. Sarah too is praised for having taken such care of her relations 'who when low are generally overlooked'. (HMC Portland IV, 406).

came often to the Queen, when the Prince was asleep, and was generally two hours every day in private with her. And', adds Sarah, 'I likewise then discovered beyond all dispute Mr Harley's correspondence and interest at Court by means of this woman. I was struck with astonishment at such an instance of ingratitude and should not have believed if there had been any room left for doubting'.[34]

Marlborough too was incredulous. His note to Sarah of June 3rd sounds naïve: 'If you are sure that Mrs Masham speaks of business to the Queen I should think you might with some caution tell her of it, which would do good, for she certainly must be grateful and will mind what you say'. But though she was not a great woman nor a very wise one, Abigail was a good deal less simple than he supposed.

The marriage was important less on account of Samuel Masham, who was of no consequence, than of Harley's promoting it; for according to Boyer it was by doing that that Harley first won the goodwill of Abigail and so the complete freedom at all hours of the Queen's back stairs. Boyer writes:

The Duchess grew weary on several accounts of a close attendance she thought she might securely ease herself [of] by leaving near her royal mistress a dependant & relation in whom she entirely confided. Mrs Hill discharged her duty to the Queen with wonderful assiduity, diligence & obsequiousness, and having a tolerable share of wit & good humour she made herself so agreeable that as the Duchess sometimes let whole months pass withour waiting on the Queen, so the Queen very easily dispensed with her absence. On the other hand the growing favourite, as 'tis usual with courtiers, as easily forgot her benefactress & whether through her own ambition or by the suggestion of others, at last resolved to set up for herself . . . Mr Harley, judging her a proper instrument for his designs, applied himself to her with all the cunning & address he was master of, showed her more respect than is generally paid by a man in his post to a woman in her station & infused such notions into her as taught her to set more value upon herself than she did before.

There grew such intimacy & confidence between them that Mrs Hill, being smitten with Mr Masham, formerly a page to the Queen & afterwards an equerry & gentleman of the bedchamber to Prince George, she did not scruple to disclose the secret of her heart to Mr Harley, who employed an old insinuating courtier & an intimate companion of Mr Masham, who plyed the latter so warmly with the alluring prospect of raising his fortune that he soon conquered his reluctancy to marry one that had little besides the Queens favour to recommend her. Thus Mrs Hill had her wishes & out of gratitude became entirely devoted to the person who had contributed to make her happy; so that by her means Mr Harley had free-er access to the Queen than any other minister. This advantage he improved so dexterously by entertaining her Majesty with diverting stories of the town that, on pretence of business, he was at last admitted into her pleasurable retirements, where he had opportunities not only to study & humour her inclinations but also to insinuate such hints of persons & things as were agreeable to his designs.[35]

Oddly enough, in none of Sarah's many ragings against Abigail does she show herself aware of the hand Harley played in this Masham match; though it might have helped explain her monstrous ingratitude to the other cousin. By Sarah's reckoning, as friendship was the greatest blessing in the world, so ingratitude was the blackest sin and of that Abigail was guilty. Yet how show gratitude to two cousins in opposite camps? Sarah, beyond question, had brought her to Court, but Harley had won her a husband. Between those good turns and the attitude of those who had done them there was a world of difference.

Of Abigail Hill, who became Mrs Masham and then Lady Masham we still, in spite of Swift and others, know too little. Even her portrait in the National Portrait Gallery carries a questionmark.* A quiet, scheming woman, placid, composed, unlovely, not without wit, she has her hour, blazes briefly, steps back into obscurity and becomes a shade. In the mind of Sarah she loomed like a Medusa, daunting and omnipotent; but she was never so. In fact, to judge by her letters, she was often frustrated and very much under Anne's thumb. Sir Winston Churchill found her 'probably the smallest person who ever consciously attempted to decide and in fact decided the history of Europe'.[36] But that too is exaggerated. It can safely be said that she smoothed the way for Harley, but her own direct influence was seldom if ever of European importance. Burnet puts

* Inscribed on back of stretcher: 'Abigail Hill (afterwards Lady Masham) favourite of Queen Anne and cousin to the 1st Duchess of Marlborough, b. 1670, d. 1734', the portrait is not in the public galleries and reproduction of it is now forbidden. In *Sarah Duchess of Marlborough* it will be found facing page 129.

his finger on it when he says that Abigail 'observed the Queen's temper with so much application that she got far into her heart'.[37] In Sarah's long absence (and it must have been long for her to have been hoodwinked) Anne desperately needed a woman of sympathy to confide in, or at least to have about her as quiet companion and nurse. In this unobtrusive servant ('Mrs Still') she thought she had found her; not, like Sarah, a pleasure to look at, but deft and quiet, even entertaining, for she could play the harpsichord. Moreover, she could mimic people and she did. In her humble – or was it so humble? – way she brought into the royal circle the missing and much needed element of humour. She was more than a little vulgar. One sees her at times as a half-solemn clown.

Sarah now saw all too plainly the explanation of Anne's behaviour in the bishoprics crisis. Her pride in her prerogative had been played up to by Harley, himself conducted by Abigail. The Queen would never have acted thus of herself; but Harley had as it were been playing at ombre, a game where one needs three sure tricks in one's hand. By appealing to Anne to assert her authority he had gained favour for himself, votes for the Tories and at the same time he had enraged the Whigs. As for Abigail, the situation, as Sarah saw it, called for a blunt letter, now lost, cautioning Anne against a low character used to low company. In what Churchill calls a masterpiece of sarcasm and polished hostility Anne, on July 18th, 1707, replied:

> I give my dear Mrs Freeman many thanks for her letter, which I received this morning, as I must always do for everything that comes from her, not doubting but what you say is sincerely meant in kindness to me. But I have so often been unfortunate in what I have said to you that I think the less I say to your last letter the better. Therefore I shall only in the first place beg your pardon once more for what I said the other day, which I find you take ill, and say something in answer to your explanation of the suspicions you seemed to have concerning your cousin Hill,* who is very far from being an occasion of feeding Mrs Morley in her passion, as you are pleased to call it, she never meddling with anything.

* When Anne wrote this letter, Abigail Hill will for some months have been Mrs Masham; but although Anne was at the secret wedding, she may for some time have continued to call her Hill.

I believe others that have been in her station in former times have been tattling and very impertinent, but she is not at all of that temper, and as for the company she keeps it is with her as with most other people. I fancy that their lot in the world makes them move with some out of civility rather than choice, and I really believe for one that is so much in the way of company she has less acquaintance than anyone upon earth. I hope, since in some part of your letter you seem to give credit to a thing because I said it was so, you will be as just in what I have said now about Hill, for I would not have anyone hardly thought of by my dear Mrs Freeman for your poor unfortunate but ever faithful Morley's notions or actions.[38]

The tone had changed. There was to be no satisfaction from the Queen; nor, when Sarah rounded upon Abigail, was there to be anything better than insolent condescension. For some time, not surprisingly, Abigail dodged her, and of this too Sarah complained to Anne, who looked grave and suggested Abigail was frightened. If so 'it was very natural and she was very much in the right'. 'It was the Queen's way', Sarah adds in her *Conduct*, 'on any occasion where she was predetermined (and my Lord Marlborough has told me that it was her father's) to repeat over and over some principal words she had resolved to use & to stick firmly to them. She continued therefore to say "It was very natural and she was very much in the right" '.

When Sarah and Abigail did meet, venom was in the air. Sarah told her it was obvious that the Queen was much changed towards her and this was due to secret management. Abigail had, as she happened to know, been often with the Queen in private, and the very fact that she, cousin and benefactress, had been kept in the dark was 'a very ill sign & enough to prove a very bad purpose at bottom. To this she gravely answered that she was sure the Queen, who had loved me extremely, would always be very kind to me'. Sarah was flabbergasted. It was some minutes, she says, before she could recover. 'To see a woman whom I had raised out of the dust put on such a superior air and to hear her assure me by way of consolation that the Queen would be always very kind to me!' It was more than any ordinary being could be expected to stand, let alone a duchess and a princess.

If Abigail was smooth, Harley was surpassing himself in acrobatics of deception. At the end of August the Whig leaders met at Sunderland's house, Althorp, and decided to get rid of him. He must have known it, but for the benefit of his managers the mask of deferential bonhomie was still worn, while Newcastle and Somerset were secretly canvassing for his new 'moderating scheme'. In policy there was nothing new about it – it was to be in tune with the Queen's notion of creaming parties to make the ideal coalition – but from the ministry implementing it there were to have been notable absentees. Sarah gasped at the man's hypocrisy. Vile though she knew him to be, it was almost beyond belief that while fawning on Godolphin and congratulating Marlborough he could at that very time be 'contriving how to ruin that glorious man in order to raise himself upon his ruins'.[39]

In Marlborough's letters that summer from his arid camp at Meldert he makes it plain to his wife that he feels anything but glorious. His thoughts turn to Blenheim where he hopes Mr Wise will make an icehouse; and Sarah should taste the fruit of every tree . . . At fifty-seven he felt old and longed for retirement. The war was going badly. His brother was being sniped at at the Admiralty. Colleagues were disloyal, favour was on the ebb. He had begun to despair of the 'quietness' he longed for. He was anxious not merely for himself but for the Queen and for Godolphin. However, 'England will take care of itself', he wrote, 'and not be ruined because a few men are not pleased. They will see their error when it is too late'.[40]

Looking back now, the scene appears a honeycomb of watertight compartments without visible connection. At Blenheim thirteen hundred men with muckrakes, or the equivalent, see no further than the 'precipice' upon which the house is to stand. At Meldert Marlborough dreams of eating Blenheim peaches, while he plans a grand descent upon the south of France. Sarah can hardly see past Abigail to Harley. Harley tunnels upwards, while Whig sappers set their mines . . . Was Anne, one wonders, conscious of a half of it? Godolphin's warning that the liberties of all Europe and the glory of her reign would depend on the next session of Parliament seemed hardly to move her. The Queen, says Sarah repeatedly, could see only one move ahead; and knowing this, Harley was careful to lure her gradually, step by fatal step. She might be blamed for trusting Harley instead of Godolphin. She can hardly be blamed for her limited view. After all, in 1707 it would have taxed someone cleverer than Anne to grasp that rule by one party was workable and desirable, and that the Cabinet needed to be monopolised by the party in power.

The disastrous flaw lay in Anne's judgment of men. At the outset she could not have chosen better, but now, as she fancied, they were letting her down. She kept being told so and she had begun to believe it. She was not shrewd enough to foresee – how should she, except that it has almost always proved so – that their successors would be a thousand times worse?

Trevelyan calls the bishoprics crisis a nice constitutional issue between Crown and ministers. Anne saw it as a direct threat to herself. 'For God's sake', she begged Marlborough, 'save me from the five lords of the Junto! . . . Do but make it your own case and consider then what you would do, and why a handful of men must awe their fellow-subjects . . . To be short, I think things are come to whether I shall submit to the five tyrannising lords or they to me'.[41]

Had she known those five tyrants better – Somers, Halifax, Orford, Sunderland and Wharton – she might have been less frightened of them, for they were not of such stuff as villains are made of; but collectively they could indeed be intimidating. They threatened Godolphin and, with the help of Sarah and Sunderland, they scared the Queen. What Marlborough in Flanders could do about it was not easy to see. At that distance there was small hope that he could control his wife and his son-in-law, though he might try. The descent on Toulon had proved a fiasco. Owing to the dilatoriness of the Duke of Savoy and the feeble support of the Emperor, who had made a truce with the French in Italy the previous March and so released their seasoned troops, Eugene, who headed the expedition, was unsuccessful. 'The news of Toulon is extremely dejecting', Godolphin told Harley on August 27th, 'and I dread the consequences of it abroad immediately and at home in the winter if we do not heartily unite ourselves to struggle with the difficulties of both. I will do my part for one'.[42] Could Harley be relied on to do his? On September 9th the point was rammed home: 'If we who have the honour to serve the best Queen in the world can't agree upon the proper measures for her service at home, whatever we do abroad will signify very little'.[43]

'I crave leave to profess to you most solemnly', replied Harley, 'that I have made it my study to serve the Queen upon an honest principle, that I have no attachment to any other person in the world but your Lordship and the Duke of Marlborough . . . I had much rather be directed than not & shall never be inquisitive to know anything but how to do my duty. It has always been my temper to go along with the company & not to give them uneasiness . . . I am satisfied to a demonstration there can be no other centre of union but the Queen by the ministration of your Lordship & the Duke of Marlborough . . . You have not a more faithful servant nor a truer nor more zealous friend in the world than myself, to the utmost of my capacity . . .'[44] Even at the time it must have made tedious reading, and it was all so futile: they had seen through him and the game was up.

With dismissal imminent Harley drafted a letter to Marlborough (it was never sent): 'As soon as I am gone, depend upon it, my Lord, the stream will run too high to be stemmed . . . and I wish that it do not prove that embracing some persons close & making others desperate do not end in truth in holding a handful of sand, the harder it is squeezed the less it is & slips through your fingers'.[45] But if by sand he meant the Junto, they could hardly prove more slippery than Robin-the-Trickster Harley himself.

October brought a bleak harvest of disasters and misunderstandings. Sailing home from Toulon Admiral Sir Cloudesley Shovell – that 'just, frank, generous, honest gentleman' – ran his flagship, the *Association*, on to the Bishop & Clerks rocks off the Isles of Scilly and was drowned.

On the domestic front a letter of Sarah's about Marlborough's brother George at the Admiralty misfired and offended both Queen and Consort. Anne complained to Godolphin. The letter is lost, but it would seem that to hit at one George was to hit at the other, which in turn meant hitting at Anne. 'If this were my last hour', Sarah anxiously assured her, 'I could safely protest that I did mean what I said of Mr Morley only as a comparison & not with any disrespectful thought or reflection upon him to show what a sort of friendship it was, and if I had thought or even heard that he had any such inclination, it would have been the last thing that ever I should have touched upon, for in my whole life I never did anything so ill bred or so foolish as to say a thing only to offend you without doing you any service, though I have ventured often to do it when I hoped it might be of use to you . . .' And so on for page after page. She had, she said, a thousand obligations to Prince George and she could she knew still count on his friendship unless the Queen had changed him. The rest of the letter is taken up with what Anne had come to call Lady Marlborough's inveteracy to poor Masham. Anne did her best to ignore it and it may be ignored now. The one thing of interest is a reference to a recent meeting between Anne and Sarah, of which there is no fuller record: 'The last time I waited upon you', Sarah reminds her, 'there were very long spaces on both sides when it was a profound silence. I never stirred once from behind the screen where I first stood, that I remember. I never in the whole conversation once pulled out my pocket-handkerchief [spelt pockitt hankerchure] till after I had taken my leave, when at the door you were pleased to give me a mark of your favour that brought tears into my eyes and I answered it as Brutus did his friend,* and I am sure no Roman was a better than I have endeavoured to be to Mrs Morley . . .'[46] A grotesque scene; but one needs to remember Anne's dread of emotional outbursts, of tears and blushing. In an undated note to Sarah she says:

By what my dear Mrs Freeman said a little before she went from me this evening I cannot help fearing she may have heard some new lie of her poor unfortunate faithful Morley and therefore I beg you to open your dear heart, hide nothing but tell me even the least thing that gives you any hard thoughts of me, that I may justify myself, which I am sure I can do, never having done anything willingly to deserve your displeasure.

I would have made this request when I parted from you, but I found my heart & eyes growing so full I durst not attempt it, being sure if I had I should not have been fit to have seen anybody. For the same reason I desire an answer to this in writing & that for Jesus' sake as

* *Julius Caesar*, Act IV, Sc. 3.

soon as it is possible, for I am on the rack & cannot bear living as we do now, being with the same sincere tender passion that I ever was my dear dear Mrs Freeman's & shall be so inviolably to my last moment.

To this Sarah coldly adds two endorsements: (i) This letter was certainly writ when she feared her kindness for Mrs Hill was discovered & therefore she would have me write, for she feared blushing when I said anything upon that subject, & she was very much out of countenance for a great while at the power she had got over her. (ii) Though she says in this letter she would not speak upon the subject for fear of not being fit to be seen, she was the least apt to cry of any person that I ever knew, but very apt to blush upon the subject of Mrs Hill for a vast long time.[47]

In such a tangle of emotions God alone knew who was being sincere. Anne is warm, Sarah freezes. Anne is benign and disarming, Sarah leaves one cold. In her own interest she plays with a sad lack of finesse. Nor is she very discerning, for while she rages against Abigail and assumes that she has Anne's confidence, there is at this time nothing of more consequence in Abigail's letters to Harley than mockery of Sarah; while Anne turns again to her 'confessor', Archbishop Sharp. On November 3rd he notes, 'She hopes I will serve her this Parliament. She seemed to intimate that she was afraid of some ruffles . . . By her talk I guess she fears lest some of her ministers should be called to account'. And ten days later, 'She spoke to me for my assistance or vote in matters that were likely to come before the Parliament with relation to the Admiralty. She said that the design was against Admiral Churchill, who was one of the ablest men for that service that could be found'.[48] Others, his brother included, thought otherwise. A fervent Tory, 'rough as the sea', George Churchill, like George of Denmark, was far too easygoing. In a private capacity that might have been excellent. At the head of the Admiralty it was disastrous. Deputations of merchants plagued Parliament with their grievances and losses. Convoys had failed them. Pirates had plundered their ships in home waters, in sight of land. Even Tallard at Nottingham knew that they were 'up in arms against the Government and particularly against Marlborough's brother, claiming that everything done at the Admiralty is by his advice . . .

In the course of an enquiry into Admiralty affairs', he added, 'the House of Commons has asked to see all Prince George's papers'.[49]

Burnet describes the Admiralty's orders as languid, which indeed would be in keeping with those who gave them. Macky found George of Denmark 'a prince of a familiar, easy disposition with a good sound understanding but modest in showing it . . . very fat, loves news, his bottle & the Queen, by whom he hath had many children but none alive . . .'[50] When during November Anne suggested he should dismiss Churchill and appoint another, he offered to resign;[51] whereupon, as it was rumoured (and it reached the Queen's ears), the mayor of Dover ordered a joyful peal of bells; but he had acted too soon. However, thanks partly to Harley's management, the Junto attack in the Commons against the Admiralty failed, at least for the time being.

On December 5th Harley outlined to Marlborough and Godolphin his 'moderating scheme' whereby, as he claimed, the ministry would be rescued and the Junto defeated. He had, he said, already convinced Somerset and Newcastle. The duumvirs agreed and Anne, with renewed confidence, issued a statement which amounted to an ultimatum to the Junto:

> Her Majesty is for the future firmly resolved to govern upon such principles as will incline her to side with the violence neither of Whig nor Tory; that she will never make bargains with either party to persuade them to do that which a sense of their duty alone ought to lead them to; but that those shall always be the object of her countenance and favour who without expecting terms come voluntarily into the promoting of her service.[52]

It was a prescription for an ideal world; but in practice, as St John once said, 'A coach may as well be driven with unequal wheels as our Government carried on with such a mixture of hands'. The strife continued. In the Lords the Tories, with Whig backing, staged a savage debate on the conduct of the war in Spain. Somers' no-peace-without-Spain motion was carried. Marlborough and Godolphin could no longer doubt that the *via media* was not for them: they must run with the Whigs or with the Tories; and the Whigs (for the war's sake) it had to be.

Some simpleton now suggested that in anticipation of the Queen's becoming an Empress (of Spain and the Indies?) she should be presented with the Pitt diamond, 'the unparalleled jewel of the world'.[53] It was declined. She is said, on the contrary, to have given Sarah a vast diamond as the 'glass' over a miniature of Marlborough; but that is untrue. It was in fact presented to Sarah by James Brydges, Paymaster General and afterwards Duke of Chandos.

Sarah, paying her Christmas visit to Anne at Kensington, learned from the page who was to announce her that Abigail had just been sent for. 'The moment I saw her Majesty', Sarah goes on, 'I plainly perceived she was very uneasy. She stood all the while I was with her and looked as coldly upon me as if her intention was that I should no longer doubt of my loss of her affections. Upon observing what reception I had I said I was very sorry I had happened to come so unseasonably. I was making my curtsy to go away when the Queen, with a great deal of disorder in her face and without speaking one word, took me by the hand and when thereupon I stooped to kiss hers she took me up with a very cold embrace and then without one kind word let me go . . .'

This was too much. Sarah owed it to herself, she owed it to Anne to write to her 'in the plainest and sincerest manner possible', and two days after Christmas she did so, complaining of 'an embrace that seemed to have no satisfaction in it' and offering her services either with 'the openness & confidence of a friend . . . or else in that manner that is necessary for the post she is in, which unavoidably forces her to be often troubling Mrs Morley upon the account of others'.[54]

Anne, in yet another soft answer, took the trouble to explain what had happened when Sarah arrived. 'I had the minute before you came into the door sent for Masham to come to prayers, she being in waiting, and as soon as you were gone I went to public prayers & the minute they were over went into my closet to make an end of my private ones & did not see Masham again till I went to supper'. The explanation was wasted. Sarah merely endorses: 'About Mrs Masham. After she had used me very ill to make me go away before Mrs Masham came'.[55]

Except for the Union with Scotland, 1707 had on all fronts been a disastrous year, and even now there was a sting in its tail. William Greg, who had spied for Harley in Scotland and had since acted as confidential clerk in his office, was discovered to have been betraying state secrets to France. Taking advantage of Tallard's correspondence, which had to pass through Harley's office (though in fact his more interesting mail did not), Greg slipped in a copy of the Queen's letter to the Emperor, dated November 28 and endorsed with Harley's and Godolphin's amendments. In it she had asked him (as it transpired, vainly) to send Prince Eugene to Spain. Greg's version, sent via Holland where it was intercepted, could have reached Versailles before the Emperor had read the original in the Queen's hand, in Vienna. Greg, arrested, confessed and pleaded guilty. In Newgate he was questioned by seven Whig lords to discover accomplices and, as they hoped, to implicate Harley; but in that they were to be disappointed. Faced with being hanged, drawn and quartered, Greg 'said over and over he had no encouragement and that it could never be made to appear that he had'.[56] His only complaint was when, after a month in prison, he begged Harley to have something done about his fetters, 'especially since a person in my circumstances can never be too often on his knees, to which duty my irons prove a great uneasiness and interruption'.[57] The Queen, it was said, sent him 'comforts and necessaries' by the hand of Dr Arbuthnot; for 'the usage he had', she protested, 'was hanging him over and over'.[58] Repeatedly cross-questioned and tempted, he languished in Newgate a hundred days. He never faltered. In the cart carrying him to Tyburn he was still proclaiming his master's innocence; and 'though the crowd and the noise were very great, Mr Harley's name was heard a pretty distance from the gallows'.[59]

Greg, like Defoe, had been a lame duck of Harley's, rescued from want and given a position of trust, though still miserably paid. Working alone through the night, censoring French prisoners' letters, he saw how easy it would be to earn a much needed bribe. Defoe had long since warned Harley of secret papers left carelessly on a table for the doorkeeper to carry to the post, and Greg himself admitted he had found the Queen's letter 'in a press where all the books lie, to which all the clerks have a key'.[60]

Though Harley had done nothing treasonable he had clearly been negligent in ignoring such a state of affairs. His career, he knew, was at stake, even perhaps his life. 'Your brother's head', Atterbury warned Edward Harley, 'is upon the block, and yet he seems to have no concern about it'.[61] But the stuff of martyrs was in Harley as it had been in Greg. He kept absolutely calm. 'I know nothing that I can do', he said, 'but entirely to be resigned to and confide in the Providence of God'. As crisis succeeded crisis (and another was imminent) his rigorous upbringing among Dissenters stood him in good stead.

CHAPTER NINE

THE YEAR OF OUDENARDE

1708

IN mid-reign Anne found a momentous year opening with what Swift was to call the greatest piece of Court skill acted these many years. It was cunningly staged by Harley, it was very nearly successful and it caused his dismissal.

During January, at private meetings with Harley, Marlborough and Godolphin continued to show approval for his 'moderating scheme', that grand compromise which was to finish faction and ensure that Anne would never be dictated to again. There seems at this stage to have been a friendly, come-let-us-reason-together atmosphere about Harley's approaches to the duumvirs, to the moderate Tories and to Whigs such as Boyle and Devonshire who were not strongly pro-Junto; while among themselves the three managers (whether they all meant it or not) agreed never to break friendship even though they should differ on points of policy.

Et in Arcadia ego . . . Into the midst of this idyll somebody hurls a bomb. Harley goes to the Queen and lays before her such damaging accusations against Godolphin that from then on she resolves to make no effort to keep him in office.[1] And Godolphin, says Sarah, 'no longer in doubt as to Harley's falsehood & insincerity', himself tells the Queen. 'The return he had for it', Sarah continues, 'was that she would believe nothing of it; for by this time she could believe or not believe just as it served the secret & real design she had then in view'.[2] Whether Harley's audience was before Godolphin's or Godolphin's before Harley's is still not known. Whichever happened, Professor Snyder believes Sarah's 'discovery' played an important part.[3]

'I did tell what I discovered', she says, 'to nobody but my Lord Marlborough and my Lord Treasurer & I believe I should always have kept it a secret if I could, but that the Queen soon after made it public herself by supporting Mr Harley against my Lord Treasurer & my Lord Marlborough after they had several proofs of his having betrayed them & endeavoured to stir up all sorts of people against them'. The Whigs were told they were being led by the nose, to be jettisoned as soon as Parliament was up; the Tories that but for Marlborough and Godolphin the Queen would employ none but Tories as long as she lived. 'Thus he blew up the Whigs and Tories', concludes Sarah, 'to mortify & ruin if he could two men that [had] made him Secretary of State'.[4]

On January 29th Godolphin sent the Attorney-General (Sir Simon Harcourt) to Harley with a formal expression of his displeasure. This of course brought protestations of innocence and of misrepresentation, to which Godolphin sent a crushing reply:

> I have received your letter and am very sorry for what has happened to lose the good opinion I had so much inclination to have of you, but I cannot help seeing and hearing nor believing my senses. I am very far from having deserved it from you. God forgive you![5]

Whatever else Godolphin's senses had told him he must by this time have realised that from Harley's 'moderating scheme' he, the Lord Treasurer, was to have been excluded. 'It is said', wrote Addison on February 13th, 'Mr Harley and his friends had laid schemes to undermine most of our great officers of state and plant their own party in the room of 'em'.[6] But the mine was sprung before Harley had made certain of full support. One cause of this was Greg (the Whigs were threatening impeachment). Another was the Almanza debate in the Commons (January 29–30), in the course of which St John admitted that of nearly 30,000 men who should have been there, only 8,660 had fought in the battle. Some said this played a part in the 'mismanagement' situation brought by Harley to the Queen's notice in evidence against Godolphin. If Swift is to be believed, Anne on February 6th told St John she had resolved to part with Godolphin. She read aloud a letter she had just written to Marlborough, telling him so, and gave St John leave to spread the news about the town.[7]

Marlborough, whether stoutly or reluctantly, decided to stand by his friend. He wrote to the Queen:

Madam,

Since all the faithful services I have endeavoured to do you & the unwearied pains I have taken for these ten days to satisfy & convince your Majesty's own mind have not been able to give you any such impressions of the false & treacherous proceedings of Mr Secretary Harley to Lord Treasurer & myself, but that your Majesty is pleased to countenance & to support him, to the ruin of your own business at home, I am very much afraid it will be attended with the sorrow & amazement of all Europe as soon as the noise of it gets abroad. And I find myself obliged to have so much regard to my own honour & reputation as not to be every day made a sacrifice to falsehood & treachery, but most humbly to acquaint your Majesty that no consideration can make me serve any longer with that man. And I beseech your Majesty to look upon me from this moment as forced out of your service as long as you think fit to continue him in it. No heart is fuller of duty to your Majesty than mine; nobody has more sincere wishes for your prosperity nor shall more constantly pray for your Majesty's long life & for your happiness both here and hereafter.[8]

Few in great office or small have not at some time longed to write such an ultimatum, and few (if wise) have sent it. Nor in this present case is it certain that Marlborough's was sent. It was drafted but then, probably, pocketed, to await his next audience: some things are much better spoken than written.

The crisis broke on February 8th, when the Marlboroughs and Godolphin met the Queen in an apartment adjoining the room where the lords of the Council were already assembled. According to Sir John Cropley, the scene then proceeded thus:

First Lord Treasurer told the Queen he came to resign the staff; that serving her longer with one so perfidious as Mr Harley was impossible. She replied, in respect of his long service she would give him till tomorrow to consider. Then he should do as he pleased, withal she could find enough glad of that staff.

Then came Lady Duchess with great duty & submission, that she had served her ever with affection & tenderness . . . The reply is said to have been: 'You shall consider of this till tomorrow, then if you desire it I shall advise you to go to your little house in St Albans & there stay till Blenheim House is ready . . .'

Lastly came Marlborough himself, with his regretful resignation, lamenting that he 'came in competition with so vile a creature' as Harley;

his sword must be put into other hands. 'And then, my Lord', said the Queen, 'will you resign me your sword? Let me tell you . . . if you do, you run it through my head'. The Queen then withdrew, bidding Marlborough follow, but he declined.

In the Cabinet room, after the Queen had entered, Harley began to deliver a report. Upon which the Duke of Somerset rose & said if her Majesty suffered that fellow (pointing to Harley) to treat [of] affairs of the war without the advice of the General, he could not serve her; and so left the Council.[9]

Somerset was supported by Pembroke and others, but the meeting continued; and the Queen still declined to part with Harley until the Commons, by refusing to pass the bill of supply, forced her hand. With him then went Henry St John (to be replaced as Secretary at War by Robert Walpole) and Harley's old schoolfellow Sir Simon Harcourt.

Anne, says Lord Dartmouth, was incensed beyond measure. Sarah adds:

Mr Harley was dismissed from his post, but not without tears in private, as some at Court then affirmed . . . This appearance of giving up that man was with his own consent & advice; the method of dealing with him in private had been settled for some time before this, that as long as Mrs Masham still continued in favour, under pretence of visiting her who was his cousin, he would have all the opportunities he himself could wish for of practising upon the passions & credulity of the Queen. But though the Duchess [of Marlborough] saw this plainly yet she resolved to try if by being easy & quiet she could regain any influence over the Queen . . .[10]

Before the dismissal Anne had stubbornly held out as long as she could. Not only were her old advisers ignored, but Harley's friend Newcastle and even Prince George were not listened to. Only Harley himself could convince her that his scheme had, for the time being, failed and must be shelved. Rather than own defeat Anne was willing to face the impossible. 'She does not seem even yet', comments the editor of her letters, 'to have realised how impotent she was'.

On February 11th Harley's seals as Secretary of State were given to Henry Boyle. As for 'the method of dealing with him in private', Harley later denied that, in pleasurable exile as he was at Brampton, he had had any sort of communication with the Queen for eight months. Nevertheless he corresponded in code with Abigail Masham, 'the heifer wherewith he had ploughed' and she, as Coke says, 'either was so inconsiderable at that time that she was overlooked or so firmly rooted in the Queen's favour that there was no shocking [shaking ?] of her'.[11] He was busy too that summer cultivating by letter the goodwill of the Duke of Shrewsbury.

Sarah, pursuing in her own way her policy of being easy and quiet with the Queen, tried to wring from her a promise that, on her retirement, her daughters should succeed to her posts;* and it was not long before she was convinced that she had succeeded. Not only, says Sarah, did Anne promise these reversions in writing. She gave further a 'solemn asseveration', upon which Sarah, as solemnly, kissed her hand. Moreover in the letter that followed, Anne said: 'If I should outlive you, your faithful Morley will remember her promise'.[12] Sarah then saw her again and thanked her, adding that she had now by her goodness left her and her husband nothing to do but pray for her. But this was going too far. Anne 'looked red and uneasy' and when pressed said she remembered nothing of it and would be glad to hear no more of it. Sarah was deeply shocked; and 'what made it the more unaccountable was that the Queen had so very extraordinary a memory that she hardly was ever known to forget anything of the smallest moment . . . But thus did words, assurances & the most serious promises bind or not bind just as humour, temper or inclination worked, and honour & truth came to be no more accounted of than her new advisers would permit'.[13]

The daughters themselves, useful though they doubtless were as spies, might not have felt comfortable if their parents had been dismissed; but the fact of the matter was that Anne had grown tired of them, 'the one cunning & dangerous to be in the family, the other silly & imprudent & lost her reputation'.[14] Anne Sunderland, the toast of the Kit-Cat as the Little Whig, was disliked by Anne on account of her husband. Harriet Godolphin was similarly handi-

* Sarah estimated that her places were worth £6,000 a year. Her enemies valued them at £9,000. She was Groom of the Stole, Mistress of the Robes, Keeper of the Privy Purse and Ranger of Windsor Park.

capped inasmuch as her father-in-law's stock was now low; but there was too her flightiness, which was to lead to the long liaison with Congreve and the birth of his daughter Mary.

The daughters might at a pinch be ignored. The mother could not be. Before Marlborough left for Flanders Anne wrote to him:

I have had a great mind to speak to you this week, but when I have met with an opportunity I have found such a tenderness coming upon me on the thought of the subject I was to speak of that I choose rather to trouble you this way with my complaints than any other. You know I have often had the misfortune of falling under the Duchess of Marlborough's displeasure and now, after several reconciliations, she is again relapsed into her cold unkind way and . . . has taken a resolution not to come to me when I am alone, and fancies nobody will take notice of the change. She may impose upon some poor simple people, but how can she imagine she can on any that have a grain of sense? Can she think that the Duchess of Somerset and my Lady Fitzharding, who are two of the most observing, prying ladies in England, won't find out that she never comes near me nor looks on me as she used to do, that the tattling voice will not in a little time make us the jest of the town? Some people will blame her, others me, and a great many both. What a disagreeable noise she will be the occasion of making in the world besides, God knows what ill consequences it may be of. Therefore for God Almighty's sake, for the Duchess of Marlborough's, your own and my poor sake, endeavour all you can to persuade Mrs Freeman out of this strange unreasonable resolution. I have not as yet ventured to make any answer to her letter, nor dare not, for till this violent humour be over all I can say, though never so reasonable, will but inflame her more.[15]

Surely a most sensible letter and surely her own. Of the tattlers, within six months Lady Fitzharding would be dead. But was the red-haired Duchess of Somerset (the Percy heiress) so observing and prying? Swift found her insinuating, but he was prejudiced. After Sarah's dismissal, Anne came in some measure to rely on her.

That a queen should dread being made a laughing-stock and take steps to prevent it seems both lamentable and reasonable; yet it was of little use just then to appeal to Marlborough; for as Sarah approached her forty-eighth birthday she was in tantrums with everyone. 'Upon my word', her husband wrote to her, 'when you are out of humour and are dissatisfied with me I had rather die than live'.[16]

'We had an unkindly Spring', Lady Pye was to remind Abigail Harley. For Anne it was particularly harsh. March began with an onslaught in the Lords on the Admiralty, deflected for a time; and on March 4th the Commons were told of the Pretender's intention to invade Scotland. Anne declared she had so much trust in God and her people that she hoped the attempt would prove fatal only to those who had undertaken it. She was not to be disappointed. Before he could leave Dunkirk the Pretender caught measles, which meant that everyone knew of his plans. When he did sail the voyage was made in westerly gales, rain and snow. He was hoping to land in the Firth of Forth, to be proclaimed in Edinburgh as James VIII of Scotland; for as Hooke, who was with him, had said, better to be King of Scotland than to remain without a kingdom at all. But even that was not to be. Pre-arranged signals to the Scots mainland were not returned, the landfall was muddled and so much time lost that Sir George Byng, who had been stormbound, managed to overhaul the Jacobite privateers and to chase them north. James, now twenty and styling himself Le Chevalier de St George, (See page 232) was still anxious to land, but he was overruled. On March 14th the chase was abandoned, the English having captured one ship, the *Salisbury*, with a handful of Jacobites aboard including old Lord Griffin and the two sons of Lord Middleton. The Pretender outsailed pursuit and returned to France.

'Sir George Byng had no instructions as to the person of the Pretender', runs James Anderson's account. 'When this particular was taken into consideration the Council broke up in confusion, for when some mentioned methods of dispatch, the moving appearance of the Queen's flowing tears prevented all further deliberation. This was a more tender & affecting point than the danger of the Crown'.[17]

Even so Anne's resentment at the attempted invasion was reflected in speeches which from then on referred to her stepbrother as the Pretender. In frank terms she denounced 'the designs of a Popish Pretender, bred up in the principles of the most arbitrary government'. Prayers of thanksgiving were offered for the defeat of an 'insolent attempt to invade her kingdom'. Prince George was congratulated. A run on the Bank of England was stopped. The Duke of Hamilton, after a few weeks in prison as the Scots Jacobite leader, was released.

The fate of the Jacobites taken in the *Salisbury* was another matter. Sunderland had a wild plan to release them on condition that all the sixteen peers returned to the Lords for Scotland should be Whigs. When Anne heard of it she accused him of using her name without authority, complained to Marlborough and Godolphin, and threatened him with dismissal. The aged Lord Griffin was a still greater embarrassment. A scaffold for his execution had been erected when the Cabinet Council, after sitting until one a.m., decided by a majority of two to reprieve him for fifteen days. After some months in the Tower and a succession of reprieves he died.

Anne, who since January had been attacked by gout, postponed going to Windsor until the end of June. Sir John Clerk, revisiting her at Kensington, found her looks even more woeful than before.

. . . Though this great Queen had made a very glorious figure in Europe by her arms & fleets abroad . . . though she was in all respects arbitrix of peace & war in Europe & by her sovereign authority held the balance of power in her hands, yet . . . she appeared to me the most despicable mortal I had ever seen in any station. The poor lady was again under a severe fit of the gout, ill dressed, blotted in her countenance & surrounded with plaisters, cataplasms & dirty-like rags. The extremity of her pain was not then upon her & it diverted her a little to see company with whom she was not to use ceremonies, otherways I had not been allowed access to her. However, I believe she was not displeased to see anybody, for no Court attenders ever came near her. All the incense & adoration offered at Courts were to her ministers, particularly the Earl of Godolphin her chief minister and the two Secretaries of State. Her palace of Kensington where she commonly resided was a perfect solitude . . . I never saw anybody attending there but some of her guards in the outer rooms, with one at most of the gentlemen of her bedchamber. Her frequent fits of sickness & the distance of the place from London did not admit of what are commonly called drawingroom nights, so that I had many occasions to think that few houses in England belonging to persons of quality were kept in a more private way than the Queen's royal palace of Kensington.[18]

No wonder few were admitted. At all costs the image of a triumphant Queen must for world consumption be preserved. At Hampton Court, on the ceiling of her drawingroom overlooking the Great Fountain Garden, Anne, balance in hand, is shown by Verrio enthroned among gods and goddesses as their equal, if not as their superior (See page 137). Mercury flies at her bidding. The three Graces adore her. She is attended by Time and History, Fame and Peace. Aquarius, her birth-goddess, juggles with water, while Envy, a three-faced fiend, is banished to a distant cell. No one stunned by this Olympus would have dreamed of dirty-like rags and bandages; nor was there need for disillusion. If the Queen was not superhuman, not perfect, at times not even presentable, she could at least be represented as though she were; and that not only at home but to the far corners of the civilised world.

In America Lord Lovelace, who had just succeeded Lord Cornbury* as Governor of New York, was told by the Council of New Jersey that Anne's reign would make a bright leaf in history and be the admiration of future ages. 'And though our distance has been disadvantageous to us', they added, 'yet we experience the effect of her princely care in putting an end to the worst administration New Jersey ever knew by sending your Excellency'.[19] Cornbury, when recalled, was in prison for debt. He had the name of a buffoon. When, formerly, he had been on the staff of Prince George he was always missing, and when at last politely exiled to New York he made his first appearance as Governor, he was dressed as a woman. It seemed reasonable to ask why. 'Because', the enquirer was told, 'I represent her Majesty the Queen'.

For herself Anne understood very well the importance of keeping up appearances. Sir Winston Churchill, admiring her tenacity right or wrong, adds, 'She had immense powers of reserve and dissimulation'. Archdeacon Coxe goes further – 'a perfect mistress of dissimulation' – and Sarah, who had the advantage of knowing her, further still when she insists that Anne was ashamed of her friendship with a bedchamberwoman and was forever trying to hide it. On

* Lord Cornbury (1661–1724), afterwards 3rd Earl of Clarendon, Privy Councillor Dec. 1711), Envoy Extraordinary to Hanover (1714). He had two daughters and a son.

Sarah's side were envy and prejudice, if not malice; on Anne's there was innocence. Even so, at that time, the friendship was not a wise one; nor was Anne wise in trying to defend it. A prince desirous of maintaining a noble character, wrote Bolingbroke, must 'observe such a decorum and keep such a guard on himself as may prevent even the suspicion of being liable to such (bad) influences; for as the reality would ruin, the very suspicion will lessen him in the opinion of mankind'.[20]

When Anne told Sarah, 'You wrong Masham and me' and 'Masham does not know one word of my writing to you', she merely laid herself open to further criticism from Sarah and from the Kit-Cat Whig she called her secretary, Arthur Maynwaring. Maynwaring was sharpwitted, worshipped Sarah, loathed Abigail, drank heavily and was apt to run to extremes. None of this would have mattered. What was regrettable was the hand he lent Sarah in her letters to the Queen, which became more and more irresponsible, impertinent and obnoxious. 'I don't wonder that this expression "Masham and me" made you sick', he tells Sarah, 'for it is very nauseous'. It reminded him of James I's 'Steeny and I' references to Buckingham. Something must be done to counter it. 'When I read over this morning', he writes again, 'the letter for Mrs Morley, as I have put it together . . . though above half of it be your Grace's . . . I am sure nobody that were to read it would guess that it were not all writ by one person, which shows that I have not imitated your style so long quite in vain'.[21] After all, if Anne could use Harley as her amanuensis, why should Sarah not employ Maynwaring? Gleefully they composed long, anonymous letters to Abigail or, in more solemn vein, long, scurrilous letters to the Queen.

Maynwaring, in one of his notes to Sarah, writes of 'the senseless farce of Harlequin & Abigail'; but this again was wishful thinking. Not for nothing were the two related. Harley in rural exile had devised a code, seemingly childish, in which the people he wanted to write or hear about were re-christened with the names of their mutual relations. 'Lady Pye', for example, was perfect for Sarah, while Anne as Abigail's 'Aunt Stephens', though with some loss of dignity, filled the part. Godolphin was 'Sir Charles Pye', Marlborough 'Cousin Nat' and Harley himself 'Cousin Robin Packer'.

The code went further to include such abstractions as courage or resolution ('ready money') and the Queen's favour ('the jointure at Chavenage'). They seem to have enjoyed it.

Between these teams Anne, who at all times sought concord and friendship, had to bear the brunt of the bickering, and to hide her gout, while at the same time trying to govern three kingdoms and win a European war. The Junto, she was told, now wanted Lord Somers appointed President of the Council. It was as she had expected. Sunderland had been merely a bridgehead. Now the rest of those tyrannising lords must be let in. She was very nearly in their clutches. But no, she would not have Somers as President. Once again personalities came into it. Somers, she said, had once disobliged Prince George. Devonshire and Newcastle then asked for his appointment without portfolio. Still she would not have him. She appealed to Marlborough, 'looking upon it', she wrote, 'to be utter destruction to me to bring Lord Somers into my service . . . it is what I can never consent to'.[22] And a fortnight later, 'I am so tired with importunities that comes from the Whigs that I have not spirits left to open my afflicted heart so freely & so fully as I intended . . .' As for ending the war, she entirely agrees with him: 'I do assure you, whatever insinuations my enemies may make to the contrary, I shall never at any time give my consent to a peace but upon safe and honourable terms'.[23]

By the end of May, when 'the most Whig Parliament since the Revolution' had been returned, Anne had worried herself sick both on her own account and on George's. On June 26th she took him to Windsor. Sarah thought this unkind. Anne's Little House there, she said, was like an oven and the Prince gasped for air. The only reason for staying there was so that Abigail might smuggle in 'such persons as she had a mind to bring to her Majesty . . . let in privately by the garden'.[24] It was as false as the Tory assertion that the Queen had been driven from her castle by Sarah and forced to live in a cottage at its gate. The truth was that the Little House with its small rooms suited Anne's way of living and of nursing her Consort. Prince George was dying of asthma and dropsy. Doctors of course were in constant attendance (Sir Richard Blackmore had just joined them) but there was little that could then be done.

On July 11th (N.S.) Marlborough won his third great victory, at Oudenarde. Had there been one more hour of daylight this battle would, in his opinion, have meant the end of the war. As it was it restored the moral superiority of the allied forces and made possible the subsequent capture of Lille. 'And if he brings home a peace next winter', wrote Maynwaring to Sarah, 'it will be as impossible for his enemies to hurt him as for the wind to blow down Mr Vanbrugh's thick walls'.[25]

For Marlborough it was undeniably a staggering achievement; 'but just look', writes Sir Winston, 'what a team he had – Cadogan, Eugene, Argyll and old Overkirk, all so experienced and comprehending, like sheepdogs perfectly trained, rounding up sheep under their unquestionably-obeyed shepherd'.[26] The French team included the Pretender, who fought well if unwisely against his own countrymen. To oppose him the Allies countered with the Electoral Prince of Hanover, one day to become George II of England. 'His horse was shot under him and for a moment men thought that England must seek another heir. But the choleric, spirited little gentleman was up and on again'.[27]

> When his warhorse was shot he valued it not
> But fought it on foot like a fury.
> Full firmly he stood as became his high blood
> Which runs in his veins so blue,
> For this gallant young man, being a-kin to Queen Anne,
> Did as, were she a man, she would do.[28]

Anne's much quoted comment when she heard of the victory – 'Oh Lord, when will all this dreadful bloodshed cease?' – was not of course reflected in her letter to Marlborough: 'I want words to express the joy I have that you are well after your glorious success for which, next to God Almighty, my thanks are due to you; and indeed I can never say enough for all the great & faithful services you have ever done me. But be so just as to believe I am as truly sensible of them as a grateful heart can be and shall be ready to show it upon all occasions'.[29]

It was a letter to keep. Marlborough by this time knew more than he liked of the sapper operations happening on his home front;

although it was not perhaps in his reckoning that his own wife, with the best will in the world, would strengthen the opposition and keep letting him down. Having contracted the rash habit of sending other people's letters to the Queen, she now sent her Marlborough's, hastily written from Oudenarde, which ended, 'I do and you must give thanks to God for his goodness in protecting and making me the instrument of so much happiness to the Queen and nation, if she will please to make use of it'.[30]

This last phrase Anne did not care for at all. She asked for an explanation. Nor were things improved by Marlborough's letter to her of July 23 in which he told her he considered her 'obliged in conscience and as a good Christian to forgive and to have no more resentments to any particular person or party, but to make use of such as will carry on this just war with vigour, which is the only way to preserve our religion & liberties and the crown on your head'.[31] He may well have been right, but was it for him to direct her conscience and was such candour (worthy of Sarah) calculated to change the Queen?

'I thank God I do forgive all my enemies', she answered, 'with all my heart, but it is wholly impossible in human nature to forget people's behaviour in things so fresh in one's memory so far as to have a good opinion of them, especially when one sees for all their professions they are still pursuing the same measures & you may depend upon it they will always do so, for there is no washing a blackamoor white . . . I can never be convinced that Christianity requires me, nor that it can be for my service, to put myself entirely into the hands of any one party'.

Lord Haversham, she continued, had warned her that the Whigs were planning an invitation to Hanover, this time to be addressed to the Electoral Prince, triumphant after Oudenarde. Such a thought, begged Anne of Marlborough, must be put out of that prince's head. She would invite none of them, 'neither the young man nor his father nor grandmother . . . it being a thing I cannot bear to have any successor here though it were but for a week'.[32]

She was prejudiced, insular, wrongheaded. She was, too, strong-willed and courageous. 'If we have called her a great queen', writes

Sir Winston, 'it is not because of her benevolence or her understanding, though both were considerable; certainly not because of her right judgment, but because of her toughness and will-power and the part they played both for good and for ill in this expansive and glorious period'.[33] Marlborough must have found her, from 1708 on, beyond words exasperating; yet he too, like his descendant, was big enough to respect her weakness and courage. 'I can't entirely agree with your opinion of the Queen', he wrote to Sarah, 'I must own I have a tenderness for her. I would willingly believe that all that is amiss proceeds from the ambition and ill judgment of Mrs Masham and the knavery and artfulness of Mr Harley'.[34]

If Abigail had, as Sarah said, been taken from a broom, she was now quickly learning, albeit in village-school hand, to use a pen. On July 21st she wrote to Harley:

My brother delivered yours safe into my hands this day & tells me he goes back early tomorrow morning, by whom I send this. I repent heartily my telling my aunt [the Queen] the reason why I desired to go to Walton [London], but did not question having leave, as I told you in my last. I thank you for your kind advice & I hope God Almighty will give me more grace than to be taken in any of their snares. I am very ready to believe they will try all ways to ruin me, but they shall never do it by any indirect action of my own. If theirs will take effect against me, God's will be done, I must submit to what he permits.

Oh my poor Aunt Stephens [the Queen] is to be pitied very much, for they press her harder than ever. Since what happened lately she is altered more than is to be imagined, no ready money [courage or resolution] at all to supply her with common necessaries; really I see it so bad, and they come so fast upon her I have no hopes of her deliverance, for she will put it quite out of her friends' power to save her.

I have heard of the court they make to Mrs Packer [Hanover], from several people, and told her all. While she is hearing it she is very melancholy, but says little to the matter . . . My Lady Pye [Sarah] is here still. I have not seen my aunt since my duty called me, which was Saturday & Sunday in the morning. Tomorrow I go again to do my duty. I don't think it any unkindness in my aunt, but because my Lady Pye is here . . . I shall be glad to have a line from you Saturday. God bless you & give you health. The papers are safe which you left with me, but if you want them let me know when you write.

Q.A.

Six days later she told him:

> I am very much afraid of my aunt's conduct in her affairs & all will come from her want of a little ready money, for hitherto you know the want of that has made her make a most sad figure in the world. I shall be very glad to have your opinion upon things that I may lay it before her, for that is all [that] can be done. I trust in God & beg of him to supply her, that she may not be so blinded but save herself while it is in her power. She will give me your book & I will keep it till I have the comfort of seeing you, which I heartily wish for.[35]

Clearly she was playing her part – a tricky composite of conspirator and angel of mercy – extremely well, her letters well peppered with invocations that would appeal to Harley, as they may have to the Queen. And if the picture she paints of Anne as Andromeda looks overdrawn, that is the picture Harley wanted: a browbeaten and terrified queen, fettered by unscrupulous favourites, themselves lustful for power and money and eager to prolong the war. No hint of course of Anne's astonishing willpower, nor of the ruthless and boundless ambitions of others. Harley, says Ralph, was ready to risk all hazards to 'rescue the devoted victim'.

Sarah's performance at this hazardous time shows less finesse. For all Marlborough's cautions she would not or could not see that onslaughts on the Queen, no matter how enjoyable, were not to be afforded. At all costs her 'inveteracy for poor Masham' was to be purged from her system, and Maynwaring was the man to help her do it. In what she called her ridiculous hand, spiky as herself, she covered page after page after page until Anne with a trembling hand begged her to stop: 'to beg you would not mention that person any more who you are pleased to call the object of my favour, for whatever character the malicious world may give her, I do assure you it will never have any weight with me, knowing she does not deserve it, nor I can never change the good impressions you once gave me of her'.[36]

Recklessly Sarah persisted. On July 26th she combined again with Maynwaring to send Anne a letter from which nothing, not even the *amours* of Charles II, was omitted. Perhaps (at least let us hope so) it was not sent. Scurrilous ballads were enclosed. The Queen was reminded of having said that of all things in the world she valued most her reputation. What, then, of this strange and unaccountable passion for Abigail, 'a woman I took out of a garret'? Could that enhance it? 'Nor can I think', added Sarah, 'the having no inclination for any but of one's own sex is enough to maintain such a character as I wish may still be yours . . .'[37] And so on and so on – jejune, irresponsible, waspish, utterly unpardonable. Sarah, a natural snob, thought her cousin vulgar and said so, but nothing could possibly have been in worse taste than some of these letters.

Of course everyone at Court and on the fringe of it knew of the new favourite. 'I had some talk about Mrs Masham', blandly reports Archbishop Sharp after an audience in April, 'whom I find she hath a true kindness for'.[38] Vanbrugh did not mince matters. 'Things are in an odd way at Court', he told Lord Manchester on July 27th, 'not all the interest of Lord Treasurer & Lady Marlborough, backed & pressed warmly by every man of the Cabinet, can prevail with the Queen to admit my Lord Somers into anything, nor so much as to make an Attorney-General. She answers little to 'em but stands firm against all they say. My Lord Chamberlain [Kent] is in a tottering way, I know he expected to be out, which he has not a mind to. He has in a trivial thing disobliged my Lady Marlborough in a great degree. She is very much at Court & mighty well there, but the Queen's fondness of t'other lady is not to be expressed'.[39]

It was enough now for Sarah and Godolphin to propose candidates for Anne to resist and oppose them. She would not countenance Somers (one of the best brains in her kingdom), nor would she have Halifax's brother for her Attorney-General. Sunderland shrugged. They might, he said, as well give up and let Marlborough and Godolphin bring in the Pretender. He, Sunderland, had no tenderness for the Queen. On the contrary, he was prepared to blackmail her now with a fullscale attack on the Admiralty. Prince George, panting for breath at Windsor, was gravely ill. The façade was in danger of cracking; yet somehow, even now, by desperate effort the vision of a triumphant Queen must be preserved.

The thanksgiving for Oudenarde was on August 19th. Sarah for the last time, before taking her place of honour in the coach beside her, arranged the Queen's jewels. Abigail, in the background, was soon to lie-in. (She gave birth to a daughter the following month). Harley stayed in the country. 'The men in office', wrote his friend Erasmus Lewis, 'acted their parts and put on their wedding garments', but the balconies were not crowded as they had been for former thanksgivings. Remembering the Blenheim occasion – herself then without ornament, Anne shimmering with diamonds – Sarah glanced at the Queen. The jewels her Mistress of the Robes had spent hours choosing and preparing had not been put on. Some would have waited until after the service. Not Sarah. She attacked her there and then and drove home her charge on the very steps of St Paul's. Worst of all, when in the portico or in the cathedral itself Anne tried to speak she was told in a harsh whisper to be silent. That at least was Anne's story; although Sarah maintained that, fearing that Anne was about to say something unfit for the mob to hear, she begged her to be quiet. No dramatist could have set a more telling scene: the whisper, the fluster, and then – organ and choir crashing into the *Te Deum* while the Tower guns thundered their salvos over the Thames.

The offence sank deep, yet it was Sarah who wrote to complain of the Queen's treatment, 'when I had taken so much pains to put your jewels in a way that I thought you would like, Mrs Masham could make you refuse to wear them, in so unkind a manner, because that was a power she had not thought fit to exercise before. I will make no reflections upon it', she ended, 'only that I must needs observe that your Majesty chose a very wrong day to mortify me, when you were just going to return thanks for a victory obtained by Lord Marlborough'.[40]

But Anne was not quite so crushed as to stand for that. Sarah, after following up with another enclosure from Marlborough, was snubbed with this:

> After the commands you gave me on the thanksgiving day of not answering you, I should not have troubled you with these lines, but to return the Duke of Marlborough's letter safe into your hands, and for the same reason do not say anything to that, nor to yours which enclosed it.[41]

One can but admire her composure. At the same time, as she sadly knew, the tiff was quite enough to make them the laughing-stock of Europe. 'I could wish', wrote Marlborough mildly to Sarah, from the siege of Lille, 'that Mrs Freeman would see what she so frequently observes that 42 [the Queen] is not capable of being changed by reason, so that you should be quiet till the time comes in which she must change'.[42] But with one woman whose goddess was Reason and another whose motto was *Semper Eadem*, what hope was there of that? Even so, early in September there seems to have been some attempt at reconciliation. Anne wrote to Sarah on the 9th, offering to see her in the gallery at Windsor, 'and shall think myself very happy', she kindly added, 'if that meeting sets everything right between us, there being nothing I am more desirous of than to have a thorough good understanding between dear Mrs Freeman & her poor unfortunate faithful Morley, who will till her last moment be so, whether you think what I shall happen to say be reasonable or just'.

Sarah went armed with a list of headings: subjects which, no matter how provocative, had to be aired – 'Mr Harley never had a good reputation . . . nobody alive more odious or more contemptible to all parties', 'Why will she not consider fairly & coolly etc.' No wonder there were raised voices and tears. Sarah makes no mention of the interview; perhaps she preferred to forget it. It was followed by another row about her lodgings at Kensington, which Abigail was said to have appropriated for her lying-in. Anne denied it and when pressed shouted, ''Tis false! 'tis a lie!' A thing she would never have done, asserted Sarah, before she fell into low company and contracted their habits.

By her own clumsiness Sarah was playing into her enemies' hands. Harley's and Abigail's letters are rich in reference to the tantrums of 'Lady Pye'. But it is no use their trying to blame him, says Harley, for the Queen's intransigence; he has not been near her. It must be due to her own good judgment and their unreasonableness, for they want to hog everything, all power and all favour. Marlborough and Godolphin have been trapped by the Junto and have no other way to turn. The Queen should be warned or all must run to ruin . . .

On the reverse of the medal we have Sunderland writing on the Junto's behalf a letter, dated October 19, 1708, which reads like an ultimatum. They have been fobbed off long enough; they still have no real power, 'they can neither obtain any right thing to be done nor prevent any wrong one'. As for the Admiralty, they found it 'under the most scandalous management of all . . . never to be cured but by the Prince's quitting, for whatever Council he has, George Churchill will in effect be always Lord High Admiral; so that they have in a body declared to Lord Treasurer that if this is not immediately done they must let the world & their friends see they have nothing more to do with the Court. The man they propose to be Lord High Admiral is Lord Pembroke'.[43] On the same day Marlborough wrote to his brother at the Admiralty, telling him bluntly that he must resign. It was hoped that his going might yet save the Queen and her Consort from a vicious attack. Lord Haversham had already declared in the Lords: 'Your disasters at sea have been so many, a man scarce knows where to begin. Your ships have been taken by your enemies as the Dutch have your herrings, by shoals, upon your own coasts . . .'[44]

The storm looked like becoming a tornado when, on October 28th at Kensington Palace, Prince George of Denmark died. In the sudden calm the Whigs were given their way: Pembroke for the Admiralty, Somers Lord President, Wharton Lord-Lieutenant of Ireland; while George Churchill retired happily to Windsor, to watch caged birds.

Anne, who had been sitting up with her dying husband night after night, was of course devastated. 'In all his illness', writes Burnet, 'which lasted some years, she would never leave his bed but sat up sometimes half the night in the bed by him with such care and concern that she was looked on very deservedly as a pattern'.[45] 'The loss of such a husband', she wrote to his brother the King of Denmark, 'who loved me so dearly and so devotedly, is too crushing for me to be able to bear it as I ought'.[46]

Two days before George died Sarah wrote to Anne:

Though the last time I had the honour to wait upon your Majesty your usage of me was such as was scarce possible for me to imagine or for anybody to believe, yet I cannot hear of so great a misfortune & affliction to you as the condition in which the Prince is without coming to pay my duty in enquiring after your health & to see if in any particular whatsoever my service can either be agreeable or useful to you, for which satisfaction I would do more than I will trouble your Majesty to read at this time.[47]

Taking the letter with her Sarah travelled all night to Kensington and delivered it herself. She was coolly received but stayed with Anne till the Prince died.

'Then I knelt down to the Queen', runs her account, 'and said all that I could imagine from a faithful servant & one that she had professed so much kindness to, but she seemed not to mind me but clapped her hands together, with other marks of passion; and when I had expressed all I could think of to moderate her grief I knelt by her without speaking for some time & then asked her to go to St James's; upon which she answered she would stay there. I said that was impossible, what could she do in such a dismal place? And I made use of all the arguments that are common upon that head, but all in vain; she persisted that she would stay at Kensington . . . I said nobody in the world ever continued in a place where a dead husband lay & I did not see where she could be but within a room or two of that dismal body'. At last she agreed to go and, handing Sarah her watch said, 'Don't come in to me till the hand of the watch comes to this place'; and as Sarah withdrew the Queen added, 'Send to Masham to come to me before I go'.

Sarah for reasons of her own thought this shocking and as she sat at a window, watch in hand, decided not to send for Abigail after all. 'I thought it would make a disagreeable noise', she explained to Anne, 'when there were bishops and ladies of the bedchamber without that she did not care to see'. Anne then called for her hoods, which Abigail's sister Alice put on, 'and as she did it the Queen whispered with her, I suppose some kind thing to her sister, who had not appeared before me at Kensington; but upon the alarm of the Queen's being to go with me to St James's, she came into the gallery with one of her ministers the Scotch doctor [Arbuthnot] to see her Majesty pass, who, notwithstanding her great affection for the Prince, at the sight of that charming lady, as her arm was upon mine which she had leaned upon, I found she had strength to bend down towards Mrs Masham* like a sail & in passing by went some steps more than was necessary to be nearer her; and when that cruel touch was over, of going by her with me, she turned about in a little passage room & gave orders about her dogs & a strong box'.

In the coach Anne spoke of the burial, that room should be left in the same Abbey vault for herself. At St James's Sarah led her to her green closet and there left her with a cup of broth. Returning that evening Sarah found the Queen at table with Abigail who left immediately 'with an air of insolence and anger'. Remembering the 'long jumbling journeys' Anne had made George take to Bath and Petworth, Sarah could not help smiling when she received from Anne this note:

> I scratched twice at dear Mrs Freeman's door, as soon as Lord Treasurer went from me, in hopes to have spoke one more word to him before he was gone; but nobody hearing me, I wrote this, not caring to send what I had to say by word of mouth; which was to desire him when he sends his orders to Kensington he would give directions there may be a great many yeomen of the guard to carry the Prince's dear body that it may not be let fall, the great stairs being very steep and slippery.[48]†

'I did see the tears in her eyes', adds Sarah, 'two or three times after his death, and I believe she fancied she loved him . . . but her nature was very hard and she was not apt to cry'.[49]

Swift's comment, albeit from a hostile critic who was not an eye-witness, is not irrelevant. 'The deportment of the Duchess of Marlborough', he wrote, 'while the Prince lay expiring was of such a nature that the Queen, then in the heights of grief, was not able to bear it, but with marks of displeasure in her countenance she ordered the Duchess to withdraw and send Mrs Masham to her'.[50] Swift very probably is quoting Abigail; but judging even by Sarah's own account it sounds to have been a quite remarkably insensitive performance.

'Thus has the Queen lost her companion', wrote Abigail to Harley, the day George died. 'Whoever succeeds in that quality, be it man or

* Mrs Masham's child had been born on September 30th.

† Reproduced in facsimile on page 342.

woman, will have a greater share in affairs than the last had'.[51] It was true that he or she could hardly have less. And yet George had had his place. Sir Winston goes so far as to call him 'one of the linchpins in that marvellous coach of state that drove so triumphantly along the roads of Europe'; and certainly the coach was to travel less safely without him. In a brilliant cast his had been a walking-on part; yet not only by Anne was he fondly remembered. 'About a year and a half after I came over', wrote Lord Westmorland, 'which was in the second year of the Queen, I was made a lord of the bedchamber to the Prince of Denmark. I am not capable to set forth the just praise due to that good man. So far I *can* say, as the facts proved themselves, that he kept the Queen from being beguiled to her dishonour by sycophants that were about her all the time of his life, for no sooner was he dead but she sullied the great glory she had gained during her reign before, by bringing in a party not able to support her . . . and putting herself into the hands of weak as well as wicked men to maintain their power brought her into an ignominious peace and, a much baser act, the desertion of her allies just ready to enter upon action, which compelled them to make also then the best peace they could. This sad change would not have been if the death of the Prince of Denmark had not happened, for he kept whisperers off and helped her judgment to stand by those who had so successfully carried on her affairs in that part of her reign'.[52]

On the last day of October Harley wrote to Abigail of his concern at hearing of 'Aunt Stephens' great loss'. 'This additional trouble', he said, 'to the persecutions she hath already undergone will, I fear, too much affect her health. But I write most earnestly to my Cousin Kath Stephens [Abigail] that she will redouble her care & attendance . . . and to omit no opportunity of being with her & diverting her, for there is nothing in the world so mischievous to body & mind as for persons to be much alone on such occasions & therefore those who are true friends should almost force themselves upon them. Otherwise they are apt to contract a habit of melancholy, which afterwards is not very easily got rid of or parted with. I will add one other consideration. Those who have already so notoriously abused the jointure of Chavenage [the Queen's favour] will take this opportunity to press the obtaining all the extravagant things which are required by the estate at Essington [Junto] . . .' The Queen is to resist them and play for time.[53]

Abigail, in her reply of November 6, writes of the Queen having lost all that was dear to her, 'the only comfort of her life', and goes on to explain that Sarah has already forced herself upon Anne. 'There is care taken', she adds wryly, 'she [Anne] shall not be alone, for since the misfortune the Lady Pye has hardly left her so long as to let her say her private prayers but stays constantly with her. My Lady's friends say it is fit she should (and they hope she always will) to keep that jade my cousin Kate from her. Oh my poor aunt is in a very deplorable condition, for now her ready money is all gone; because I will not trouble you with a melancholy story (give me leave to repeat your own words), she has shut & bolted the door upon herself. Oh what can one say to all these things when I know what wise & good advice you have given her & yet she rejects it to satisfy those monsters who she knows will ruin her. When you come to town I desire you will give me leave to wait upon you & the rest of my good friends, whom I shall have the greatest value for to the last moment of my life'.[54]

For the winter Anne shut and bolted the door upon herself at St James's, haunting the gloomy closets (one overlooking a court where Abigail hung out washing) where George used to make little models of ships. Sarah was mystified. 'I thought nothing was more natural', she said, 'than to avoid seeing of papers or anything that belonged to one that one loved when they were just dead'. In this belief – for she could imagine no different outlook – she had taken upon herself to remove George's portrait from Anne's bedroom. The Queen sent her a note:

> I must desire you to bespeak a purple quilt and three cushions, against I see company, but they must not be of any glossy thing, and if you please send one of your servants to the upholsterer to know the size of the bed, that they may be made fit. I cannot end this without begging you once more for God's sake to let the dear picture you have of mine be put into my bedchamber, for I cannot be without it any longer.[55]

While she remained Groom of the Stole, Mistress of the Robes and

Keeper of the Privy Purse Sarah, no matter how unwelcome, had every right to be there. Indeed it was her duty, until recently neglected, to deal with petitions and to organise the large and elaborate operation of putting the Queen and her household into mourning. Anne at this time saw practically no one, although Sarah suspected that some were secretly admitted. Even so it was, thought Sarah, her duty to bring to Anne's notice the case of Mrs Howe, a penniless widow with five young children; for, Sarah adds, she thought it would give the Queen 'an air of being grieved for the Prince to be touched upon that melancholy subject'; and so it proved. 'My artifice', Sarah continues, 'succeeded just as I expected, for her Majesty put on a very melancholy air as if she felt a great deal upon that subject & said yes indeed, I do know how to pity her, I will look over a list of the lodgings at Somerset House; and for the pension she said she would do anything that was reasonable. But she had a hum which she always has when she does not really care for what she does, and answered it would be time enough to say what she would give her when she had spoken to my Lord Treasurer'.[56]

And as for mourning, Sarah's neat accounts, page after page of them, again speak for themselves; but the sudden change is striking. Instead of crimson and gold mantoes and petticoats, Mr Alexander sends only purple and black. Even Mr Smith the pin man sends black pins only with two black pincushions. Mrs How makes a purple weed, with ribbon; Mrs Wilkins supplies a long black veil, a fine black fox muff and a short black crêpe hood with a double crown; Mrs Hawker nine yards of fine purple cloth for another weed and petticoat. There are purple fans and purple shoes, sable tippets and black stomachers. A 'bill of mourning for the six maids of honour, by her Majesty's order' comes to £600.[57] At St James's even the steps outdoors were draped with black flannel, while indoors the sconces were oxydised black. The Court circular, sent to peers, laid down that 'no person should use any varnished or bullion nails to be seen on their coaches, chariots or chairs'.[58]

Prince George, who was fifty-five, was buried by torchlight, on November 13th, in Westminster Abbey, 'after the same manner as King Charles II, which was privately, at twelve at night'.[59]

'Every honest man', wrote a contemporary, 'must have a due sense and concern for what the whole nation suffers by the death of so gracious a Prince and particularly for the Queen's extreme grief on the loss of her royal Consort with whom her Majesty had lived for many years in such an happy and uncommon union'.[60]

CHAPTER TEN

BEHIND THE FAÇADE

1708 - 1710

'I WAITED upon the Queen, who received me very kindly', wrote Archbishop Sharp the day after the funeral. 'At my first coming in we both wept. She is in a very disconsolate condition'.[1] Throughout that black winter at St James's those who had to be seen were received, once a week, in the royal bedchamber, where Anne in black sat beside a purple bed. She dined alone. On Sundays she attended the Chapel Royal, to which no one wearing anything coloured (not even a handkerchief) was admitted. The prayer for the Queen to be a happy mother of children was dropped.

It is Victoria with a difference. One sees Anne as widow and invalid driven in upon herself and her 'family' (the very name seems a mockery): a household already divided against itself. Few women were ever more in need of friendship, but she had learned her lesson and would never completely unbosom herself again. Those she now naturally leaned on most were churchmen and doctors, and of these last a new recruit had just joined her staff.

As a doctor and as a figure in history Sir David Hamilton, FRS (1663–1721) is of no very great importance. As a diarist, from the end of 1709, when he began to write, until the Queen's death in 1714, he is invaluable. In the course of duty he was often alone with Anne, who confided in him; and though his style is not to be compared with Sarah's, he would seem to have been a good deal less prejudiced and far better tempered. In psychiatry, if not in medicine, he was centuries before his time, again and again begging Anne to avoid 'disquiets and uneasiness', which he recognised as the worst possible things for her 'gout'. When his counsel went further – on such hazardous subjects as Hanover and the Pretender – she was at least prepared to listen; and every now and then he notes comments and exclamations which not only ring true but, not having been published, are extremely interesting and revealing. One could wish he had been in attendance for the whole reign; or alternatively, that Abigail had turned diarist.

Until the Queen's birthday on February 6th, when Anne made a brief public appearance, the world at large saw only a black curtain, behind which, apart from personal grief, they were supposed to imagine that all was well. Marlborough, ever victorious, had moved on from Oudenarde to capture Lille. They were not to know of course that, during that long siege, peace-feelers had been exchanged between Marlborough (again offered a vast bribe) and his nephew the Duke of Berwick. Nothing came of them. Nor can they have known of Marlborough's frequent threats to resign: 'a thing', wrote the Queen, 'I can never consent to'. He and Godolphin had lost the Queen's confidence and that confidence had not passed to the Junto, now that they had power. 'The Queen', observes Churchill, 'was estranged. Instead of being their strength she was henceforth their bane. Sarah and Godolphin were her aversion, Marlborough a splendid but oppressive fact'.[2] Marlborough himself wrote repeatedly that he was 'impatient for quiet'. He had washed his hands of politics. He would be a soldier, at times a diplomat, nothing more.

Realistic as always, the French had no illusions. 'The authority of Princess Anne', runs a secret memorandum of November, 1708, 'is not enough to uphold Marlborough against his enemies, and even if she could it is doubtful whether this Princess, governed by others, would be willing to use her power to maintain a former favourite . . . Marlborough risks the hatred of the British, with whom popularity is more capricious than with any other nation . . . If he works sincerely for the peace he will be rewarded to the tune of three million *livres* . . . He need not be asked to dethrone Anne and put the Pretender in her place, but somehow she must be made to nominate the Pretender her successor. This will obviate all the Hanover unpleasantness, now a source of constant grief and disgust'.[3]

For one whose avarice was said to be his one great fault, the bribe must have been as tempting as the rich governorship of the Netherlands. Both had to be refused; nor, when the French again turned secretly to the Dutch, were their peace overtures more successful. The Allies had won the war against France and lost it against Spain.

In pride and shortsightedness (and to honour the agreement with Portugal) they told each other they must soldier on: 'No Peace Without Spain!' Not quite everyone in England however was so blind, nor so scrupulous. St John, writing to Harley on November 6th, exclaimed, 'For God's sake let us be once out of Spain!'[4] He urged Harley to rally the Tories and oust the Whigs. Power must be lodged where it naturally belonged: with property, i.e. with the Tory owners of land. (The Whig landowners, it seemed, must be won over or written off).

The new year (1709) brought throughout Europe snow and devastating frost. On January 28th, in a remarkably ill-timed address from her Parliament, the Queen, within a few days of her forty-fourth birthday, was begged to marry again. This should of course never have gone farther than the halfwit who in the Commons proposed it: a Whig called Watson, nicknamed the Fillet of Veal.[5] Anne was outraged, nor was she mollified by the ballad *The Hasty Widow or the Sooner the Better*, now hawked about the streets. With dignity she replied: 'The subject of this address is of such a nature that I am persuaded you do not expect a particular answer'. The humour of the thing, if any, was of the crudest: a bucolic jest to help pass a long winter's evening. ''twould make a dog die with laughing', wrote Abigail Harley to her nephew, 'to think of the matrimonial address, which looks like the result of a consultation of superannuated women rather than senators, since they won't allow her Majesty the decent retirement that all the sex may justly claim upon such occasions . . . Methinks the next step shall be to make it penal for anyone to live a month a widow, which I hope would not want the royal assent'.[6]

The other ludicrous affair was the case of the Russian Ambassador, arrested in London for debt. No one would have given it a second thought nor bothered about the officious bailiffs who had bundled him into a sponging-house. He owed money. There had been a scuffle. That was all. But the wrath of his master, Peter the Great, was savage and Olympian. He demanded the heads and hands of the bailiffs. Failing this, with the northern war hovering over the borders of the Empire, Russia was in a strong position to offer reprisals. At first it was hoped that a soothing letter to the Czar from the Queen 'under her own royal hand, to remain to posterity a glorious and unequalled monument of her friendship and esteem', might prove enough; but no, the Russians were out for blood: heads must roll. Another tack was tried. 'It cannot be supposed', wrote the embarrassed Secretary (Boyle) 'that so merciful a Prince as his Czarish Majesty would have any service or satisfaction in the death of one or two mean persons'. Such punishment in Britain, he added, was wholly impracticable, unless it could be proved that there had been a plot to assassinate. Not even to please the Czar could we be expected to 'break in upon our constitution and overturn the foundations of our Government'.

Things looked very black for the fourteen culprits rounded up; and blacker still when, on February 15th, a jury 'chosen particularly for the purpose', in a court packed with peers including Sunderland and Halifax, found all save one guilty. After this however luck – and British justice – began to run their way. Lord Chief Justice Holt, who presided, whether or not he cared a fig for their fate, had enormous respect for the law he administered and represented. There had been no injury and he could find no precedent for severe punishment nor any law to justify it. They might lie in prison a while (they had done so), but they must soon go free. For months the Russians continued to rage. As our envoy in Moscow explained to Boyle, 'The methods of this Government and especially their administration of justice differ more from those of Great Britain than the severity of their climate from the gentleness of English air and therefore 'tis no wonder they are so little understood'.[7] Lord Chief Justice Holt (may his name shine in gold till the Day of Judgment) remained unmoved, and a *nolle prosequi* was entered. The Queen expressed her 'true sisterly sorrow' to the fuming Czar, and as a sop had Parliament pass an Act of Diplomatic Immunity which, though from time to time abused, has probably, in two hundred and sixty years, done less harm than good.

When immediate legislation was called for, the seemingly cumbrous machinery of Anne's Parliament seems to have worked. On April 20th an Act for the Queen's Most Gracious & Free Pardon was rushed through both Houses, receiving the royal assent the same day. The reason for it was not made public, but the tale at Court was that a letter of Godolphin's to St Germains had fallen into the hands of Wharton, who had threatened exposure unless the two remaining Junto lords without office, Halifax and Orford, were instantly brought in.

Pressure from the Junto, at home and abroad, was still relentless. To a vital conference at the Hague, for the Barrier Treaty, they insisted on sending their own emissary, Lord Townshend,* to act for Britain with Marlborough in guaranteeing Holland a long list of Barrier towns in the Netherlands. Holland for her part was, if called upon, to send troops to Scotland to secure the accession of the House of Hanover, on the death of Anne. Townshend was inexperienced and not in the confidence of Marlborough, who refused to sign the treaty. But indeed the lack of trust all round was enough in itself to kill the new promise of peace. The Dutch, accused of trying to go it alone, protested: 'Their High Mightinesses will never agree to any conditions whatever until all the Allies have full satisfaction'. Peace-preliminaries from France, brought over from the Hague by Walpole, promised all that could reasonably be asked for. Even the throne of Spain was to be surrendered by Philip of Anjou to Charles of Austria. So confident was Marlborough that the Allies would be satisfied that he sent for a chair of state (for himself as plenipotentiary), 'made so as that it may serve for part of a bed when I have done with it here, which I hope will be by the end of the summer'.[8] It was never to be used. By article 37 of the treaty, should Philip refuse to leave Spain, Louis XIV his grandfather had to guarantee to take up arms and drive him out, an imposition so manifestly unjust and impracticable that everything foundered on it. Louis refused to sign and appealed to his people. Facing famine as they were, they rose like a phoenix in a flame of indignation; and the Allies marched on to fight them in the blood bath of Malplaquet.

At home, almost literally on the Queen's doorstep, strange things were happening in St James's. Sarah, while still on tolerably good terms with Anne, had begged a long lease of Crown land adjoining the Palace on the east, for building what was to be called Marlborough House. It meant giving up part of the Palace garden: that pleasance of espaliers and wilderness where Verrio had a bothy. It meant too

* Townshend was more acceptable to Marlborough than Halifax, who desperately wanted the job but was not supported by Somers.

that when Anne was in residence she could not be more closely neighboured. 'If the house be set in an equal line with her Majesty's Palace', Maynwaring told Sarah, 'it will have a view down the middle walk of her garden . . . and being removed from all manner of dust & from the smoke of the houses in the Pell-mell, you will live & sleep as it were in the middle of that great garden'.[9] Had the house been built in 1702 this might strongly have appealed to both women. Sarah laid the foundation-stone, inscribed *Anno Pacifico*, on May 5th, 1709 and moved in, before the walls were dry, in 1711; but by that time they were no longer on speaking terms. 'The house is to be built after the model of the Duke of Buckingham's',* wrote Peter Wentworth, 'upon which account there is struck up a great [friendship] where there has lately been a coolness, the said Duke & his Duchess with her Grace of Marlborough visit their work very often together . . . His Grace is the chief architect'.[10] But that was not literally true. Sarah had hoped to demonstrate that by choosing her own architect – not Vanbrugh, not Buckingham, but Wren – and directing him, that she could quickly raise 'the best and strongest house that ever was built'. Wren and his son were willing enough, but she soon fell out with 'the poor old man', as she called him, and decided to finish the place herself.

The temptation to tease the Queen was irresistible. With favour gone and nothing more to lose Sarah took a delight in it. There was no shortage of ammunition. Abigail could and did fill chapters or, as Sarah called them, notums and narratives, often with bulky enclosures. But there were other grievances such as interference in her offices (e.g. the promotion of a starcher without her authority) and of course lodgings, that never-failing source of contention throughout the Court. Anne had long since tired of them all, as she had of the droned burden of Long and Faithful Service rewarded with coldness and ingratitude. Marlborough was wiser. 'I know very well there

* Buckingham House, built in 1705, preceded Buckingham Palace. The Duke was accused, while laying out his grounds, of encroaching upon Crown land and 'going further into the Park than he had leave from the Queen to do'. Marlborough House, a well-mannered building in brick with stone dressings and niches, was unexceptionable but showed how dull Blenheim might have looked in more orthodox hands. It has since been much altered and added to.

is no more tenderness', he wrote sadly, 'and I have taken my measures never to expect any . . . It has always been my observation in disputes', he added later, 'especially in those of kindness and friendship, that all reproaches, though ever so reasonable, do serve to no other end but the making the breach wider'.[11] But this of course made no impression. Sarah sailed in among the mournful closets of St James's and demanded lodgings to make a better entrance to her own apartments. When Anne told her they had been promised to Abigail's sister, and servants must be found rooms, she bridled: 'Your Majesty, then, does not reckon Lord Marlborough or me among your servants?' So it amounted to this, that after all Marlborough's conquests the Queen still chose to refuse him 'a miserable hole to make a clear entry to his lodgings. 'I beg therefore to know', she asked Anne, 'whether I am at liberty to repeat this to any of my friends'. After a long pause Anne said yes she might.[12]

All this was at St James's before Marlborough House was finished. It was at Windsor however, where Anne had had the Little House hung with black for the summer, that the nadir in bickering over trifles was reached. The storm, audible at a distance, had according to Lord Dartmouth arisen from Anne's having, without telling Sarah, ordered her laundress, Mrs Abrahall, a bottle of wine a day. When Sarah raged, Anne said nothing but rose to leave the room; whereupon Sarah (if Dartmouth is to be believed) 'clapped her back against the door and told her she should hear her out'.[13] The report may be exaggerated, but the letters following that interview remain: one drawing attention to Mrs Manley's scandalous *New Atlantis*, containing 'stuff not fit to be mentioned of passions between women',[14] and another enclosing passages from the Prayer Book and Jeremy Taylor's *The Whole Duty of Man*. Sarah's only satisfaction was in sending them. There was to be no acknowledgment, unless as she said you could count the Queen's smile on her way to Communion, and even that, Sarah on reflection decided, was probably meant for Taylor rather than for herself.

Anne may by now have regarded Sarah as no longer able to pierce her composure; but that would have been to underestimate her. Her letters could still sting. On one such occasion Anne, 'with a great deal of stiffness and reservedness in her looks', complained to

Godolphin of 'a very extraordinary letter' from Sarah, of which she was not then composed enough to mention particulars.[15] Sarah when told of it was not disturbed. She found comfort in the uncritical admiration of Maynwaring, who doubtless had helped to compose the letter. 'If your Grace had any passion or tenderness', he wrote, referring to Anne and Abigail, 'I know it would be impossible to endure this, but since there is nothing of that, I should think the fondness there is in another place, as it is ridiculous to all the world, should be only sport and diversion. Though that expression "Sure I may love whom I please" was an extraordinary one, yet it will always be true that one cannot help loving what one loves. The humour must spend itself, let the object be ever so leperous; and so in the name of wonder let it'.[16]

He then mocks at Anne's Court: 'This great and famous Queen, the arbitress of Europe, whose history will be the greatest that ever was read . . . never willingly draws any of her nobles from their own seats but seems to think her Court wants no further decoration when it is set off with the Bug and Lady Frescheville and with those shining lights the Scotch Doctor [Arbuthnot] and Abigail'.[17] And as for this last, red in the face and with her fan working like a windmill, he never saw anyone so odious. 'I do really believe the creature is rotten', he concluded, 'and should be removed as Wolsey was designed to be for his stinking breath, lest Sacred Majesty should be infected'.[18] It was the Kit-Cat touch.

Abigail, who reminded Swift of 'Mrs Malolly that was once my landlady in Trim', had been writing again to Harley. She hoped she might read his last letter to her friend, who still showed 'so little courage & resolution'; but nothing should be written that Anne might be cross-questioned about: it was better for her not to know. Abigail expected to lie-in again in October and in the meantime could get no leave. 'I can't tell you', she adds, 'what use my friend has made of the advice given her in your letter, but she heard it over & over. She keeps me in ignorance & is very reserved, does not care to tell me anything . . .' And again, 'My aunt will not let me go . . . She is afflicted with very sore eyes, which makes her mighty melancholy, together with the thoughts of Lady Pye's being to be near her this night & is to stay as long as my aunt does . . .'[19]

Sarah had had to be sent for to Windsor to present Mrs Danvers' daughter Belle as a bedchamberwoman. It was a detestable duty. Belle, later to marry an Irish bishop, 'did not', says Sarah, 'look like a human creature'; while her mother, having once regaled Sarah with 'a great deal of the wickedness of Abigail', had since gone over to the enemy; and Sarah's own candidate for the job, a Mrs Vane, had been turned down. Anne, sending for Sarah, writes of Mrs Danvers' long and faithful service and says she now grows very infirm.[20] Peter Wentworth adds:

> The Queen sent for the Duchess from London to present Belle Danvers, till when her Grace had not been there since the Queen was at Windsor. The town talk as if the Duchess has thoughts of resigning the Groom of the Stole & that upon the condition Lady Sunderland should succeed her, but they say the Duke of Somerset contests the matter for his Duchess, which is what keeps the Duchess of Marlborough from quitting. The Duke of Somerset does keep close to Windsor, I don't think he has been three days absent this season.[21]

That was the Court view (Wentworth was an equerry). Sarah thought she saw a good deal further:

> . . . and though Mrs Masham & Mr Harley were the first causes of bringing all this mischief about, they were helped & supported by the Duke of Shrewsbury; for the Queen always thought the Duke of Somerset to be a fool & used him only as a tool, & all her favour to the Duchess of Somerset was affected only to cover that to Mrs Masham, as she hoped, for she certainly was ashamed of it a great while & had a mind to have the world think at last that she had a great kindness for the Duchess of Somerset, but in reality there was no such thing.[22]

If Sarah played into the hands of the enemy, as most surely and rashly she did, so now, most surprisingly, did Marlborough; for in October, when he asked to be made Captain-General for life, he made the biggest miscalculation of his career. Though a fair case might have been made for it (to re-establish his credit and to give him the authority he needed to end the war), it was disastrously mistimed.*

* Dr Snyder believes Marlborough's request was first made in the spring of 1709 and was repeated. 'He knew that if the Whigs fell he would lose his job.' See Snyder: *The Duke of Marlborough's Request* . . . Army His. Research Journal, Summer 1967.

The Queen was alarmed: 'as if', says Swift, 'she apprehended an attempt upon the Crown'. Her new counsellors whispered 'Cromwell' and 'King John' . . . a most dangerous situation. She refused him. She went further and begged him to call to order his impossible wife:

> I saw very plainly your uneasiness at my refusing the mark of favour you desired, and believed from another letter I had from you on that subject you fancied that advice came from Masham, but I do assure you you wrong her most extremely, for upon my word she knows nothing of it, as I told you in another letter. What I said was my own thoughts, not thinking it for your service or mine to do a thing of that nature. However, if when you come home you still continue in the same mind I will comply with your desires.
>
> You seem to be dissatisfied with my behaviour to the Duchess of Marlborough. I do not love complaining, but it is impossible to help saying on this occasion I believe nobody was ever so used by a friend as I have been by her ever since my coming to the Crown. I desire nothing but that she would leave off teasing and tormenting me and behave herself with the decency she ought both to her friend and Queen, and this I hope you will make her do . . . Whatever her behaviour is to me, mine shall be always as becomes me . . .[23]

The teasing, as Sarah owned to Maynwaring, was deliberate, and in it she was urged on by the Junto lords, whose ambitions, with the appointment of Orford as Lord High Admiral in place of Pembroke, were now all but fulfilled. They had taken another castle but, did they but know it, in Shrewsbury they had lost a key man. From his letter to Harley of November 3 it is easy to see how he had been indoctrinated.[24] Harley's gospel was simple and not without some truth: 1. The nation longed for peace. 2. Chances to make a good peace had been thrown away. 3. The Whigs wanted to prolong the war. 4. The Tories must get rid of them and make the peace.

As with foreign enemies, so it has always been with political parties: one has but to endure until the opposition cracks; for sooner or later and usually from some quite unforeseen cause the rift opens or, better still, the fire kindles within and the foe vaporises as it were by spontaneous combustion. As the grim year 1709 dwindled, Harley thought the explosion overdue; but if Dr Sacheverell had not, with his tedious sermon in St Paul's, touched it off, Harley and his men might have stayed in the wilderness much longer. The Whigs would have done well to shrug off the man and his sermon (on 'in perils among false brethren': II Corinthians, 11, 26) as, in Sarah's phrase, an heap of bombast; but this was not easy. The provocation had been blatant: a seditious blast released on the anniversary of William's landing (November 5), preached before a High Tory Lord Mayor and printed. Godolphin, stung by his reference to Volpone (another of his nicknames) and encouraged by Sunderland and Wharton, decided to impeach. 'So solemn a prosecution for such a scribble', wrote Dr Stratford to Harley, 'will make the Doctor and his performance much more considerable than either of them could have been on any other account'.[25] The trial was arranged to begin in February.

In her speech at the opening of Parliament on November 15th the Queen was made to refer scathingly to France's attempts to divide the Allies by 'amusing' them with 'false appearances of peace'. They had failed and the succeeding campaign had been 'as glorious as any of the former'. Neither of those things was true. She seemed, said Maynwaring, to have changed. Her voice was fainter, her whole manner more careless and less moving. Neither publicly nor privately did she mention Marlborough's victory at Malplaquet, and for the thanksgiving on the 22nd she went to her own chapel (she was still in mourning), not to St Paul's. In December she had gout. Her Physicians-in-Ordinary were now Lawrence, Lister, Hamilton and Arbuthnot, and in that order, with Shadwell as Physician Extraordinary.

Hamilton, consulted 'about the beginning of December', found the Queen 'inwardly affected with an uneasiness' and cautioned her against 'disquiets'. 'Her receiving this advice with so much goodness (I may say thankfulness)', he adds, 'convinced me how right my conjecture was'. Godolphin's great gravity and forbidding countenance did not usually, says Hamilton, invite confidence. On December 9th however he stopped the doctor on the back stairs and asked after the Queen. Hamilton said she was better and taking no medicine but spirit of millipedes, to which Godolphin remarked, 'The oftener boards are washed, the sooner they are impaired'.

Having swallowed this, Hamilton made bold to suggest that the Queen should be protected as much as possible from disquieting business and more especially 'at some certain seasons'. Would Godolphin co-operate? 'With wonderful good nature and seeming pleasure' he said he would. If Hamilton would inform him of every such season, 'he would do his utmost to keep her easy'. This seemed well enough, but on Christmas Eve Godolphin grew testy and 'broke out, saying "You think I disquiet the Queen. What trouble can it give her Majesty for me to read a letter or two to her, or to make her walk to the Council & hear her Lords discourse upon her affairs? It's uneasiness from tattles that injures her most & craving from her that which would not look so well for her to grant" '.[26]

Seventeen hundred and ten opened with what Wentworth called a great hurlyburly at Court. It was a trial of strength devised by Harley and the last chance for Marlborough and the Whigs to make a stand. Lord Rivers, calling on Marlborough, asked if he would object to his succeeding the late Earl of Essex in the sinecure known as the Lieutenancy of the Tower. Marlborough, ever polite and at the same time confident that in this Anne would consult him, told Rivers he might ask the Queen. Rivers lost no time and without further word to Marlborough Anne gave him the job. On the same day Marlborough learned that Essex's regiment of dragoons, promised by him to an experienced officer, General Meredith, had been given instead to Abigail's brother, Honest Jack Hill. 'It was obvious', comments Sir Winston, 'that an insult of the most carefully studied character was intended by the Queen's secret advisers'; the idea being – undermine them enough and the Marlboroughs might feel bound to retire.

Marlborough absented himself from the Council and withdrew with his wife to Windsor Lodge. Sunderland and Maynwaring pleaded strongly for a showdown: let the Queen choose once and for all between Marlborough and Abigail. But Godolphin demurred. An address to Parliament, threatening, blackmailing the Queen? He was 'much distracted' at the prospect. It could not be. And so it was that Marlborough's ultimatum, its sting removed, ended with nothing stronger than a plea for protection against 'the malice of a bedchamberwoman'.

Anne's relief was obvious. To part with Abigail had been almost as upsetting a notion as had been that, so long ago, of having to part with Mrs Freeman. In panic she had appealed to friends and sent a gardener (Wise?) with a note to Harley. Now all was well again. She could smile on Marlborough and wish him God speed as he left for Holland. She was less pleased when a little later she found that his list of promotions stopped just short of Jack Hill and Samuel Masham. However, a compromise was patched up and Anne consoled Hill – once rescued by Sarah as 'a boy naked and wanting bread' – with a pension of a thousand a year. Another day, as a general, he would lead the disastrous expedition against Quebec. ''Tis thought', said Sarah, 'the Queen will see her errors when 'tis too late, as her father did before her'.[27]

> For she was pinch'd and pull'd, she said,
> And he by friar's lantern led.

It was a rich time for rumour. 'The Queen has promised the Duke of Beaufort', runs a mutilated scrap dated January 20, 'that there shall be a thorough remove, and Mr Harley says the same. It is believed Lord Sunderland & some others will lose their heads'.[28] ''Tis said the Queen has been so provoked', wrote Wentworth ten days later, 'as to declare to more than one she has been so slighted by the Duchess of Marlborough that she can't endure the sight of her'.[29]

'She told me she was under great vexation', runs Hamilton's entry for February 10, 'but such as my Lord Godolphin could not help her in, probably from her being secretly pressed to put him out, as well as my Lady Marlborough, which I am satisfied from her own words and after-actions she was most unwilling to do . . .' Next day he congratulated her on a visit from Lady Charlotte, 'as if she had been but twenty years old'. This came from warding off disquiet. If only she could continue so, but of course she could not. Under February 27 he notes: 'Another succeeding occasion of uneasiness happened in the affair of Dr Sacheverell, some insisting that he should be punished more mildly & others that his punishment should be more severe. Her own opinion she expressed to me was that there ought to be a punishment but a mild one, lest the mob appearing of his side should occasion commotions & that his impeachment had been better let alone'.[30]

When she had read it Anne told Burnet it was a bad sermon and Sacheverell deserved well to be punished for it. Later, when Abigail questioned her about it, she said her friends' advice was not to meddle. All the same, she was determined to attend the trial.

Wren, asked to run up stands in Westminster Hall, told the Lords plainly that the Queen was positive she would have nobody over her head, 'which made the House laugh, coming so pat to what had been so lately the discourse of the town'.[31] As she rode in her chair to the trial the mob is said to have acclaimed her with the tongue-twisting shout: 'We hope your Majesty is for the High Church and Dr Sacheverell!' But she 'appeared very pensive'. From Sacheverell in custody she had had a strange letter, addressed to her as Most Dread Sovereign, in which resignation and adulation competed. 'But this is my comfort in the midst of my trouble', he wrote, 'that I have a Prince whose mercy & goodness extends itself with equal concern to the meanest of her subjects as a tender mother of her people'. He dared to hope for 'the same royal compassion your Majesty has hitherto vouchsafed towards the loyal clergy of the Church of England, of whom I am the least & most unworthy'.[32] Ungrammatical charlatan though he might be (Burnet calls him a bold, insolent man with a very small measure of religion, virtue, learning or good sense), his style echoed Harley, if not St Paul.

In Westminster Hall, still hung with the captured standards of Blenheim, it soon became obvious that Sacheverell, a natural actor revelling in his part, was playing the lead in a political epic, produced on the Blenheim scale. Resistance or non-resistance, toleration or persecution, Divine Right, the Revolution – all these and more were aired and fought over. Lord Chief Justice Holt died during the hearing and was quickly replaced by an equally brilliant though less scrupulous judge, Thomas Parker, later Lord Macclesfield. Sacheverell's ninety-minute oration – 'so many falsehoods and so many appeals to God' – is said to have been composed by Atterbury and Swift. His delivery was irresistible: 'in so fine a manner, in such moving terms, with so harmonious a voice', Abigail Harley told her nephew Edward, 'that the poor ladies wet all their clean handkerchiefs, nay the men could not refrain [from] tears, as they tell you the Duke of Leeds, Lords Rochester & Nottingham showed their tenderness that way. I question whether ever the Doctor did such a feat in his pulpit . . . Yesterday was taken up by the Doctor's counsel in reading passages out of several books full of the horridest blasphemy that ever was vented among those called Christians; others full of base reflections upon the Queen & her family, one passage that she had no more title to the Crown than my Lord Mayor's horse . . . The Queen heard all this'.[33] She heard too Lord Wharton declare that but for the Revolution she was no true Queen and nearly all the lords were traitors. No wonder she looked pensive. Was she for or against? She had been against, then ('not to meddle') neutral; but now her thoughts were running a different way.

'Mr Harley', writes Swift, 'who came up to town during the time of the impeachment, was by the intervention of Mrs Masham privately brought to the Queen and in some meetings easily convinced her Majesty of the dispositions of her people, as they appeared in the course of that trial, in favour of the Church and against the measures of those in her service. It was not without a good deal of difficulty that Mr Harley was able to procure this private access to the Queen, the Duchess of Marlborough by her emissaries watching all the avenues to the back stairs and upon all occasions discovering their jealousy of him'. However, 'Mrs Masham . . . had taken all proper occasions of pursuing what Mr Harley had begun. In this critical juncture the Queen, hemmed in and as it were imprisoned by the Duchess of Marlborough and her creatures, was at a loss how to proceed'. Anne made it clear to Harley that she welcomed his secret visits, and he 'from that time began to have entire credit with her'.[34]

Sarah's behaviour at the trial was characteristic. She ignored the hearing and watched those about the Queen: did they stand or sit? She herself, after standing for three hours near the Queen, seated *incognita* behind a curtain, sought and obtained her permission to sit for the rest of the trial. When however she and Lady Burlington were joined by the Duchess of Somerset and Lady Hyde, Sarah noticed that they insisted upon standing. Early next morning Sarah cornered the Queen. Were her ladies-in-waiting to stand or were they to sit? Anne looked angry and snapped her up, saying she had very little time . . . But Sarah persisted. She was fearful, she said, of doing anything the Queen might dislike. This infuriated Anne, who 'answered very brutally, "I thought I should have been troubled no more with it" '.[35] She needed all her reserve to keep control.

When after a three week's trial Sacheverell had been voted guilty, his light sentence of suspension from preaching (his sermons were to be burned) was almost as much a mockery as the trial itself and the 'nonsensical harangue' of his sermon. Far more significant was the fact that not only Sharp and Compton but the Dukes of Shrewsbury, Somerset and Argyll had all voted in Sacheverell's favour. Scattering blessings and kisses Sacheverell now set out on a triumphal progress; the mob, when not cheering him, burning chapels and threatening to storm the Bank of England. Sunderland, commanded to send the Queen's own guard to disperse them, was reluctant to leave her person unguarded at night. When told of it Anne said God would be her guard.[36]

She was never afraid of the mob, but to others, whether Sarah or Abigail, Harley or the Junto, each besetting her in turn, if not together, she was alarmingly vulnerable. It was not long since Sarah had been plaguing her about the preferment of bishops. Now it was the bedchamberwoman's turn. On March 10th Abigail wrote to Harley:

> Last night I had a great deal of discourse with my aunt & much of it about the two men that are named for bishops.* I told her what a wild character Barton had & that her father never made a worse man one than he is. She said very little to me, but by what she did say I suspect she has promised he shall be one as well as Bradford . . . Now nobody can serve her if she goes on privately doing these things every day when she has had so much said to her as I know she has, both from myself & other people; and because I am still with her people think I am able to persuade her to anything I have a mind to have her do, but they will be convinced to the contrary one time or other. I desired her to let me see you. She would not consent to that & charged me not to say anything to you of what had passed between us. She is angry with me & said I was in a passion. Perhaps I might speak a little too warm, but who can help that when one sees plainly she is giving her best friends up to the rage of their enemies? I have had no rest this night, my concern is so great, and for my part I

* The vacant sees were those of Bristol and St David's and Bristol.

should be glad to leave my aunt before I am forced from her & will see you very soon to talk about that matter, whether she will give me leave or no . . .[37]

Sarah would have been transported to know that Abigail, so new to her role of tormentor, had been checked by Anne's obstinacy; but she was not the only one who believed that Abigail ruled the Queen.

> Bright Masham's the whirlwind that turns us about,
> One whiff of whose breath can bring in or put out.

Shrewsbury told Sarah that Abigail could if she wished it make Anne stand upon her head. It was not true. As a Stuart she would always have a will of her own. She could be teased, nagged, bullied, but she could and would still say no.

On April 4th Anne greeted Dr Hamilton with the remark that if uneasiness could hurt her, she had enough of that now. Hamilton guessed that things had reached that pitch between the Queen and the Duchess that Anne wanted to dismiss her, but not if it meant parting with Godolphin as well. She had hoped that though Marlborough and herself had failed to make her see reason, Godolphin might yet have succeeded; but she now realised it was a hopeless case.

On April 5th Anne, proroguing Parliament for Easter, told the Lords she could 'heartily wish men would study to be quiet rather than busy themselves in disputes which must be with an ill intention since they could only tend to foment their divisions.' She hoped God would 'continue to make her the happy instrument for uniting the hearts of all her subjects';[38] and in that frame of mind, suppressing her own troubles, she prepared for her Easter Communion.

This was the moment Sarah chose to press for a private audience. In a note dated April 3rd Anne had asked her to write, but that, replied Sarah, would not in the circumstances be possible. She must see her before Easter Communion. Anne again asked her to write, adding that gout permitting she would be at Kensington; and it was there, on Maundy Thursday (April 6th) that Sarah, as dusk was falling, ran her to earth.

There was a long pause before she was admitted; during which, Sarah guessed, the Queen was being taught her lines. Sure enough when at last she was shown into the gloomy closet she found Anne armed with parrot-phrases beyond which she knew, from former arguments, it would be fatal to go. Two phrases – 'Whatever you have to say you may put it in writing' and 'You desired no answer and you shall have none' – were, in the same maddening manner practised by James II, repeated again and again. It must, said Maynwaring afterwards, have been like addressing a statue filled with earth. Even Sarah was baffled. She had heard, she said, that the Queen had been told she had said things of her which she was no more capable of saying than of killing her own children. The truth was she seldom in company referred to the Queen at all and never without respect. Anne dared to say that without doubt there were many lies told. Pressed further, however, she fell back on her set part and stonily refused to discuss the matter. Nor could Sarah's sobs (Anne was too used to them) make any impression. It was a macabre scene to which Sarah's thoughts and pen kept returning throughout the rest of her long life. Herself, after Anne's death, the sole eye-witness, she owed it to history to write down every word; and there in her *Conduct* it is: the perfect dialogue with the perfect ending –

Sarah: I am confident your Majesty will suffer for such an instance of inhumanity.

Anne: That will be to myself.

'Thus ended', says Sarah, 'this remarkable conversation, the last I ever had with her Majesty. I shall make no comment upon it. The Queen always meant well, how much soever she might be blinded or misguided'.[39]

On the stage it is very convincing. But then, turning to alternative drafts for *Conduct* and to Dr Hamilton's diary, one finds that the interview, which lasted an hour, did not in fact go quite so neatly. Sarah owns she held forth about the Somersets (the Duchess, as she thought, still impatient for her gold key) and adds that what she said about them was heard with marked attention. What was more, after Sarah had left the Queen and sat in the gallery to dry her tears, she decided to return to exact Anne's promise that should she continue to wait upon her in public she would not be affronted. Instead of denying her an answer Anne then assured her 'very easily' that never in her life had she done such a thing to anyone.[40]

'Upon the whole', wrote Maynwaring to Sarah, 'I think what you did & said was mighty right & what happened to you whilst you were speaking would have moved anyone that had not been insensible'.[41]

Some women thrive on emotional scenes, others recoil from them. Anne was determined that, at least in the case of Sarah, this should be her last. There would inevitably be letters, but on no account would she ever receive her again.

'The Scheme of the Queen's new counsellors to make her ministers quit her service or engage her to discard them', notes Sarah, 'began now to appear without disguise. They durst not tell her Majesty at once all they designed but, proposing to her only one thing at a time, led her by insensible degrees to the accomplishment of the whole'.[42] To the dismissal of Kent – the only Lord Chamberlain never to have been summoned to Anne's Cabinet – no one other than the Bug himself could object, and he would be recompensed with a dukedom. The vital thing was the appointment in his place of the Duke of Shrewsbury. The deed was suddenly done while Godolphin was at Newmarket, and it was from there that he wrote to Anne, '. . . your Majesty is suffering yourself to be guided to your own ruin & destruction as fast as it is possible for them to compass it to whom you seem so much to hearken . . .' Shrewsbury, he went on, had been his friend for years; but capable though he was, what would the world make of the Queen's appointing, without consulting her ministers, a man known to have sided with Harley and, notably in the Sacheverell trial, to have voted against the Government? If this was to be her policy, it must lead to ruin; and for himself he must once more beg leave to retire.[43]

Anne was not to be moved. 'Her Majesty told me', says Hamilton, 'she had made the Duke of Shrewsbury with less trouble than she expected'. Godolphin, too kind, too timorous, was backpedalling. However the Queen chose to act, he assured her, he would do his duty. No one, except possibly Shrewsbury and Somerset, was finding her service easy. Abigail, desperate for leave to see Harley, wrote, 'I have a mind to do it without her knowledge & so secret as to be impossible for any but ourselves to know it, but . . . I dare not stay out of this house past ten o'clock without my aunt's leave'.[44] Even

Harley, who had thrown off the cloak of compromise and was now trying to insist that the Queen must 'govern by one party or the other but not by both', was finding her (and no wonder) sluggish and difficult to convince.[45] In one way and another everything seemed to have gone heavy. Something lighter, something diverting seemed overdue. And so it chanced that for one of his first duties as Lord Chamberlain Shrewsbury was called upon to present to the Queen the four Indian Kings.

Few people in England had seen or imagined such exotics. When Verelst painted them they wore warpaint, blankets and elaborate, beribboned boots; and although in London they had been provided with gilt-edged scarlet mantles, they had at the audience, the Court still being in mourning, to wear black over all. Through an interpreter they told the Queen that they represented the Six Nations inhabiting the wilderness between French Canada and the New England States. 'We have made', they said, 'a long and dangerous voyage that we might have the honour to see and relate to our great Queen what we thought absolutely necessary for the good of her and of us her allies which are on the other side of the great water . . . We were mightily rejoiced last year', they added, 'when we heard that our great Queen desired to send an army and reduce Canada, and were extremely sorry it was prevented for that season . . .' They had brought belts of wampum and necklaces of shells, which they now presented, receiving in return 200 guineas, the Queen's portrait and arms, looking-glasses, a magic-lantern, four laced hats, kettles, razors, scissors and knives, guns and swords. The Archbishop of Canterbury sent Bibles, with an eye to their conversion to Christianity. This too was appreciated. 'We have', they admitted, 'some knowledge of the Saviour of the World and have often been importuned by the French, by priests and presents, to come over to their interest, but had ever esteemed them men of falsehood; but if the great Queen would send some to instruct us, they should find a most hearty welcome'.[46] This last suggestion, it was thought, had been made to them by the Society for the Propagation of the Gospel; but though missionaries were later sent and a chapel was built within an Indian stockade, the country proved for some years too savage and the chapel at Fort Hunter had to be abandoned.

Wherever the Kings went in and about London – to Dr Flamsteed's at Greenwich, to Windsor and Hampton Court, even to a special performance of *Macbeth* – crowds followed and cheered them:

O Princes, who have with amazement seen
So good, so gracious and so great a Queen,
Who from her royal mouth have heard your doom
Secured against the threats of France & Rome,
Awhile some moments on our scenes bestow . . .[47]

But indeed amazement was mutual. Their visit was compared with that of the Queen of Sheba to King Solomon. Thoughts flew to the Magi . . . 'They were men of good presence', says Coke, 'and those who conversed with 'em said that they had an exquisite sense and a quick apprehension'.[48] At the beginning of May they returned to their own countries, leaving England less colourful and the Queen still in mourning.

Anne's main aims at this moment were to dismiss Sunderland and – a very big and very personal worry – to retrieve from Sarah her own private letters ('strange scrawls', as she called them) before they were published. But Sarah had other views. She continued to bombard the Queen with letters, one of them enclosing a note from Somerset 'in which the Queen was treated with little ceremony'. It was not returned. Her persistence might seem like madness, perhaps it was, but she had her purpose. Somerset, she knew, was secretly seeing Harley, and 'that fool', as she told Maynwaring, 'must be exposed and run down'.[49] She knew too (it was the talk of the coffee-houses) that Sunderland was in danger, and she believed as always that the best defence was attack. A forlorn hope was no worse than a challenge. She would go on battering the Queen till she dropped. As for the letters, it had not occurred to her to print them (or so she says) until Shrewsbury and Hamilton began asking for them back. She then saw how foolish she would be to part with a weapon which, even though never used, might be reserved as the very one she would need to protect Sunderland, Godolphin, Marlborough and herself. Indeed in any case for her own defence their evidence was priceless. She showed some of the letters to Hamilton, who quoted them to Anne. She said, 'When people are fond of one another, they say many things, however indifferent, they would not desire the world to know'. Precisely. At the same time she had sense enough to realise that were some of those letters published in her lifetime they would make her the laughingstock of Europe. Sarah for her part told Hamilton frankly that she cared most for self-vindication; for 'she took more pleasure in justifying herself than the Queen did in wearing her crown'.[50]

No doubt Hamilton enjoyed his role of confidential go-between, and no doubt at this time he was useful, whether calming and cautioning Anne or advising Sarah to part with the letters and to address her own only to him, that he might read them aloud to the Queen. It seemed a good plan, if only because Hamilton would be able to tell her how the Queen reacted. The Duchess had her suspicions but she complied – only to be told that Anne usually listened in silence and made no comment.

Nothing the Marlboroughs or Godolphin pleaded could save Sunderland. Indeed Anne, who had never liked him, seemed to take some delight in this thrust to the Whig heart. On June 13th she sent Godolphin a blunt letter:

> Just before I saw you I had sent for Mr Secretary (Boyle) in order to give him my directions to fetch the seals from Lord Sunderland, and I do not see why the Duke of Marlborough's letter should make me alter my resolution, unless I could agree with him that I had done him some hardship, which I am not conscious to myself I have, and I can't but think that all impartial people will be of the same opinion.
>
> It is true indeed that the turning a son-in-law out of his office may be a mortification to the Duke of Marlborough, but must the fate of Europe depend on that and must he be gratified in all his desires and I not in so reasonable a thing as parting with a man who I took into my service with all the uneasiness imaginable and whose behaviour to me has been so ever since, and who I must add is obnoxious to all people except a few? I think the Duke of Marlborough's pressing so earnestly that I should delay my intentions is using me very hardly, and I hope both he and you, when you have considered this matter more calmly and impartially, will not wonder that I do not comply with his desires.

Whoever composed the letter (Sarah found the grammar typical but was certain Anne would never have written 'obnoxious') pursued it next day with another:

> ... I have no thoughts of taking the Duke of Marlborough from the head of the army, nor I dare say anybody else. If he and you should do so wrong a thing at any time, especially at this critical juncture, as to desert my service, what confusion would happen would be at your doors and you alone would be answerable and nobody else ...[51]

Today resignation would be automatic; but of course a comparable situation could not arise. At the Opposition's bidding the Queen (herself neither absolute nor absolutely limited) was using her prerogative to fly in the face of her chosen ministers and so, ultimately, to deliver them into their enemies' hands. Convinced though she may well have been that she was acting for peace and for her country's good, she was still betraying her staff and she must have known it. Marlborough, for a while, was still needed; she had finished with the rest. And Marlborough could not resign without letting down the Allies; nor could Godolphin if Marlborough and the war were to continue to have Whig support.

Sunderland, whose words when offered a pension ('If I cannot have the honour of serving my country I will not plunder it') are perhaps the most quoted of any in Anne's reign, was replaced by the Earl of Dartmouth, described by Macky as a short, thickset man (St John called him a pigmy) who loved to make jokes and laugh at them. A Tory and the son of a Jacobite, he was, surprisingly, Anne's choice, not Harley's. 'I was known', says Dartmouth himself, 'to be no zealous party man'. Heavens no; the last thing she wanted was another Sunderland, 'reflecting in a very injurious manner upon all princes ... as a proper entertainment for her'.[52] Better surely to be served by nonentities and sycophants than mocked by republicans and 'enthusiasts'.

On June 15th, the day Dartmouth was sworn in, the Queen received a deputation from the Bank of England. They, the Governors headed by Sir Gilbert Heathcote, humbly sought her assurance that no further dismissals were intended. 'I have no present intention', she told them, 'to make any further changes, but should I alter any of my ministers it shall be no prejudice either to the Bank or to the common cause'. It was an equivocal answer. Godolphin's letter of dismissal, though not sent till August 7, was drafted early in July.[53] The Tories however regarded the Governors' call as outrageous: were subjects to presume to dictate policy to their Queen? Certainly she should never have been put in such a false position; but that was not their affair. Hamilton afterwards blamed the Queen's advisers for 'loading her character with falsehood . . . Her piety', he felt certain, 'would never suffer her to break her word, as she has been of late charged, it proceeding from too much trust to [in] others & her ignorance in her own affairs by means of this trust, and her repeated indispositions'.[54]

Even now she hesitated, as well she might, to dismiss Godolphin. There was no personal dislike, as there had been with Sunderland; and while it might be true that, as Harley said, the Treasurer every day grew sourer and ruder, Anne's chief objection was that he was so abjectly under the thumb of Sarah. 'It is wonderful', wrote Harley to Newcastle, 'that the passion of a madwoman should so far influence the public affairs and overrule a wise man'.[55] It was Anne's frequent complaint. She would come to a decision with Godolphin, only to find it quickly reversed by Sarah. 'O that my Lord Godolphin would be parted from the Duchess of Marlborough!' she exclaimed to Hamilton, 'I should be very happy but . . .' She knew it was impossible. They were related by marriage, their friendship was lifelong; and had not Anne herself laid it down that 'we four must never part till Death mows us down with his impartial hand'? Hamilton guessed that 'the pressing & teasing of her Majesty had been increased and had succeeded'. Yet she dreaded the consequences. The dismissal itself (must she see him?) would be bad enough, but what of the City? It would be in uproar. The repercussions, she had been warned, might be shattering not only to Britain but to Europe, now heading for peace. She may have hoped that Godolphin's spleen would betray him and provide the excuse for ridding herself of her friend. What he is supposed to have said in the Queen's presence still is not known. Whatever it was it had to serve; and now the long-kept letter of dismissal was amended and sent:

The uneasiness which you have showed for some time has given me very much trouble, though I have borne it, and had your behaviour continued the same it was for a few years after my coming to the crown I could have no dispute with myself what to do. But the many unkind returns I have received since, especially what you said to me personally before the lords, makes it impossible for me to continue you any longer in my service. But I will give you a pension of four thousand a year, and I desire that instead of bringing the staff to me you will break it, which I believe will be easier to us both.[56]

No thanks, no kindness, not even the offer of a farewell interview; nothing of all his guiding and schooling, nothing of friendship or service, nothing but peevishness at 'unkind returns'. When on August 7th he had asked her directly, 'Is it the will of your Majesty that I should go on?' She had answered yes; yet her letter of dismissal bore that same date. She never did a meaner thing. The pension was never paid.

Godolphin in his dignified answer signed himself 'the most humble and most dutiful of all your subjects'. It was painfully true.

Stocks fell. Sarah, knowing it would be retailed to the Queen, told Hamilton how ungenerous she thought it to send Godolphin – 'for so many years consulted as a father' – his dismissal by the hand of Somerset's coachman. If Shrewsbury had not found things too much for him, she said, Harley would have stayed behind the scenes; but as it was, Godolphin had had to go to make way for Harley. Shrewsbury had refused to serve in the Treasury, which would now need to be made a Commission, with the egregious Lord Poulett at its head. Harley became Chancellor of the Exchequer.

Three years later, when Anne was complaining to Hamilton that there was no one she could trust, she remembered that 'she had been dealt insincerely with and teased to do many things against her own inclination, particularly that of turning my Lord Godolphin out'. At the same time she reminded her doctor of how he had repeated to her something he had said to Harley – 'that people said he [Harley] would learn her to equivocate'.[57] That too was true.

CHAPTER ELEVEN

THE GREAT CHANGE

1710 - 1711

'THE Earl of Oxford [Harley] and Lady Masham', writes Swift, 'were the sole persons who brought about that great change'. He then goes on to say that had he been appointed historiographer he would, 'from a sincere honest design of justifying the Queen . . . against a load of scandal . . . thrown on her memory with some appearance of truth', have shown posterity the Queen and her ministers in a true light. 'The scheme I offered', he adds simply, 'was to write her Majesty's reign'.

And why not? We have far too much from Sarah and far too little from the Tory side. Swift blames it on the negligence of Anne, Abigail and Harley that his account of the 'first springs of that great change at Court after the trial of Dr Sacheverell' is imperfect. Yet all this is to oversimplify. Swift, returning from Ireland with Wharton on August 31st, 1710, intent on winning Queen Anne's bounty for the Church in Ireland, received coldly by Godolphin and warmly by Harley, was never, as he so fondly fancied, completely in the know. True he was astonishingly soon in the innermost Tory circle with Harley (the Dragon), St John (Mercurialis), Abigail (Mrs Still) and her sister Alice (the Queen of Prudes). Understandably he flattered himself that none of their many secrets was kept from him.

'He was elated', wrote Lord Orrery, 'with the appearance of enjoying ministerial confidence. He enjoyed the shadow: the substance was detained from him. He was employed, not trusted; and at the same time that he imagined himself a subtle diver, who dexterously shot down into the profoundest regions of politics, he was suffered to sound only the shallows nearest the shore & was scarce admitted to descend below the froth at the top'.[1]

For Harley's purpose – to banish Whigs and Marlboroughs and end the war – that froth, in the pen of Swift (for no other could have done it) was enough. Of intrigue at Versailles and St Germains Swift was told nothing. The Queen too was kept from him.

Abigail had, for good reason, to know a little more. She was required to watch the Queen and to watch Shrewsbury, whose support was vital. Perhaps only she knew that at this very time (August 1710) Harley and Shrewsbury were sending peace-feelers to France. At midnight she writes to Harley:

> My aunt is not very well tonight, so I did not stay long with her. She has flying pains about her as she used to have before a fit of the gout, but I hope the warm weather will prevent that. Say nothing of it to anybody, for without she is laid up with it she does not care to have it known till it is so bad she cannot hide it. I would fain have entered into some discourse which might have led us to have talked of the main point in hand, but whenever I said anything relating to business she answered, 'Pray go, for if you begin to talk you will make it so late I shall not get to bed in any time'. Though I think she is in good humour and has not a desponding countenance as sometimes she has. God Almighty send you health.[2]

In another note to Harley, excusing herself for not 'talking of public matters to Mr Anthony' (Shrewsbury?), she adds, 'You know my shyness & backwardness of talking freely to anybody but such a dear friend as yourself'. And again, 'The Queen is much better today than she was & I hope will be able to see you soon, for I know she desires it very much. I have not named anything to her of business, she has been in such pain. I cannot fix any time of seeing you while the Queen is so very lame . . .'[3]

With Britain's future in the melting-pot – yes, even Europe's – it seemed just then as though the fate of millions hung upon the efficacy of the spirit of millipedes, the only medicine that was being prescribed for the Queen. Her misery and frustration can but dimly be imagined. Knowing and fearing her own helplessness (physical and mental) in any emergency, she was yet too ill even to see the ministers she relied on.

'Depend upon it', Halifax wrote to Newcastle on August 17th, 'your country is at stake and in more danger of being lost than I fancy you imagine . . . I have helped them with the Bank & preach to everybody that the public credit ought to be supported, but if they give continual alarms, make new changes and dissolve this Parliament, we must all sink'. Two days later Somers told Newcastle, 'If we may have a new Parliament & those elections should go ill, as far as I am able to judge we are utterly undone & must not think of a peace with France but upon the terms France will give'.[4]

That was exactly it. The danger was real and Harley knew it, but as always calmest in a crisis, he methodically picked his team: Rochester President of the Council, Buckingham Lord Steward, Ormonde Lord-Lieutenant of Ireland (instead of Wharton), Harcourt Attorney-General, St John Secretary of State (northern division. Dartmouth had succeeded Sunderland for the southern). He would have liked to retain Lord Cowper and so would the Queen, but he would have none of it. 'They carry on things', he protested, 'by trick and contradiction and shuffle, which will make the Queen lose her honour and the affection of her people'.[5] Harley tried all his wiles to keep him – 'All should be easy . . . The danger of going out . . . A Whig game intended at bottom . . .' – but was far too plausible and at the same time almost unintelligible. 'To keep in when all my friends were out', Cowper told him, 'would be infamous'.[6] Though the Queen rejected his resignation half a dozen times, she at last had to yield.

At a meeting of her Privy Council Anne called for a proclamation to dissolve Parliament and, when Harcourt had read it, refused to have it discussed. On September 21st the dissolution dreaded by the Whigs came about. 'I am almost deaf with the huzzas for the Queen and the Church', the obsequious Beaufort told Harley, 'Prosperity and success to the new faithful ministry, a good Parliament and a speedy & lasting peace'.[7]

Not everyone was so pleased. Somerset, Peter Wentworth reported, had left 'in a pet for Petworth', raged at his servants and vowed Harley had tricked him; 'for all he intended to do was to free the Queen from the power of the two great men & was promised that things should be carried no further'. He had reckoned neither on a dissolution nor on being left out of the new deal; but he had not been clever. Now, having flirted with the enemy to no purpose, he was 'looked upon with very contemptible eyes by both parties'.[8]

Marlborough, despairing of the Queen – 'She will risk England',

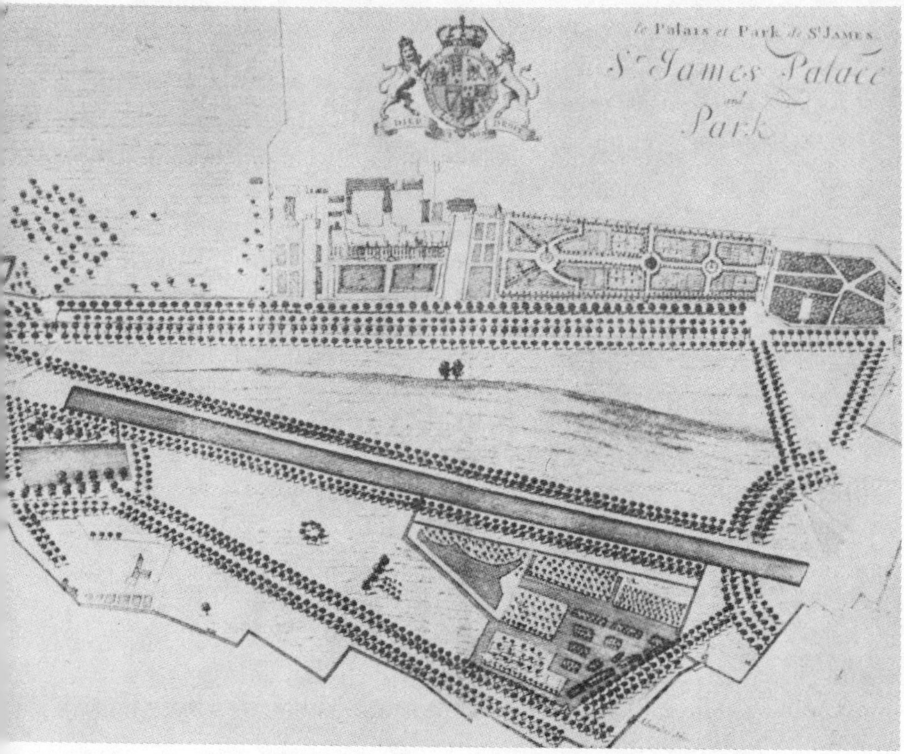

St. James's Park: the Palace gardens running eastward to a formal wilderness. Foreground: the canal and duck-decoy which preceded the lake

Robert Harley, First Earl of Oxford and Mortimer

Belle: James Francis Edward Stuart (The Old Pretender)

Henry St. John, Viscount Bolingbroke

The Duke of Shrewsbury

The Duchess of Somerset

he told his wife, 'rather than not vex you' – turned again to her successor at Hanover. Since 1708, when the Elector had taken offence at not being consulted before the battle of Oudenarde, Marlborough had worked hard and effectually to restore goodwill. Now he warned George against those who were plotting to overturn the Protestant Succession while pouring poison about Hanover into the Queen's ear. He was on a pretty safe wicket, for though George might be fooled, his mother Sophia, with Leibniz at her elbow, could not be bamboozled. Harley's emissary to Hanover, the rakish Rivers, was coldly received; nor did letters from Harley himself make any better impression. 'I have taken the liberty', he wrote, 'to write this in English because I know your Electoral Highness has an English heart and that you may be assured it comes from a heart entirely devoted to your service'.[9] It was not a letter Anne would have been charmed to see. Dr Hutton, a Tory agent then at the Hague, wrote more interestingly. The Queen, he told George in September, was adored by her people. For the past four years she had wanted to be rid of Godolphin and Marlborough but had been prevented. Now Sarah had been banished. The Elector, it was rumoured, was to lead the allied troops as Generalissimo. This would make him the most glorious prince in the world and would win him the love of the British.[10]

Simultaneously Gaultier, in France, was hearing a different story. Abigail, he learned, could be thanked for the fall of Godolphin and for the disgrace of Sarah. Anne would prefer to be succeeded by her stepbrother the Pretender and not by Hanover. Might he not reign in Scotland or settle in England as heir-presumptive?[11]

In Scotland, if Defoe was to be believed, there were not a few Jacobites and Highlanders who 'did not look for their Saviour's coming with half the assurance they did for that of the Pretender'.[12]

Whatever lay locked in the Queen's heart, the façade remained unexceptionable. Opening Parliament at the end of November she said she would employ none but such as were heartily for the Protestant Succession in the House of Hanover, the interest of which family no person could be more truly concerned for than herself.

The October election had given Harley a Tory majority, but he was faced now with a financial crisis grave enough to daunt a Godolphin – and in Treasury matters he was far from that. 'The public credit is fallen past retrieve', Halifax told Newcastle, '... till men's minds are better satisfied of the intentions of the new ministers nothing can raise it ... There are many black clouds gathering from all quarters'.[13]

The Whigs were dismayed but not in despair. Harley too had brilliant men on his side and knew how to use them. Defoe, he remembered, was economist as well as writer. Swift in *The Examiner* had already taken the field. Marlborough loathed and despised lampoons and satires. Harley recognised them as ammunition and was quick to take advantage of the growing power of the press. The main lines of Tory propaganda laid down by Harley and St John were as uncomplicated as were many of the minds at which they were directed. Envy was to be roused, envy of Whig profiteers in the City, who had gained by the war and wanted it to last, and envy of the Captain-General, the biggest profiteer of all. As for the Queen, she was to be pictured as a prisoner, now at long last free to reign as Queen indeed. In his November *Examiners* Swift, anonymously, went at it hammer and tongs:

> Let any man observe the equipages in this town, he shall find the greater number of those who make a figure to be a species of men quite different from any that were ever known before the Revolution; consisting either of generals and colonels or of those whose whole fortunes lie in funds and stocks; so that power which ... used to follow land is now gone over to money ... If the war continues some years longer a landed man will be little better than a farmer of a rack-rent to the army and to the public funds ... The wealth of a nation that used to be reckoned by the value of land is now computed by the rise and fall of stocks.[14]

This was the gospel according to (Henry) St John and it was exactly what Tory landowners, groaning beneath the Land Tax, wanted to hear. Why in the name of fortune should they to their own ruin continue to subsidise a war no one in England wanted? Their money, it was plain to see, enriched army officers and those Whigs who juggled with shares and reaped where they had not sown. Oh no, it was not good enough, England was better than that. The country should be run as it had been by responsible landowners and men of property and by no one else.

Three weeks later Swift followed up with his famous onslaught on the Marlboroughs who, he reckoned, had got away with a good deal above half a million. His Bill of British Ingratitude, which included the cost of building Blenheim, came to £540,000; his Bill of Roman Gratitude, which included laurels for the conqueror's brow (tuppence) came to £994 11s 10d. At least founded on fact, it was skilfully done and must have raised many chuckles. Unhappily and foolishly he went on to accuse Sarah of pocketing £22,000 a year of the Queen's money, which was so manifestly false that it cast doubt over the whole attack.[15] Everyone knew that Sarah, though in some ways preposterous, was scrupulously straightforward about money. The charge might surely be ignored. But no; for Sarah, self-vindication was now everything; the Queen must be told and Hamilton must see to it. He did. Anne's comment, when the libel had been read to her, was typical. 'Everybody knows', she said, 'cheating is not the Duchess of Marlborough's fault'. But Hamilton was not sure that this would satisfy her. 'A woman of sense and passion provoked', he warned the Queen, 'does often turn malicious'. As it was, she had sent in a bill for £16,000: eight years' back pay of the £2,000-a-year she had refused to accept. Anne blushed, appeared very uneasy and 'looked out of countenance and as if she had much rather not have allowed it', but she did allow it.

On the subject of the *Examiner* Sarah was fairly well informed. 'I have very good reason to believe', she told Hamilton, 'that Mr St John's is the chief instruction of the person that writes it, who has not one single qualification of any merit and is notorious for being of a scandalous & profligate life & conversation . . . It is pretty difficult to be silent under such provocations and . . . very hard & unjust in Mrs Morley to suffer such things'.[16] She persuaded Maynwaring to reply in *The Medley*, which he did, claiming that Marlborough's conquests had enriched the Allies by some eight million pounds.

In this last, post-mortem stage of their friendship Anne felt fear and dislike, Sarah disgust and hatred. Dining at Lord Cowper's Sarah told him the Queen had no original thoughts on any subject, was 'neither good nor bad but as put into'; that she had much love and passion, while pleased, for those who pleased her, and could write pretty affectionate letters, but could do nothing else well.[17]

Anne's affectionate letters to Sarah were still matter for concern. Hamilton's entry for November 30 reads as follows:

> The Queen discoursing of having her original letters from the Duchess of Marlborough, in order to make what she said of less value, for if it was seen or printed *that she wished never to see heaven if ever she parted from her*, how reflecting that would be. And since the letters could not be taken away by force, perhaps upon my Lord's coming over, matters might be so settled as that she might have them. The Queen said all these promises were nothing now. I said she knew that best but that I durst not say so, and would endeavour if possible to obtain them from the Duchess, because I found her extremely willing to gratify her Majesty in many things . . . I having no by-end but her Majesty's honour, health and quiet of mind.

Under December 9 he notes: 'The Queen positive she would never see her more, and it would look odd to keep her in and she never come to her'. The thought of Sarah busy with her *Conduct* increased Anne's uneasiness. It was all very well for her to take such pains with her side of the picture, but what of the other side? 'She says that she says no shocking things to me', observed Anne, 'but that I say them all to her'. Quick to accuse the Queen of doing and saying wrong things, she 'never owned herself doing or saying so'. Consider one example, when at the close of their last interview she had warned Anne that 'God would punish her either in this world or in the next for what she had done to her that day'. The idea of 'passing a sentence upon anybody' was shocking; that, said Anne, was 'a thing between God and themselves'.

When Sarah spoke, she added, it was always in passion, 'which is uneasy to me'. That was why she had told her to write. Sometimes indeed she had stormed so fiercely that the Queen had felt bound to detain her until it had blown over. She had to her face called her a liar and had repeated it to others. She had further accused her of spending hours in her late husband's closet with Abigail when in fact, said Anne, 'I was there on melancholy occasions'. Once she went so far as to say she hoped Anne might some day need her help so that she might have the pleasure of withholding it.

In view of all this the notion that Sarah should keep her offices without coming to Court was plainly ridiculous. As Anne reasonably said, 'If the Duchess offered to kill me, must I not put her away? And does she not go about to take away my name and reputation, which is all one?[18] For Christmas Anne would come out of mourning for George; but she could manage well enough without her Mistress of the Robes. An arbitrator? A priest to mend their quarrel? God forbid! 'Pray', she begged Hamilton, 'keep her from that'.

It was of course an impossible situation, a crisis beyond even Marlborough to settle. 'He was told', wrote St John, 'that his true interest consisted in getting rid of his wife, who was grown to be irreconcilable with the Queen, as soon as he could and with the best grace he could . . . What is the effect of all this plain dealing? He submits, he yields, he promises to comply . . .'[19] When told of the affection with which Marlborough still spoke of her Anne 'melted'. He longed, he said, to 'have his wife quiet. For himself, he was all duty and submission, asking nothing but the Queen's smile.' When he arrived, Anne said she was sorry to see him looking so broken; but a day or two later, noticing some improvement, she said she thought it could only have been fatigue. Others however were shocked at the change in his looks. 'Marlborough has suffered so much,' wrote Count Gallas, 'he no longer looks like himself'.[20]

By January 17th Anne had finally decided that Sarah would have to go. 'Visiting the Queen', notes Hamilton, 'she ordered me that if they [the Marlboroughs] spoke of her laying down [Sarah's resigning], to give into it, but not to mention it either to him or her as of myself; the Queen saying that if my Lord cried a little it would then be over. I mentioned how ill he was and how affected, and said that his dependance was on the Queen's compassion for him'. The same day Hamilton, having advised Marlborough to await a favourable moment, told Sarah, 'I am of opinion today is most fitting. There seemed to be great tenderness'.[21] Accordingly Marlborough went, taking with him Sarah's letter of submission in which she apologised and promised to do anything the Queen thought reasonable. She feared, she said, that unless an end were put to Marlborough's sufferings on her (Sarah's) account, he could not live another six months. It was an abject and moving letter, which left Anne cold and adamant. At first she refused to read it at all and when she did she said, 'I cannot change my resolution'. Marlborough begged for time. Only postpone the blow until the end of the campaign, when they both might retire together . . . an honourable retreat . . . nothing ill meant . . . barbarous to deny so small a favour etc.

Anne was as unyielding as she had been with Sarah. Marlborough, well briefed, was determined at least to discover what exactly was laid to his duchess's charge. Anne would not answer. Something was mumbled about her honour, and that was all.[22] She demanded Sarah's gold key of office: it must be brought to her within three days. Marlborough on his knees pleaded for ten. 'Two days', said Anne. He was now at a loss. His other purpose had been, as Captain-General, to protest vehemently against the dismissal of three of his best officers for, as he had been told, drinking his health; but the Queen cut him short. 'I will talk of no other business', she said, 'till I have the key'. It was not an edifying scene. 'Let us make haste', writes Sir Winston, 'to draw the curtain upon an unnatural spectacle which reduces the stature of a soldier without raising the majesty of a queen'.[23]

Sarah, says Dartmouth, threw the key on the floor and insisted on its being returned to the Queen at once. '. . . and the true reason why I was in so much haste to have it given', she wrote afterwards, 'was because I hoped he might have been allowed to have quitted upon the affront in the affair of the officers and I had a mind to have the key given before this came out, that people might not say he quitted upon the account of my places, which many thought was wrong, though I confess I thought using his wife so ill was as great an affront as any, but could not be sure I was not too partial in that matter . . . I must not forget', she adds, 'that when Lord Marlborough delivered the key I desired to know what her Majesty was pleased to say upon it, but he could give me no other account than that she mumbled something which he could not understand nor make anything of, by which I concluded that speech was her own; and indeed after they had got the key it was needless for them to make any more speeches for her upon that subject, which would have been so much labour lost, besides the pains of getting them by heart; and she has an easy way that I have often known her practise with great success upon many occasions when she has not known what to say, which is to move only her lips and make as if she had said something when in truth no words were uttered.'[24]

With so accomplished a diplomat on his knees before her – friend, prince, saviour of Europe – silence cannot have been easy. And yet what could she say? There were moments, Marlborough thought, when she looked as though she wanted to speak. But where to begin, where end? Better, surely, to say nothing at all. For some things – looks, scenes, tones of voice – words are inadequate; and as Sarah added darkly, 'There are yet many things untold for which there wants a name'.

Hamilton's entry for January 18th is chatty and domestic: 'The Queen told me the Duke had been there and was not so tender as one might have expected, and said it would be more for his and her quiet to prevail with her to lay down [with Sarah to resign]. He said he would endeavour it & if in a fortnight he could not accomplish it, she might do what she thought best; and this being concerted, [the Queen] ordered me not to go [to the Marlboroughs] unless they wrote'. This does not tally with other accounts. However, under January 19 he adds, 'The Queen told me the Duke had brought the key last night'.[25]

The Christmas junketings, with the Queen out of mourning, had, says Boyer, been 'much appalled by the ill news from Spain'. By their defeat at Brihuega, where Stanhope was taken prisoner, the Allies' hopes of victory in Spain were finally extinguished. Louis XIV ordered another *Te Deum*.

In England the most Marlborough could do for his cashiered officers was to obtain leave for them to sell their commissions; for not only had they drunk confusion to his enemies, but they had also, it was said, fired at a scarecrow they had made and labelled Harley. For himself, as he said, nothing would have been easier than to throw England and her Allies into confusion by resigning. He could not bring himself to do it. The Hanover envoy Robethon, reporting this to the Elector, added:

> The Queen can be led where she does not think she is going. I cannot

describe to you to what degree her favourite & Mr Harley control her. They can raise & lower her mood at their pleasure. The poor Queen has still from time to time this winter had openings of heart to me, which have made me realise to what a point these people have laid hold of her mind . . . The best policy for the present is for your Highness to humour the Queen as much as possible & to live with her Majesty & with her ministers on the best terms.[26]

On all sides the air seems heavy with hypocrisy and bluff. Harley as always thrives on it. And Marlborough? Bluffing the enemy has long been part of his profession. Among Harley's undated musings at Longleat there is this:

Either the Duke of Marlborough is in earnest or not . . . If not in earnest then he only designs to amuse us in order to cover some other purpose. If this be the case it will be right to amuse him & to keep on such a treaty with him as may not let him despair on one side & on the other may oblige him to give fresh assurances or proofs which may obtain credit that he is not carrying on a double game.[27]

The double game in which all were involved had a double title: the Peace and the Succession. Provided cards were face down, any number could play and rules were made and broken as one went along. The Queen was known to hate Hanover, while going through the motions of loving it or at least of approving its succession to her crown, as by law established. But what if the Pretender should turn Protestant, or suppose that Hanover should further offend the Queen? To the very end she would keep them guessing; for as Swift said, 'There was not perhaps in all England a person who understood more artificially to disguise her passions'.[28]

In January 1711 the Abbé Gaultier, with the connivance of Harley and Shrewsbury, was smuggled through the lines to Paris with orders to test the possibilities of beginning discussions for peace. Gaultier had been chaplain to Marshal Tallard, himself regarded in France, after his capture at Blenheim, as their most promising peacemaker. Since then the *Abbé* had schemed with the Jacobite Earl of Jersey, married to a French Catholic, while acting as chaplain to the Austrian Ambassador. Gaultier was in fact the accredited emissary of Louis XIV's minister de Torcy, whom he later requested to prepare for the British ministers in London a 'spontaneous offer' of negotiations for peace.

Gaultier is said also to have approached Berwick with the suggestion that 'Queen Anne should enjoy the Crown in tranquillity during her life, provided she confirmed the possession of it to her brother after her death';[29] but if Gaultier did so, he was almost certainly exceeding his brief. The Queen knew nothing of it.

Harley was exactly suited to these stratagems. He now turned from France to Hanover, to tell George of Sarah's dismissal. 'The causes of this lady's disgrace', he wrote, 'have been so public and of so many years' continuance that it will be needless to trouble your Electoral Highness on that head. The places will be speedily disposed and the chiefest will fall to the share of the Duchess of Somerset . . . I shall think myself extremely happy', he ended, 'if any occasion shall be ever offered me to manifest the great veneration & duty wherewith I am, may it please your Electoral Highness, your Highness's most humble, most dutiful and most obedient servant'.[30] Since the days when he had sworn lifelong devotion to Marlborough and Godolphin, Harley's style had not changed; for though to Anne's successor he had not yet offered to bare his soul, there were signs that by scattering bugwords, as Sarah called them (Highness, Majesty and the rest), he was hoping to make a good impression. On his desk one morning he found an anonymous note:

> Be not unmindful of a counter mine! It hath by some been observed that the Queen is pleased with another Duchess, by whom a scheme is formed which (if it succeeds) you cannot approve of.[31]

There might be something in it; but he had taken his measures. Abigail was now Keeper of the Privy Purse and while she was in attendance he could be certain that the Duchess of Somerset would be closely watched. But if only she had been a Tory! Swift feared the Whigs meant to play with her the same game that had been played against them.

Lord Cowper, calling on the Marlboroughs the day after Sarah's dismissal, was astonished to find her sitting beside Marlborough's bed (himself languidly stretched upon it) and raging aloud about the Queen. When he whispered to Marlborough he was assured in his plaintive voice that nobody minded her when she was in a passion, which she pretty often was.[32] She would not of course be at the Queen's birthday celebrations, now boycotted by most of the Whig women. The Tory duchesses however glittered so dazzlingly, it was said no finer Court had been seen since 1660. The Princess (Duchess of Buckingham) and Lady Poulett were 'scarce able to move under the load of jewels'. Gout was forgotten. The Queen, in green flowered satin embroidered with gold, was treated to 'an Italian dialogue in her Majesty's praise, set to excellent music by the famous Mr Handel, a retainer to the Court of Hanover in the quality of Director of His Electoral Highness's Chapel . . . and sung by Grimaldi & the other celebrated voices of the Italian Opera, with which her Majesty was extremely well pleased. The Duke of Marlborough did not appear at this festival, having with her Majesty's leave set out the Friday before for Blenheim House with the Governor of Brussels'.[33]

At Blenheim Marlborough congratulated Wise on his fruit trees, which had shot to admiration, but showed some anxiety about Vanbrugh's gigantic bridge. Would there be earth enough to join it to the sides of the valley? Wise assured him there would. The Queen's gardener needed to be versatile. Back in London he was commanded to ship immediately ten brace of spotted deer from the royal parks to the Emperor of Morocco. He demurred. The does were pregnant; in the heat they might die. He was overruled and several of them died on the voyage. The Moroccan Ambassador was desolate. Addressing Anne as 'the Most Glorious of the Greatest Princes that are Followers of the Messiah, Chosen and Separated by God to the Highest Dignity Among Christian People', he threatened reprisals on captured Britons if his master – Descendant of the Family of Ottoman Whose Reign May God Perpetuate to the Day of Judgment – were not compensated with instant replacements.[34] It was another urgent job for Wise.

Nothing was easy. Harley was finding the Queen intractable. Supply bogged down and St John, his righthand man, whoring after October Club extremists and writing treacherously to France. By the end of February Harley was facing a crisis.[35]

'We are plagued here', Swift told Stella on February 18th, 'with an October Club, that is a set of above 100 parliament-men of the country, who drink October beer at home and meet every evening at a tavern near the Parliament to consult affairs and drive things on to extremes against the Whigs, to call the old ministry to account and get off five or six heads . . . The Queen, sensible how much she was governed by the late ministry, runs a little into t'other extreme and is jealous in that point even of those that got her out of the others' hands'. And again on March 4th: 'They have cautioned the Queen so much against being governed that she observes it too much'.

It was irony indeed for those who had 'rescued' the Queen to find that they had but reinforced her obstinacy. Did she trust them? Harley yes, but St John . . . one might judge him by his company.

The Marquis de Guiscard, once employed by Marlborough as a captain of Huguenots, and received by the Queen at Windsor, had since become one of St John's drinking companions, shared one of his mistresses and was suspected of being a spy. On his pension of £500 a year he was comfortable enough in London until Harley suddenly reduced it to £400. He was furious and began to intrigue with France, using Lady Dorchester (once James II's mistress) as go-between until his letters fell into the hands of her husband, Lord Portmore, who told Harley. Harley then had de Guiscard watched and early in February was rewarded with two incriminating packages of letters addressed to British officers in Flanders. They contained Cabinet secrets.

For the accession-anniversary on March 8th Harley wore the same waistcoat (silver and blue, embroidered with gold brocade flowers) he had first put on for the Queen's birthday. Under it he wore flannel and on top of it a heavy buff coat. It kept him warm but as armour it was to prove barely enough.

De Guiscard, arrested in St James's Park, was brought for questioning to the Cockpit. The Council met in the room where Greg had been interrogated, Harley sitting next to St John. Two clerks sat at a table. De Guiscard, a remarkably handsome man, was truculent and remained so even when faced by the treasonable letters. After further questions St John rang for messengers to take the prisoner away. De Guiscard, shouting 'J'en veux donc à toi!' sprang at Harley and stabbed him twice with a pen-knife he had found in an outer room. There was complete confusion. St John, shouting

'The villain has killed Mr Harley!' broke his sword on de Guiscard who, three times wounded, begged the Duke of Ormonde to finish him off. ''tis for the hangman', said the Duke. When the messengers burst in one of them, Wilcox 'a very robust & strong man', grappled with de Guiscard and gave him bruises, one of which, in the back, was afterwards judged to have caused his death.[36]

St John wrote of Harley, 'I who have always admired him never did it so much. The suddenness of the blow, the sharpness of the wound, the confusion which followed could neither change his countenance nor alter his voice'.[37]

The penknife, transfixing a gold flower in the waistcoat, broke off or it might have killed him. As it was, Harley was very ill. The Queen thought he was dead and would not at first believe otherwise. She wept for two hours and, after sleepless nights, was found by four of her doctors (summoned at five a.m.) to be in a fever. 'Her solicitude for his health and safety after his recovery . . . became almost obsessive'.[38]

By keeping de Guiscard alive it was hoped to make him confess that he knew of a plot for a Jacobite invasion and that he had meant to kill the Queen. He had been seen in the neighbourhood of the back stairs and of the bakery where, it was guessed, he intended to poison the Queen's bread. But all this he denied. The Queen, he said, was a good woman and had always treated him very civilly. He refused to let anyone dress his wounds from which 'he wished he might die'. He died in Newgate on March 17th. Soon afterwards the keeper of the prison sent in his bill:

For chickens, broths, water gruel, jellies & brandy for bathing his bruises etc.	£3 2s 6d
Expended on the jury	£7 9s 10½d
Expended in wine at my house	£2
Expenses of his burial	£3 6s
A new bed & furniture spoiled	£8
To repair the damages done to the floors & ceilings of two rooms by the salt water that ran out of his coffin	£5
For his lodging in my house with the inconveniencies attending it & for my extraordinary care, attendance & watching, having no salary for	

the same & being at £200 p.a. charges only for the accommodation of unhappy gentlemen £64 10s

On March 9th Parliament presented an address to the Queen, that they would effectually stand by and defend her person and those employed under her against all attempts of her enemies; that she would please to take care of herself and issue a proclamation to banish all Papists ten miles from London.[40]

Dartmouth, who was apt to exaggerate, asserted that on the evening before his attempt on Harley de Guiscard was actually in the Queen's presence, 'and nobody in the outer room but Mrs Fielding or within call but Mrs Kirk who was commonly asleep'.[41] There could be no doubt that, although on paper her household was large and there was strong competition for sinecures, the security arrangements were dangerously crude. Shrewsbury was appalled. Wherever she was, he reminded Harley (and none knew it better than he did) her back stairs were made 'the common way to come to her . . . I have lived in four Courts', he said, 'and this is the first where I have ever seen anybody go up the back stairs unless such as the Prince would have come to him unobserved'.[42]

Harley, slowly recovering from his wounds, received another anonymous letter:

> The writer hereof this morning dreamt that a parcel of discontented captains & soldiers [spelt soulgiers] was drawn up within the courtyard at the new house next St James's [Marlborough House] and whilst one party of them went & seized the guards at St James's, another party with leaders hauled [themselves] out of the cellars of the new house, got over the wall into the Queen's gardens & got into the house of a sudden & seized the Queen before anybody could come at her. I hope never such a thing will come to pass, yet revolving in my mind that I have heard of dreams that have come true, I make bold to write this letter to your Lordship, thinking it can do no hurt to let you know it. I will make no observation but leave it to your Lordship that if any have such ill thoughts to attempt such a thing, that house is ill situated.[43]

The de Guiscard affair was of course a gift to any political writer, and Swift was much tempted.* In the event however and most reluctantly (knowing that St John claimed that de Guiscard's knife had

* Swift did in fact publish a 'St John' version in *The Examiner* (15 March 1711).

been meant for himself: a most delicate situation), he found it prudent to pass the job on to one of those hacks he called his under-spur leathers: Mrs Rivella Manley, author of the *New Atlantis*. He could have done worse; she was not ungifted. Her weakness, apart from being totally without principle, was one which persists in some writers to this day. Her fancy could not be bounded. She wrote luridly and euphorically, as though for a novelette:

> He generally carried a bottle of poison and . . . it is almost past doubt that he did design to kill the Queen and, failing of his attempt there, stabbed Mr Harley, as by his own confession he would have done Mr St John, because they were the two important lives that gave dread and anguish to that monarch [Louis XIV] who has so long and often been the terror of others. The Queen, all merciful and saintlike as she is, had herself the goodness . . . to appoint two surgeons and two physicians to attend him in Newgate with whatever was befitting a man of family. This gracious treatment could depart only from a mind so conversant with Heaven, so near of kindred as that of our pious Queen. Her cares and prayers were the balm that healed Mr Harley's wound. The honour that was done by the address of Parliament will never be forgotten, nor her Majesty's gracious answer. It is remarkable that when it was brought into the House of Lords the Whigs all went out except one . . .

After heaping Harley with every imaginable virtue and accomplishment ('We talk with veneration of the Cecils, but posterity shall boast of Harley as a prodigy in whom the spring is pure as the stream'), Mrs Manley rounded off her eulogy with – 'We have now a Queen and ministry of consummate piety, prudence and abilities, who know the true interest of England and will pursue it'.[44]

It was, once more, the heaven-on-earth picture Harley wanted the mob to admire: an angelic Queen attended by ministers but a little less saintly than herself. For him, after all, an angel in the guise of an assassin had overnight made him a martyr, the role for which nature would seem to have designed him. The one drawback was the length of his convalescence. It meant that St John would have to be told of the secret peace-feelers. It meant too that he would leap at the chance to further his own schemes (notably the expedition to Quebec) and to try to cultivate the Queen.

The Queen too took time to recover. Her guards were doubled, the locks were changed. She remained ill and shaken. Hearing that de Guiscard's corpse, pickled in a trough, was being exhibited for money, she commanded that it instantly be buried. 'In this month of March', notes Hamilton, 'the Queen's fever took away the opportunity of converse'. He too had been ill and on his recovery, talk turned to doctors:

> The Queen told me Dr Radcliffe was the last man she would take in and gave me leave to say so. Dr Mead moved for [suggested] steel, but she did not go into it . . . He said one thing she never heard before, that Bath was not proper for the gout.[45]

On March 20th Peter Wentworth noted that the Queen was 'quite rid of her ague' and went on to say, 'They kept it a secret till the danger was past, how many fits she had had; so that when Dr Radcliffe heard her physicians had given her the bark [quinine] upon her first fit . . . he said the Elector of Hanover was to pay the Queen's doctors'. And on the 27th: 'The Queen was at the Chapel last Sunday and was so well as to see company in her bedchamber afterwards'.[46]

'The Queen is well', Swift told Stella on April 28th, 'but I fear will be no long liver, for I am told she has sometimes the gout in her bowels'. It became common knowledge that the Queen's health had been shaken, and even when in the spring she moved to Windsor she continued to give audience in her bedchamber, her macaw perched behind her upon an Indian screen.

Very gradually and reluctantly the secrets of the peace preliminaries were leaking out. At first only Harley and Shrewsbury knew; then the Queen. In April it was the turn of St John and the rest of the Cabinet. Sooner or later and preferably later the Allies would have to be told. But it would still be important not to tell Marlborough. He had won the war but he was to have nothing to do with making the peace.

'Upon the whole', wrote Shrewsbury to Harley on April 26th, 'I could wish the Queen would speak of it tonight to the Cabinet, as a paper come to her hands without saying how, and in the Cabinet let them debate in what manner it should be sent to the Pensioner [of Holland]'.[47]

But a few days before, the whole situation had been changed by the death from smallpox of the Emperor Joseph of Austria. By inheriting his vast possessions his brother Charles could no longer be regarded, even potentially, as King of Spain. The young man who had insisted upon kissing the hem of Anne's robe at Windsor was now Emperor. In England 'No Peace Without Spain!' sounded more nonsensical than ever, while in Holland 'the project of driving Philip of Anjou out of Spain was looked upon to be a pure chimera'.[48]

Looking back to that spring of 1711 one sees, with St John, expediency triumphant; and, with the Jacobites, wishful thinking disguised in the cloak of conviction. Holland is told that the peace proposal comes not from us but from Louis XIV. Lord Jersey never questions but that the Pretender's claims will form part of the peace treaty. One had to be realistic. 'If he changes his religion or even remains a Roman Catholic in private, well and good. Otherwise he could not reign two years in England without meeting the same fate as his father. Why not marry him to a Protestant princess? His mother must remain in France. She will be paid a pension on condition she never returns to England'.[49] Lord Middleton, writing from St Germains to de Torcy, adopts the same no-nonsense style: 'When the Princess of Denmark dies, the King of England [Pretender] is resolved to go at once to England, and to this end measures are being taken to keep him well posted'.[50]

Anne was to be persuaded, once the peace-treaty had been signed, to let the Pretender return to England, on the understanding that she should enjoy the Crown for life. But this was underestimating Anne. During her lifetime, as she had said, no successor, whether from Hanover or France, would be tolerated in her country, no, not even for a week. And as for the Pretender, though there had at one time been tenderness to the point of tears, his abortive attempt upon her crown in 1708 had brought her to her senses; and Sarah testified that in all the years she had known her she never once heard Anne say a good word for him. Even so, Anne had a conscience; and as she neared her end the one thing everyone wondered and the one she was determined to keep to herself, whatever she might choose to tell them, was how in her heart of hearts she felt about her stepbrother James Francis Edward and the Succession. Hanover was odious, a Roman Catholic equally so. Yet what if he should change or, like Charles II, dissemble his religion? Procrastination was her answer. Things changed, princes died (France had lost its Dauphin, Austria its Emperor), anything could happen, the world might end (they kept saying it would), one had but to wait and see.

Harley, like the Queen, was better, though not fully recovered. In May his South Sea scheme was approved by both Houses. Its ingenuity spoke of Defoe, though his name was not mentioned. Harley alone was congratulated upon 'finding a way to satisfy immense public debts and opening such a vein of riches as may make this nation more than sufficient amends for the vast expenses of two successive tedious wars'.[51] At its launching in 1711 the South Sea Company, offering Government investment at six per cent, did what it set out to do, restored credit. Lord Stanhope calls it far more specious than solid. Perhaps it was. But the wild speculation which burst the Bubble in 1720 and ruined thousands (including Sir David Hamilton) could not fairly be laid at Harley's door.

On May 29th Harley was rewarded with the Lord Treasurership and an earldom; and to judge from the preamble to his patent of honour one would suppose him to have rescued the nation from daylight robbery. He had taken his title 'from the city where learning flourishes in so high a degree, himself the ornament of learning and patron of learned men'. Because his claim to the earldom of Oxford was disputed by the Berties, Harley was allowed to add 'and Mortimer' to his title. If the Bertie claim succeeded (regrettably it did not), he could always fall back on the alternative. 'This man', wrote Swift admiringly, 'has grown by persecutions, turnings out and stabbing'. How much farther was he to go?

Three days after his promotion the new Lord Treasurer was faced with a bill for £28,036 for equipping St John's expedition to Quebec which, led by Abigail's brother, Jack Hill, had sailed for Canada in April. St John, furious at having the bill queried, 'procured the Queen's positive pleasure to have it paid'. Oxford, who with the late Earl of Rochester had vainly tried to stop the whole project, investigated and found that from this one contract St John and his friend Arthur Moore had creamed £21,000 to line their pockets.

For the rest of the year most of Oxford's time was spent in peace-negotiations not only with the rest of Europe but with his own colleagues, St John, Dartmouth and Abigail, who quarrelled with him and among themselves.[52] Most if not all of this bickering could for the time being be kept from Anne. It was better that she should hear of the crimes of others, of millions lost in Whig peculation or of Sarah's plundering the lodgings she was leaving at St James's of marble chimneypieces and brass locks.* It was to be Anne's last wound from that quarter and not a serious one. Nevertheless she was incensed.

Reading between a great many lines, most of them Sarah's, one gathers that she stripped the lodgings (almost certainly earmarked for Abigail) of everything except the chimneypieces, which Marlborough had from Flanders begged her to leave. Abigail, seeing the desolation, ran to fetch the Queen, whose reactions were as she had calculated: dismay and fury. She took her humour from Abigail, says Sarah, and reflected her anger. Very well, other people's houses might be left in the same condition. In the code of the day Sarah was told, '42 is so angry she says she will build no house for 39 [Marlborough], when 240 [Sarah] has pulled hers to pieces'.[53] Blenheim, as far as Anne was concerned, might remain unfinished. The only thing was, grants for that building could still be used as an inducement for Marlborough to stay at the front until everyone was prepared for his dismissal. In August Swift was able to tell Stella, 'The Queen has ordered £20,000 to go on with the building at Blenheim, which has been starved till now since the change of the ministry. I suppose it is to reward his last action of getting into the French lines'.[54]

As one may still judge from the Blenheim tapestries, Marlborough was as proud of passing the *ne plus ultra* lines at Bouchain as he was of any of his better known victories; and indeed throughout Europe it was regarded, as Sir Winston has said, as his finest stratagem and manoeuvre. It was his last great work. 'If I could in quietness and without great inconveniency of old age enjoy two or three years of yours and my children's company', he wrote to Sarah, 'I should bless God and think myself happy . . . I know the intentions of those

* If, as seems likely, the locks were by the Queen's locksmith Josiah Key (or Kay), they would be worth taking. Key was known in his day as 'the most ingenious man in Europe'.

that now govern is that I am to have nothing to do in the peace. This is what I am extreme glad of, but they must not know it'.[55]

His enemies tried to write off Bouchain as the taking of a dovecote, which St John said had cost the Allies nearly seven million pounds: the total the war had cost them for the campaign of 1711. It had become fashionable to decry everything he had ever done, although at the time, as Sarah put it, the public had seemed pleased with it. Talking to the Queen, of Marlborough, Hamilton told her, 'The Duke asked me what people said of his conduct to the Queen and nation. I told him some gave him as great or greater character for that victory over himself under provocations than for all his other victories'. The Queen too, thought Hamilton, deserved praise for her patience. Her new tormentors, he said, should be warned that 'nothing lessened love like the objects of it giving disquiet. This was what [had] lessened her affection for the Duchess of Marlborough and would again do the same to those who gave her uneasiness. But I must say', Hamilton adds, 'Her Majesty was to me a pattern of patience, and her bearing so much turned her into a subject to be afraid, instead of a Queen to cause terror in others. This I can demonstrate by letting the whole world know that she has denied even her own inclinations that she might not provoke those about her and so by provocation be made uneasy in her own mind; which often forced her to have conversation with me *incognita*, both to keep herself quiet and me from being injured, which she often said was pity when I sought no by-end but only aimed at her health and quiet'.[56]

Hidden amid this labyrinth of words one suspects the presence of a human being, of whom his fellow-doctors were jealous; while beneath that heavy disguise of brocades and bandages there still seemed a fair chance of finding (or so thought Hamilton) a compassionate woman.

CHAPTER TWELVE

THE PEACEMAKERS

1711 - 1712

FROM the summer of 1711, a time of peacemaking, until her death in 1714, Anne's existence, as Pope wrote of Sarah, was one warfare upon earth. Again and again her Stuart willpower needed to be drawn on to overcome pain and force herself to attend Cabinet meetings or even to career along her chaise-ridings in her crazy high-wheeled gig. Her health, never good, was steadily declining. At forty-six she was huge and unweildy and prematurely aged. All she wanted was peace for herself and for her country, and that she was impatient for it did but reflect, as her humour often did, the spirit of the nation. In a typical note to Harley, now Earl of Oxford, she says:

I have been in so much pain all the last night and this day that it is not easy to me now to write, and therefore I hope you will excuse me for only thanking you for your letter and assuring you I do not at all doubt of the sincerity of your friendship for her that is with all sincerity your very affectionate friend . . .

. . . and the postscript: 'If it please God to send me a tolerable good night I intend to write to you again tomorrow morning'.[1] Ten days later she is hoping with the help of a stick to be able to walk to Council. Yet only the previous month Swift was telling Stella of Anne's driving like Jehu and hunting the stag for forty miles until four in the afternoon. His description of Anne's drawingroom that summer is a masterpiece of considered flatness:

August 8. There was a drawingroom today at Court but so few company that the Queen sent for us into her bedchamber where we made our bows and stood, about twenty of us, round the room, while she looked at us round with her fan in her mouth and once a minute said about three words to some that were nearest her and then she was told dinner was ready and went out.[2]

Anne dined alone; but Swift managed to eat well at another of her tables, provided by the Board of the Green Cloth: 'much the best table in England and costs the Queen £1,000 a month while she is at Windsor or Hampton Court . . . the only mark of magnificence or hospitality I can see in the Queen's family'.[3] Food in the summer would be good, if a little dull. In the winter even for the rich there was not much meat besides venison; a balanced diet was not thought of. Anne almost certainly ate and drank unwisely, though according to Sarah, not to excess. In drinks she is said to have favoured chocolate, often last thing at night; and if for gout she took laudanum on toast floating in brandy (a prescription at Blenheim), no sufferer could possibly blame her; there was nothing much else to take.

That summer, but for the Somersets and Oxford, she would have been very much alone. Hamilton was recuperating from gout at Bath. Abigail, away for two months, gave birth on August 15 to a son. Somerset's attempted return to the Council was frustrated by St John, who refused to sit with him. His wife however, in Abigail's absence, was steadily gaining favour with the Queen. Not surprisingly, Anne was cautious, but she smiled on her enough to cause the utmost anxiety among the Tories. It was agony for them to see a Whig gaining ground; and they had never a doubt but that absence cooled the Queen's heart, whether the absentee were Sarah or Abigail; and for no matter how valid a reason. There was one good thing: Sarah was out of the running; and Marlborough and his dovecote might be forgotten while thoughts turned to Versailles. Even now the dove of peace in the guise of three emissaries (Mesnager, Gaultier and Matthew Prior)* should be winging its way back to London, swiftly and secretly, with the news the Queen most wanted to hear.

How lovely are the messengers that preach us the gospel of peace!

And how mortifying when, owing to officiousness and bad

* '. . . I always thought it very wrong to send people abroad of mean extraction; but since you think Mr Prior will be very useful at this time, I will comply with your desire'. Anne to Harley 19 Nov. 1711.

management, they are arrested at Deal. Centuries after the event St John's rage when he heard of it can still be sensed, as can also the dismay of John Macky who, recognising an old acquaintance in Matt Prior, sent off an express to Marlborough at Bouchain. Macky was lucky not to lose more than his livelihood. The amateurishness of the operation was beyond belief. As Boyer says, 'It appeared so strange and improbable either that Mr Prior should in this clandestine manner be sent to France upon so important affair as the negotiation of a general peace or if he were, that better care were not taken of his free going to and fro undiscovered, that many doubted the truth of the general report'.[4] It was just as well that they did. Holland must on no account be allowed to know in advance details of preliminaries which might not be to her taste or advantage.

On September 21st Mesnager was able to send de Torcy an account of his winings and dinings in London with the Tory ministers. The claret was excellent. 'Je leur trouvais', he writes, 'le visage un peu allumé, surtout celui de Milord Shrewsbury'. In that close and secret circle with Oxford, St John, Dartmouth and Shrewsbury, they all felt they could relax. So they drank the healths of Louis XIV – now regarded, said Oxford, as England's good ally . . . Everything went merrily until, perhaps rather unfortunately, Mesnager mentioned Canada. It was, he said, absolutely worthless to England. Why, it could not even produce wine! Now, Rio de Janeiro, that was worth infinitely more . . . There was general embarrassment. 'I gather', wrote Mesnager afterwards, 'that it was neither the good earth nor the extent of Canada that appealed to them, but the concern they have here for Hill, brother of Madam Masham the Queen's favourite'. The long silence was at last broken by St John, who changed the subject by observing that peace could not be made while the Pretender remained in France. It was Mesnager's turn to be nonplussed. He said this was something new, for which he had no instructions.[5]

A week later Mesnager, admitted by the back stairs, wished Anne many years of peace. She replied, 'I have no liking for war and shall do all I can to end it as soon as possible'.[6] When he had gone she wrote to Oxford:

I have the business of the peace so much at heart that I cannot help giving you this trouble to ask if it may not be proper to order Mr Secretary, in case he finds M Mesnager very averse to the new proposition [the Pretender's removal from France], not to insist upon it; and if you think it right I hope you will take care Mr Secretary has such an order in my name, for I think there is nothing so much to be feared as the letting the treaty go out of our hands.[7]

It was something that she could write to him in such terms. No matter how worried she might be, reported Mesnager, her new Lord Treasurer could always cheer her and leave her composed and happy. Oxford's own composure was remarkable and she counted upon him. With his anti-Marlborough doctrine he had been entirely successful. 'I think the Duke of Marlborough shows plainer than ever by this new project his unwillingness for a peace', she wrote to him in September, 'but I hope our negotiations will succeed and then it will not be in his power to prevent it'.[8]

By the end of September even Swift had been vouchsafed some inkling of what was happening. 'We have already settled all things with France', he tells Stella on the 28th, 'and very much to the honour and advantage of England, and the Queen is in mighty good humour. All this news is a mighty secret; the people in general know that a peace is forwarding. The Earl of Strafford is to go soon to Holland and let them know what we have been doing and then there will be the devil and all to pay, but we'll make them swallow it with a pox'.[9]

This was no time to be squeamish; and if Swift was, as Sarah said he was, past blushing, what of St John? Working night and day he was determined that, cost what it might, nothing on earth should stop England from making peace. Repeatedly let down by the Allies, she had as Europe's packhorse borne the full burden of the war. Surely, so his argument ran, she had every right to make her own terms for peace and in her own way; 'given out by degrees, intermixing some truth and falsehood together' – as Lord Cowper called it, a dripping peace.[10] For such difficult work one needed encouragement; but for St John and Abigail nothing could have been more disheartening than the news that reached them now of the fiasco in Canada. Honest Jack Hill had not stormed the heights of Abraham, he had never seen them. What with storms, fogs, mismanagement and muddle, nearly a thousand lives had been lost and Hill was limping home with what was left of the strongest force that, up to that time, had ever crossed the Atlantic.

'The news of Mr Hill's miscarriage in his expedition came today', wrote Swift on October 6th, 'and I went to visit Mrs Masham and Mrs Hill, his two sisters, to condole with them. I advised them by all means to go to the music-meeting tonight to show they were not cast down etc. and they thought my advice was right and went. I doubt Mr Hill and his admiral made wrong steps; however we lay it all to a storm etc. . . . The Secretary [St John] is much mortified about Hill, because this expedition was of his contriving and he counted much upon it; but Lord Treasurer was just as merry as usual'.[11]

Oxford, while convalescing from de Guiscard's attack, had begged the Queen not to sanction the expedition; and his merriment now did nothing to endear him to St John and Abigail. Even a smile at such a time could be offensive. The cracks were beginning to show.

St John was further put out by the tornado of political pamphlets now swirling about him. It was high time, he told Harcourt, to put a stop to such 'insolence and licentiousness reflecting on her Majesty and her administration'. The fourteen booksellers, printers and publishers already arrested should be prosecuted with the utmost rigour the law allowed. One such by the name of Collins had had the effrontery to say that the Queen was a mechanic (automaton), the daughter of a collier, her father a rogue and Collins himself better born than she was. Another had published a ballad called *Ye Welcome to Ye Medal.*[12] This was particularly serious because, as everyone knew, the Duchess of Gordon, by presenting the Pretender's medal to the Faculty of Edinburgh, had insulted the Queen. The silver medal minted in Holland carried the Pretender's head and the words *Cujus est*? ('Whose superscription is this?'), and on the reverse a map of England with the word *Reddite* ('Render . . .' etc.) With Defoe industriously blowing up the coals the thing soon became a conflagration, and then as soon died down. The balladmonger may have hoped to revive it, but the excitement was over. However, the various prosecutions made useful propaganda, highlighting as they did the outraged innocence of the Queen's loyal ministers.

Oxford's illness that autumn gave St John a free hand with the French and he used it. His aim now was not only to please the Tories but to stagger the Whigs with the trade concessions he meant to wring from France in return for allowing Philip of Anjou to stay on the throne of Spain. In this Holland, guaranteed equal commercial rights by the Barrier Treaty of 1709, would be ignored. Our gains would include Gibraltar and Port Mahon, Acadia and Newfoundland; Dunkirk would be dismantled; and for Oxford's South Sea Company there would be the heartening bonus of admission to the monopoly in the Spanish-American slave trade known as the Assiento. When these demands were first broken to de Torcy he said they would ruin trade for all Europe except Great Britain; but the haggling went on, and Tallard was given four months on parole in France to work behind the scenes.

On October 13th Count von Gallas of Austria had the peace-preliminaries published in the *Daily Courant*. For this he was banned the Court. 'Most people', says Boyer, 'found them captious and insufficient . . . They had been made to expect glorious and advantageous terms for all the Allies and that the Peace would be lasting, safe and honourable'. The *Post Boy*, by printing another six articles not yet communicated to foreign ministers, made matters a great deal worse. What were called the preliminary articles of October, containing (according to St John) 'more advantages for your Majesty's kingdom than were ever perhaps stipulated for any nation at one time', were found to have been signed in London by Mesnager for France and by the two Secretaries of State for England. None of the Allies had been represented.

The dismay of the Dutch was as nothing compared with the anger of Austria. George of Hanover too was disgusted. 'Leave Spain and the Indies to Philip of Anjou', he wrote to Oxford, 'and we lose all the fruits of victory. France would soon be in a position to dictate to Europe'.[13] But nothing could check St John and nothing could deter Anne. Armed with words by Oxford she defied the Dutch advocate William de Buys. His people, she told him, were delaying peace by withholding passports from the plenipotentiaries. St John went further. Knowing all the ropes of propaganda he fell back on the trustiest of all: blaring the reverse of the truth so loudly that none dared question it. 'As to any separate treaty with France', he told Strafford in Holland, 'there is no such thing. The Queen would never think of taking so dishonourable a course'.

On November 10th the Dutch reluctantly agreed to allow the plenipotentiaries their passports. 'This', wrote Abigail, 'will prolong the Queen's life'. She was still suffering from gout and had just written to Oxford from Hampton Court: 'When the Duke of Marlborough comes I should think it will be best for me just to begin to open the matter of the Peace to him and to refer him to you and Mr Secretary for a fuller account of all that is passed'.[14] The victor of Blenheim might not always be counted on to kneel in submission; and indeed, if he and his friends chose to oppose the peace with vigour, they still had trumps to play. George of Hanover was continuing to harp on 'a perfect union between the Allies, without which all Europe will fall into confusion and sooner or later into slavery'. Nearer home, if the Whigs could make certain of a majority in the Lords, they might block the Peace till kingdom come or at least till the terms were made more acceptable to those who had backed us.

'Dismal' Nottingham, the High Tory earl who had long ago set his heart on suppressing Occasional Conformity, suddenly became a key figure. Since votes in the Lords were all-important, Nottingham, it was decided, must be lured over to the Whigs. It was a barefaced bargain: he had but to join them and vote against the peace terms. They in return would guarantee his heart's desire: the Occasional Conformity Bill, thinly disguised, should at last be smuggled through and passed. He agreed. Lord Poulett told Oxford:

> I find Nottingham as sour & fiercely wild as you can imagine anything to be that has lived long in the desert. I am so sensible of your observation on the would-be King [Marlborough] that I own to you I am a great deal concerned how your numbers may answer in our House, for I think the Queen's enemies at present generally understand one another much better than her friends & servants but . . . as old Leeds says, you have a budget full of miracles upon all occasions.[15]

It was true. Under whatever guise they knew him – Robert Harley, Earl of Oxford & Mortimer, The Dragon, Robin the Trickster – they knew that as a worker of miracles he could be relied on. He who had conjured from thin air the South Sea talisman might well have a trick or two in store to make his audience gasp. On neither side was quarter expected. In Oxford's master moves there would be the same lack of scruple as the Whigs had shown in kidnapping Nottingham, or St John in his hoodwinking of Holland. Even so the double blow was staggering: Swift's *Conduct of the Allies*, and the instantaneous creation of twelve Tory peers.

On November 17th (the anniversary of Queen Elizabeth's birthday) Marlborough landed at Greenwich with George of Hanover's righthand man Baron von Bothmar.* A demonstration of welcome, planned by the Kit-Cat, in the course of which effigies of Oxford, Sacheverell and the Pope would have been burned, was suppressed. Ten days later, while Bothmar was telling Anne bluntly what her successor-apparent thought of the Peace, Swift published the most powerful pamphlet ever known in Britain, *The Conduct of the Allies*.

In the shortcomings of our Allies – the reluctance of the Dutch to risk their troops in battle, the failure of Austria to send promised contingents, the almost total inadequacy of Portugal, and so on – Swift had a strong case and put it devastatingly. With a touch neither too light nor too heavy for his audience, Marlborough was damned. A Captain-General-for-life might too easily have become a King. There had been a conspiracy to prolong the war, which from first to last had been one vast deception with England draining herself of blood and money to enrich the Allies, the generals and the Whig speculators and to set an unwanted Austrian on the throne of Spain. And as for the Queen, had she not been hounded from castle to cottage and very nearly shoved from her throne? Except for this last, written in Manley style for the groundlings, the whole piece was most skilfully done; and it had its effect.

* '. . . The Duke of Marlborough came to me yesterday as soon as I had dined, made a great many of his usual professions of duty and affection to me. He seemed dejected and very uneasy about this matter of the public accounts, stayed near an hour and saw nobody here but myself . . .' Anne to Oxford 19 Nov. 1711.

Less subtle was the speech Anne found prepared for her at the opening of Parliament on December 7th. 'I am glad that I can now tell you', she said, 'that notwithstanding the arts of those who delight in war, both place and time are appointed for opening the treaty of a general peace'. Even though Marlborough's stock, with Swift's help, might have reached its nadir, this opening was thought unworthy of a great Queen. Cowper was indignant. 'It looked', he said, 'like a libeller in a garret, with a reflection on a general, and not like a Queen, who should not have thundered in that way'. Even Hamilton considered it mean to speak so from the throne: 'It had been better said in her chamber. It did not go with her calm temper'. Anne, taxed with it, showed surprise. She had meant no more, she said, than to quote from the Prayer Book. [Psalm 68, verse 30: 'Scatter thou the people that delight in war.'][16]

After she had made her speech the Queen disrobed and returned to the Lords *incognita* 'to hear the debates and by her awful respectable presence to moderate any heats that might arise'.[17] It was a brave thing to do. She heard Nottingham say that though he had a numerous family he would readily give half his income rather than acquiesce in a peace which he thought unsafe and dishonourable to his country and to all Europe. He was followed by Marlborough who, after bowing to Anne, said his age and the fatigues of war made him wish for retirement and repose, to think of eternity. Having been generously rewarded he could not have the least desire to continue the war. If however he could but crawl along he was always ready to serve to obtain an honourable and lasting peace. He was supported by Burnet, Cowper and Halifax. When the vote was taken the Government was defeated (though uppermost on the same vote in the Commons); and when Anne came to be led from the Lords she markedly chose the arm of Somerset who, for all his flirtation with Oxford, had just proved 'louder than any in the House against the Peace'.

Swift panicked. The Queen was false, he declared, or at best very much wavering, and the Tories were ruined; and all because Oxford was too negligent to get rid of Somerset's wife and those who encouraged her: 'This is all your damned Duchess of Somerset's doings'. 'Poh poh', said Oxford, 'all will be well'. The hearts of kings, he observed, were unsearchable.

At such times there is never a dearth of soothsayers. The Queen, barely able to walk with a stick, was beset with them. Burnet thundered about Doomsday – 'We are ripening for judgment' etc. – and threatened her with Popery and the Pretender; while the aged Bishop of Worcester chimed in with Armageddon which, he said, must end Pope and Popery at a blow. To prove his prophecy he went in search of a Bible, 'but when he returned, the company began to move off'.[18] Oxford, it seemed, knew the scriptures even better than he did.

More serious were the December onslaughts upon Anne of Oxford and St John. Time pressed. They knew what had to be done and were ruthless about doing it. Marlborough, she was told, must be disgraced. The Somersets too must go.* And on top of all this, if the Peace were not to be further impeded, twelve new lords must be made at once to ensure a Tory majority. Between them they won most of the day. With Anne it was still possible to do this by teasing and bullying. The bogey of King John was half-believed. They added 'peculation'. Did she and her people not long for peace? And who but Marlborough and his friends would obstruct it? To sack the Somersets St John would, he found, need a separate set of libels, and in that perhaps Swift might again be set to work . . .

Swift did in fact spend a strange Christmas. To begin with he found on December 21st he had forgotten that Christmas was imminent; which for one in holy orders was strange enough. Then followed this:

December 23. I have sat at home all day & eaten only a mess of broth & a roll. I have written a Prophecy which I design to print, I did it today & some other verses.
December 24. My Prophecy is printed & will be published after Christmas Day. I like it mightily. I don't know how it will pass . . .
December 26. I called at noon at Mrs Masham's, who desired me not to

* Oxford was content with the dismissal of the Duke of Somerset as Master of the Horse, and even that was postponed until January. The Duchess, he realised, might still prove a useful go-between with the Whigs, should he need one. The scheme for creating twelve peers is attributed to Oxford alone.

let the Prophecy be published, for fear of angering the Queen about the Duchess of Somerset, so I writ to the printer to stop them . . .[19]

It was too late. The shaft had gone home.

'We must certainly fall', Swift had written, 'if the Duchess of Somerset be not turned out, and nobody believes the Queen will ever part with her'. Eager himself to meet the challenge, and in what he called his hobbling measure, he wrote this:

> . . . And, dear England, if ought I understand,
> Beware of carrots from Northumberland.
> Carrots sown thynne a deep root may get,
> If so be they are in Somer set.
> Their Conyngs mark thou, for I have been told
> They assassin when young and poison when old.
> Root out these carrots, oh thou whose name
> Is backwards and forwards always the same, [Anna]
> And keep close to thee always that name
> Which backwards and forwards is almost the same. [Masham]
> And England, wouldst thou be happy still,
> Bury those carrots under a Hill.

He must have hugged himself for his puns, and kicked himself afterwards for letting them lose him a bishopric. Still there it was – 'They do but jest, poison in jest, no offence in the world'. The red-haired Duchess's history – first married to Thynne of Longleat, who was shot by Königsmark – was common knowledge and few, very few can have thought the doggerel funny. On Boxing Day Cowper told Hamilton that the Duke of Somerset had persuaded his wife not to retire. The Queen, he added, should be prepared, for with the *Windsor Prophecy* 'endeavours against the Duchess' had already begun. Somerset took it for 'a design to lessen her and to make her fall a sacrifice to Mrs Masham, because Swift was notoriously employed by the Ministry'.

All this Hamilton repeated to Anne, whom he found much relieved at the Duchess's not going. When he produced a copy of the *Windsor Prophecy* she refused to read it and ordered him to tell no one he had mentioned it. It could never affect her respect for the Duchess. With Sarah, owing to her own temper and carriage, things had been different. This Groom of the Stole would never behave like that. Hamilton fervently agreed. None knew better than he how much the Queen needed 'an agreeable friend to open to in order to lessen the ill effects of her disquiets'. Would not Anne unbosom herself to this heaven-sent Duchess? No she would not, she had been bitten too savagely before. She was unfeignedly glad of her company all the same. Hamilton was crestfallen. 'I hoped', he said, 'she had an openness to draw your Majesty outward and to open to her what are your Majesty's disquiets; else your Majesty's reservedness and secrecy might lose you the greatest pleasure of conversation'.

Oxford decided to play two trumps on the last day of the year. Nottingham's son-in-law Dartmouth, now an earl, was never more surprised in his life than when the Queen drew from her pocket, like twelve spare aces, a list of twelve names and asked that all should immediately have warrants for titles. It was but his duty, he said, to warn her that such an inundation would have 'a very ill effect in the House of Lords and no good one in the kingdom'. She thanked him, adding that she liked it as little as he did, 'but did not find that anybody could propose a better expedient'. Those to be ennobled included Abigail's husband Samuel Masham, described by Sarah as a soft, goodnatured, insignificant man, always making low bows to everybody and ready to skip to open a door. He had been chosen as an afterthought, almost by chance, when another lord-to-be had declined to be honoured; and now the notion of Abigail as a great lady did not please the Queen. It would not, she observed, become a peeress to lie upon the floor and do inferior offices. Besides, she was a useful servant and must continue so.[20]

The hilarity at the Kit-Cat can be imagined. Wharton rose in the Lords to ask the new members if they meant to vote individually or by their foreman. It was indeed Oxford's packed jury and Hamilton told Anne so. 'King William made more', she said. 'Not at one time', he answered, and anyway this was 'not to reward merit but to make votes'. Swift thought it 'a strange unhappy necessity the Queen had drawn upon herself by her confounded trimming and moderation'.[21] Others said it was unprecedented and invidious and made the Lords the property of the Court. At best it tarnished the Crown, itself further to be debased that same day by the dismissal of Marlborough.

There was no man then living who had not marvelled at his victories. Like everyone else he had accepted vast perquisites but, unlike many, he had given much more than he had received. He would not have bungled the attack on Quebec, nor let his secret agents be taken at Deal. One needed to be cynical as St John to call him a villain; although now, as Coke says, 'his very successes began to be interpreted as crimes'. And so (as Sarah puts it) what plausible pretence was there to remove so successful a general, with his country still at war? The answer was 'a frivolous and groundless complaint in Parliament about certain perquisites he had claimed as belonging to his station'. As with the making of the lords, no better expedient was proposed. The fact that the Allies had been happy to pay him their share of those perquisites (and said so) and that exactly the same payments were continued to his successor the Duke of Ormonde, had to be ignored. Anne managed to persuade herself that he 'had not carried himself well to her since he came home; she did not mean to her personally, but in her business'.[22]

Her letter of dismissal Marlborough threw into the fire; nor were words minced in his reply. His enemies, he said, had made her believe 'a false and malicious insinuation contrived by themselves and made public when there was no opportunity for me to give in my answer' (Parliament was not sitting); and he ended by warning her against 'a man who . . . puts your Majesty upon all manner of extremities', and against friendship with France.

In England few wanted to hear him, a prophet without honour. France and Germany seemed far more alive to his value. Louis XIV, told of his disgrace, said, 'The affair of displacing the Duke of Marlborough will do all for us we desire'. Sophia of Hanover's comment was equally trenchant. Accused by Lord Rivers of taking Marlborough's part she replied, 'If the Queen had made a monkey her General and he had won so many battles and taken so many towns, I would be for him just the same'.[23] What she says in the same letter of Marlborough's opinion of Anne has too its glimmer of humour. 'When speaking of the Queen', she remembers, 'he always said she was a very good woman. This he repeated often. It did not seem to us like praise for so great a Princess'.

At Marlborough's expense the balladmongers were busy:

A widow kept a favourite cat,
At first a gentle creature,
But when he was grown sleek and fat
With many a mouse and many a rat
He soon disclosed his nature . . .

Swift may have written it, but neither he nor Defoe relished savaging a man when he was down. That was left to Mrs Manley (now 'very homely and very fat') in *The Examiner*. Her recriminations however, like herself, were not taken very seriously. It might be thought of more moment that Robert Walpole, on another trumped-up charge, was sent to the Tower, where the lions usually on show had just died.

On January 5th, 1712 Prince Eugene landed. His visit, except to Marlborough whom he publicly praised and befriended, was an embarrassment. Anne received him and then, pleading gout, passed him on to Oxford and St John. It was to them that he protested, on behalf of the Emperor Charles, against the terms of peace. His hearers listened politely and congratulated themselves that he had come too late to save Marlborough or to prevent the peace conference from opening at Utrecht, even though the Emperor might choose to have no truck with it.

At Utrecht our plenipotentiary Lord Strafford, too proud to be linked with Matthew Prior ('a person of so mean extraction'), was sent instead John Robinson Bishop of Bristol who, to everyone's amazement, had succeeded the late Duke of Newcastle as Lord Privy Seal. The Bishop, who for twenty-five years had served as chaplain and Minister Resident in Stockholm, knew what was called for. He made his entry into Holland in a black velvet gown enriched with gold loops and a long train upheld by two pages in ash-coloured coats laced with silver orris, and waistcoats of green velvet. Without doubt Strafford, if not the Dutch, appreciated it; but nothing could have been more sluggish than their proceedings. Prince Eugene said it was Babel. On the question of whether or not to remove the Pretender from France they looked like arguing forever. Strafford's brother, Peter Wentworth (stuck in a rut as equerry forever) kept him posted from London:

17 January. The Queen took all her clothes & divided them herself in six several heaps & stood by while the bedchamberwomen chose as they were eldest. Lady Masham took in her turn & 'tis given out as if she will continue bedchamberwoman.
22 January. [Of Somerset's dismissal] . . . and when he came home from St James's he pulled off the Queen's liveries from his men, so 'tis known he's out.[24]

Marlborough's daughters, Harriet Godolphin and Anne Sunderland, had both resigned as ladies of the bedchamber; Harriet being succeeded by Lady Catherine Hyde, daughter of Lord Rochester, who had died the previous May. 'The Queen and Lord Treasurer', Swift told Stella, 'mortally hate the Duke of Marlborough and to that he owes his fall . . . I do not love to see personal resentment mix with public affairs'.[25]

Anne, still with gout in knee and feet, forced herself on her birthday to present Prince Eugene with a diamond sword. It was a full dress occasion. Oxford brought his family and the Mashams, the ladies 'monstrous fine' while their Whig counterparts 'all undressed' looked cynically on from neighbouring windows. For the evening reception at St James's it was ruled that all flamboys were to be extinguished on arrival, 'the chairs of all persons of quality to be ranged in the Little Court between the great staircase and the back stairs . . . The bonfire not to be lit nor the strong drink given to the soldiers till ten o'clock at night'.[26] Even the little exercise the Queen took within her palace, noted Swift, seemed to do her good. 'Her friends wish', he added, 'she would use a little more'.[27] Certainly, one might think, a woman of such resilience and fortitude deserved better health. 'I hope', wrote Shrewsbury, 'her indisposition is over, which I believe was occasioned by a cold she got taking the air last Tuesday in her chaise whilst the sun was warm but the wind easterly and so sharp that at the same time it was very hot or very cold as her Majesty turned her face to or from the wind'.[28]

A motorcar would have been a godsend, and so would television. She was carried to her chaise; she was carried to a sofa and there lay, hoping her 'sore eyes' would allow her to read. Books were usually beyond her. The most she could manage was a letter or a newspaper, and those had often to be read to her. 'Every time the post comes in from Holland', Gaultier told de Torcy, 'the Queen never fails to ask for the *Gazette de Paris* and she delights in reading the articles headed *Londres*. Therefore your friends here request you to give directions that henceforth there may be nothing in those articles that could displease this Princess. And if your Excellency could now induce the King to write to her, such a step on the part of his Majesty would engage her very far in our interest and our affairs would proceed much the faster. Montgoulin [Pretender] might take the same opportunity to declare his sentiments to Madame Protose* [the Queen] and assure her that he will always follow with pleasure the advice or the injunctions which may be given him in her name'.[29]

Thus were princes manipulated. Without hesitation Louis XIV and the Pretender both wrote to Anne. Louis, in mourning, assured his 'sister' that he longed for a perfect reconciliation, and his references to friendship were echoed in Anne's reply. No one, she added, knew better than she did how to sympathise in his bereavement.† Piety alone could lighten the burden for them both.[30]

The Pretender's letter was longer and livelier. He could not believe, he said, that she had ever seriously intended to exclude him from the throne of their joint ancestors. After touching upon 'the splendour of our House' he went on to remind her of their father 'who loved you tenderly' and of the son he left to be his successor. He would submit to whatever plan she prescribed, but hoped she would not hesitate to follow her natural wish to prefer her own brother to strangers, and so to perpetuate the Stuart succession'. Interesting as this was, the original draft was more so. In that he had said the voice of God and of Nature called her [to restore him]; and if that were not enough, she should remember too the public good, the preservation of their family and the promises she had made to James II. To ignore all this might well mean civil war. And after all, what was Hanover? Sophia was the most distant relation they had and Anne had no reason to count on her friendship. The Hanoverians spoke another language and had different interests. Moreover if they

* Protozoa: Animals of the simplest or most primitive type. *O.E.D.*

† In February 1712 Louis XIV's son, daughter-in-law and grandson died of smallpox. The survivor, another grandson, a sickly infant of two, became Louis XV.

came they would bring with them a pack of Germans to enslave the British; whereas the Pretender, on the other hand, would change nothing, not even the Church of England. Her happiness, her peace of mind, the glory of her reign, all must depend upon her justice now . . .[31]

It was the sort of thing Swift meant when he wrote of 'passages which the curious of another age would be glad to know the secret springs of'. Here one would like to know how much reached Anne and how deeply, if at all, it impressed her. In public and in private she continued to deny and disown any sympathy for her stepbrother as her successor. Doubt persisted. The warmingpan was nonsense. It was unnatural and unjust to disown one's own blood. She hated Hanover. The sum, as most people reckoned, did not add up to what she insisted it did. 'I can't but fear', wrote Bishop Trelawney, 'the Pretender is next ours. If so, the coffin is bespoke for the Queen, for Popery is always in haste to kill when they are sure of taking possession'. Swift might assert that 'the Queen hated and despised the Pretender', Sharp deny 'the least suggestion of any kind for the Pretender's interests'. Both may have been misled. The Queen's conscience, her heart of hearts, was to remain the most secret as well as the most intriguing thing about her. 'That', as she once said to Sarah, 'will be to myself'.

And if Anne could dissemble her feelings, what of her ministers? It is Swift again who loyally writes of them 'I could never hear one single word let fall in favour of the Pretender'. Yet St John, after Anne's death, was to fly to the Pretender; while Oxford took delight in mesmerising his contemporaries, posterity and himself. Mystery was his element. 'His whole management', says Bolingbroke, 'was to keep up a kind of general indetermination in the party about the succession'. When on March 15th Cowper met him at St James's he found him a miasma of hints and winks. Speaking 'as always very dark and confusedly, interlacing all with broken hints of his discoveries', he seemed to suggest that everyone except himself had been flirting with the Pretender. He of course had always been and still was for Hanover, as was the Queen, who would abdicate rather than let the Pretender in. Marlborough was in every sort of intrigue;

Sophia a very cunning woman. And as for the Peace, had we been at the gates of Paris we could not have had a better.[32]

Oxford, and with good reason, still felt confident of the Queen's friendship. She showed it again when, with Mohawks about, she begged him to take more care. It was kind, but he was scornful of bodyguards. 'I would be a worm rather than a man', he said, 'if I did not believe a Providence'.[33]

Anne's own unshaken belief was reflected in her continuing to touch for the Evil. Among a batch she touched in March was Samuel Johnson, then but thirty months old.* He had, he said, 'a confused but somehow a sort of solemn recollection of a lady in diamonds and a long black hood'. He remembered too, when he went to the palace, hearing a boy crying.[34] That could of course have been any child, but it may conceivably have been Abigail's six-months-old son. 'He has a swelling in his neck', noted Swift on February 14th, 'I fear it is the Evil'.[35] Abigail, again pregnant, was ill. Lady Strafford reported in April, 'Lady Masham has not been with anybody or received any visits at home this six weeks and some say the Queen has ordered her to live very privately that she may not get the envy of the people like the Duchess of Marlborough'.[36] Still, there were tiny comforts: Abigail's two-year-old daughter had been given the £1,000-a-year sinecure of Chief Ranger of St James's Park.[37] She could if she chose give orders to Henry Wise.

On his return to Vienna Prince Eugene described those he had met at the English Court: Oxford smooth and insinuating and 'with such an ascendant over the Queen, she approves his every action'; St John the bold bulldog; Harcourt equally bold; Dartmouth pliable; Buckingham sanguine and in favour; Shrewsbury less resolute than Buckingham and more easily browbeaten . . . But the party, he said, was divided against itself and if Marlborough used his money with the skill he had shown in getting it, he could speed its fall. Marlborough's successor Ormonde he found a fine cavalier

* Boswell says Johnson's scrofula 'disfigured a countenance naturally well-formed and hurt his visual nerves so much that he did not see at all with one of his eyes'. Raymond Crawford, author of *The King's Evil*, adds: 'Johnson carried with him to the grave abiding testimony of Anne's ineffectual handiwork'.

prepared to sacrifice all for Church and Queen, but he 'acted most by direction and had no great sway in the Cabinet'.[36]

Ormonde was unfortunate. When in May St John sent him the notorious restraining orders, forbidding him to engage in any siege or hazard a battle, he found himself in the worst quandary a commander can ever have known: not allowed to collaborate with his allies, nor permitted to tell them why.

Years afterwards St John (then Bolingbroke) wrote that when he first heard of the restraining orders, less than an hour before he sent them, he was so surprised and hurt that if he could have had a moment in private with the Queen he would 'in the first heat' have opposed them.[39] Even when they went into Council St John is said to have begun to object, but Anne 'made a sign with her fan at her mouth' to silence him.[40] There was no option but to send Ormonde the Queen's 'positive command' and this he did, adding that she wished him to disguise receipt of the order. 'I had almost forgot to tell your Grace', the message ended, 'that communication is given of this order to the Court of France, so that if the Maréchal de Villars takes in any private way notice of it to you, your Grace will answer accordingly'.[41]

Ormonde was spared nothing. When by well planned manoeuvres the allied troops found themselves presented with 'the best opportunity of beating the French army that could be wished for', and at the same time a British commander refusing to give the order to advance, they demanded to know why. He could not tell them. Desperately he groped for excuses. Four times he wrote to Oxford, imploring him at least to let him explain. It was treachery on the grand scale. Burnet, who blamed Oxford, said it was not only resented by the whole army but 'struck us here in England with amazement . . . it seemed we were neither to have peace nor war'.[42] The Whigs at once staged a debate in the Lords. Had such orders, they asked, in fact been sent to Ormonde? But Oxford was not to be so easily caught. 'They who had the honour to serve the Queen', he said, 'could not reveal the orders she gave her General without a particular direction from her Majesty, and in his opinion those orders were not fit to be divulged'.[43] When it was further suggested that the ministry was set on a separate peace, Oxford bridled.

'Nothing of that nature', he insisted, 'was ever designed. Such a peace would be so base, so knavish and so villainous a thing that every servant of the Queen must answer for it with his head to the nation'.

The next step was to stop the pay of all foreign troops before (again without consulting our Allies) declaring a cessation of arms. All this was done. The Allied armies, with some bitterness, broke up; Ormonde, as they left him, wishing them luck and hoping that no disaster might befall them. It very soon did. At Dénain the French fell upon the Dutch and the Austrians and losses were heavy.

Sophia told Strafford she considered the Queen's action a breach of treaty and of friendship. Marlborough in the Lords was even more outspoken and contemptuous. 'The measures pursued in England for a year past', he said, 'are directly contrary to her Majesty's engagements with the Allies, have sullied the triumphs and glories of her reign and will render the English name odious to all other nations'.[44]

What the ordinary people of Britain thought went for the most part unrecorded. Only when informers exposed them did the blunter ones unwillingly get a public hearing; as when a victualler was arrested for saying that the Duke of Marlborough had done the nation service and deserved better treatment; and further said she was a bitch. When asked could he possibly mean 'Our Governess', he said simply 'Aye'.[45]

CHAPTER THIRTEEN

THE RIVALS

1712 - 1713

FRANCE had lost the war. She had not the least intention of losing the peace. Through the summer of 1712 her ministers' secret memoranda spoke for themselves: 'Peace is to be made on conditions that will be glorious to France'; and to Marshal Villars: 'No one knows better than you the importance of separating the Allies and above all an ally as considerable as the Queen of England'.[1]

It was not easy for Oxford to convince Hanover. His cousin Thomas, sent there as Ambassador Extraordinary, was told by the Elector, 'The Queen is a young woman and I hope will live a great many years. When she dies, my mother is before me . . . In the meantime speak to me as a German prince and a prince of the Empire. As such I must tell you I cannot depart from what I take to be the true interest of the Empire and the Dutch'.[2] His mother Sophia was just a little more realistic; for while, as she told Strafford, it was natural for her House to take the Emperor's part, the notion of conquering Spain without England's help was as hopeless as trying to bite the moon.[3]

Before leaving for Windsor Anne, in the Lords, had once more publicly acknowledged the Hanoverian Succession and had promised 'the removal of that person out of the dominions of France who has pretended to disturb this settlement'. Nevertheless in many minds, if not in hers, the rivalry persisted, as did that of Oxford and Henry St John. This last, since de Guiscard's attempt, had grown from envy to enmity. St John, ever thrusting and driving, lost all patience with Oxford's dilatoriness – 'sometimes asleep and sometimes at play' – with which he now seemed to have infected the Queen. The Dragon was altogether too easygoing. It was foolhardy to tolerate near the Queen such Whigs as the Duchess of Somerset or to allow anyone to attempt to obstruct the Peace. His newest grievance, and to him it was a huge one, was being made Viscount Bolingbroke instead of, like Oxford, an earl – 'dragged into the House of Lords', as he put it, 'in such a manner as to make my promotion a punishment, not a reward'. The earldom had been extinct in his family for only a year and he had counted on its restoration. Taken aback with the disappointment he 'fell into the utmost rage and . . . continued raving and railing at the Queen, Lady Masham, the Treasurer and everyone else'.[4]

King Jemmy fights for England,
Queen Anne did die for France,
And he that at St James's
His interest would advance
To Paris straight must go . . .[5]

In an attempt to pacify the new viscount, Oxford sent him to Paris, where indeed he was fêted. He was welcomed to Fontainebleau by Louis XIV, made love to a countess and in Paris was honoured with a gala night at the opera, where the Pretender appeared in a neighbouring box. No greetings passed; but Anne, when she heard of it, said that Bolingbroke should have left at once. On his return to England he was displeased to hear that Oxford had awarded himself the Order of the Garter.

Abigail too nursed a grievance. She had hoped that when Lord Rivers died his post of Master General of the Ordnance would go without question to her brother Jack;[6] but Oxford had given it to the Jacobite Duke of Hamilton and appointed him at the same time Ambassador Extraordinary to France. A grievance shared is a grievance doubled: after comparing notes with Bolingbroke, Abigail found they had more in common than she had supposed.

But the main thing of course was to make certain of the Queen's favour; and by this time both Oxford and Bolingbroke suspected that they were being steadily undermined by each other. Oxford, said Bolingbroke, neglected the thread of business and negotiated by fits and starts. Bolingbroke, said Oxford, fell out with everyone; so much so that both Swift and himself despaired of a reconciliation. Inveteracy was once again at the Queen's door.

Anne's health when for the summer she moved to Windsor appeared to improve. The move itself was always a performance, with a long string of coaches for the 'family' and luggage piled high on what was listed in Sarah's accounts as a 'shashmaree' (*chaise marine*). No sooner was Anne settled, however, than she went chaise-riding in the forest. With a sudden change of weather in September forty of the staff at the Castle went down with a 'fever' which was probably influenza. Anne did not catch it, yet she was clearly unwell. Arbuthnot, who sat up with her all one night, diagnosed a fit of the gravel. 'You never saw such countenances as we all had', Swift wrote to Stella, 'such dismal melancholy'; but the Queen herself, in spite of pain and sickness, was 'only a little dispirited'. By the end of the month, except for gout in one foot, she had recovered.

During Anne's illness Godolphin died at Holywell, the Marlboroughs' house at St Albans. ''Tis a good jest', wrote Swift, 'to hear the ministers talk of him now with humanity and pity because he is dead and can do them no hurt'.[7] Godolphin, who had stood by James II and Mary of Modena, witnessed the birth of the Pretender and guided Anne as she stumbled to the throne, had declared towards the end that the game was scarce worth the candles. When Dartmouth told Anne of his death she wept. 'She could not help it', she said, 'for she had had a long acquaintance with him and did believe that whatever offence he had given her was owing to the influence the Marlborough family had over him; but she did not think him to be naturally an interested man'.[8] Just as the pension had been withheld in his lifetime, so now there was to be no generous tribute. That was left to Sarah, who wrote in her Bible: 'The best man I ever knew'.

In October the Court, still at Windsor, was 'very thin'. Oxford was ill in London. Abigail, after quarrelling with her chairmen, fell in the forecourt and had since gone to lie-in at Kensington. Swift asked Arbuthnot if the Queen had dropsy and was told no. She was said again to be using Henry VIII's pulley-chair to take her from floor to floor, rather than the stairs. On October 9th she was carried to her Little House, where next day she was seized by a violent fit of the gout. Two days later she made herself sit at a Cabinet Council.[9]

At Utrecht it was rumoured that the Queen's life was 'very precarious and in all appearance would be very short'. It was further said that Bolingbroke had exceeded his brief in France and had 'made several advances in favour of the Pretender', so that the Dutch were beginning to wonder whether 'the present ministry in England were for having the Pretender succeed the Queen'.[10] In this of course they were by no means alone. Dr Hamilton took it upon himself to tackle Anne. It was being said, he told her, that though the Pretender's coming in might not happen directly with her consent, 'yet they might bring her to do such things as would necessarily force her to yield to it'. Anne's comment – 'Can any think me so blind as not to see through these things?' – was non-committal. Hamilton was not to be put off. At a second interview on the same subject, at Windsor on October 11th, he repeated Cowper's assertion that Jacobites were being given key posts, so that 'things looked as though the Pretender was designed'. This stung the Queen. 'Oh fie!' she exclaimed, 'there is no such thing. What, do they think I'm a child and to be imposed upon?' He assured her that he himself was certain she was not 'in the Pretender's affair'; indeed he had just given that assurance to Richard Steele. And what had Steele said? 'If he thought that', he had said, 'he would go home and sleep sounder than he had done for many nights'. At this point Hamilton, not surprisingly, thought he might have gone too far. 'I asked her', he adds, 'if I said anything I ought not. She said no, but the less I talked with them of it the better'.[11]

Anne must by this time have realised that her doctors were almost as helpless as she was; but she liked always to hear the talk of the town. She might call it twittle-twattle; she would still listen to it. From Hamilton, a natural gossip, she could learn what the Whigs were saying without having to see them. Besides, a doctor could sense her mood and if need be act as shock-absorber. He would doubtless choose his time before telling her, for example, that when Cowper read in the *Flying Post* that the Pretender was calling himself Duke of Gloucester he said, 'How can that be cured but by entering into the warmingpan again?' And if the reaction was unfavourable, as it surely was, Hamilton sugared the pill by doubting the word of Mary Beatrice's midwife, who was a Roman Catholic and had since vanished. It worked. 'Her Majesty', he notes, 'received this with cheerfulness and by asking me several questions about the thing'.

The warmingpan might be a discarded bygone, but at least it was encouraging to know that one's doctor still doubted if the Pretender was 'the real son of James II'.[12] In that direction even the flimsiest scrap of comfort was welcome.

The Commissioners of Accounts, busy searching for grounds to prosecute Marlborough, had to Anne's distress now nosed their way into her late husband's papers. She begged Oxford to call them off. 'To have an account of what money the poor Prince called for, for his own private use, laid before the Parliament', she wrote, 'would be very shocking to me and in my poor opinion very improper'.[13] On October 21st she wrote again. There was friction between her Secretaries: Dartmouth, 'roughly used' by Bolingbroke, spoke of retiring. She had no wish, she said, to part with him.

In his diary, for November 8th, Hamilton noted: 'The Queen mentioned the box which was sent to my Lord Oxford with a pistol in it; and my Lord Marlborough's going abroad. She said it was prudent in him'. [14]The Band Box Plot, as it came to be called, was generally supposed to be meant as a harmless practical joke, but Swift, who was with Oxford (he was shaving) when the box arrived and undid it for him, liked it to be thought that he had saved his life. What Swift saw were 'two large inkhorns charged with powder and ball, two linen bags of gunpowder and two quills filled with wildfire; the two barrels designed to discharge different ways'. Others maintained that there was nothing more lethal than a bundle of squibs.[15] Swift, sending his account of it to Stella, added, 'I wish myself more and more among my willows'. Though in more ways than one he had saved the lives of these ministers, there was still no preferment. As Anne told Hamilton, Swift was good for some things, but the rumour that he was to be Dean of Wells was false.

On November 13th Anne wrote to Oxford:

> . . . Should not Duke Hamilton be hastened again? . . . Care should be taken that he has no just pretence for staying . . . I think one may reasonably hope now the great work of the Peace is in a fair way of coming to a happy conclusion. When you come next pray order it so that you may be here [Windsor] by daylight and take more care of yourself and be assured of my being most sincerely your very affectionate friend.[15]

Anne was anxious for the Duke of Hamilton to take up his duties as Ambassador in Paris. Two days later he and his adversary, Lord Mohun who 'gave the affront and yet sent the challenge', were both killed in a duel in Hyde Park. Swift hurried to comfort the Duchess; even the porter at her door was in tears. Anne was said to be 'stupefied with grief'. Shrewsbury was persuaded to go to Paris instead. His Italian duchess was delighted.

Rumours from abroad that the Queen's life was about to be attempted at Windsor now reached her ministers. 'Disaffected persons' had been seen lurking near the Little House. Some said they were only sightseers, others that they had climbed the wall. The guards were doubled. On November 21st Anne assured Oxford, 'These accounts that are come of a design against my person does not give me any uneasiness, knowing God Almighty's protection is above all things, and as He has hitherto been infinitely gracious to me, I hope He will continue being so'. In a postscript she wished him joy of his new cousin:[17] Abigail's son, Samuel. A week later, just before leaving for London, she wrote to him again, but less cordially:

> I have just now received your letter, for which I give you many thanks, and am very sorry anything I said on Tuesday morning should make you think I was displeased with you. I told you my thoughts freely, as I have always and ever will continue to do on all occasions. You cannot wonder that I who have been ill used so many years should desire to keep myself from being again enslaved. And if I must always comply and not be complied with, it is I think very hard and what I cannot submit to and what I believe you would not have me . . .[18]

The over-zealous convert to freedom was once more proving intractable – a theme to which Swift constantly returns: 'They have cautioned the Queen so much against being governed that she observes it too much'.[19] Her natural caution, reinforced by experience and by Oxford's teaching, now resulted in chronic obstinacy, indecision and procrastination. Swift and others due for promotion might wait and go on waiting. She was, he says, 'extremely cautious and slow and after the usual mistake of those who think they have been often imposed on, became so very suspicious that she overshot the mark and erred in the other extreme . . . so that Oxford had no other remedy but to let her Majesty take her own time, which never failed to be the very longest that the nature of the thing could suffer her to defer it'.[20]

If this was frustrating for Oxford, with 'the jealousy and discontents of his friends on one side and the management of the Queen's temper on the other', for the Man of Mercury, Bolingbroke, it was insufferable. And if Oxford had learned to wear two faces – one for the Queen, another for Hanover – Bolingbroke, like Cerberus in Verrio's allegory, wore three, the third turned to the Pretender. 'Desirous to begin in right earnest some measures for the interest of Montgoulin [Pretender]', as Gaultier told de Torcy, Bolingbroke now asked for the names of those Whigs who, some eighteen months previously, had offered their services to the Chevalier; but in that he was to be disappointed. James replied that he would never dream of betraying his supporters; to buy restoration at that price would be infamous. Except for vague compliments he had had nothing from Marlborough for at least two years, and the same applied to the rest. He was now moving (but as slowly as possible) towards Lorraine. What he urgently wanted was a plan, agreed on with Oxford, that could be put into operation the instant Anne died. Ormonde's zeal, he felt sure, could be counted on, but could he bring over the army he commanded? De Torcy was unable to reassure him. No, they must not count on Ormonde's capacity to dispose of the British army; and as for Anne, she simply must not die before the peace treaty had been signed.[21]

As de Torcy saw it, the situation was hazardous. At the same time he could not resist a jest with Monsieur de Montplaisir (his codename for Bolingbroke) at the expense of Mathieu (Prior) who, with the Duke of Shrewsbury in Paris, was making desperate efforts to speed the peace. If he failed, suggested de Torcy, they would hang him.[22]

On November 30th Marlborough, threatened with prosecution, embarked for 'a sort of pilgrimage' to the Continent. With Anne there was to be no leave taking. 'It was confidently reported', says Boyer, 'that his Grace was denied the favour of paying his personal duty to the Queen before he left England'. In England indeed there seemed nothing to keep him: the Queen estranged, Godolphin dead,

Blenheim at a standstill. Maynwaring died ten days before he left. There was something about his going that had a dying fall. 'On assure que le départ de Monsieur de Marlborough', de Torcy told the Pretender, 'est la dernière preuve de la décadence de son party'. But it was more than that. It was almost as though he carried with him much of the glory of her reign. His progress across Europe to Antwerp, via Mindelheim, Aix, Maestricht and Frankfort, was as leisurely as that of the Pretender himself. Nor did Sarah, who viewed it as exile, hurry to join him. Her packing (120 large 'parcels') took time and so did her distribution of presents. Rummaging among discarded oddments she came across a miniature of Anne as a young woman, in a diamond-studded frame; and after adding the diamonds to the pile her grandchildren were to raffle for, she gave the miniature to an old pensioner, Mrs Higgins, who promptly sold it to Oxford for £100. 'Was ever there such an ungrateful beast as that Duchess?' Swift asked Stella, 'takes off the diamonds and gives away the picture to an insignificant woman as a thing of no consequence and gives it her to sell like a piece of oldfashioned plate. Is she not a detestable slut?'[23]

Sarah had in fact hoped that 'some flattering fool would buy it' and so benefit the beldam. 'It did not enter my head', she wrote from Frankfort, 'that anybody should think it reasonable for me to keep a thing that could put me in mind of one that had used the Duke of Marlborough and myself so barbarously'.[24]

Thanks to various pens – Swift's, Lady Strafford's, Dr Hamilton's . . . – the December scene at St James's is pretty clear: Abigail moving into new lodgings, but still paying no calls. (Swift wanted her son to be called Robin, but she insisted on naming him after his father); the Queen out in the snow, or at basset in some closet with the Spanish Ambassador, his hands the dirtiest Lady Strafford ever saw. On the 18th Oxford saw his daughter Elizabeth married to Carmarthen, eldest son of old Danby, Duke of Leeds. Lady Poulett was there 'in all her fine true-lover's knots of diamonds set in as much silver as would make a pair of candlesticks'. On the 19th Lord Fitzharding died and so quitted two valuable sinecures: Treasurer of the Chamber and Teller of the Exchequer.[25]

Hamilton, visiting Anne, found her (though reluctant to admit it) disconsolate at the absence at Petworth of the Duchess of Somerset. In his view, there was still too much reserve on both sides – 'It had been still happier for the Queen if her Grace had been more open . . . she had so much uneasiness elsewhere from other hands'. He had watched the Duchess at Anne's bedside when she was ill, heard her soft, courteous way of speaking and seen the good effect it had had. Even when no words passed between them, he thought he detected an inward delight and a union of souls. This Duchess, he noticed, 'never pressed the Queen hard; nothing makes her more uneasy than that'.

A little before Christmas Hamilton again found Anne 'disquieted' and with gout in her hand. He knew she was being 'teased to prefer Dr Swift' but would not yield; and he told her should he meet Abigail or Oxford he would beg them to keep off business and especially disquieting business. 'She answered softly that I need not do that, to which I replied that she kept all within, whereas nothing was so injurious as disquiet lodged within one's self. I also said that the Duchess of Somerset's calmness made her a most suitable companion to her Majesty; to which she said, "So she is" . . . I presumed to say', adds Hamilton, 'that if the Duchess of Marlborough had been of the temper of the Duchess of Somerset, she had never gone out. "No", says she'. Even so there was a world of difference between the two friendships. To this second Duchess – so cool, so calm, so ineffably well bred – there was no question of catching every post with 'strange scrawls'. When Hamilton asked if he might let her know of Anne's gout he was told no, "she had wrote on Tuesday, and a servant wrote to her every day" '.[26]

Anne had had such pain in her hand at Christmas that she was not expected to appear on New Year's Day. However, she did, receiving in a small, crowded bedroom and even talking of holding drawing-rooms every day. No detail escaped her. When someone mentioned that a chaise from France was being sent over for Abigail, Anne asked Oxford to prevent it. Oxford at this time was receiving both threats and presents: two lamprey-pies from the mayor and corporation of Gloucester, and from someone less benevolent a letter beginning 'Your death is designed by a blunderbuss loaded with a number of balls . . . betwixt Charing Cross and Westminster before next

Candlemas Day'.[27] It was not however by blunderbuss that he was to be dealt his second martyrdom.

Swift, with a bad cold, saw the new year in at Abigail's, where he talked business till out of humour – 'a thousand things wrong, most of them easy to mend, yet our schemes availing at best but little and sometimes nothing at all. One evil which I twice patched up with the hazard of all the credit I had is now spread more than ever'.[28] Oxford and Bolingbroke were as irreconcilable as Anne had been with Sarah.

Early in January 1713 Louis XIV's Ambassador the Duc d'Aumont, scattering largesse, was mobbed on his entry into London by people shouting for the Queen, the Peace and the King of France. Like most foreigners he was stunned by the unpretentiousness of Kensington Palace; it seemed hardly respectable. The household too was unimpressive. Some semblance of a Court was being made by afternoon receptions, now held three times a week. Anne managed to rise from her armchair to greet him and then sank back to talk (or so he said) of the strangeness of her people. D'Aumont from the first had taken against them: proud, independent bourgeois, corruptible with cash. In spite of their welcome he found them a vile mob, doubtless dangerous in the hands of those who knew how to sway them. Perhaps they sensed his hostility. On the Queen's birthday the house where he was staying was burnt to the ground. The Ambassador escaped, but Anne was extremely upset. Already, d'Aumont reported, she had been suffering from gout in feet and stomach, and now she was too scared to show herself at a window. He called her birthday a *jour de crise*. At table with Buckingham he received an anonymous note threatening assassination if he went to the palace. However, he drove to St James's that evening without incident, arriving at seven to find a large, disorderly crowd, showing no respect for anyone. He played basset with the Queen, who was carried through the rooms in a chair, and when she had left he stayed to watch the dancing, marvelling at the difference between St James's and Versailles, one so glittering and polished, the other a drab world of ambition, fleeced by faction of 'what little politeness the British character permits'. After touching upon Anne's plans for the Pretender ('ses intentions ne regardent que son frère'), for whom he himself was scheming, he told Louis Parliament could not be opened until the arrival of 'several men from Scotland', without whom Oxford could not be certain of a Tory majority.[29]

Though there were plenty to notice how conveniently the Queen's illness chimed with the Treasurer's reluctance to have the session begun (it was postponed seven times), she did not in fact walk, that year, from January until July. At Oxford's table Swift raised a laugh by suggesting that when she did make her speech the Queen should begin:

'My Lords and Gentlemen . . . In order to my own quiet and that of my subjects I have thought fit to send the Duchess of Marlborough abroad after the Duke'.[30]

Sarah sailed in February, taking with her forty mantoes and petticoats, and the draft of her *Conduct*, shown a year since to Walpole while in the Tower and now to be rewritten and polished. Like the furious author she was she had wanted to publish instantly, but Walpole had counselled postponement. It was postponed for thirty years.

On March 5th Abigail miscarried. 'I am told that Lord Treasurer and Lady Masham begins to be jealous of one another', wrote Lady Strafford. ''tis now again talked of the Duchess of Somerset's being out and the key is named for the Duchess of Ormonde or Lady Rochester'.[31] But there she was misinformed: the Whig duchess was to stay.

Swift, his preferment ever in the balance, dined on March 8th with Oxford. 'He showed me some of the Queen's speech', he told Stella, 'which I corrected in several places and penned the vote of thanks for the speech; but I was of opinion the House should not sit on Tuesday next unless they hear the Peace is signed, that is provided they are sure it will be signed the week after and so have one scolding for all'.[32] This was cynicism itself; but at least Anne had sense and conscience enough not to make him a bishop. All Abigail's influence did not run to that, nor Oxford's teasing. If Ormonde as Lord-Lieutenant of Ireland chose to make him Dean of St Patrick's, that benefice was his to give. For herself, she had not forgotten the *Windsor Prophecy*.

The Peace was not signed (and then not by Austria) until March

31st. 'The Queen delivered her speech very well', Swift noted, 'but a little weaker in her voice. The crowd was vast'. She spoke of the 'perfect friendship' (Oxford had altered 'harmony' to 'friendship') now existing between herself and Hanover; and of the unparalleled licentiousness of current libels. The town was indeed clamorous with pamphlets and ballads:

> A treaty's on foot, look about, English boys,
> Stop a bad peace as soon as you can,
> A peace which our Hanover's title destroys
> And shakes the high throne of our glorious Queen Anne.
> Over, over, Hanover, over,
> Haste and assist our Queen and our State.
> Haste over, Hanover, fast as you can over,
> Put in your claims before 'tis too late.[33]

Defoe's satirical *Reasons Against the Hanover Succession* was taken literally, which meant an S.O.S. to Oxford to save him from going again to gaol. Oxford usually left such letters unanswered. He was too busy writing to Hanover and trying to wean George from Marlborough and the Whigs. It was futile. What Marlborough had told Sarah in 1710 still applied: 'I have more real power with his Highness than any man in England'.

But the balladmongers were still busy:

> She gave up all her honour,
> Her treaties and her word
> In quitting of her Allies
> And Charles for James the Third,
> And to Lorraine we may go, we may go . . .[34]

The more Anne denied her preference for the Pretender, the less in some quarters it was believed. Hamilton returned yet again to the charge. He had told everyone, he said, that she was not in the Pretender's interest. Did he do well? 'She said yes, you may [say] so with the greatest truth'. He then went on to tell her that Sir Richard Vivian had said he knew England so well, especially the West, that were there any question of bringing in the Pretender, they would turn against Oxford as one man. This pleased the Queen; and when mention was made of the Pretender's nominating a cardinal she said, 'Poor creature, he has influence to do nothing'.[35]

Others felt that they must have reassurance from her own lips; though when Kent and Dorset were shown in for that purpose, 'she spoke so low about the Pretender that they could not tell what to make of it'. It did not please her to be told of it. 'The Duke of Kent came of himself', she said, 'and did they expect I should speak in a passion?'[36] There was no need for Hamilton to remind Anne that Oxford was 'a secret man'. Everyone knew it. But how much of him was genuine and how much sheer trickery and bluff? Here for example is Gaultier reporting to de Torcy from London on March 20th:

> Six days ago M Vanderberg [Oxford] sent for me on a matter of consequence. In effect he opened his heart and let me see his feelings for Montgoulin [Pretender] and the longing he has to serve him directly peace is made. He will bring Protose [Anne] into line and in that he will have no difficulty for she is of his mind.[37]

But after all, if Marlborough could play cat and mouse with the Pretender, so could Oxford, if only to make certain of the Jacobite vote. With friends failing him at home (and how much longer could the Queen's health and favour last?), insurance abroad, in both directions, was the obvious thing. Bolingbroke and Ormonde had seen to it. Abigail and Arbuthnot passed for Jacobites. The Queen herself was suspect. Only a fool would fail to hedge his bet. Swift of course must know nothing of it. To him all his friends must be solidly for Hanover; and so things should remain. He might carry his illusions to Ireland, they could do no harm.

Abigail was nursing her eldest son, who was ill at Kensington. 'She is so excessively fond', wrote Swift, 'it makes me mad. She should never leave the Queen, but leave everything to stick to what is so much the interest of the public as well as her own. This I tell her but talk to the winds . . . She said so much to me of what she had talked to the Queen and Lord Treasurer, the poor lady fell a-crying, shedding tears openly. She could not bear to think of my having St Patricks etc. I was never more moved than to see so much friendship'.[38] It was not long since he had been sighing for his Irish willows. Now he was less sure. Might he not feel in his own country as much an exile as the Shrewsburys did in Paris or the Marlboroughs in Antwerp?

'The Duchess of Shrewsbury has never had a week's health in this country', the Duke now wrote to Oxford, 'and therefore joins with me in thanks for leave to come home . . . To wish the Queen life and health and happiness', he added, 'is no compliment, for all our happiness, I am sure, if not lives, depend upon hers'.[39] It was not perhaps the best of omens that a phoenix, sent to the Queen with two lions, a tiger and an eagle, by the Emperor of Morocco, had just died, as had also the eagle and one of the lions. The voyage had been long, it was explained, the winds contrary. Even for a phoenix resilience had its end.[40]

Shrewsbury was trying to persuade Oxford to give his favourite architect, Thomas Archer, Vanbrugh's job of Comptroller of the Works, since Vanbrugh had 'fallen so much under her Majesty's displeasure that it is supposed he will be removed from his employment'. All Vanbrugh had done was, in a letter to the mayor of Woodstock, to refer to 'the continual plague and bitter persecution' Marlborough had 'most barbarously been followed with for two years past',[41] but it was enough to wreck his career. He consoled himself as best he could by moving into the ruins of Woodstock Manor ('and very pleasant too, although in the middle of rubbish'), and at Rosamund's Well musing amid 'those scenes of love he was so much pleased with'. From the Manor roof he could see the half-finished house called Blenheim. Marlborough was in exile – *qui sait quand reviendra*?

Sarah, who had at first been charmed by her reception in Flanders, wrote now, "tis much better to be dead than live out of England'. Lady Mohun had sent her Addison's *Cato* and told her of Bolingbroke's congratulating Booth (in the name part) for his stand against a dictator, when as everyone knew (or so said Lady Mohun), Cato represented Marlborough. The point was taken. Had she been there, Sarah replied, she would have risen and pointed at Oxford 'whenever a perfidious villain was named that ruined his country to set up himself'.[42] Distance had done nothing to lessen her resentment. She wrote and rewrote, fuming that without Anne's letters her *Conduct* could not be finished and published abroad. One particularly telling passage, omitted from the published version, might have been headed *Semper Eadem*:

When I reflect upon all this I sometimes think that when Posterity shall come to read the annals of our times: a scene of glory, conquest, victory without intermission, at last ending in this manner, were there not authentic records to the contrary they must certainly conclude that just in the most unhappy crisis of time Queen Anne the wise, the good, the just, the honourable, unfortunately died and that she was succeeded by another of the same name but of a temper and principles directly opposite; one who loved only those whom her predecessor hated and hated those whom she loved, one glorying in breaking the contracts and unravelling the scheme in which her predecessor had triumphed, one taking a pride in raising those up whom she had cast down as public enemies and in casting those to the earth whom she had seated on thrones, one in a word untouched with a sense of the miseries of her country and posterity, unmoved with the unhappiness of the world about her, giving back as it were in sport the glories and victories purchased with her subjects' blood and treasure and abusing them to their own unhappiness and misery; one uncapable of understanding or of following the good counsels which had made her predecessor so great; but selfish, passionate, headstrong, preferring the satisfaction of her own private humour or resentments before the safety of her own people and of all Europe.

But when they shall be assured by all the monuments and records of history that this was one and the same Queen Anne who filled this whole period of time; the same who, after having fought so long and so successfully against France, raised it to a greater pitch of power than it ever enjoyed before; the same who, after having made Charles King of Spain, presently dethroned him; the same who, after having entered into the most solemn alliances and contracts, broke through them with so much resolution and ease; the same who, after having owed the quiet and security of her life to her great General and other faithful ministers, afterwards rewarded them with all the ignominy and disgrace she could heap upon them; who . . . but I am weary of recounting these unpleasing things. When posterity comes to be assured of this, will it not shake and surprise them? And will not many be apt to ask what part her justice had in this procedure? What her pity, what her gratitude, what her honour, what her faith and what her constancy? I will give no further answer . . . Facts speak too plainly to be denied.[43]

It was beautifully done; and in the face of such professionalism to quote Hamilton again may seem inadequate and naïve. Nevertheless he spoke as he found, and what he found tallied near enough with what Sarah herself in old age admitted: 'Her kindness to me was real, and what followed afterwards was compassed by the contrivance of such as are in power now'. Sir David Hamilton wrote in his diary:

> I only thanked her Majesty for giving me leave to mention any little concern of mine which gave me trouble and doing me the honour to interest herself therein by advice which I had found successful. To which she answered that it would make her appear very unkind, after my showing so much concern for her health and quiet, not to do it. This was from herself and without the knowledge of others; and everything that came to me from herself was of the same sort; so that I cannot but say that the Queen in herself had all the goodness of temper, of courtesy and breeding, of compassion and inclination to serve the world; and what had another appearance was from outward influence and none of the Queen. Not being intimate with such I am not capable to accuse particular persons, but having spoke to and known so much of the Queen, as to what sprang from herself, I should be false in the highest degree and ungrateful to the countenance she gave me not to maintain to my last breath this character of her, to the honour of her memory.[44]

CHAPTER FOURTEEN

TEMPESTUOUS STATION

1713 - 1714

IN 1713, as spring turned to summer, it was a twilight time between war and peace. Treaties might be signed and peace proclaimed, but Austria still abstained from signing; while in England the Succession was in the balance; and between Anne's chief ministers there seemed nothing better to hope for than a truce.

Visiting the Queen on April 29th Hamilton begged her to take more care of her health, 'for if she happened to die, it was very probable that the nation would be in blood'. To preserve her health, he reminded her, there was nothing like peace of mind. 'Nothing could disquiet her but two things, either the Government, which is left to the ministry, or the Family; each of which she could frown down when she pleased'.[1]

When on May 5th peace was officially proclaimed, Anne said she was well pleased. Austria's absence was a pity, but then 'the Emperors always stood out from coming into a peace'. The next thing must be the thanksgiving . . . 'Blessed are the peacemakers for they shall be called the children of God . . .' Beautiful. How did it go on? 'I have looked in the New Testament', Dartmouth wrote on May 15th, 'and find the verse your Majesty objects to is the tenth, and the Archbishop proposes to end with the ninth . . . which seems a very proper conclusion upon that occasion'.[2] Yes indeed, verse ten – 'Blessed are they which are persecuted for righteousness' sake for theirs is the kingdom of heaven' – would have been quite irrelevant. Dartmouth might at times be too pliable, but he knew his duty. On the eve of the thanksgiving (postponed from June 16 to July 7) he again made bold to advise the Queen:

I humbly beg leave to propose to your Majesty whether it were not better these words were left out: 'For which I have ventured so much and with so great success as obliges me to return thanks to Heaven and next to the affection of my people'. There seems to me to be no occasion for them. Thanking Heaven is a poetical expression and I believe never used from the throne before. 'Thanks to the affection of my people' is not good English . . . but if this is not your Majesty's own opinion I beg it may go no further and that you will pardon the presumption . . .[3]

Anne had been hoping to drive to St Paul's and hear the Tower guns, in their last salute to war, echo the *Te Deum*, specially composed by Handel;* but her gout was still troublesome and Hamilton advised against going. She might, he thought, have recovered sooner had it not been for her uneasiness about Scotland, clamouring again for dissolving the Union. 'Meeting Lord Mar at the back stairs', Hamilton noted on June 4th, 'I desired him not to tease the Queen now the gout was upon her, for what teased the Queen weakened her spirits, whereas by the strength of them illness was to be thrown outwards'.[4] She was encouraged when an attempt to repeal the Union was defeated (though narrowly) in the House of Lords.

On the thanksgiving night a float of barges chained together near Whitehall made a platform for a triumphal arch fifty-two feet high, bearing Anne's arms, crown and motto – all to go up in flames and fireworks. The scene sketched by Thornhill (See page 329) looks too good to burn, but the effects – rockets and cannon, fountains and balloons, 'large water-pyramids and large and small bee-swarms half of which were set with lights to swim on the water' – were, it was mildly said, 'surprising'. But neither Queen, Treasurer nor doctor was well enough to see them. For most of July Oxford was absent with the gravel and eye trouble. Hamilton had gout and was disgusted with Oxford for keeping him three years in arrear with his pay – a thing, he told Anne, Godolphin would never have dreamed of doing. The present Treasurer, he added, promised but did not perform; no wonder he was unpopular. Anne said Oxford was crazy† and if anything happened to him it would be a great loss to her.[5] Throughout July she continued to send him sympathetic letters.

Burnet noted on July 18th that the Queen's end-of-session speech

* By composing a *Te Deum* for the peace thanksgiving Handel offended George of Hanover, who disapproved of the Treaty of Utrecht.

† Crazy formerly meant cracked in the sense of being frail or indisposed.

in the Lords was 'severely reflected on . . . The sharpness with which she expressed herself was singular and not very well suited to her dignity and her sex'.[6] She had made no mention at all of Hanover, and the Lords had taken offence at being called factious. Sarah would have blamed it all on Abigail, for it was she, Sarah said, who had taught an otherwise wellbred woman to vent her spleen.

Visiting Anne on August 1st Hamilton found Abigail in a tantrum – 'a great passion of crying in the Queen's hearing and scolding at Mrs Foyston and Mrs Smith lest they had thrown her child down in the Queen's room on purpose. I took notice', he adds, 'of my Lady Masham's passion as unsuitable to the Queen's temper, and of the Duchess of Somerset's [as] more suitable, to which she [the Queen] replied "Yes by far"; but suitable to her natural goodness made an excuse for my Lady Masham's loud passion, because the child had been lately ill and she was afraid of any hurt to come to it'.[7] Four days later the Queen left for Windsor.

In her absence her business languished. The Duc d'Aumont, reporting to Versailles on August 7, said that Bolingbroke was treated by Anne with extreme reserve. Oxford was ill and Shrewsbury was the only one who could rouse him.[8] He did however pull himself together for the wedding of his son Edward to Lady Henrietta Cavendish, daughter of the late Duke of Newcastle. Her fortune of £12,000 a year had been much angled for, Somerset, on behalf of Hertford his heir, being chief fisherman. To the disgust of the Duchess of Newcastle, however, the match was won by Oxford who, after obtaining leave of absence from Anne at Windsor, slipped away to Wimpole for the wedding. The bride's father had, on marrying the former Newcastle heiress, been honoured by William with a dukedom; and so now what, thought Oxford, could be more reasonable and charming than that the compliment should be repeated, there being no direct male heir? With infinite caution and humility the Queen was sounded. She paused. According to Bolingbroke, she 'presumed to hesitate on so extraordinary a proposal', so that Oxford sensed at once that he had offended. He withdrew, sulky and suspicious. A year afterwards Abigail told Hamilton that Oxford 'had never acted right in the Queen's affairs since his being refused the title of Duke of Newcastle'.[9] He himself called it his never enough to be lamented folly. In his mind it seemed comparable with Marlborough's gaffe in asking to be made Captain-General for life.

Even before his favour had been asked, the Treasurer had received from Anne what Sarah would have called her first peevish letter. 'I desire you would not have so ill an opinion of me', she wrote, 'as to think when I have determined anything in my mind I will alter it'.[10] With a blunt and disheartening truth he had been called to order; and from then on he steadily declined.

If Anne is unlucky in Sarah, as biographer and critic, Oxford is unlucky in Bolingbroke. Like Sarah he puts his own case shiningly. Even his flight to the Pretender is very nearly explained away. But when he writes of Oxford he is venomous and every drop of poison tells:

> He pretended to have discovered intrigues which were set on foot against him, and particularly he complained of the advantage which was taken of his absence during the journey he made at his son's marriage, to undermine him with the Queen. He is naturally inclined to believe the worst, which I take to be a certain mark of a mean spirit and a wicked soul . . . I never knew a man so capable of being the bubble of his distrust and jealousy. He was so in this case, although the Queen, who could not be ignorant of the truth, said enough to undeceive him. But to be undeceived and to own himself so was not his play. He hoped by cunning to varnish over his want of faith and of ability . . . The sum of all his policy had been to amuse the Whigs, the Tories and the Jacobites as long as he could and to keep his power as long as he amused them. When it became impossible to amuse mankind any longer, he appeared plainly at the end of his line.[11]

Before the rift became absolute, Bolingbroke had made a last appeal. 'Separate in the name of God the chaff from the wheat', he begged Oxford. 'Let the forms of business be regularly carried on in Cabinet and the secret of it in your own closet'.[12] What could be more practical? But Oxford's reshuffle was not at all what Bolingbroke had had in mind. Dartmouth was appointed Lord Privy Seal in the place of Bishop Robinson, who was to be Bishop of London. Sir Thomas Hanmer was made Speaker instead of Bromley, now to be Secretary of State for the southern division with jurisdiction over affairs at the Hague. The Earl of Mar was made Secretary of State for Scotland, where Bolingbroke had had some control. Shrewsbury was to be Lord-Lieutenant of Ireland, Sir William Wyndham* (another Jacobite) Chancellor of the Exchequer. In the autumn election the Tories were again returned with a clear majority.

Bolingbroke looked to his defences. The Lord Chancellor, Harcourt, he knew he could count on, and the same went for Wyndham and for Atterbury, whom Anne under pressure – knowing he would be 'as meddling and troublesome as the Bishop of Salisbury' – had made Bishop of Rochester. At Court, though Bolingbroke himself might never thaw the Queen's reserve, it seemed possible that another might do it, at a price. At any rate it was worth trying. And so while Oxford was at Wimpole, Bolingbroke applied himself to cultivating and captivating Abigail. Even to the most sophisticated courtier, the bribing of a favourite must always be a delicate business. There must never of course be mention of cash. What Bolingbroke dangled were shares in Oxford's South Sea Company; and Abigail saw at once that she had earned them and that it would be foolish and churlish to say no. Only Oxford could obstruct the deal and he did. The result was lamentable. Abigail, 'finding the Treasurer could not be brought into those corrupt measures that might fully gratify her avarice, set herself with all the malice that passion could inspire to prejudice the Queen against the Treasurer'.[13] That was why, or so Oxford thought when he returned to Windsor to present the bride and bridegroom, he found the Queen cold and Abigail distant. In October he seriously thought of resigning, but was persuaded by Lord Trevor to stay. Shrewsbury, in a friendly letter, cautioned him against 'late hours of eating and sleeping';[14] but things had gone farther than that.

During the summer the Queen, though still carried from room to room at Windsor, had been in better health. 'After a visit to Windsor in September, the Hanoverian resident wrote almost lyrically of the intense joy felt by the whole Court when on the 13th the Queen had walked for the first time since the previous February. True she had been carried to the Royal Chapel, but she had actually walked back, needing no other help except her Spanish cane in her right hand and the support of the Duke of Shrewsbury'.[15]

* Sir William Wyndham, Bart., (1687–1740), son-in-law to the Duke of Somerset.

Naturally, Jacobites at home and abroad – in Scotland, France and Holland – buried her time and time again. 'The general conclusion comes out', Oxford now heard from Amsterdam, 'that she can't live three months longer . . . but since these three months have continued for these three years, I find they begin to be weary of this'.[16] Defoe was shocked, or for Oxford's benefit pretended to be, at the Whig attitude: 'It is with horror I mention to your Lordship their treatment of the Queen. How visibly they discover in their very faces a secret satisfaction at any indisposition her Majesty may suffer, eagerly enlarge the account and report every trifle of that kind to be fatal'.[17] In his new pamphlet *But What If the Queen Should Die?* Defoe said that while the Queen lived, no one in his senses could imagine one who from infancy had declared her horror and aversion to Popery favouring a Roman Catholic successor, but – Lord have mercy upon us – what if the Queen should die? 'We must with a deep sigh reflect upon the precarious circumstances of the nation, whose best privileges hang uncertain upon the nice and tender thread of royal mortality, and say we are happy while these last and these may last while her Majesty shall live, but what if the Queen should die?'

The question echoed and re-echoed for a year. Would not the Queen's collapse automatically result in a race for the throne? From Lorraine, where the Pretender now was, it might take only three days. And from Hanover . . . ? There were two obvious solutions, or at least precautions. One was to have one of the Hanover family here in residence. The other was to compel the Pretender to move farther off, preferably to Rome, where he might seem to belong. Both plans looked sensible and easy. Both proved impracticable.

'The whole conduct of our ministry', wrote Marlborough from Antwerp to Robethon at Hanover, 'leaves no reason to doubt of their intentions to bring in the Pretender . . . No step in earnest has been made towards removing him out of Lorraine'.[18] The Queen's last plea in that quarter had brought more than was palatable. The Duke of Lorraine, she learned, was by no means prepared to abandon to the rage of his enemies an innocent and distressed prince whose only crime was being the last male heir to the illustrious line on which she herself had shed so much lustre. 'He wants only to be seen', the Duke added, 'to be admired, and needs only to be known to command the utmost respect . . . so bright a wit, such solid judgment, so upright a heart . . .'[19] From portraits (See page 232) and from other contemporary accounts the Pretender – full-lipped and prominent-nosed – appears to have been personable but not always impressive. In his father's opinion, 'never child had a greater resemblance of his parents, both in body and mind'; but in manhood he was found to be reserved and subject to melancholy. Bolingbroke, who eventually fell out with him, said he was unfit to be a king.

In November Bolingbroke, discussing Oxford with a friend said, 'I and Lady Masham have bore him upon our shoulders and have made him what he is, and he now leaves us where we were'.[20] It was the new pairing-off, reminiscent of Anne's 'Masham and me': a bowing to partners in the course of the minuet. Oxford had just suffered another blow in the death of his daughter, Lady Carmarthen. 'The Queen is in a great deal of concern for you', Abigail told him on November 21st.[21]

Baron von Schütz of Hanover, who had not seen Anne for four years, found her this autumn looking fresh and healthy and less red than before. When seated, he said, her corpulence was masked by her robes. But her feelings against Hanover were bitter. 'Her hatred against us is so strong', he told the Elector, 'that she will endeavour to leave the crown to the greatest stranger rather than allow it to fall to the Electoral Family'.[22]

By December Anne was clearly growing testy with Oxford: '. . . Now that I have a pen in my hand I cannot help desiring you again when you come next to speak plainly, lay everything open and hide nothing from me or how else is it possible I can judge of anything? I spoke very freely and sincerely to you yesterday and I expect you should do the same to her that is sincerely your very affectionate friend'.[23]

Her own position remained unenviable. She knew how Shrewsbury felt when writing to Oxford from Ireland he said, 'I hope her Majesty will recall me and name some other Governor more fitly qualified for this tempestuous station'.[24] She was not made, like Marlborough, to ride in the whirlwind and direct the storm.

At Windsor on Christmas Eve Anne was taken violently ill and terrified the Court by remaining unconscious for hours. Dr Shadwell, who diagnosed 'a violent inflammatory fever, not an ague', was against her taking quinine and prescribed bleeding. In this he was backed by Dr Lawrence, but they were overruled by Arbuthnot. The Queen, at one stage, was seized with 'a violent rigour and horror' and had a fluttering pulse. She had a pain in her thigh and recurrent fever. 'God in his mercy to these kingdoms preserve her', wrote Bolingbroke to Oxford, 'Let us see you here without delay'. And on Christmas Day: 'The Queen expressed a desire to see you . . . surely you should be here . . . Lady Masham is continually attending the Queen . . . Pray lose no time in coming. Her Grace of Somerset will be here tonight'.

To the general astonishment Oxford declined to go. 'You know she has every year an ague', he reminded Prior. To dash down to Windsor might cause public panic and a run on the Bank. Ever calm in crisis he would drive around London openly and so set people's fears to rest. Directly he heard that the Queen was better he would go down. 'Whenever anything ails the Queen', he said, 'these people are out of their wits, and yet they are so thoughtless that as soon as she is well they act as if she were immortal'.

The Duchess of Somerset, like Oxford, had hoped to enjoy a quiet, family Christmas; but in this – her sojourns at Petworth – the Queen's complaints of Sarah's long absences were being repeated. Claims of husband and family took priority. 'It must be so sometimes', Anne resignedly told Hamilton, 'He will have it so'. Hamilton, putting his patient first, was disposed to differ; and when he took the Duchess to task she sounded reasonable. Neither the smiles nor the frowns of the Court, she said, would prevent her from doing her duty, but that clearly was twofold: she owed a duty to her family as well as to the Queen, with whom she spent every spare minute. To give all her time to the Queen was impossible.[25] When she received Arbuthnot's summons to Windsor she set out at once and on reaching the Castle found that the danger was over. 'She was received with some coldness', says Coke, 'and was expostulated with about the reason for her non-attendance'. Her excuse that the message had been delayed was accepted, but for the future, said Anne, there would be special messengers for Petworth and signed receipts.[26]

'I find here in town they had her dead on Sunday', wrote Mar to

Lord Findlater on December 29th, 'and some people thought fit to show (as I am told) but very undecent countenances upon such an occasion'.[27] This was echoed next day by Defoe to Oxford:

> . . . it fills every honest faithful subject of her Majesty's with indignation to see these men brighten their faces and betray a secret satisfaction at the appearance of that danger which every good man trembled at, and now how they do feign a joy at her Majesty's recovery, which anyone may see is rather a visible disappointment to them.[28]

It might sound sententious, but Bolingbroke recognised it at once as the very stuff propaganda is made of. To the sick Queen he made the most and worst of the Whigs' joy (if any there had been) over her illness, and found her never more receptive and impressionable. Mrs Manley was directed to write *A Modest Enquiry Into the Reasons for the Joys Expressed by a Certain Set of People Upon the Spreading of a Report of Her Majesty's Death.* Oxford's schemes for a coalition were finished. Anne wished to hear no more of the Whigs. She was back where she had started – indeed in this she might claim that she had never changed – a true Tory in the bosom of the Church. Her health seemed to be mending, or so from the symptoms her doctors thought: 'Her Majesty is lame in both hands', runs the report, 'She now begins to complain of her knee. It is hoped the gout will fall into her feet'. But Abigail, writing to Oxford at the end of January, remained anxious: 'The Queen continues better but is still in my opinion far from well . . . What I write concerning her health she knows nothing of, neither would I for the world have her know it, for our business must be to hearten her; she is too apprehensive already of her ill state of health'. And again on the 27th: 'I was unwilling to send a messenger on purpose, there are so many people upon the watch; but the Doctor has given you his thoughts upon our dear Queen's condition, which makes me hardly able to hold up my head, and I shall only tell you that I pray God you may be able to come here on Friday . . . I am so much out of order I know not what I write . . .'[29]

Two days later Anne wrote to the Lord Mayor of London, referring to the 'aguish indisposition succeeded by a fit of the gout' which had kept her at Windsor and expressing her resolve to open Parliament on February 16th. In the meantime she asked him to 'discountenance malicious rumours spread by evil-disposed persons to the prejudice of credit and to the hazard of public peace'.[30] It seemed that Oxford's gay progress in his chariot had not after all been enough to prevent a run on the Bank. To the best of the City's belief, the Queen was 'a percher' and her coffin bespoke; and though some Whigs might rejoice at the prospect of their party's restoration, if Anne's death let in the Pretender, that might well mean a 'sponge' to wipe out all loans to her Government. The signs were not good. In her looks Anne had changed completely. 'She did not look like the same person as before', says Coke, 'and therefore 'twas expedient to use paint to disguise the discolourings; but this was kept so secret that it never was as much as whispered in her lifetime . . . Count Gallas said she could not live till the following Christmas'.[31]

She did not venture the coach journey to London until February 17th, when Hamilton and the rest welcomed her. Disagreement among her doctors would seem to have been almost if not quite as serious as that between her ministers. Hamilton more than hints at suspicion and malice. 'I imagine', he says, 'the differences among the ministers were then rising to a height and so raised more a jealousy of anybody that stayed long with the Queen'. Anne asked him to leave her door open just in case . . .[32]

Was there anyone for Anne to turn to? Archbishop Sharp was dead, ministers and doctors were divided, the Whigs (including Cowper, whom she now thought party-biased and 'hard as steel') not trusted, the Duchess of Somerset distant, Abigail (as Anne told Dartmouth) listening at keyholes . . . In casting out Sarah and her set she had made way for seven other devils. Was there not in her whole Court one single disinterested soul to be trusted? 'I believe', wrote Anne Sunderland to her sister Mary Montagu, 'God Almighty could hardly find three honest men to save this country as there was in Sodom'.[33]

Bolingbroke was working till two in the morning, at times so exhausted that he nearly fell from his chair. Oxford's lethargy was hopeless; Bolingbroke must do all himself. Whatever happened, he told Shrewsbury, the Queen must never be suffered to 'revert back to that state of thraldom [from] which your Grace was a principal instrument of her deliverance'.[34] And to the Earl of Anglesey:

... the Queen has only one life and whenever that drops, if the Church interest is broke, without concert, without confidence, without order, we are of all men the most miserable. The Whigs will be united and ready to take any hand which their leaders shall give. I will not say that the inclination of the House of Hanover is to the Whigs. I intend to be for them and therefore hope better things of them but . . . I shall be sorry to see it in any degree made their interest to give in to that party whose tyranny we have felt . . .[35]

Thanks to Oxford, wrote Bolingbroke afterwards, the Tories were powerless to exert the strength they had –

We saw our danger and many of us saw the true means of avoiding it, but whilst the magic wand was in the same hands this knowledge served only to increase our uneasiness, and whether we would or no, we were forced with our eyes open to walk on towards the precipice. Every moment we became less able, if the Queen lived, to support her Government, if she died, to secure ourselves . . . We knew that we were out of favour at the Court of Hanover, that we were represented there as Jacobites and that the Elector had been rendered publicly a party to that opposition, in spite of which we made the peace.[36]

Bolingbroke, Oxford, the Queen all found clouds of words (or even, on occasion, lip-movements without words) the most effectual screen for their innermost thoughts and intentions; although compared with the others, Bolingbroke, master both of the spoken and of the written word, was an amateur at dissimulation. Himself the most cynical of occasional conformists, it did not occur to him until it was flung in his face that the Pretender would be mad enough not, for a crown, to change his religion. At worst, most surely, he could like Charles II dissemble it. What could be easier? Without some such move he would stand no chance. Too vividly remembering, as most men did, James II, even a Lutheran was to be preferred to a Roman Catholic.

On February 6th, 1714 the case was bluntly put to the Chevalier by the Abbé Gaultier: 'It is absolutely necessary', he told him, 'that you dissemble your religion or change it entirely'. From a priest this might seem shocking but, as he pointed out, it was to save a nation. On the other hand, he went on, 'you must give your countrymen to understand that you will never touch their religion, their laws, their privileges . . . Your compatriots, you must remember, are very jealous (while not having much of it) of their religion, their liberty and property: all the schemes of the King your father foundered on these three things . . . Encourage Marlborough to make proposals and pretend to welcome them. Oxford asks this and has his reasons . . . Write often in English and be sure to say something flattering about the Queen; and remember never to mention Bolingbroke in any letter I am to read to Oxford'.

Later the same month Gaultier told de Torcy he planned to get Oxford to ask the Queen, in her will, to nominate the Pretender her successor on condition that he changed his religion and conformed to the laws and customs of England.

The same day (February 26th the Pretender, from Bar-le-Duc in Lorraine, launched his bombshell. 'To my last breath', he declared, 'by the grace of God I will maintain my religion . . .' Dissimulation? Never! He was amazed at the suggestion. He would give his life for his country, his conscience and honour never . . .

What a pity, Gaultier commented. Oxford had just told him that, provided the Pretender turned Anglican, measures would next year be taken in Parliament to repeal the Act of Settlement.[37] For Bolingbroke, knowing beyond all doubt that the Pretender could never hope to gain London without first abandoning Rome, the blow was devastating. For himself there might still be time for re-orientation; but what if the Queen should die? The Pretender by his refusal, says Professor Plumb, sealed the fate of Oxford and Bolingbroke, as well as his own.

If, as is now generally supposed, Bolingbroke at this point despaired of the Pretender and turned to Hanover, few of his immediate actions accorded with it. True, he assured France's new Ambassador d'Ibberville that the British would rather have the Grand Turk than a Catholic; but at the same time he took a series of measures consistent only with a Jacobite restoration, the chief of them being a purge of the army to make certain that it was staffed only with officers who would 'serve the Queen without asking questions'.

And what of Anne herself? Her reaction to the Pretender's adamantine refusal is not positively known. Sir Winston, without quoting a reference, says she was staggered, as of course she may well have been. 'She feared that his accession would fatally injure the Church of England, her rock in tribulation. She therefore allowed events to drift on their course, and implored Oxford and Bolingbroke to be reconciled to each other'.[38]

On March 2nd Anne, carried to the Lords to open Parliament, referred to factious rumours that the Hanoverian Succession was in danger. 'Attempts to weaken my authority', she said, 'or to render the possession of the crown uneasy to me can never be proper means to strengthen the Protestant Succession'. The speech caused astonishment. It contained, Schütz told the Elector, coarse expressions, its truculence smacked of Bolingbroke. The *Flying Post* was scathing. On all sides, it said, one might see Jacobites drinking the Pretender's health; yet no loyal subject might dare suggest the Succession in danger until he heard that the Pretender and a French fleet were again in the Firth of Forth or at the mouth of the Thames.[39]

At a crowded Court on March 4th the Queen addressed half a dozen inaudible words to d'Ibberville. On the 5th she touched for the Evil. On the 9th she appeared at her drawingroom looking well and took a hand at basset. Two days later she was again taken violently ill. Dr Shadwell* wrote secretly to Shrewsbury in Ireland:

> On Thursday March 11th the person was seized with a chilliness, vomiting, a pain in the leg, the pulse very disordered and in every manner as two months ago except that the person did not shiver, but the chilliness and cold continued twelve hours and was then succeeded by very great heat, thirst and all the symptoms of a very high fever, which lasted till the next evening . . . On Sunday things were so well that a chicken was eaten with great appetite . . . but this appearance does not cure me of my fears for what may happen to the limb, but everybody else is very happy . . .[40]

'Some of her physicians', says Boyer, 'were for administering the snakeroot, but Dr Shadwell opposed it . . . He feared the erysipelas

* Dr John Shadwell FRS (1671–1747), Physician Extraordinary (9 Nov. 1709), Physician-in-Ordinary (9 Feb. 1712) in succession to Dr Martin Lister. He disagreed with the Queen's other doctors and complained of 'having suffered very much for not agreeing that her Majesty's disease was an ague'.

of the leg might turn to an impostumation, which it did not long after and proved at last the immediate cause of the Queen's death'.[41]

Sophia of Hanover, after reading the reports from England, said she had supposed that Anne was about to 'décamper hors de ce monde'; but again she recovered; while in press and Parliament the tempest continued to rage. Where the cry had been 'The Church is in danger!' it was now 'The Succession is in danger!', both equally invidious and upsetting to the Queen. The Whigs, after narrowly losing their motion to declare the Succession in danger, again insisted that the Pretender must be expelled from Lorraine. But the one thing that agitated Anne most was the thought of Hanover. The question of inviting one of that detestable family over had yet again been hinted at and Anne was positive that she would rather risk the crown than consent to it.[42]

In *The Crisis* and in *The Englishman* Steele had directly accused the Government of jeopardising the Succession, and though defended by Walpole, he was expelled the House. Swift's anonymous counter-attack, *The Public Spirit of the Whigs*, was equally violent and as a matter of form its printer and publisher were arrested. Oxford sent Swift £100 for the printer; and an informer claiming the £300 reward for discovering the author was ignored.

In the spring of 1714 the stage was set for the last act, but the chief actors appeared to be lurking behind the scenes, and with no written parts. The more listless and resigned Anne and Oxford grew, the more desperate it made Bolingbroke and the Lord Chancellor, Harcourt. 'The concern I am under is inexpressible', wrote Harcourt to Oxford on March 17th. 'It is most certain everything may be set right if your Lordship pleases, but . . . should you give way to your resentment,* consider how the Queen will be affected by it, what confusion in every part of the public service must inevitably follow . . .'[43]

Oxford, as his habit was, jotted down that March his seemingly unconnected thoughts: 'Mr Sec. sent me word that I had lost the Queen's favour. He was sensible of it himself in relation to his own concerns . . . I have had all my faults displayed to the Queen . . .

* Oxford was threatening to resign.

complains I never come in time . . . A misunderstanding with the Lady Masham . . . Now is the time to retire'.[44]

Abigail wrote to him on March 22nd: 'I am surprised at your Lordship desiring me to name what I know will be so disagreeable to her Majesty. I did not expect you ever would send me of [sic] such a message. You must excuse me, for I never will carry it, and I hope your Lordship will consider better of it both for the Queen's sake and your own'.[45] She refused to carry his resignation.

A week later Edward Harley, alarmed at his brother's chronic lethargy, tried to insist on his making an effort to drag himself free from 'the leeches of time', to devote himself singlemindedly to the Queen's business. 'The indulgence that some very great men have shown in little passions or habits scarce discerned by themselves till it was too late', he dared to add, 'has proved very fatal to them'.[46]

Indolence, all too obviously, could not be afforded. To imagine for a moment that the Whigs had not taken their measures would be folly indeed; and so good was their Intelligence that nothing was overlooked. Marlborough in Antwerp, for example, was kept well posted of the Queen's day-to-day condition. As Boyer puts it,

> Though the better to conceal the true state of the Queen's health, a trusty physician only [Arbuthnot] was for a long time admitted to see her leg, yet those who were for the security of the Protestant Succession did not want intelligence of the dangerous condition the Queen was in and accordingly took all possible measures to defeat any attempt that should be made to bring in the Pretender on or before a demise.[47]

Marlborough knew perfectly the plans made by Stanhope and Cadogan and shaped his own accordingly. At a double game he was literally a past master, who could beat Oxford and Bolingbroke hands down. Nothing could be more deft than his obtaining from the Pretender a pardon and from the Elector a commission to command the anti-Pretender troops. A fleet must of course be ready, he told Hanover, to thwart any attempted invasion, and the Dutch were preparing one. The danger would be greatest should the Queen linger on for some weeks, for that might 'give the ministers time to concert everything with France for bringing in the Pretender even whilst the Queen was alive'.[48]

As for Anne, she might, wrote Bolingbroke later, have saved herself from all those mortifications of the last months of her reign if only she had bestirred herself; but she was enfeebled by illness and 'that fatal irresolution inherent to the Stuart race hung upon her'. Oxford, he adds, looked on as though he were in fact no more than an onlooker. The same might have been said of the Queen.

CHAPTER FIFTEEN

THE NICE AND TENDER THREAD

1714

In April the Queen recovered or at least appeared to recover. She was able to walk, and to touch for the Evil twice a week. Barring some major crisis she might, it was thought, steadily improve through the summer and perhaps even live for years. 'Krakende Wagens', observed Sophia, 'gân lang'.*

But that was not to be. The Succession alone was a consuming worry, and on April 7th Hamilton found her 'extremely grieved about the talk of some of the Family of Hanover coming over'. Oxford's cousin Thomas Harley had been sent to Hanover with a vague promise of 'further securities'; and so here was the Queen being taken at her word. On the 12th Baron Schütz told Harcourt that the Electress had asked for a writ of summons to the Lords on behalf of her grandson the Electoral Prince (George II-to-be) as Duke of Cambridge. It was nicely timed and contrived.

In a recent Lords debate, when Wharton had proposed a reward for anyone taking the Pretender dead or alive, Lord North & Grey had protested that, devoted though he was to the Hanover Family, 'they must excuse him if he would not venture damnation for them'. Anne's own retort – 'I do not at this time see any occasion for such a proclamation' – was considered a dry answer which 'did not a little revive the hopes and expectations of the friends of the Chevalier de St George', while at the same time it damped the Whigs and the Tory 'Whimsicals' who leaned towards Hanover.[1]

Sophia said afterwards she had meant no more than to enquire about the writ for the Duke of Cambridge, not to demand it. Without telling son or grandson she had sent her message and if, she said, it had happened to reach the Queen by irregular channels, she could not be blamed.

* Creaking waggons travel far.

Anne was enraged. Oxford, writing to his cousin in Hanover on April 13th, said he had never seen her so much moved in his life. If such a message had to be sent at all, Anne should have received it from a Secretary of State, not from the Lord Chancellor. The breach of etiquette was in itself an insult. But the message too was monstrous. As Anne told her Cabinet, it insinuated that though she had often expressed her friendship for the House of Hanover, they would not accept it. Her authority was slighted. She was treated with scorn and contempt . . . and so on, blowing up the coals and heaping the faggots on her own rage. Baron Schütz, the tool of 'rash, angry people', must go. And as for Cambridge's coming over, that, Oxford told his cousin, would automatically convert the Hanover-versus-Pretender contest into one between present possessor and future successor, to the advantage of the Jacobites. 'I could add many other reasons', he ended, 'which [would] make such an attempt stark madness . . . It is the mutual interest of the Queen and the Elector to have a firm friendship, and that the world should know it so. If the world should get it in their heads that a Queen so much beloved is hardly used, God knows what may be the consequence'.[2] By law the demand for the writ could not be refused; but nothing was ever sanctioned with worse grace.

The writ did damage, but at least it could be thanked for rousing Queen and Treasurer from their lethargy. Oxford in his letters to Hanover poured out his soul in protestation: 'I do in the most solemn manner assure you that next to the Queen I am entirely and unalterably devoted to the interest of his Electoral Highness of Hanover . . . I may without vanity say that I had the greatest hand in settling the Succession . . . I am sure', he added, 'that Lady Masham, the Queen's favourite, is entirely for their [Hanover's] succession. I am also sure that the Queen is so'. It would, he thought, be most unfortunate if the Elector should one day find himself King of one party only, and that a party which could not last. He, Oxford, would pawn his life that any advances of kindness from Hanover now would be met with immediate proofs of the Queen's friendship.[3]

The tribute to Abigail's love of Hanover was remarkable, particularly since in the Harley Memoirs it would later be asserted that the writ 'very much alarmed the Queen; and, as I have been told, Lord

Bolingbroke and Lady Masham took this occasion to insinuate that this was a contrivance of the Treasurer's . . . whereas in truth it was by means of the Treasurer and Mr Thomas Harley's conduct there [Hanover] that the Prince's coming over was prevented . . . A letter from Lord Oxford to the Elector fell into the Duke of Marlborough's hands and the Duchess sent it to England, where Lord Bolingbroke got it printed'. Anne was further displeased when told that Oxford's fulsome letter had been printed by his own direction.[4]

News reaching the Marlboroughs at Antwerp was anything but reassuring. The Duke, told of the death of his daughter Elizabeth Bridgwater, from smallpox, fainted. Sarah had for months been convinced that the Pretender would succeed Anne. A relative wrote to her on April 16th, 'I can't believe but that 5 [the Queen] will soon be forced really to declare whether 'tis 13 [Pretender] or 14 [Elector of Hanover]'.[5] Three days later Oxford jotted down a significant memorandum:

> . . . insinuating by half-hints and dark expressions . . . that HM, Lady Masham and HM's chief servants are against the Protestant Succession in the House of Hanover . . . a growing mischief that may have fatal consequences unless a proper remedy be found . . . In my poor opinion the Queen may immediately beat down these reports effectively . . . if HM will have the goodness to send for such persons of the clergy and laity, Lords and Commons as she in her great wisdom shall think fit and let them know from her own mouth HM's thoughts about the Succession . . . that she is desirous to give all public testimonies of her friendship to that family [Hanover] and for confirming their succession which are consistent with her own safety and honour.[6]

But for a number of rather too obvious objections, notably Anne's dread of Hanover, it would have been the ideal plan. As things were, had she not already protested too much? She had been told as much a month before, after she had condescended to reassure personally a couple of doubting earls. 'I told her', Hamilton noted, 'Lord Hervey asked me if a person had not reason to be jealous of his wife if she was always endeavouring to prove her own chastity; asking me if it looked chaste in the Queen, from the Pretender, to send for those noblemen to vindicate herself from being for the Pretender'.[7] Must the royal word be given again and yet again? She cannot have relished it, yet she made herself do it, sending for Sharp's successor at York, Sir William Dawes, and once more solemnly asseverating, in his presence, that she was for Hanover and no other.

But if she was believed in England, and that was doubtful, her intentions were still being called in question abroad. From the Hague Oxford now received details of a projected invasion: '... the Pretender having landed without opposition, the Queen will appear on her throne and will declare to the two Chambers that being convinced in her heart that the Pretender is her brother and consequently the heir presumptive to the crown, that on account of her bodily infirmity she can no longer support alone the burden of the two crowns, she is resolved to associate with him in the Government... This finds much credit here and secret measures are being taken to support the House of Hanover... It is told me confidently that the Pretender's party flatters itself with getting Lord Bolingbroke into its interests, and he would work to ruin your Excellency in the mind of the Queen; indeed it is said that he has already succeeded in doing that...'[8]

The ingenuous plan that Anne should share her throne with the Pretender – an oddly mixed brace of Stuarts – was said to have originated in the mind of Marlborough's gallant nephew the Duke of Berwick. He knew France better than England and James better than the Queen. Oxford of course knew all about Bolingbroke and the Pretender and what was whispered to the Queen, but what more could he do? In his strange, doodling way he jotted: 'The Queen has offered her friendship, wishes returns... You take no care to court her...'[9]

Remembering the Pretender's last futile attempt at invasion, no one believed that anything he designed would prove a walkover. Schütz had reported to Hanover in February, 'Although of every ten men in the [British] nation nine should be for us, it is certain that of fifteen Tories there are fourteen who would not oppose the Pretender in case he came with a French army'. On the other hand Bolingbroke told d'Ibberville it could never be a question of foreign troops but of English hearts. 'The bulk of this nation will be true to their oaths', he added, 'but they will among these oaths in the first place remember that of allegiance to the Queen'. Meanwhile he spoke at length in the Lords in favour of the Protestant Succession, without once mentioning Hanover, and was congratulated by Argyll and Anglesey as 'the only man of honour in his party'.[10] Parliament, reported d'Ibberville, was in tumult and full of bitterness. Bolingbroke hoped never to see such another: 'All the confusion which could be created by the disunion of friends and the malice of enemies has subsisted at Court and in Parliament'. He had had more than enough.

Both Bolingbroke and Oxford are said to have assured Gaultier, on April 26th, that after Anne's death they would recognise no King but James.[11] The astonishing thing was that a Court so divided could still, for public occasions, make a calm and convincing show. 'Yesterday being the anniversary of her Majesty's coronation', runs a newsletter account dated April 24, 'there was a vast appearance of the nobility and gentry at Court to wait on her Majesty . . . In the evening a drawingroom, bonfires, illuminations and other demonstrations of joy . . . The effigies of Jenny Man* the coffee woman and Richard Steele Esquire were attended to a bonfire with the usual ceremony, both of them having made themselves famous for affronting the best of Queens in the most odious manner possible'. And under May 1: 'On Thursday the Queen took the air as far as Kensington and yesterday touched for the Evil and it is observed that she never was better'.[12]

The façade still mattered. Whatever the Queen's trouble, whether gout or doubt, the world must for as long as was humanly possible be kept in the dark. 'Yesterday in the evening', Erasmus Lewis told Thomas Harley on May 7th, 'the Queen returned from Kensington to St James's very much indisposed, which is attributed partly to a cold she is supposed to have taken and partly to the reports generally spread and believed here that the Court where you are [Hanover] is determined to keep no measures with her . . . I saw your friend Dr Arbuthnot this afternoon, who told me her Majesty was much better'.[13] All Hamilton has to say, under the same date, is: 'A new

* 'Whig army officers found their natural habitat at Old Man's in the Tilt Yard. This establishment, stoned by a Tory mob during Sacheverell's trial, was kept by that staunchest of Whig hostesses, Jenny Man'. Holmes: *British Politics in the Age of Anne*, 23.

illness returning, my mouth was stopped. Probably about Family of Hanover coming to Britain'. He was not pleased with Arbuthnot's new rota, allowing the Queen's doctors to be admitted 'one a day, in his own turn' and not oftener.[14] It sadly reduced his time for gossip.

In their formal reply of May 7 to Anne's offer of further security, Sophia and her son now asked for four things: the removal of the Pretender – 'full of plans for a descent on the north of Great Britain' – from Lorraine; a grant sanctioned by Parliament for Sophia as heiress-apparent; British titles for Electoral Princes; and an establishment in England for a member of the Electoral House.[15] All reasonable enough; yet to expect Anne's compliance was, as Sophia had said of Spain, like trying to bite the moon. Her letters to Hanover of May 19 were so harsh that the Electoral Princess Caroline suspected they had been inspired by Bolingbroke. In them Anne said she felt certain that the Elector would never tolerate the least encroachment on his authority. Very well – nor would she on hers. She then turned to his son. 'Nothing', he was told, 'could be more dangerous to the peace of my kingdom, to the right of succession in your line, nor consequently more disagreeable to me at this juncture than such a *démarche*' [as his coming over].

To Sophia Anne wrote: 'There are here – such is our misfortune – a great many people that are seditiously disposed . . . Propose whatever you may think may contribute to the security of the succession. I will come into it with zeal provided that it do not derogate from my dignity, which I am resolved to maintain'[16] – a proviso comparable with Sarah's when, writing to Blenheim's clerk of the works, she ends: 'I am your friend if you do as I bid you'.

Oxford at his oiliest seized his chance and once again, for Hanover's benefit, bared his loyal soul. 'I profit of this occasion', he wrote, 'to lay myself at your feet. I have no enemy who knows me that is not just enough to allow me to be inviolably attached to your Succession. Nothing comes in competition with that because I know I please the Queen when I am zealous for the service of your Serene House . . . I am sure the Queen is most heartily for your Succession . . . As I am sure your Royal Highness's great wisdom would not choose to rule by a party, so you will not let their [the Whigs'] narrow measures be the standard of your Government . . .'

Sophia too was assured that as her Serene Family were to reign over the whole British nation, so she would be too wise to attach herself to one party. 'It is a steady and fixed resolution in the Queen', Oxford added, 'to secure and confirm your Succession; and as I have never varied in my zeal for it, so I shall make it my study to watch every occasion to promote the interest of your Royal Highness, and particularly to cultivate that friendship with the Queen which is so necessary for this good end, which I know her Majesty sincerely desires'.[17] That Hanover should at this stage turn Tory was as devoutly to be wished and as unlikely as that the Pretender should turn Protestant. Still, it had to be attempted.

Sophia, in contrast to Anne, had always been a calm person; but all this was too much for her; the letters – especially Anne's – 'cast such a damp upon her spirits' that she could not shake it off. She gave orders for two of them to be printed, 'that the world might see it was not her fault if her children lost three kingdoms'. She then tried to regain her composure. On June 8th she was walking with Princess Caroline and a lady-in-waiting in the grounds of Herrenhausen when it began to rain. She hurried for shelter, collapsed suddenly and, without doctor or priest at hand, died. Some said the Queen's letter had killed her. Certainly Anne's attitude was extraordinary. 'I asked her', says Hamilton, 'if Princess Sophia's death added anything to her quiet or disquiet, to which she said that Princess Sophia was chipping-porridge, it would neither give more ease nor more uneasiness'.[18] To tender official sympathy she then sent to Hanover as Envoy Extraordinary the new Earl of Clarendon, the same who, as Lord Cornbury, had represented her in New York in woman's dress.

Clarendon was instructed to explain more fully how it was that the Queen, with the best will in the world, was unable to fall in with Hanover's wishes. The Pretender in Lorraine was beyond her control (even a letter would be treason); but the Queen thought herself fully secured by treaties and by the duty and affection of her people against all attempts whatsoever. As for the suggestion that one of the Electoral Family should live in England 'to take care of the security of her royal person, of her kingdoms and of the Protestant Succession, this God and the laws have entrusted to her Majesty alone'. It would be dangerous and unconstitutional to attempt to share it. And titles? In view of what had just happened over the dukedom awarded to the Electoral Prince, the Queen felt little encouragement to grant more; but in any case, in William's reign titles for foreigners had caused so much dissatisfaction that Parliament had since ruled against them.[19]

Anne, still constantly warned by Hamilton of the danger of disquiet in cases of gout, saw nothing but dissension. 'We are the most unhappy nation under the sun', Halifax wrote to Oxford, 'running to inevitable destruction'.[20] In May Bolingbroke had the Schism Bill, aimed against the dissenters' academies, introduced into the Commons as 'a mine to blow up the white staff' and with it Oxford who as Treasurer held it. Wharton rose in the Lords to express his surprise and pleasure at seeing 'some men of pleasure on a sudden become so religious as to set up for patrons of the Church; but he could not but wonder that persons who had been educated in dissenting academies, whom he could point at, should appear the most forward in suppressing them . . .' The only reason for this behaviour that he could think of was 'apprehension lest they might produce still greater geniuses that should drown the merits and abilities of those great men'.[21] After heated debate the Bill narrowly passed the Lords on June 25.

At the end of May Oxford read Anne at Kensington an anonymous letter, threatening her life.[22] She left at once for St James's, but 'finding herself somewhat better' returned to Kensington on June 10th. Apart from indigestion, after eating rice cakes, she seemed pretty well and made plans for Windsor. Three weeks before her death a direction was issued: 'This is the proper time for repairing the roads between London and Windsor. Her Majesty will be going thither very shortly and care must be taken that the persons liable thereunto do immediately repair the same'.

Her Court was, as usual, dull. 'Nothing but ceremony, no manner of conversation', complained Lady Orkney, 'My Lady Burlington in good earnest and imitated in perfection; the Duke of Somerset sitting at a little table by, that the ladies (and most of them his own daughters) might have room, without one bit of meat upon it till the other table had done; the Duke of St Albans a-jesting, Lord Arran sleeping, my Lord Burlington eating with his eyes. We played after dinner, drank tea, bowed extremely and so returned'.[23] It was the scene Pope painted:

> Here thou, great Anna, whom three realms obey,
> Dost sometimes counsel take – and sometimes tea.*
> In various talk th'instructive hours they pass'd,
> Who gave the ball or paid the visit last.
> One speaks the glory of the British Queen,
> And one describes a charming Indian screen;
> A third interprets motions, looks and eyes:
> At every word a reputation dies.
> Snuff or the fan supply each pause of chat,
> With singing, laughing, ogling and all that.[24]

Few, reported d'Ibberville, saw the Queen at all and of those few the Duchess of Somerset, though married to an extreme Whig, had all her confidence. There was much speculation, he added, as to what might happen at her death, both Whigs and Tories betting on civil war. Clarendon's being prepared for Hanover was suspicious. True, as Cornbury he had been the first to desert James for William, but now he was a zealous Jacobite.[25]

Early in June Shrewsbury returned from Ireland, 'resolved to act a cautious and reserved part'. Anne begged him to try to reconcile Oxford with Bolingbroke, but where she and Swift had failed, there seemed slight hope even for the King of Hearts. On June 9th Oxford sent the Queen his *Brief Account of Public Affairs Since August 8, 1710 to June 8, 1714*, in which he accused Bolingbroke of peculation. As for himself, 'Do with me what you please', he wrote, 'displace me or replace me . . .' And then (though this may have been struck out – it was in the draft): 'Your affairs are looked upon to be desperate'. Indeed they were.

At one stage, according to d'Ibberville, Shrewsbury put Oxford's case so strongly to Anne that she sent for Bolingbroke and told him

* Tea (pronounced tay) reached England from China (not yet from India) via Holland and was expensive. A bill at Blenheim shows that Sarah bought tea for Queen Anne at £2 a pound.

sharply that if he could not get on with the Treasurer he must resign. He told her he had no other wish. It was vital to her health and to that of her kingdom that they should learn to agree. 'The Duke of Shrewsbury led her into the Council Room', Peter Wentworth noted on June 14th, 'She has not been able to walk so far for some time past.'[26]

Three days later Marlborough, about to leave Antwerp for England, wrote to Hanover: 'My best friends think my being in England may be of much more use to the service than my continuing abroad'.[27] His movements were anxiously watched. 'We are all frightened out of our wits', wrote Prior, 'upon the Duke of Marlborough's going for England'.

Count Bothmar, sent from Hanover in place of Schütz, found Anne, when she gave audience on June 29th, pale and gracious. In his report to Hanover he referred to Oxford's unfathomable duplicity and gave it as his opinion that both he and Bolingbroke favoured the Pretender, whose head now carried a reward of £100,000. Oxford was astute, Bolingbroke rash. Neither was to be trusted. Each was hoping to overthrow the other.[28]

In the first week of July Bolingbroke looked to be the loser when he, Arthur Moore and Abigail were named as having shared a large sum from the Assiento slave-contract, assigned to the South Sea Company by the Treaty of Utrecht. Oxford's refusal to sanction Abigail's bonus had finally lost him her friendship; and now, with Moore censured and dismissed from the South Sea, awkward questions were asked in the Lords as to the Queen's share in the same contract.* No one of course begrudged her her profit from the slave trade, but who were her mysterious assignees? Did anyone, for example, know Manuel Manasses Gilligan Esquire? Nobody did. On July 9th Anne drily told the Lords that she would dispose of her share of the profits as she should judge best for the service. This, though it raised a Tory laugh was 'very ill relished by the Whigs'.[29] Indeed, Wharton called it an affront to the House. It still would not have saved Bolingbroke had not the Queen, finding her Parliament

* In November 1713 the Assiento agreement was found to include a $22\frac{1}{2}\%$ share of trading profits for Queen Anne. Under pressure she ceded this back to the Company in June 1714. See Dickson: *The Financial Revolution in England*, p. 67.

'in a flame', promptly prorogued it. Supported to the throne, she spoke firmly and audibly, but again made no mention of the Succession. Bothmar, reporting this to Hanover, added that Bolingbroke was expected to bring over the Pretender before the next session (August 10), if only to save himself from impeachment.

On July 12th Hamilton found the Queen upset. The cause was said to be from something she had eaten, but he guessed the real trouble to have been 'the hot speeches made upon her answer to the address of the House about the South Sea'. There was some misunderstanding about Lord Cowper. Mischiefmakers had been 'putting confusion and commotion among persons she trusted, which she hated as any mortal poison'. While careful to name no one Hamilton insists that Anne was being deliberately misled and forced to yield to others, 'for', he adds, 'by management few were admitted to give her a contrary account to what was habitually sounding in her ears'.[30]

One wonders to what extent if any Anne still trusted Abigail. Oxford had been trying to regain her favour. In May he had adopted a chiding tone: 'You disable a fine friend to serve you and thereby you help nobody. You cannot set anyone up, you can pull anyone down. You have nobody about you does not tell stories . . . What is your scheme? What will the world say? The first point is to support the Queen and encourage her. Do not terrify her with differences of her fast friends. The enemy make their advantage at your coldness or anger to me. What view can you have in it? It is the pretence (to wise people) for their jealousies. Has it not done hurt enough to the Queen already? If you hate me, however, counterfeit indifference, for the Queen's service'. It did no good and on June 8th he told the Queen, 'Lady Masham was right, if she did not meddle against me, to say she would not meddle for me'.[31]

Arbuthnot kept Swift posted. Writing to him on June 12th he said Abigail had some time since told Oxford she would carry no more messages nor meddle nor make. And on the 26th: 'The Dragon [Oxford] dies hard. He is now kicking and cuffing about him like the Devil . . . no hopes of any settlement between the two champions'. On July 6th Swift heard from Erasmus Lewis: 'The two ladies [Anne and the Duchess of Somerset] seem to have determined the fall of the Dragon and to entertain a chimerical notion that there shall be no M le Premier, but that all power shall reside in one and profit in the other'. This, thought Lewis, would suit Bolingbroke, but his faults were glaring and 'we cannot find there is any scheme in the world how to proceed'. On the 17th he repeated to Swift what Abigail had told Oxford 'in her own house last Thursday morning: "You never did the Queen any service, nor are you capable of doing her any". He made no reply but supped with her and Bolingbroke . . . His revenge is not the less meditated for that. He tells the words clearly and distinctly to all mankind. Those who range under his banner call her ten thousand bitches and kitchenwenches. Those who hate him do the same and from my heart I grieve that she should give such a loose to her passion, for she is susceptible of true friendship and has many sociable and domestic virtues'. On the 24th Swift heard of Arbuthnot's being stormed at by Abigail – '. . . that I did not care if the Great Person's affairs went to entire ruin so I could support the interests of the Dragon. That I did not know the half of his proceedings. Particularly it was said, though I am confident it was a mistake, that he had attempted the removing her from the favour of a Great Person. In short, the fall of the Dragon does not proceed altogether from his old friend, but from the Great Person, whom I perceive to be highly offended, by little hints that I have received . . . I have been', ends Arbuthnot, 'but indifferently treated myself by somebody at Court, in small concerns. I can tell who it is [Hamilton?], but mum for that. Adieu'.[32]

As the last crisis approaches, Oxford's jottings, when legible, read sometimes like the musings of a drunkard – 'The Queen's name used dangerously. What have I done? Send for the Duchess of Somerset, nobody else can save us . . . After this it is direct madness to depend upon you, nobody will believe you act by yourself . . . You manage so as neither to be for Hanover nor for the Pretender . . .'[33] – yet it may well be that to him these self-addressed memoranda, meant only for himself, were clear enough: they may have helped him to unfuddle his mind. In this case 'The Queen's name used dangerously' must refer to Shrewsbury's complaint that orders were sent him in Ireland without Cabinet sanction: a lapse which made the Queen furious. And the last lines would appear to be addressed to Bolingbroke. But what a set! As Buckingham wrote when he was turned out of office –

> How has this poor nation been governed in my time? During the reign of King Charles II we were governed by a party of French whores; in King James II's time by a parcel of popish priests; in King William's time by a parcel of Dutch footmen; and now we are governed by a dirty chambermaid [Abigail], a Welsh attorney [Trevor?] and a profligate wretch [Bolingbroke] that has neither honour nor honesty.[34]

Not surprisingly Anne now owned to Hamilton that she had no one to trust. She excepted himself and, supposedly, a small handful of others including the Duchess of Somerset and Henry Wise. The sunk garden Wise had made from a gravel-pit at Kensington (answered with a mount) was as soothing a place to sit in as was her Greenhouse beside it; and now at Windsor he was perfecting the Maestricht garden close to the Thames. (See back end-paper). She looked forward to seeing it. In the meantime she gave him fresh orders about the Emperor of Morocco's spotted deer. No time must be lost in replacing the ones that had died. The Emperor was manifestly a barbarian, but there were good reasons for humouring him. If sixty-nine British prisoners were to be freed, the Emperor must 'with the utmost expedition' have the deer plus 'two dozen of the largest china dishes that can be had' plus 'two large copper tea-kitchens and a little fine tea'. On top of all this he demanded an exchange of prisoners: '60 Moors, 30 of which must be ready at the delivery of the Christians . . . He has ever demanded from other nations', it was knowingly added, 'two Moors for one Christian'.[35]

On July 23rd Hamilton had a long and emotional interview with the Queen, their talk ranging from the Pretender to the dismissal of Godolphin (now regretted); and taking in on its rambling way Oxford's boast that he would teach the Queen to equivocate, and Cowper's scorn for tricking and shuffling. It was a melancholy recapitulation, for Anne must have seen all too clearly where she had gone wrong. She had meant well. She had been misled. It was now too late . . . 'This discourse', says Hamilton (and would that he had reported it more fully), 'melted me to that degree that Lady Masham was surprised to see me come out with such a violent heat'. To her he pleaded bashfulness, but in fact he was flushed with 'resentment at those, whoever they were, who had brought her [the Queen] to that distress of mind, and from the pleasure I had to see her trust in me as a reward of my faithfulness as her physician and my unbiased regard to her as her subject'.[36]

Revisiting her at Kensington on the 27th Hamilton thought to please her by saying, on good authority, that the Electoral Prince would not be coming over. She said 'that gave her no uneasiness now'. She seemed eager to write secretly to the Elector to tell him that 'the changes she was about to make should not injure him nor lessen her friendship to him unless he was the cause of it himself by personal ingratitude, and that if he would write to her upon this her profession of friendship, she would immediately answer it with her own hand without the knowledge of any of her ministry, and desired that his writing might be without the knowledge of any of his. For most of them sought themselves, they had neither regarded her health, her life nor her peace; but at the same time', adds Hamilton, 'she asked me if I could find no excuse to go to Hanover, without people's suspicion of being sent. To which I said yes, by removing my son from Oxford and settling him at Leyden or Utrecht I could have the excuse of going over with him, having now no family . . .' His mission would have been 'to settle a sincere friendship with the Elector and remove all occasions of jealousy, and in such a way as would give herself least disquiet . . . He [George I] was to ask leave to come over to pay a visit to her for three or four weeks, by which means he would have entire satisfaction and she quiet, she resolving to put it upon him to make changes. This confidence affected me even to tears . . . but sudden death coming in prevented her going on; for she told me Lord Oxford would be out that night, and upon telling her that [Lord] Bolingbroke was said to get [succeed to] the staff, she said no; as also upon my telling her that persons said the reason why my Lord Oxford was to be out was because he had hindered her Majesty from giving grants to Lady Masham, to which she answered that if he said so he was very ungrateful to Lady Masham'.[37]

It was an astonishing interview, showing beyond all doubt that Anne, knowing her brother would never change his religion, had finally thrown him over in favour of Hanover. How much this decision had cost her and when she had made it – tragically late – will never be known. But for Hamilton we would not know so much. Now at the eleventh hour, mistrusting her ministers, she was prepared to abandon protocol and with it her profound reluctance to have her successor near her even for a week. She had once made a bishop Lord Privy Seal and plenipotentiary. Now she would send her doctor – the only man in her 'family' she could still trust – as secret envoy to Hanover. It might have worked, but again it was too late.

The Queen dismissed Oxford that same day; and in the manner of it he was luckier than Marlborough and Godolphin had been, and herself braver, sending for him as she did and talking with him for 'above two hours'. His own account of that interview compares favourably with the reasons Anne baldly gave her Cabinet Council for his dismissal. In those, grants to Abigail did not of course figure; though when Hamilton had probed, she had prevaricated. There were, to her mind at least, several better reasons: 'that he neglected all business, that he was seldom to be understood, that when he did explain himself she could not depend upon the truth of what he said; that he never came to her at the time she appointed; that lastly, to crown all, he behaved himself towards her with bad manners, indecency and disrespect'.[38]

In contrast to this (to Swift from Lewis) we have Defoe's fascinating, if in parts sickening, *Secret History of the White Staff*, thought to have been dictated or directly contributed to by Oxford himself. In this the Dragon nearly turns phoenix, or would have us believe so. He is viper too. The Queen, at that last interview, is warned against those plotting her ruin: the black designs of men pretending to serve her, who had sacrificed her peace for their own avarice and ambition. These traitors 'aimed at things which, if they did not directly advance the interest of the Pretender, yet tended to the prejudice of the House of Hanover . . .' A lurid background against which Oxford, 'leading the Queen by the hand to a clear view of the gulf they were going to sink her into', shines with a clear pure light. It is heady stuff. 'A discourse of this nature', Defoe dutifully goes on, 'was too moving not to affect even her Majesty herself. She felt the return of those kind sentiments which had taken such deep root in her mind in favour of the White Staff [Oxford] on former occasions; and I have been informed that from this moment her Majesty formed some new resolutions on this affair, that although she did at present receive the staff, yet [that was] not immediately to gratify the instruments in the placing it; and in a short while [she meant] to restore it to the same hands again, upon the foot of such schemes as he had laid before her'. Of such table-turning in extremity only Oxford of all men then living was capable. When Harcourt heard of it he was enraged. ' "The Blast of Hell and the rage of a million devils be on this cursed Staff", said he, slinging the purse on the ground, "It is he that has ruined us and broken all our measures . . . I told you always it was impossible to supplant him with the Queen; that she could never hear him speak, such was the magic of his tongue, without being enchanted with his words and that if he got but the liberty for five words he would undo us all" '.[39]

The evening after Oxford's dismissal Bolingbroke gave a dinner party for the younger Whig leaders – Stanhope, Craggs, Pulteney, Cadogan, (Walpole was absent) – at his house in Golden Square. Whatever his desperate scheme was, it failed. As he left, Stanhope told his host, 'Harry, you have only two ways of escaping the gallows. The first is to join the honest party of the Whigs; the other to give yourself up entirely to the French King and seek his help for the Pretender. If you do not choose the first we can only imagine that you have decided for the second'.

It was too late to switch, too late even to worry; yet the ferment increased. That night's Council, for naming the new Treasury commissioners, lasted till two in the morning. In the Queen's presence Oxford, with nothing to lose, flung everything – corruption, peculation, disloyalty, treason – into Bolingbroke's face.* For himself, he would be revenged and 'leave some as low as he had found them'. Anne, silent and seemingly withdrawn, told Arbuthnot afterwards that she would hardly outlive it. She slept little and next day (Wednesday) was low-spirited and again at Council said little.

Hamilton, summoned with the other doctors on Thursday morning, found she had 'a trembling in her hands, a pain and heat in her

* In Mr Holmes's opinion this confrontation may have occurred on July 25 or 26. The contemporary accounts are conflicting.

head, with sleepiness, and a little bleeding at the nose'.[40] It was decided to cup her (she preferred that to phlebotomy) and this gave her some ease. 'Towards seven o'clock she woke again and finding herself pretty well rose from bed and got her hair combed. This done, towards eight her Majesty went to look on the clock,* and Mrs Danvers, taking notice that she fixed her eyes a long time upon it, asked her Majesty what she saw in the clock more than ordinary. The Queen answered her only with turning her head and a dying look, at which Mrs Danvers being frighted she called for help. The physician in waiting, judging that she was seized with a fit of apoplexy, caused her to be let blood'.[41] She then became unconscious for about an hour and on coming to, heard a thud. Abigail had fainted.

That Thursday Abigail wrote to Swift:

> My good friend . . . The Queen has got so far the better of the Dragon as to take her power out of his hands. He has been the most ungrateful man to her and to all his best friends that ever was born. I cannot have so much time now to write all my mind because my dear mistress is not well and I think I may lay her illness to the charge of the Treasurer, who for three weeks together was teasing and vexing her without intermission, and she could not get rid of him till Tuesday last . . . Will you leave us and go to Ireland? No, it is impossible. Your goodness is still the same, your charity and compassion for this poor lady who has been barbarously used won't let you do it. I know you take delight to help the distressed and there cannot be a greater object than this good lady who deserves pity . . . I must go to her for she is not well . . .[42]

'Poor woman', wrote Lewis to Swift, of Abigail, 'I heartily pity her. Now is not the Dragon born under a happy planet to be out of the scrape?'

Two duchesses – Somerset and Ormonde – were in waiting. The first, asking the Queen how she did, was answered 'Never worse. I am going'. The second sent urgently to the Privy Council in session at the Cockpit, to hurry to Kensington, which they did, there to be joined by Somerset and Argyll. Their sudden appearance unbidden

* Possibly the superb Tompion bracket-clock still to be seen in a closet of Anne's at Kensington Palace.

caused astonishment. As Privy Councillors however they had every right to be there, and Shrewsbury made them welcome.

On Friday morning (anniversary of the death of Gloucester) Anne was in convulsions and thought to be sinking, but again she rallied and, with help, put the Treasurer's staff into the hands of Shrewsbury. The effect of this on the Jacobites, Defoe wrote afterwards, was like a clap of Christmas thunder to a female soothsayer. They were 'in an astonishment that divested them of all power . . . We are told some of them had the assurance to ask her Majesty if she knew what she did; to which she gave such an answer as they deserved'.[43] The Queen would have needed to be even farther gone than she was to have handed the staff to Bolingbroke, and he knew it.

Messengers from the Privy Council sped to the Governor of the Tower, the Lord Mayor, judges, mayors, lord-lieutenants, to ports and garrisons. Troops were summoned from Flanders, the drums of the trained bands were heard everywhere and judged an ill omen for the Jacobites.

'The thunder had long grumbled in the air', wrote Bolingbroke, 'and yet when the bolt fell most of our party appeared as much surprised as if they had had no reason to expect it. There was a perfect calm and universal submission through the whole kingdom. The Chevalier indeed set out as if his design had been to gain the coast and to embark for Great Britain, and the Court of France made a merit to themselves of stopping him and obliging him to return. But this to my certain knowledge was a farce, acted by concert to keep up an opinion of his character when all opinion of his cause seemed to be at an end'. In the circumstances, an attempted invasion would, as Bolingbroke told the Pretender afterwards, have been 'in the last degree extravagant'.[44]

News and rumour flew about the country:

July 30 (Friday). Lord Lansdowne to Oxford: 'I am this moment come from Kensington. The Queen is very dangerously ill, and little hope but from the working of the blisters . . . The Council resolved unanimously to desire her to put the Treasurer's staff into the Duke of Shrewsbury's hands, which she did, being perfect in her senses.[45]

July 30. Newsletter: People are in a strange consternation upon this sudden illness of her Majesty . . . I am informed that when Dr Radcliffe was sent for he answered tomorrow would be time enough; but the insolence of this expression makes me scruple the truth of it.

July 30. Peter Wentworth to Lord Strafford: 'I got to Kensington about six o'clock and whilst I was there her Majesty had the benefit of vomiting thrice by the help of cardis. Dr Arbuthnot said 'twas the best symptom they had had today and that she felt pain in her feet, there being garlic laid to 'em, which likewise was well, and was gone to sleep ... I overheard Dr A in a whisper say 'twas ten thousand to one if she recovered; which was dismal to me. The chaplains desired the Queen's servants that were in waiting to come and pray for the Queen, so I and three or four more was the whole congregation'.[46]

July 31. Ford to Swift: 'Her disorder began between eight and nine yesterday morning. The doctors ordered her head to be shaved & while it was doing she fell into a fit of the convulsion or as they thought an apoplexy. This lasted near two hours & she was speechless & showed little sign of life ... but came to herself upon being blooded. As soon as she recovered, my Lord Bolingbroke went to her & told her the Privy Council was of opinion it would be for the public service to have the Duke of Shrewsbury made Lord Treasurer. She immediately consented & gave the staff into the Duke's hands ... She continued ill the whole day. In the evening I spoke to Dr Arbuthnot & he told me he did not think her distemper was desperate. Radcliffe was sent for to Carshalton ... but said he had taken physic and could not come ... This morning when I went there before nine they told me she was just expiring. That account continued above three hours & a report was carried to town that she was actually dead. She was not prayed for even at her own chapel at St James's & what is more infamous, stocks arose three per cent upon it in the City. Before I came away she had recovered a warmth in her breast & one of her arms & all the doctors agreed she would in all probability hold out till tomorrow; except Mead, who pronounced several hours before, she could not live two minutes & seems uneasy it did not happen so ... The Council sat yesterday all day & night ... Last night the Speaker & my Lord Chief Justice Parker were sent for, and the troops from Flanders. This morning the Hanover Envoy was ordered to attend with the black box [nominating thirteen Lords Justices as regents], and the heralds to be in readiness to proclaim the new King ...[47]

The small room where she died, in Kensington Palace, sounds to have been very full indeed. Lady Frescheville was sent for to join the two duchesses, Abigail, Mrs Danvers and the rest; the Bishop of

London, with chaplains, stood ready to administer the last rites; and there were no fewer than seven doctors: Lawrence, Shadwell, Arbuthnot, Sloane, Hamilton, Blackmore and Read.*[48] It was hardly surprising that Radcliffe declined to join them. 'I knew the nature of attending crowned heads in their last moments too well', he wrote later, 'to be fond of waiting upon them without being sent for by a proper authority . . . However, ill as I was I would have gone to the Queen in a horse-litter had either her Majesty or those in commission next to her commanded me so to do . . . But the people about her', he adds, 'the plagues of Egypt fall on them! put it out of the power of physic to be any benefit to her'.[49] Heavily censured for not going, he was in fact dying and in three months was dead.

The person who sent for Radcliffe is said to have been Abigail; but Burnet maintains that the Duchess of Somerset was 'by much the greatest favourite when the Queen died'. It was she, it seems, and not Abigail who at the last proved the most comfort. 'The town tell a world of stories of Lady Masham now', wrote Peter Wentworth, 'as that a-Friday she left the Queen for three hours to go and ransack for things at St James's . . . I hope people wrong her, for she would be a monster in nature to be ungrateful and to forget a Queen so soon that raised her from nothing'.[50]

Queen Anne, after lying in a coma for several hours, died at half-past seven on Sunday morning, August 1st. She was forty-nine. 'My dear mistress's days were numbered', wrote Arbuthnot to Swift, 'even in my imagination, and could not exceed certain limits, but of that small number a great deal was cut off by the last troublesome scene of this contention among her servants. I believe sleep was never more welcome to a weary traveller than death was to her; only it surprised her too suddenly, before she had signed her will, which no doubt her being involved in so much business hindered her from finishing . . . My case is not half so deplorable as poor Lady Masham's and several of the Queen's servants, some of whom

* According to Radcliffe, Dr Mead also prescribed, but Trevelyan omits his name from those in attendance at the deathbed. Sir William Read was oculist-in-ordinary to Queen Anne. There is also mention in the Downshire Papers (page 902) of a Dr Daniel Malthus.

have no chance for their bread but the generosity of his present Majesty'.[51]

'My sister Arundell has had much sitting up', noted Peter Wentworth, 'and has behaved herself with much more decency after the breath was out of the Queen's body than any of the bedchamber-women . . . Lady Masham, Mrs Hill and Danvers are cried out upon for their behaviour; though they roared and cried enough whilst there was life, but as soon as there was none they took care of themselves . . .'[52]

The chaplain of St John's College, Oxford, asked to pray for King George the First, protested that surely Queen Anne was not dead. 'Dead?' he was told, 'she is as dead as Julius Caesar.' The unsigned will was of course a disappointment: '. . . My body shall be buried within the Chapel of our royal ancestor King Henry VII . . . in the same vault with and near unto the body of my dear husband the Prince of Denmark deceased'. The funeral was to have 'the same solemnities as were used upon the decease of my said dear husband'. All servants were to be paid their arrears, and £2000 was to be given to the poor. After that came space for legacies, a space not filled, except for five words: 'the residue for our Successor'. The draft-will ends with the expected formula: 'In witness whereof we have signed these presents with our own hand and caused our royal signet and the great seal of Great Britain to be put and affixed thereto'; but there is no signature and no seal; nor is the successor named;[53] nor, on her deathbed, was her stepbrother mentioned.

In their search for a signed will at St James's Palace the Regents found a packet of papers 'the thickness of four fingers, sealed with her Majesty's seal and written on the outside in her own hand that she desired these papers should be burnt'. To this the Regents and Bothmar from Hanover agreed. Somerset threw the packet into the fire and as the sheets fell apart Bothmar noticed that they were all written in the same hand, a hand he took to be that of the Pretender.[54] Mystery must always hang about that packet – or was there another? 'Anne', says a writer in the Stuart Papers,* 'for a long time past and even in her husband's lifetime, always carried about her and put every evening under her bolster a sealed packet of which she changed

* HMC Stuart Papers I, li. See also Wentworth Papers, page 414.

the envelope when it got dirty or worn, which was suspected to be a will concerning the Pretender'. No such will was found.

Much of Hamilton's* last long entry is taken up with, as it seems needlessly, 'vindicating the Queen's constitution' against 'all the stories of her ails and complaints . . . the monstrous description of dropsical swelling' and so on which, he insists, were utterly false. This is followed by a panegyric – 'civility and good breeding . . . pious . . . calm and courteous in conversation . . . dutiful to a husband and one of the best mistresses to servants' etc. He ends:

'Such a mind upon the Throne, does it not resemble the sun in the firmament; but when a cloud is before it, how are its beautiful aspect and influence changed and lessened, while the sun itself is the same'. Clouds had been cast about Anne by her ministers, while she – *semper eadem* – stayed flawless and constant.[55]

On Anne's accession the sun had shone – so people said – as never before. On the day she died it was eclipsed. But the clouds had still to be scattered.

* Lady Cowper, who copied out Sir David Hamilton's *Diary*, arranged for him to continue to practise in the Court of George I and to be made Physician-in-Ordinary to the Princess of Wales.

Epilogue

Princess, the world already owns thy name!
Go mount the chariot of immortal fame,
Nor die to be renowned; Fame's loudest breath
Too dear is purchas'd by an angel's death.

But O the parting stroke! Some heav'nly power
Cheer thy sad Britons in the gloomy hour;
Some new propitious star appear on high,
The fairest glory of the western sky,
And Anna be the name.

Isaac Watts

THE hush was impressive. 'Everything has been so quiet since her death' . . . 'Everything goes very smoothly and I believe the great men of yesterday will submit very quietly . . .' 'Everything is in tranquillity and the stocks rise upon the bettering of the times. Indeed to tell the truth, the Queen and her ministry seem very clear of the charge some people made against them of endeavouring to bring in the Pretender. Whatever thoughts she had upon that subject she is gone to answer for to Him who only can judge of thoughts'.[1]

George I, proclaimed on August 1, the day Anne died, made no haste to come over. Though there were said to be (Roman Catholics included) fifty-seven better claims than his to the British crown, the race had been called off. The Act of Settlement was working. The Regents were in charge. When George did come he brought a staff of ninety, two mistresses, two Turks and a dwarf. His Queen was in prison, for adultery. Lady Mary Wortley Montagu pronounced him an honest blockhead.

On August 2nd the Marlboroughs, delayed by contrary winds, landed at Dover and were soon making their triumphal entry into London. There were cheers and flowers and a few hisses. 'One forgives him the fireworks', wrote d'Ibberville, 'but – artillery with drums, and his servants shouting "Behold your liberator!" All this from one who used to slink into London *incognito* after the most glorious campaigns. A City spokesman came to the door of his carriage and said, "My Lord, you come too late. We proclaimed another three days ago"'.[2] The Jacobites called it insulting the Queen's ashes, with 'so good and gracious a mistress lying a corpse . . . The scurvy mob that followed cried out with huzzas: God Bless King John and Queen Sarah Our King and Queen Protectors of England! and after went and thought to have mobbed the Earl of Oxford but were prevented'.[3]

Marlborough was hurt at not having been named among the Regents, but the slight was unintentional and when at last the King arrived, on September 18, he said, 'My lord Duke, I hope your troubles are now all over'. By the first warrant George signed Marlborough was reinstated as Captain-General. The troubles in store for him were no more than are common to all men: bereavement, sickness and death. The loss of his second daughter Anne Sunderland in 1716 wounded him deeply. He suffered his first stroke and became infirm, a frequenter of spas with Sarah, who dosed him with ass's milk and Sir Walter Raleigh's Cordial. In 1719 he moved into Blenheim. In 1722 he died. So the same year did the Duchess of Somerset. A year later the Sovereign (Somerset) sought Sarah's hand and would not take no for an answer until she had found him another wife. He had mellowed and disclosed a sense of humour. Sarah lived on, falling out with everyone – children and grandchildren, painters and architects – until in 1744 she died. She was eighty-four and had seen Charles II, James II, William and Mary, Anne and the first two Georges. Her *Conduct* made little stir when at long last it was published in 1742.

For Anne there was no public lying-in-state, although at the Prince's Lodgings, near the Lords, the coffin under a purple canopy was attended by 'some of the ladies' throughout the night. The funeral on August 23rd (postponed 'by reason the ladies could not get their clothes ready'), though elaborate, was 'private', that is to say it took place at night. The Marlboroughs were not there; nor was the Duchess of Somerset, who was ill. The bills for the funeral and mourning show an item: 'For covering and hooding eight large Flanders horses', the same that had taken her to thanksgivings. This time they drew a hearse 'altered from an open to a covered chariot, by the Lords Justices' order'. The horses were 'covered all over with purple cloth; bits and buckles varnished purple; with eight large tailcases, silk reins, large purple silk tassels and all manner of large purple tops to the horses' heads'. When Sarah found herself presented, after Marlborough's funeral, with a similar bill for forty-eight yards of black cloth she remarked that it was enough to cover her garden. Now, for Anne, everything had to be thought of (though not by Sarah), from 'fine purple-in-grain cloth for a large state-bed' to 'a purple velvet cushion with pearl-mould tassels' for 'a crown of tin, chased and gilt with fine gold'.

To put into mourning the yeomen of the guard and the children of the chapel might seem straightforward. It was not so. Stephen Toulouse, embroiderer, charged for 'taking off the bullion-badges from 140 laced coats and putting them on 140 mourning coats, on back and breast, and for taking off the letter A and substituting the letter G.' And he was further responsible for embroidering 'a black cloth livery-coat, on back & breast, with the letters & crowns, and on the arm with rats & wheatsheaf, as formerly, for Samuel Stubbs the ratkiller'. The children of the chapel were provided with 'fine hats and hairbands, black lambskin gloves and sixty pairs of waxleather shoes'.

At St James's Palace the beds needed purple and black bedding and all sconces were blackened. Furniture made for the occasion included lacquered chairs and tables, stools and 'a large arch-glass' by Gerrit Jensen, in a purple frame. Fourteen carpenters, who at some stage carried the body, were provided with black cloth caps. It was remarked that though Prince George's coffin had been bulky, Queen Anne's was more nearly square.[4] Covered with a pall of purple velvet it was carried to the Abbey by 'ten or twelve yeomen of the guard'. Six dukes supported the pall, the chief mourner, in the Duchess of Somerset's absence, being the Duchess of Ormonde. 'Poor Lady Masham almost dead with grief' was there with her sister Alice, Mrs Danvers, Mrs Arundell and two other bedchamber-women. At the west door the procession was met by the Dean

Kneller: Allegorical sketch of Queen Anne presenting Blenheim Palace to Military Merit

Thornhill: Firework display to celebrate the Treaty of Utrecht

hames July 7th 1713, being the Thanksgiving day for the Peace
QUEENS
PACIS
MDCCXIII
achine or Frontispeice was 52 foot high 64 foot wide, which made a surprizing effect; as soon as the Machine was on fire
s possible to fire, And evey 4 minuts 2 Rocket Chests with 6 Balloons in the Air, till ye whole was Consumd
, 5 large Water Pyramides, 4 water Fountains, 13 Pumps, 27 standing Rockets wth lights all swimming on ye Water
ere Composd of different sorts of Fire, as Starrs, Reports, Gold & Silver rain fire, Squibbs &c.
rection of ye Board of Ordnance

The Rysbrack statue of Queen Anne erected for Sarah Duchess of Marlborough at Blenheim

(Atterbury), prebends and choir, 'all having wax tapers in their hands'. The service was read by the Jacobite Dean, the same who, on the day of Anne's death, had suggested proclaiming the Pretender at Charing Cross.

At minute intervals, throughout the funeral, the Tower guns were fired. After the committal and anthem John Vanbrugh as Clarenceux King of Arms (in the absence of Garter) advanced to the vault and over it read the Queen's style and titles:

> Thus it has pleased Almighty God to take out of this transitory life to his Divine Mercy that late Most High, Most Mighty and Most Excellent Princess Anne by the Grace of God Queen of Great Britain, France and Ireland etc., Defender of the Faith . . . Let us beseech Almighty God to bless and preserve with long life, health and honour and all worldly happiness the Most High, Most Mighty and Most Excellent Monarch Our Sovereign Lord George, now by the Grace of God King of Great Britain, France and Ireland etc., Defender of the Faith.[5]

On the last of the reigning Stuarts the vault was then sealed. There was her effigy in wax and there would be statues, but there was to be no stone, no stylito statue (there was to have been one in the Strand), no royal monument, no fitting memorial, other than the churches she had sponsored by Hawksmoor, Archer and Gibbs.* For William and Mary Grinling Gibbons, directed by Wren, had designed an elaborate tomb, never made; and so for Anne also there was to be nothing. In the Abbey today the only mention of her is, by strange chance, in a plaque on the north wall of the Lady Margaret Chapel, a plaque 'presented by Trinity Church, New York in 1966 in grateful memory of King William III . . . and of Queen Anne, who in 1705† granted Trinity Church the Queen's farm and garden on Manhattan Island'.

It would be left to Sarah, in old age, to raise that 'very fine thing' to her, the Rysbrack statue in white marble at Blenheim (See opposite page), and to write inscriptions:

* An Act of 1711 provided for fifty churches to be built 'in or near the cities of London and Westminster or the suburbs thereof'. The few that were built were noble. See Howard Colvin: *Fifty New Churches.*

† Trinity Church, New York. The date given in SP 44/104, f 228 at the Public Record Office is March 12, 1703.

Queen Anne was very graceful and majestic in her person, religious without affectation, she always meant well. She had no false ambition . . . her journey to Nottingham was never concerted . . . had no vanity in her expenses nor bought any one jewel . . . never refused her private charity to proper objects . . . extremely well bred, treated her chief ladies and servants as if they had been her equals . . . her behaviour to all that approached her was decent and full of dignity and showed condescension without art or meanness . . .

As Sarah explained, 'I never flattered anybody living, and I cannot be suspected of it now the Queen is dead'. Her private opinion however – and one not of course to be incised on the pedestal – was different. As she told her friends, 'She certainly meant well and was not a fool, but nobody can maintain that she was wise, nor entertaining in conversation. She was ignorant in everything but what the parsons had taught her when a child, and she never failed in performing exactly the rules given her by them, with great sincerity . . . but their directions were not the most material part of religion . . . Being very ignorant, very fearful, with very little judgment, it is easy to be seen she might mean well, being surrounded with so many artful people, who at last compassed their designs to her dishonour . . . And one thing I will say more, that she was as good as an angel and as wise as Solomon in comparison of some that I have had the honour to know . . . She certainly was as decent in her behaviour as I have formerly represented her, till the latter end of her reign when a very brutal woman got into her favour . . .'[6]

Not everyone considered Abigail brutal. Swift, writing a week after the Queen's death, assured her she had been 'the best and most faithful servant that ever any sovereign had. And although', he added, 'you have not been rewarded suitably to your merits, I doubt not but God will make it up to you in another life and to your children and posterity in this'.[7] They were, as befitted the Dean of St Patrick's, lofty thoughts, but concern for her worldly audit was wasted. For months before Anne's death the Secret Service funds had systematically been raided. The Mashams in their quiet retreat at Langley were never to be in want. At Court she was no longer *persona grata.* In her twenty-year retirement she would, as Lewis predicted, be *persona muta*, her *Conduct* (more's the pity) never written. 'Lady

Masham died yesterday', wrote Lady Compton on December 7th, 1734, 'she had long been ill and in doctors' hands, 'tis said she had great riches. Left only an only son and a granddaughter about seven years old who always lived with her'.[8] Oxford had pronounced her 'cunning, but willing to be thought much more so than she was. She had insinuated herself into favour more by the want of merit in those that went before her than by any real significancy in herself'.[9] As Cinderella at Court she had, slyly and quite adequately, played her part and, as Sir Winston remarked, no one can say she had not had her hour.

The case of Bolingbroke and his gamble with time is fascinating. By the Queen's death, he told Swift, he had lost all but his spirit. He then told d'Ibberville that to complete his plans he had needed six weeks. In that short time, so he reckoned, 'on aurait mis les choses en tel état qu'il n'y aurait eu rien à craindre de ce qui vient d'arriver'; although in that case England, though he did not say so, would very likely have been landed with civil war. It was, declared Bolingbroke, all Oxford's fault – the collapse of the Tories, the quenching of Stuart hopes, the death of the Queen: 'le chagrin l'a tuée'.[10] Now he awaited with impatience the arrival of George I, since he, Bolingbroke, was then prepared either to retire philosophically to the country or to continue as Secretary provided the ministry were not all Whig. It was, and thanks to Walpole would for a century remain so.

Writing to Strafford, a fortnight after Anne's death, Bolingbroke told him, 'Indeed the Queen's death was a very great surprise, for though I did not imagine she could hold out long, yet I hoped she would have got over the summer'. As for any Jacobite plots he might have heard of, all that of course was nonsense. 'Sure there never yet was so quiet a transition from one government to another . . . the nation never was in a better temper . . . For my own part I doubt not but I have been printed in fine colours to the King. I must trust to my conduct to clear me. I served the Queen to the last gasp as faithfully, as disinterestedly, as zealously as if her life had been good for twenty years and she had had twenty children to succeed her. I do not repent doing so, nor envy those who did otherwise. On the same principle will I serve the King if he employs me'.[11]

Even before George had landed, Bolingbroke was dismissed and his papers were seized. By them it was hoped to incriminate both him and Oxford; but that risk had been thought of. Nevertheless the Whigs were out for blood and Anne's Tory ministers were in jeopardy. Bolingbroke later denied that his flight to France the following April was 'in a panic terror improved by the artifices of the Duke of Marlborough'. Yet Sir Winston's account of their last interview – Marlborough smooth as a serpent, Bolingbroke panic-stricken – stays in the reader's mind.[12] Slipping away, between the acts at Drury Lane, Bolingbroke was just in time to help the Pretender with the invasion of '15 – and to be blamed for its failure. As a patriot king the Chevalier proved disappointing; nor did Bolingbroke, as subject and secretary, appeal to James.* Bolingbroke's doubts had been fed that October by the Pretender's Declaration in which he said he had had no reason to doubt Anne's good intention, which had only been thwarted by her sudden death. That was rash enough; but his censoring of the draft was positively petty. In the passage about Anne, from 'of blessed memory' James struck out 'blessed', and 'When it pleased Almighty God to take her to Himself' was changed to 'When it pleased Almighty God to put a period to her life'. No prince deserving of his loyalty could be so small-minded. They parted. Bolingbroke remained in exile until 1723, when George's German mistress the Duchess of Kendal was bribed into securing his pardon. He returned but was not allowed to sit in the House of Lords. By going to France he had hoped, he told his friends, to help his party. It had the contrary effect. To quote a modern historian (Professor Plumb): 'The enormity of this decision cannot be too strongly stressed . . . he did his party irreparable harm by making it far easier for Whig propaganda to label all Tories as Jacobites'.[13] What, then, apart from fear, was his real motive? He answers himself, and in this we can believe him: 'I abhorred Oxford to that degree that I could not bear to be joined with him in any case. Nothing contributed so much to determine me as this sentiment'.[14]

* James Francis Edward in 1719 married Princess Maria Clementina, daughter of Prince James Sobieski, eldest son of the King of Poland. Their son Charles was the Young Pretender. James died in 1766.

The idea of being linked in a twin impeachment with the Dragon was more than he was prepared to face. He chose exile.

On George I's landing at Greenwich, Oxford hurried to greet him. He was (to quote Bolingbroke) treated with the most distinguishing contempt. In the following summer impeachments were declared against Oxford, Bolingbroke (in his absence) and Ormonde, who escaped to the Pretender. Strafford too was accused. Matthew Prior, said to have been composing an ode to Anne when told of her death, was sent to prison for a year. Oxford, in pain with the gravel, went to the Tower. Loaded with trouble – sickness, disgrace, discomfort – he behaved magnificently. Bolingbroke had long since told him he was cut out for destruction. He seemed indeed made to be a martyr, and now his second martyrdom had begun. 'Your heroic and Christian behaviour', wrote Swift, 'astonisheth everyone but me, who know you so well and know how little it is in the power of human actions or events to discompose you'. His wife nursed him in the Tower through a fever; he was crippled with rheumatism and lost much weight. He wrote down his meditations, in Latin. He stayed in prison for nearly two years. When at last he was brought to trial the lords assembled in Westminster Hall found that, due to muddle and craft, no prosecutor was going to appear. Though Sarah was said to be distracted with disappointment, Oxford was acquitted and so was free to retire to his splendid library at Wimpole.

In his last public speech Oxford had declared that he was 'unconcerned for the life of an insignificant old man, but', he went on to say –

> I cannot without the highest ingratitude be unconcerned for the best of queens: a Queen who heaped on me honours and preferments, though I never asked for them, and therefore I think myself under an obligation to vindicate her memory and the measures she pursued, to my dying breath . . . I shall lay down my life with pleasure in a cause favoured by my late dear royal mistress.

He died in 1724, having outlived Marlborough and most of the rest of his antagonists. Of the Junto, Wharton, Halifax and Somers all died in 1715, Sunderland in 1722. Dr Johnson, after reading Sarah's *Conduct*, observed, 'The picture of Harley is partially drawn: all the deformities are heightened and the beauties (for beauties of mind he certainly had) are entirely omitted'. Musing further upon the letters Sarah had published from Anne, he found in them 'nothing insolent or overbearing, but then there is nothing great or firm or regal, nothing that enforces obedience and respect or which does not rather invite opposition and petulance. She seems born for friendship, not for government, and to be unable to regulate the conduct of others otherwise than by her own example'.[15]

In default of an Abbey inscription, two epitaphs may be quoted. This from France:

Ci git la Reine Anne Stuart,
Morte trop tôt, morte trop tard:
Trop tôt pour l'ancien ministère,
Trop tard pour le party contraire.
Tout calculé, tout rabattu,
Voici ce que j'en ai conclu –
Trois ans plus tôt le Roi de France
N'aurait pas vu tourner la chance.
Six mois plus tard les Protestants
Auraient fort mal passé leur temps.*
Qu'on la loue, qu'on la condamne,
Grace à Dieu, ci git la Reine Anne.[16]

And the other from Anne herself, in a letter to Godolphin, of 1707:

. . . as long as I live it shall be my endeavour to make my country and my friends easy and though those that come after me may be more capable of so great a trust as it has pleased God to put into my poor hands, I am sure they can never discharge it more faithfully than her that is sincerely your humble servant.[17]

* Though the Schism Act came into operation on August 1, 1714, the day Anne died, and remained in the Statute Book, her death rendered it in effect a dead letter.

APPENDIX I

Notes on the Health and Death of Anne

Queen Anne died sadly worn out with a complication of distempers.

Lady Mary Wortley Montagu.

ANNE as an infant was not strong. For her health's sake she was sent out of London to stay at Richmond. No details of early ailments are given, with the exception of what was called a defluxion of the eyes. At the age of five she had treatment for this in France; but off and on it continued to trouble her for the rest of her life and to limit her capacity for reading. Boyer says, 'The only blemish in her face was owing to the defluxion she had in her infancy in her eyes, which left a contraction in the upper lids that gave a cloudy air to her countenance'. Her sister Mary too suffered from chronic eye-trouble, vaguely referred to as 'sore eyes'.

In 1677 when Anne was twelve she had smallpox. She recovered, and nothing more is heard of her health until after her marriage, at eighteen, in July 1683, to Prince George of Denmark. In May 1684 the long series of births and miscarriages begins:

1684 May 12 a still-born daughter.
1685 June 2 Mary or Marie (died 8.2.1687).
1686 June 2 Anne Sophia (died 2.2.1687).
1687 Between January 20 and February 4 a miscarriage.
1687 October a miscarriage (male).
1688 April 16 a miscarriage.
1689 July 24 William Duke of Gloucester (died 30.7.1700).
1690 October 14 Mary (two months premature, lived two hours).
1692 April 17 George (born at Syon, lived a few minutes).
1693 March 23 a miscarriage (female).
1694 January 21 a miscarriage.
1696 February 18 a miscarriage (female).
1696 September 20 a double miscarriage ('a son of 7 months' growth, the other of 2 or 3 months').
1697 March 25 a miscarriage.
1697 December a miscarriage.
1698 September 15 a miscarriage (male).
1700 January 25 a miscarriage (male).

In 1698, when Anne is 33, we have the first mention of gout which, from then on, begins to affect various parts of the body: both hands, both feet, elbow, knees and eventually (as then diagnosed) stomach and head. In 1701 she was 'extremely afflicted with gout', and the following year, at the age of 37, she had to be carried to her coronation. Whether or not her 'gout' was in fact gout (a disease not common in women) cannot now be decided. Her helplessness could be accounted for by the miscarriages and what they led to alone. From time to time she complains of the vapours, worries about blushing, suffers from the gravel (1712) or has 'symptoms of an ague' or 'an aguish fever'.

From 1708 on, when Sir David Hamilton joined her household, he repeatedly warned her against emotional disturbance – 'disquiets and uneasiness' – reacting on gout. She paid attention, but there was little she could do. Whenever there was a crisis – e.g. de Guiscard's attempt on Harley in 1711 or trouble from Hanover in 1714 – she was ill, sometimes with storms of weeping, sleepless nights and disabling attacks of 'gout'.

In the summer, at Windsor, her health usually improved. There and at Hampton Court she drove many miles a day in her one-horse gig. Apart from that she took little exercise and towards the end became unwieldy and gross. It has been said that she ate and drank to excess. Sarah denies the drinking part of it. About her diet too little is known, but it is not likely to have been well balanced. She was fond of drinking chocolate, often last thing at night. Her husband ate and drank heavily and suffered from gout and asthma. She had sometimes to sit up with him all night.

In 1713 at Christmas Anne was very ill indeed and lay for some hours unconscious. Her doctors could not agree on a diagnosis of her 'fever', some insisting that it was 'aguish' and so prescribing quinine, others (particularly Shadwell) standing out against it and pronouncing it 'inflammatory'. They were overruled by Arbuthnot and quinine was given. After her death on August 1st 1714 Shadwell said 'ever since Christmas last he not only thought her to be in ill circumstances, but made the prognostic of the danger of an impostumation, which accordingly happened in her leg about two months before her death, though it was kept secret, the discharge of which abating and the gouty humour translating itself upon the brain were the immediate occasions of her death'.

During those last six or seven months the Queen appears to have had an abscess on her thigh, but diagnosis even then was made practically impossible since Arbuthnot was the only doctor allowed to examine it. When her last illness began, on July 29th, it came as a surprise to her and to most people because for some weeks she had seemed very well. Hamilton found that morning she had 'a trembling in her hands, a pain and heat in her head, with sleepiness and a little bleeding at the nose'. Later she had convulsions, and for the last few hours could not speak. 'From infancy to death', writes Hamilton, 'she had no complaint but what was the common effect of a sharpness in her blood, discharging outward in the common forms of ails to preserve her constitution, till within those few years a succession of disquiets happened which weakened her nerves and prepared them for receiving a translation of this sharpness, threatening first to discharge on the foot and knee in the form of gout, but her spirits being weakly at the time, it would not perform it and translated upwards upon the nerves and brain; so that all the stories of her Majesty's supposed ails and complaints were utterly false. . . How many have mentioned to me a monstrous description of dropsical swelling of her Majesty's limbs and elsewhere, when I have been vindicating her constitution as without any tendency to it; and though her royal body when dissected declared the truth thereof, yet the reproaches hold on, they breathing out their venom by saying she was tapped the night before'.

In an attempt to break through all this to some scientific fact the writer approached physicians and surgeons distinguished in their various fields. All responded generously, though with caution, qualifying their opinions by insisting upon the impossibility of diagnosing with any certainty a disease or condition affecting someone who lived centuries ago. This being understood, and with their kind permission I quote as follows:

Dr Ida Macalpine: The question of her numerous miscarriages is unanswerable with certainty. Porphyria may have played a part, but there is no certainty. One can exclude that she was rhesus negative, because in this condition the first child is all right but subsequent ones are either very ill or born dead. Her son of course was the third child. It is also a peculiar fact that her son (Gloucester) was malformed, and nobody will be able to make anything of that either.

Professor Chassar Moir: The information available is too vague . . . I don't think rhesus immunization very likely, as there would be a history of a *first* baby carried normally to term. Nor would it cause *early* miscarriages (and I think that most of her disappointments *were* early miscarriages). It might however cause premature labour with the birth of a dead child, or one that survives only a few hours or days. Syphilis is also probably ruled out, for it does not cause *early* miscarriage (better termed abortion), but may cause the death *in utero* of the foetus from the fourth month onwards. Typically, these women later have a living baby which however dies soon after birth; or if it survives, may show various defects – 'stigmata' – including blindness or deafness of varying degree. There are other causes of 'habitual abortion', but it would be impossible to identify them in retrospect.

Dr Frank Bevan: The evidence for syphilis (congenital or otherwise) is by no means conclusive; the porphyria theory seems equally untenable. Such details of her last illness as survive suggest a possibility of kidney failure. However, after every scrap of contemporary evidence has been considered, it is impossible to make a conclusive diagnosis. The eye-trouble plus miscarriage plus Gloucester's hydrocephalus (sic) might together seem to point to syphilis; but when studied in detail that pattern fails to fit. 'A defluxion in the eyes' is too vague; miscarrying can be due to a number of causes; and Gloucester's complaint could have been rickets. One would like to know something about her blood-pressure, and what effect gout (if it was gout) had on her kidneys. The 'impostumation' (abscess) may have been inflammation of the lymph glands in the upper part of the thigh, perhaps secondary to some infected area in the lower part of the leg or foot. I find no evidence of 'ague' (malaria) and therefore no occasion for quinine. All things considered, the wonder to me is that she lived to be forty-nine.

Mr Barton Gilbert of Salisbury, Rhodesia: To my mind the obstetrical history does not fit in with the disease of syphilis. I can find nothing in this story to support that idea. A diagnosis of a deformed pelvis would be absurd, because she clearly passed full-time babies through it, apparently with no great difficulty. She may have developed a uterine retroversion, a very common sequel of labour and delivery and cause of abortion. If after the last miscarriage in January 1700 she developed chronic pelvic-inflammation, this would explain why she did not conceive again. Chronic pelvic-sepsis is to my mind the likely diagnosis: she would have been chronically sick with back-ache, abdominal pains, recurrent fever etc. She would have absorbed toxic products over the years. In those days they developed amyloid disease and toxic myocarditis etc., and I am therefore not astonished to read that she became gross and dropsical – her kidneys are unlikely to have been an exception to the general toxic state.

The remedies prescribed for Queen Anne were typical of the time: ass's milk, hiera picra, oil of millipedes, spa water, steel, quinine, Sir Walter Raleigh's Cordial and for pain laudanum. She was quite often bled, but preferred cupping.

See also: *Some Royal Deathbeds: Queen Anne*
(British Medical Journal 12 November 1910).
Idols and Invalids
by James Kemble ChM, FRCS (Methuen, 1933).

APPENDIX II

Aquarius*

The following excerpts from *Astrology* by Evangeline Adams (Harrap, 1928) are quoted with the kind permission of the author and publisher.

AQUARIUS, pouring water from an urn, indicates graphically the child-like tendency to give of those who are undeveloped and the love of imparting knowledge by those who have reached self-control under this sign . . . There is a strong sympathy between the native of this sign and the interests of humanity at large . . . It is natural to him to live on a slightly higher plane . . .

Aquarius has influence over all vessels of the body which contain fluid, particularly the lymphatic system. One may say indeed that the lymphatic temperament is characteristic of this sign . . .

Nature progresses by excesses, but Aquarius always tries to progress without upsetting existing conditions . . . tolerance both broad and deep . . . Aquarius never leaves the balance. People of extreme kinds of mind are thoroughly annoyed by the calm and moderation of the Aquarian method . . . The natural man always wants to rush to extreme action . . . Deliberation may sometimes look like temporising . . . But there is a defect in the temperament in that it finds difficulty in coping with emergencies when they really arise. There are occasions when the most violent action is absolutely necessary . . . In undeveloped types this defect is a serious matter, for where wisdom is not based upon the very widest possible experience almost every circumstance is new. The uneducated or semi-educated, with no knowledge of history and with little experience of their own, are helpless in quite ordinary emergencies . . . As a rule the mind of the Aquarian is not rapid in its action and this may become a tendency to let things slide . . . new things are apt to confuse him.

There is undoubtedly a certain coldness in the type . . . the heart is too big to narrow itself down to a single, trivial instance . . . The Aquarian respects himself . . . does not fall in love easily and is likely to feel affection

* Queen Anne, whose birthday was February 6th 1665, was born under the sign of Aquarius.

as strongly for one sex as for the other. When he loves, his general amiability leads him to do all in his power to gratify the feelings of the other ... The strongest point in his whole make-up is his capacity for friendship. He is much better here than in love or marriage ... can be relied on never to quarrel or to do anything to break up an existing situation ...

Nothing gives him a greater incentive than some genuine, ultimate value to humanity ... He will never yield to fanaticism or allow himself to be rushed into a violent decision . . . The common people, those whose voices are never heard, represent a substratum of practical wisdom and it is to these people that the Aquarian always appeals. He will never satisfy extremists but will express the subconscious feeling of the great mass of humanity ... His function begins only when the battle is fought and the true necessity is to calm the violence of partisanship ...

Pisces (Prince George of Denmark, born 29 February).
The type is not very longlived. Gout is the characteristic disease ... Alcohol is exceedingly dangerous to natives of this sign ... His character is really negative ... As a business associate he makes a splendid sleeping partner ... In the active conduct of public affairs Pisces will be utterly hopeless if he is ever entrusted with anything of the sort, which he hardly ever is ...

Gemini (Sarah Duchess of Marlborough, born 29 May).
People born between May 22 and June 22, when the sun is in the airy, intellectual sign Gemini, are naturally sympathetic and helpful to those born under Aquarius ... in speech and correspondence exceedingly eloquent, logical and clear but ... not very honest in method of argument ... it is possible for accurate statement to convey profound falsehood . . . quick to retort, finds no difficulty in winning the argument – as if argument settled everything or indeed anything. An extreme freedom of thought and speech is characteristic, but ... there is apt to be a great lack of heart.

APPENDIX III

Facsimile of Anne's note to Sarah, on the death of Prince George of Denmark, October 1708

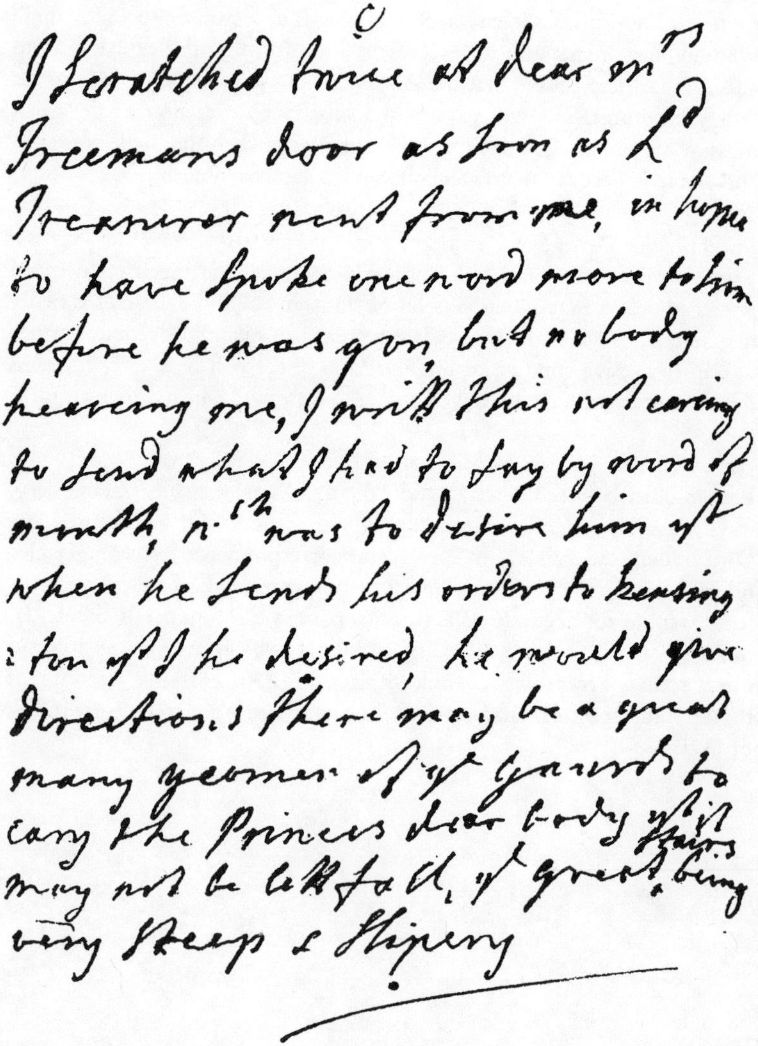

I scratched twice at dear Mrs
Freemans door as soon as Ld
Treasurer went from me, in hopes
to have spoke one word more to him
before he was gon, but no body
hearing one, I writt this not caring
to send what I had to say by word of
mouth, wch was to desire him yt
when he sends his orders to Kensing
:ton as soon as he desired, he would give
directions yt there may be a great
many yeomen of ye guards to
carry the Princes dear body yt it
may not be lett fall, ye great stairs being
very steep & slipery

Bibliography

NB The Jacobite sources for this period need to be referred to and quoted, if at all, with great caution. Sir Winston Churchill, after referring to them as a mare's nest, discounts all the Nairne and Macpherson Papers and in his life of Marlborough alleges (I, 310–20) that James II's memoirs, after 1660, were written by Mary of Modena's almoner William Dicconson. This last contention however has been challenged by Mr Maurice Ashley who, in his *Churchill As Historian* quotes evidence in favour of J. S. Clarke's *Life of James II* and shows that James II continued to write memoirs until 1695, if not later. With due allowance for prejudice, the Baschet transcripts in the Public Record Office would seem to be genuine and dependable.

MANUSCRIPT SOURCES

Althorp: The Spencer Papers

Blenheim Palace: The Marlborough Papers.

British Museum: Additional mss., Lansdowne mss., Portland Loan (BM 29), Stowe mss.

Hertfordshire County Record Office: Panshanger mss: Sir David Hamilton's *Diary* (in the hand of Mary Countess Cowper).

Longleat: Portland Papers (Harley, Godolphin and Masham correspondence).

Public Record Office: Baschet transcripts. Calendars of Treasury Books State Papers Domestic etc.

PRINTED SOURCES

Historical Manuscripts Commission (165 volumes, the most important for this present work being the Bath and Portland Papers).

Dictionary of National Biography (A. W. Ward's long contribution on Queen Anne etc.).

Contemporary newspapers, notably the *Examiner*, *Post Boy* and *Flying Post*.

AITKEN, G.A.: Life and Works of John Arbuthnot (1892).

ASHLEY, MAURICE: Churchill As Historian (1968). The Stuarts in Love (1963).

ASHTON, J.: Social Life in the Reign of Queen Anne (2 vols.).

BATHURST, LT-COL THE HON. BENJAMIN: Letters of Two Queens (1924).

BEATTIE, J.M.: The English Court in the Reign of George I (1967).

BOLINGBROKE, HENRY ST. JOHN VISCOUNT: A Letter to Sir William Wyndham; The Idea of a Patriot King (Works 5 vols., 1754).

BOYER, ABEL: History of the Reign of Queen Anne digested into Annals (3 vols., 1703–13).
The History of the Life and Reign of Queen Anne (1722).

BROWN, BEATRICE CURTIS: The Letters of Queen Anne (1935).

BURNET, GILBERT, BISHOP OF SALISBURY: History of His Own Times (6 vols. and supplement, 1823).

BURTON, IVOR: The Captain-General (Marlborough) (1968).

BUTLER, IRIS: Rule of Three (1967).

CARPENTER, CANON E. F.: The Protestant Bishop (Compton) (1956).

CARSWELL, JOHN: The Old Cause (1954).

CHAPMAN, HESTER: Queen Anne's Son (1954).

CHURCHILL, SIR WINSTON: Marlborough, His Life and Times. (2 vols., 1947).*

CLARENDON, HENRY EARL OF: Diary (1687–90). Life & Corresp. (1828).

CLARKE, J. S.: The Life of James II (2 vols., 1816).

CLERK, SIR JOHN: Memoirs (1845).

COKE, ROGER: A Detection of the Court & State of England (vols. 2 & 3, 1719).

CONNELL, NEVILLE: Anne the last Stuart Monarch (1937).

COWPER, MARY COUNTESS: Diary (1865).

COWPER, WILLIAM 1ST EARL: Diary (1833).

COXE, ARCHDEACON WILLIAM: Memoirs of John Duke of Marlborough (6 vols., 1820). Shrewsbury Correspondence (1821).

CRAWFURD, RAYMOND: The King's Evil (1911).

DALRYMPLE: Memoirs of Great Britain (3 vols., 1790).

DEFOE, DANIEL: Political Tracts including The Secret History of the White Staff (1714).

DICKSON, P. G. M.: The Financial Revolution in England (1967).

EVELYN, JOHN: Diary (ed. de Beer, 1955).

* I am most grateful to the publishers, George G. Harrap & Company, for allowing me to quote so freely from the signed copies of the two-volume edition given to me by the author in 1952.

D.B.G.

EVES, C. K.: Matthew Prior (1939).
FEILING, SIR KEITH: History of the Tory Party (1924).
FOOT, MICHAEL: The Pen and the Sword (1957).
GREEN, DAVID: Blenheim Palace (1951). Gardener to Queen Anne (1956). Grinling Gibbons (1964). Sarah Duchess of Marlborough (1967).
HAILES, LORD: Opinions of Sarah Duchess of Marlborough (1788).
HAMILTON, LADY ELIZABETH: The Backstairs Dragon (Harley) (1969).
HART, A. TINDAL: The Life & Times of John Sharp Archbishop of York (1949).
HART, JEFFREY: Viscount Bolingbroke (1965).
HERVEY, JOHN 1ST EARL OF BRISTOL: Letterbooks (1894).
HOLMES, GEOFFREY: British Politics in the Age of Anne (1967).
HOLMES, GEOFFREY AND W. A. SPECK: The Divided Society (1967).
HONE, CAMPBELL: The Life of Dr John Radcliffe (1950).
HOPKINSON, M. R.: Anne of England (1934).
KENYON, J. P.: Robert Spencer, Earl of Sunderland (1958).
KRAMNICK, ISAAC: Bolingbroke and His Circle (1968).
LAKE, DR EDWARD: Diary (1677–8). (1847).
LEDIARD, THOMAS: Life of John Duke of Marlborough (1736).
LEVER, SIR TRESHAM: Godolphin, His Life and Times (1952).
LEWIS, JENKIN: Memoirs of Prince William Henry, Duke of Gloucester (1789).
LUTTRELL, NARCISSUS: A Brief Historical Relation of State Affairs (6 vols., 1857).
MACALPINE, IDA AND RICHARD HUNTER: Porphyria – a Royal Malady (1968). George III and the Mad-Business (1969).
MACKY, JOHN: Memoirs of Secret Services (1895).
MACPHERSON, JAMES: Original Papers (1775).
MANLEY, MARY DE LA RIVIERE: The New Atlantis (1709).
The Secret History of Queen Zarah (1743).
MARLBOROUGH, SARAH DUCHESS OF: An Account of the Conduct of the Dowager Duchess of Marlborough (ed. Hooke, 1742).
Letters at Madresfield Court (1875).
Private Correspondence (2 vols., 1838).
MARY II, QUEEN OF ENGLAND: Memoirs (1886).
MICHAEL, WOLFGANG: England Under George I (1936).
MISSON, M.: Memoirs & Observations in his Travels Over England (1719).
MONTAGU, LADY MARY WORTLEY: Letters (1893).
OLDMIXON, JOHN: History of England (1735).
OMAN, CAROLA: Mary of Modena (1962).
PAUL, HERBERT: Queen Anne (1906).

PETRIE, SIR CHARLES: Bolingbroke (1937). The Jacobite Movement (1959).

PLUMB, J. H.: The Growth of Political Stability in England (1967). Sir Robert Walpole (vol. I, 1956).

PRIOR, MATTHEW: Works (2 vols., 1959).

QUENNELL, PETER: Alexander Pope (1968).

RALPH, JAMES: The Other Side of the Question (1742). [1914).

REID, J. STUART: John and Sarah, Duke and Duchess of Marlborough

ROBB, NESCA: William of Orange (vol. 2, 1966).

ROWSE, A. L.: The Early Churchills (1956). [1825).

SHARP, THOMAS: The Life of John Sharp, Archbishop of York (2 vols.,

SHEPPARD, EDGAR: Memorials of St James's Palace (2 vols., 1894).

SICHEL, WALTER: Bolingbroke and His Times (1901).

SMITHERS, PETER: Joseph Addison.

STANHOPE, EARL: History of England: Anne (1870).

STRICKLAND, ELIZABETH: Lives of the Queens of England (Mary and Anne) (1847).

SUTHERLAND, JAMES: Background For Queen Anne (1939).

SWIFT, JONATHAN: Correspondence (ed. Ball, 1911). Journal To Stella (ed. Williams, 2 vols., 1948). Prose Works (13 vols., 1953).

TERRY, C. S.: The Chevalier de St George (1901).

TREVELYAN, G. M.: England Under Queen Anne (3 vols., Fontana edition, 1965).

UFFENBACH, Z. C. VON: London in 1710 (1934).

WALCOTT, ROBERT: English Politics in the Early 18th Century (1956).

WARD, A. W.: The Electress Sophia (1909).

WENTWORTH PAPERS (ed. Cartwright, 1883).

WILKINS, W. WALKER: Political Ballads of the 17th & 18th Centuries (2 vols., 1840).

Articles and Transactions

ANSELL, PATRICIA: Harley's Parliamentary Management (Bulletin of the Institute of Historical Research, 1961).

BEVAN, BRYAN: Queen Anne's Sporting Interests (Country Life, 30 July, 1964).

BENNETT, G. V.: Robert Harley, the Godolphin Ministry and the Bishoprics Crisis of 1707 (English Historical Review Oct. 1967).

BURTON, I. F., P. W. J. RILEY AND E. ROWLANDS: Political Parties in the Reigns of William III and Anne (Bulletin of the Institute of Historical Research, Nov. 1968 supp. 7).

COLVIN, H. M.: Fifty New Churches. (Arch. Review, March 1950).

DICKINSON, H. T.: Henry St John: a Reappraisal of the Young Bolingbroke (The Journal of British Studies, May 1968).

GARRATT, JOHN G.: The Four Indian Kings, 1710 (History Today, February 1968).

HOLMES, GEOFFREY: The Attack on the Influence of the Crown, 1702–16 (Bulletin of the Institute of Historical Research, May 1966).

HOLMES, GEOFFREY AND W. A. SPECK: The Fall of Harley in 1708 Reconsidered (English Historical Review, October 1965).

LEGG, WICKHAM: De Torcy's Account of Prior's Negotiations at Fontainebleau in July 1711 (English Historical Review, 1914).

Jacobite Correspondence 1712–14 (English Historical Review, July 1915).

MCINNES, ANGUS: The Appointment of Harley in 1704 (Cambridge Historical Journal, 1968).

PLUMB, J. H.: The Organisation of the Cabinet in the Reign of Queen Anne (R.H.S. Transactions, 5th Series, vol. 7).

REITAN, E. A.: The Civil List in 18th Century Politics (Cambridge Historical Journal, 1966).

SNYDER, HENRY L.: Godolphin and Harley, a Study of their Partnership in Politics (Huntington Library Quarterly, 1966–7).

The Formulation of Foreign & Domestic Policy in the Reign of Queen Anne (Cambridge Historical Journal, 1968).

The Defeat of the Occasional Conformity Bill and the Tack (Bulletin of the Institute of Historical Research, November 1968).

The Duke of Marlborough's Request of his Captain-Generalcy for life (Journal of the Society for Army Historical Research, Summer 1967).

SPECK, W. A.: The Choice of a Speaker in 1705 (Bulletin of the Institute of Historical Research, No. 37 (1964)).

SYKES, N.: Queen Anne and the Episcopate (English Hist. Review 1935).

TOYNBEE, MARGARET: Anne As a Patroness of Painters (Burlington Magazine, March, 1970).

WARD, A. W.: The Electress Sophia of Hanover (English Historical Review, July, 1886).

ANON.: Some Royal Deathbeds: Queen Anne (British Medical Journal, 12 November, 1910).

CORRIGENDA

p. 133 l. 13	For Seccession read Succession
p. 329	The reference Howard Colvin: *Fifty New Churches* should read Howard Colvin: Fifty New Churches, *Arch. Review*, March 1950.

References to Manuscripts and Printed Books

Abbreviations

Blenheim: mss in the muniment room at Blenheim.

HMC: Historical Manuscripts Commission.

DNB: Dictionary of National Biography.

Churchill: *Marlborough His Life & Times* (two-volume edition) (1949).

Conduct: *An Account of the Conduct of Sarah Duchess of Marlborough* (1742).

Boyer *History*: *The History of the Life & Reign of Queen Anne* (1722).

Boyer *Annals*: *The History of the Reign of Queen Anne Digested Into Annals* (1703–13).

Brown: *The Letters of Queen Anne* (edited by Beatrice Curtis Brown) (1968).

Hamilton: *Diary*: The Diary of Sir David Hamilton (Panshanger mss).

CHAPTER ONE – AQUARIUS

1 BM Add ms 15900
2 Blenheim G–I–8
3 *Conduct*
4 Churchill: *Marlborough* I, 166
5 HMC IX, 474
6 Bolingbroke: *A Letter To Sir William Wyndham*
7 Clarke: *The Life of James II*, I, 630
8 Oman: *Mary of Modena*, 150
9 *The Works of John Sheffield Duke of Buckingham*
10 Clarke: op. cit., I, 502–3
11 Lake: *Diary* (1677–8)
12 Blenheim G–I–9
13 Kemble: *Idols & Invalids*, 178–9
14 Boyer *History*
15 Blenheim E 25

16 & 17 Burnet: *History of His Own Time*, VI, 204
18 Blenheim G–I–7
19 Lake: op. cit.
20 Burnet: op. cit., II, 132
21 & 22 Lake: op. cit.
23 Marlborough mss at Althorp, book A
24 Brown: *The Letters of Queen Anne*, 6
25 HMC XV, App. 1, 321
26 Brown: op. cit., 20
27 Boyer *History*, 15
28 Blenheim E 38
29 Blenheim E 17

CHAPTER TWO – REVOLUTION

1 Feiling: *The Tory Party*, 361
2 Coke: *A Detection of the Court & State of England*, III, 118
3 Clarke: op. cit., I, 730. Churchill: op. cit., I, 158
4 HMC VII & XIV, App. 4, 143
5 Bathurst: *Letters of Two Queens* (21.3.1683)
6 Kenyon: *Robert Spencer Earl of Sunderland*, 87
7 Bathurst: op. cit., (4.6.1683)
8 HMC III, App., 289
9 HMC VII, 22
10 Churchill: op. cit., I, 169
11 Boyer *History*, 4
12 Bathurst: op. cit.
13 Brown: op. cit., 11
14 HMC IX, App. 2 .The letter from Prince George to Bellasyse, from Windsor (3 May 1683) appears to be wrongly dated. He reached England that July.
15 *Conduct*
16 Brown: op. cit., 19
17 Burnet: op. cit.
18 DNB (Ward)
19 Brown: op. cit., 19
20 *Conduct*
21 Sarah Duchess of Marlborough: *Corresp.* II, 120
22 Blenheim E 17
23 Coke: op. cit., 340–1
24 Blenheim G–I–9

25 Brown: op. cit., 16–17, 19
26 Ibid, 20–21
27 Hopkinson: *Anne of England*, 98
28 Brown: op. cit., 26–7
29 Ibid, 27–8
30 Luttrell: *A Brief Historical Relation of State Affairs*, I, 398
31 Brown: op. cit., 28
32 Glyn Mills mss (Sarah to Lord Marchmont, 15.6.1734)
33 Petrie: *The Jacobite Movement*, 73
34 Clarendon: *Diary* (1687–90)
35 Brown: op. cit., 33
36 Ibid, 35
37 Boyer *History*, 4
38 Plumb: *The Growth of Political Stability in England*, 62
39 HMC XII, App. 5, 119
40 Boyer *History*, 6
41 Clarke: op. cit., II, 160
42 Brown: op. cit., 37–8
43 Clarke: op. cit., II, 213
44 Connell: *Anne the Last Stuart Monarch*
45 & 46 Clarendon: *Diary*, 196
47 Brown: op. cit., 40
48 Clarendon: op. cit., 179
49 *Conduct*
50 Lediard: *The Life of John Duke of Marlborough*
51 Pepys
52 DNB (Ward)
53 Clarke: op. cit., II, 226
54 Clarendon: op. cit.
55 Brown: op. cit., 43–4
56 Ibid, 44–5
57 HMC (Leyborne-Popham) Dr Clarke's autobiography
58 Clarke: op. cit., II, 229
59 Churchill: op. cit., I, 265
60 Bath mss at Longleat (Portland XI, f 46): John Sheffield Duke of Buckingham
61 Clarendon: op. cit.
62 Higgons: *Short View of English History*
63, 64 & 65 Clarendon: op. cit.
66 Ibid, quoting Ralph

CHAPTER THREE – WILLIAM AND MARY

1 Burnet: op. cit., Supp. 496
2 Kenyon: *The Stuarts*
3 *Conduct*
4 & 5 Mary II: *Memoirs*
6 Clarke: op. cit., II, 306
7 Clarendon: op. cit.
8 Clarke: op. cit., II, 329
9 & 10 *Conduct*
11 Lewis: *Memoirs of William Duke of Gloucester*
12 Blenheim G–I–9
13 *Conduct*
14 Burnet: op. cit., Supp. 313
15 Clarendon: op. cit.
16 Mary II: op. cit.
17 Ibid
18 Blenheim E 19
19 Blenheim E 18
20 Burnet: op. cit., VI, 373
21 Strickland: *Lives of the Queens of England*, II, 240–1
22 Churchill: op. cit., I, 343
23 *Conduct*
24 Blenheim E 17
25 *Conduct*
26 Mary II: op. cit.
27 Blenheim E 48
28 *Conduct*
29 Coke: op. cit., 124
30 Boyer *History*
31 *Conduct*
32 Clerk: *Memoirs*
33 Brown: op. cit., 55–6
34 & 35 *Conduct*
36 & 37 Blenheim E 17
38 Ibid
39 Blenheim G–I–7
40 Brown: op. cit., 60–1
41 Hone: *Life of Radcliffe*, 50
42 Blenheim E 18

43 Strickland: op. cit., II, 329
44 Clarke: op. cit., II, 525
45 HMC II, App. 1, 170
46 Clarke: op. cit., II, 559–60
47 *Conduct*

CHAPTER FOUR – WILLIAM

1 Blenheim G–I–8
2 Burnet: op. cit., V, 7
3 Bolingbroke: *The Idea of a Patriot King*
4 HMC XII, App. 5, 173
5 Burnet: op. cit., Supp. 387
6 Kenyon: *Sunderland*, 270
7 Blenheim E 17
8 Blenheim E 18
9 Sarah Marlborough: *Corresp.* II, 120
10 Blenheim G–I–9
11 Blenheim E 17
12 Blenheim E 19
13, 14 & 15 Blenheim E 17
16 Blenheim E 19
17 Blenheim G–I–7
18 Burnet: op. cit., V, 333
19 Ibid, V, 380
20 Buckingham: Works, II, 139
21 Lewis: op. cit.
22 Blenheim E 17
23 Blenheim E 19
24 HMC II, 286
25 HMC XII, App. 2, 365
26 Blenheim E 18
27 Ibid, E 19
28 Luttrell: op. cit., IV, 235–6
29 Ibid, IV, 269
30 Dalrymple: *Memoirs* III, 87
31 Whistler: *Sir John Vanbrugh*, 64
32 Luttrell: op. cit., IV, 328
33 & 34 *Conduct*
35 Clerk: op. cit., 93–4
36 Burnet: op. cit., VI, 216

37 Luttrell: op. cit., IV, 664
38 Ibid, IV, 673
39 Strickland: op. cit., 439
40 Macpherson: *Stuart Papers* II, 223
41 Bath mss at Longleat: Portland XI, f 32
42 Burnet: op. cit., V, 8
43 Coke: op. cit., III, 480
44 & 45 Ward: *The Electress Sophia*
46 Hamilton: *The Backstairs Dragon*, 1–3
47 HMC Portland II, 111
48 BM Stowe mss 242, f 66
49 Plumb: op. cit., 135
50 Snyder: *Godolphin & Harley* (Huntington Lib. Quarterly 1966/7)
51 Bolingbroke: *Letter to Sir Wm. Wyndham*, 8–9
52 Coxe: *Shrewsbury Corresp.*, 182
53 Trevelyan: *England Under Q. Anne: Blenheim*, 144–5
54 Clarke: op. cit., 598
55 Luttrell: op. cit., V, 89 & 91
56 Brown: op. cit., 67–8
57 Somers Tracts: IV, 82–3
58 DNB (Ward)
59 Clarke: op. cit., 602
60 Luttrell: op. cit., V, 107–22
61 Boyer *Annals* VIII
62 Stanhope: *Hist. of England: The Reign of Anne*, 35
63 *Conduct*

CHAPTER FIVE – SEMPER EADEM

1 Burnet: op. cit., V, 1
2 HMC Egmont II, 121
3 Boyer *Annals*
4 HMC IX, App. 2, 399
5 Blenheim E 40
6 & 7 Burnet: op. cit., V, 2
8 HMC VII, 246
9 & 10 Burnet: op. cit., V
11 HMC II, 242
12 Churchill: op. cit., I, 504–5
13 Ralph: *The Other Side of the Question*, 219
14 Burnet: op. cit., VI, 133

15 HMC Portland IV
16 Blenheim G–I–8
17 Blenheim Library mss
18 Fiennes: *Journeys*
19 Boyer *History*, 177
20 Blenheim G–I–8
21 Swift: *Memoirs Relating to That Change . . .*
22 Blenheim E 19
23 Swift: *Journal to Stella*, 363
24 Switzer: *Nobleman, Gentleman & Gardener's Recreation*
25 PRO Treasury Papers (2 Oct. 1716)
26 Strickland: op. cit., II, 361
27 HMC Portland IV
28 Boyer *History*
29 Macky: *A Journey Through England* II, 143
30 & 31 Blenheim E 19
32 Blenheim E 17
33 Churchill: op. cit., I, 505
34 HMC Portland VI (20 Oct. 1710)
35 PRO SP 44/108, f 70
36 BM Add. mss 28055 (9 Aug. 1702)
37 Ibid, ff 13–14
38 BM Add. mss 29588 f 193
39 Ibid, f 275
40 PRO SP 44/101, f 309
41 Blenheim E 45
42 Burnet: op. cit., V, 54
43 HMC Portland IV (10 Nov. 1702)
44 Ibid
45 Holmes: *British Politics in the Age of Anne*, 57
46 Luttrell: op. cit., V, 238–9
47 Churchill: op. cit., I, 614
48 Ibid, I, 619
49 Swift: *Memoirs of the Queen's Ministry*, III, 172
50 Boyer *Annals*
51 HMC Bath I (Harley to Godolphin, 10 Sept. 1707)
52 HMC XII, App. 5, 173

CHAPTER SIX – BLENHEIM

1 & 2 Boyer *History*

3 & 4 Blenheim E 19
5 HMC Portland IV, 59
6 Blenheim E 19
7 Blenheim G–I–7
8 PRO SP 44/104, f 228
9 PRO Treasury Minutes
10 Trevelyan: op. cit. (*Blenheim*), 293
11 Bath mss at Longleat: Misc. (13 Aug. 1703)
12 Blenheim E 19
13 Burnet: op. cit., VI, 217–8
14 Churchill: op. cit., I, 700
15 Boyer *Annals*, IX
16 & 17 HMC Portland IV
18 Blenheim E 19
19 Burnet: op. cit., V, 104
20 Blenheim E 2
21 Ibid G–I–8
22 BM Birch mss 4221, art. 6, f 22
23 Boyer *Annals*
24 Connell: *Anne the Last Stuart Monarch*, 132
25 Holmes: *Brit. Politics in the Age of Anne*, 303
26 Swift: *Letters* (16 Dec. 1703)
27 *Conduct*
28 Sarah Marlborough: *Corresp*. II, 147
29 *Conduct*
30 Brown: op. cit., 129
31 Blenheim G–I–9
32 HMC XII, App. 5, 178–9
33 Boyer *History*
34 HMC XII, App. 5, 178–9
35 HMC X, App. 5, 337
36 Sharp: *The Life of John Sharp*, 344
37 Strickland: op. cit., XII, 102
38 Boyer *History*
39 Blenheim Long Library mss
40 HMC XV, App. 7, 352
41 HMC Portland IV (4 Nov. 1703)
42 Ibid, May 1704
43 Ibid, July 1704
44 Churchill: op. cit., I, 716

45 Ibid, I, 719
46 Ibid, I, 721
47 Boyer *History*
48 Bolingbroke: *The Idea of a Patriot King*
49 Boyer *History*
50 McInnes: *The Appointment of Harley in 1704* (Hist. Journal XI, 2)
51 HMC Portland IV (29 Aug. 1704)
52 Bolingbroke: *A Letter to Sir William Wyndham*
53 PRO Baschet Transcript 3/191, f 124
54 McInnes: op. cit., 270
55 Churchill: op. cit., I, 916
56 Brown: op. cit., 150
57 Hervey Earl of Bristol: *Letterbooks* (8 July 1704)
58 HMC II, part 2
59 HMC XIII, App. 7 (5 Sept. 1704)
60 HMC Portland IV (28 Sept. 1704)
61 Boyer *Annals*
62 Evelyn: *Diary* (7 Sept. 1704)
63 Boyer *Annals*

CHAPTER SEVEN – 'THIS BOILING NATION'

1 PRO SP 44/105, 5 185
2 Burnet: op. cit., V, 94
3 Coke: op. cit., III, 182
4 Burnet: op. cit., V, 182–3
5 Boyer *Annals*
6 HMC Portland IV
7 Ibid
8 Spencer mss quoted Snyder (IHR Bulletin, Nov. 1968)
9 Snyder: *Defeat of Occasional Conformity Bill* (IHR Bulletin, Nov. 1968)
10 Boyer *History* (17 Jan. 1705)
11 Defoe: *Tour Through Great Britain*
12 Blenheim E 18
13 & 14 Blenheim E 19
15 PRO Baschet Transcript 3/192
16 Churchill: op. cit., I, 937, 982
17 HMC Portland IV, 178
18 Boyer *Annals*
19 Wren Soc. XIX, 114
20 HMC Bath I

21 Bath mss at Longleat (Misc.) ff 113-4
22 HMC Bath I, 74
23 HMC XII, App. 4, 63 (19 Sept. 1705)
24 HMC Portland V
25 PRO Baschet Transcript 3/192, f 112
26 Boyer *Annals*
27 Brown: op. cit., 153
28 Ibid, 172
29 Bennett: *Harley, the Godolphin Ministry & the Bishoprics Crisis* (EHR Oct. 1967)
30 HMC XV, App. 7, 267
31 Holmes: op. cit., 114, 295. See also McInnes: op. cit., 260
32 Burnet: op. cit., V, 225, 228
33 Brown: op. cit., 177
34 PRO Baschet Transcript 3/31/192, f 157
35 Brown: op. cit., 177
36 *Conduct*
37 Earl Cowper: *Diary*
38 Trevelyan: op. cit. (*Ramillies*), 78
39 HMC Bath I, 76
40 HMC Frankland-Russell-Astley mss
41 Mary Countess Cowper: *Diary*, 8
42 Bennett: op. cit.
43 Earl Cowper: op. cit., (6 Jan. 1706)
44 Brown: op. cit., 185
45 Ibid
46 Churchill: op. cit., II, 119
47 Luttrell: op. cit., V
48 Churchill: op. cit., II, 124
49 Brown: op. cit., 189
50 Blenheim C–I–16
51 HMC Portland IV
52 Boyer *Annals*
53 BM Stowe mss 241. f 72
54 HMC Portland IV
55 Boyer *Annals*, V (Intro.)

CHAPTER EIGHT – THE ARBITRESS

1 Clerk: *Memoirs*, 62–3
2 Earl Cowper: *Diary*

3 Churchill: op. cit., II, 196
4 Ibid, 198
5 Ibid, 198–9
6 Blenheim G–I–7
7 Churchill: op. cit.. II, 202
8 Brown: op. cit., 196–7
9 Blenheim A–I–37
10 Sarah Marlborough: *Corresp.* I, 52
11 Churchill: op. cit. II, 209, 278
12 BM Loan 29/10/4, quoted Bennett: op. cit.
13 BM Loan 29/9/4 quoted Plumb: *Walpole*, 128
14 Brown: op. cit., 19 9
15 HMC Bath I (15 Oct. 1706)
16 PRO A01/2480/278
17 Aitken: *Arbuthnot*, 36
18, 19 & 20 PRO Baschet Transcript 3/31/193
21 HMC Bath I (4 Jan. 1707)
22 Ibid (30 Jan. 1707)
23 Ibid (22 May 1707)
24 Ibid, 169
25 PRO Baschet Transcript 3/31/193
26 Burton: *The Captain-General*
27 PRO Baschet Transcript 3/31/193
28 Brown: op. cit., 219–20
29 Bennett: op. cit.
30 BM Add. mss 52540 L
31 Bennett: op. cit.
32 Brown: op. cit., 230–1
33 & 34 *Conduct*
35 Boyer *History*
36 Churchill: op. cit., II, 286
37 Burnet: op. cit., V 326
38 Brown: op. cit., 227
39 *Conduct*
40 Churchill: op. cit., II, 291
41 Blenheim B–II–32
42 & 43 HMC Bath I
44 & 45 Ibid
46 Blenheim G–I–7
47 Blenheim E 18

48 Sharp: *Life of John Sharp*, I, 301–2
49 PRO Baschet Transcript 3/31/193
50 Clerk: *Secret Services of John Macky*, 33–4
51 HMC XII, App. 5, 187
52 Bennett: op. cit.
53 HMC XIII, App. 3
54 *Conduct*
55 Blenheim E 19
56 Blenheim C–I–16
57, 58 & 59 HMC Portland IV
60 Blenheim C–I–16
61 HMC Portland V, App.

CHAPTER NINE – THE YEAR OF OUDENARDE

1 Holmes & Speck: *The Fall of Harley in 1708 Reconsidered* (EHR, Oct. 1965)
2 Blenheim G–I–9
3 Snyder: *Godolphin & Harley* (Huntington Lib. Quar. 1966–7)
4 Blenheim G–I–8
5 HMC Bath I (30 Jan. 1708)
6 Addison: *Letters* (ed. Graham)
7 Sichel: *Bolingbroke*, 195–6
8 Churchill: op. cit., II, 312–3 & f.n.
9 PRO 30/24/21/150, quoted Holmes & Speck: op. cit.
10 Blenheim G–I–9
11 Coke: op. cit., III, 323–4
12 Blenheim E 18
13 Blenheim G–I–9
14 Panshanger mss: Hamilton: *Diary*, f 23
15 Brown: op. cit., 244–5
16 Blenheim E 4
17 BM Birch mss 4221, f 22
18 Clerk: op. cit., 71–2
19 Boyer *Annals*, VII, App.
20 Bolingbroke: *The Idea of a Patriot King*
21 Blenheim E 26
22 Brown: op. cit., 246
23 Blenheim E 18
24 *Conduct*
25 Trevelyan: op. cit. (*Ramillies*) 388–9

26 Ashley: *Churchill As Historian*, 235
27 Trevelyan: op. cit. (*Ramillies*) 382
28 Swift: *Jack Frenchman's Lamentation*
29 Brown: op. cit., 252
30 Churchill: op. cit., II, 382
31 Ibid, 410
32 Ibid, 413
33 Ibid, 316
34 Ibid, 408
35 HMC Portland IV, 495–9
36 Blenheim E 19
37 Green: *Sarah Duchess of Marlborough*, 318–21
38 Sharp: op. cit., 330
39 Vanbrugh: *Letters* (ed. Webb) 25
40 & 41 *Conduct*
42 Blenheim E 4
43 BM Lansdowne mss 1236, ff 246–9
44 Churchill: op. cit., II, 476
45 Burnet: op. cit., V, 380
46 Connell: *Anne*, 203
47 Coxe: *Memoirs of John Duke of Marlborough* II, 360
48 Ibid, II, 362
49 Sarah Marlborough: *Corresp*. I, 412–6
50 Swift: *Prose* V, 369
51 HMC Portland IV
52 HMC X, App. 5, 49
53 Portland mss at Longleat X, f 59
54 HMC Portland IV, 510–1
55 Blenheim E 19
56 Blenheim G–I–8
57 Blenheim Long Library mss
58 Boyer *Annals*
59 Luttrell: op. cit. (30 Oct. 1708)
60 BM Add. mss 37357, f 7

CHAPTER TEN – BEHIND THE FAÇADE

1 Sharp: op. cit., 331
2 Churchill: op. cit., II, 486
3 PRO Baschet Transcript 31/3/195
4 Portland mss at Longleat, VI

5 Wentworth Papers, 75
6 HMC Portland IV, 519–20
7 BM Add. mss 37357, ff 25, 45, 104, 113
8 Churchill: op. cit., II, 548
9 Blenheim E 26
10 Wentworth Papers, 89
11 Churchill: op. cit., II, 650
12 Ibid, 651
13 Burnet: op. cit., V, 440, f.n.
14 Blenheim G–I–7
15 Blenheim E 20
16 Sarah Marlborough *Corresp.* I, 255–6
17 Blenheim E 27
18 Blenheim E 25
19 HMC Portland IV, 524–5
20 Blenheim E 18
21 Wentworth Papers, 98
22 Blenheim G–I–8
23 Churchill: op. cit., II, 640–1
24 Portland mss at Longleat, VI
25 HMC Portland IV, 530
26 Hamilton: *Diary*, f 4
27 Blenheim G–I–8
28 HMC III, 270
29 Wentworth Papers, 105
30 Hamilton: *Diary*, f 5
31 Wentworth Papers, 111
32 Portland mss at Longleat, XI, f 51
33 HMC Portland IV, 534
34 Swift: *Memoirs Relating to That Change . . .*
35 Blenheim G–I–8
36 Boyer *Annals*
37 HMC Portland IV, 536
38 Coke: op. cit., III, 376
39 *Conduct*
40 Hamilton: *Diary*, f 28
41 Blenheim E 27
42 & 43 *Conduct*
44 HMC Portland IV, 540
45 Holmes: op. cit., 379

46 PRO SP 44/108, ff 211–2
47 *Macbeth* prologue, quoted Garratt: *The Four Indian Kings* (History Today, Feb. 1968)
48 Coke: op. cit., III, 382
49 Churchill: op. cit., II, 709
50 Hamilton: *Diary*, f 12
51 Brown: op. cit., 303–4
52 Burnet: op. cit., VI, 7
53 HMC Portland V, 647, quoted Churchill II, 739
54 Hamilton: *Diary*, f 14
55 HMC Portland IV, 213
56 Brown: op. cit., 305
57 Hamilton: *Diary*, ff 66–7

CHAPTER ELEVEN – THE GREAT CHANGE

1 Orrery: *Letters to his Son*, 5
2 & 3 HMC Portland IV, 29, 38
4 HMC Portland II
5 Hamilton: *Diary*, f 18
6 Earl Cowper: *Diary*
7 HMC Portland IV, 585
8 Wentworth Papers, 143
9 BM Stowe mss 223, f 408
10 Ibid, ff 372–7
11 PRO Baschet Transcript 31/3/196, ff 118, 122
12 HMC Portland IV (18 Nov. 1710)
13 HMC Portland II
14 *Examiner* No. 13 (2 Nov. 1710)
15 *Examiner* No. 16 (23 Nov. 1710)
16 Blenheim G–I–8
17 Earl Cowper: *Diary* (14 Oct. 1710)
18 Hamilton: *Diary*, f 29
19 Churchill: op. cit., II, 791–2
20 Ibid, 798
21 Coxe: op. cit., III, 175
22 Blenheim G–I–8
23 Churchill: op. cit., II, 797
24 Blenheim G–I–8
25 Hamilton: *Diary*, f 29
26 Churchill: op. cit., II, 799–800

27 Bath mss at Longleat (Harley, unclassified)
28 Swift: *Memoirs*
29 Churchill: op. cit., II, 876
30 BM Stowe mss 241, f 142
31 Bath mss at Longleat (Harley: anon.)
32 Hopkinson: *Anne of England*
33 Boyer *Annals*
34 PRO SP 44/110, ff 306, 425 & SP 44/112, ff 45–8
35 Elizabeth Hamilton: op. cit., 176
36 Boyer *Annals*
37 Stanhope: op. cit., 476
38 Holmes: op. cit., 197
39 PRO SP 44/111, f 128
40 Luttrell: op. cit.
41 Burnet: op. cit., VI, 39
42 HMC Bath I (25 Apr. 1711)
43 Bath mss at Longleat (Harley: anon.)
44 Swift: *An Enquiry Into the Behaviour of the Queen's Last Ministry*, 333 et seq
45 Hamilton: *Diary*, f 31
46 Wentworth Papers, 188, 215
47 HMC Bath I (26 Apr. 1711)
48 PRO SP 44 116
49 & 50 PRO Baschet transcript 31/3/197
51 Boyer *Annals* IX (dedication)
52 HMC Portland V, 464
53 Blenheim E 25
54 Swift: *Journal to Stella*, 336 (19 Aug. 1711)
55 Blenheim E 5
56 Hamilton: *Diary*, ff 31, 36–7

CHAPTER TWELVE – THE PEACEMAKERS

1 HMC Bath I (21 Aug. 1711)
2 & 3 Swift: *Journal to Stella* I, 324, 328
4 Boyer *Annals* X
5 & 6 PRO Baschet Transcript 31/3/197
7 Portland mss at Longleat III
8 Brown: op. cit., 340–1
9 Swift: *Journal to Stella* II, 372
10 Coke: op. cit., III, 412–3

11 Swift: *Journal to Stella* II, 378
12 PRO SP 44/111
13 BM Lansdowne mss 1236, f 277
14 Brown: op. cit., 355
15 HMC Portland V
16 Hamilton: *Diary*, f 33
17 Boyer *Annals*
18 HMC Portland V
19 Swift: *Journal to Stella* II, 444
20 Burnet: op. cit., VI, 36
21 Swift: *Journal to Stella* II, 451
22 Hamilton: *Diary*, f 38
23 BM Stowe mss 241, f 195 (8 Jan. 1712)
24 Wentworth Papers, 252, 257
25 Swift: *Journal to Stella* I, 452–3
26 HMC XII, App. 2, 99–100
27 Swift: *Journal to Stella* I, 480–1
28 Portland mss at Longleat VI
29 Macpherson: *Original Papers* II, 295
30 & 31 PRO Baschet Transcript 31/3/198
32 Earl Cowper: *Diary*
33 HMC Portland V
34 Johnson: *An Account of the Life of Dr Samuel Johnson*
35 Swift: *Journal to Stella* I, 488
36 Wentworth Papers, 285
37 HMC Portland V, 15
38 Ibid, 142
39 Bolingbroke: *A Dissertation On Parties*
40 HMC Hardwicke II, 482
41 Stanhope: op. cit., 522–3
42 Burnet: op. cit., VI, 119
43 Elizabeth Hamilton: op. cit., 225
44 Stanhope: op. cit., 526
45 PRO SP 44/112, ff 515–6

CHAPTER THIRTEEN – THE RIVALS

1 PRO Baschet Transcript 31/3/199
2 Boyer *Annals* XI
3 BM Stowe mss 241, f 238
4 HMC Portland V

5 Wilkins: *Political Ballads*
6 BM Add. mss 22226, f 221
7 Swift: *Journal to Stella* I, 557
8 Burnet: op. cit., VI, 133
9 Boyer *Annals*
10 HMC Portland V, 237
11 Hamilton: *Diary*, ff 44, 46
12 Ibid, ff 46–7
13 Brown: op. cit., 382
14 Hamilton: *Diary*, f 46
15 Boyer *Annals*
16 Brown: op. cit., 390
17 Ibid, 393
18 Ibid
19 Swift: *Journal to Stella* I, 206
20 Swift: *An Enquiry Into the Behaviour* . . . 288–9
21 & 22 PRO Baschet Transcript 31/3/200
23 Swift: *Journal to Stella* I, 658–9
24 Sarah Marlborough: *Letters at Madresfield Court*, 72
25 BM Add. mss 22226, f 252
26 Hamilton: *Diary*, ff 49–52
27 HMC Portland V
28 Swift: *Journal to Stella* I, 589, 593
29 PRO Baschet Transcript 31/3/201
30 Swift: *Journal to Stella* I, 604
31 BM Add. mss 22226
32 Swift: *Journal to Stella* I, 635
33 & 34 Wilkins: op. cit.
35 Hamilton: *Diary*, f 53
36 Ibid, f 54
37 Wickham Legg: *Jacobite Corresp*. (EHR XXX, 503)
38 Swift: *Journal to Stella* I, 645, 658, 661
39 HMC Bath I (5 May 1713)
40 PRO SP 44/113, ff 408–9
41 Vanbrugh: *Letters* (ed. Webb), 54
42 BM Stowe mss 751, f 39
43 Blenheim G–I–9
44 Hamilton: *Diary*, ff 47–8

CHAPTER FOURTEEN – TEMPESTUOUS STATION

1 Hamilton: *Diary*, f 56
2 & 3 HMC XI, V, 315–6
4 Hamilton: *Diary*, f 57
5 Ibid, f 59
6 Burnet: op. cit., VI, 167
7 Hamilton: *Diary*, f 59
8 PRO Baschet Transcript 31/3/201
9 Hamilton: *Diary*, f 66
10 Brown: op. cit., 401
11 Bolingbroke: *Letter to Sir William Wyndham*, 20
12, 13 & 14 HMC Portland V
15 Holmes: op. cit., 193
16 HMC Portland V, 308
17 Ibid (18 July 1713)
18 BM Stowe mss 242, f 14
19 HMC V, 240 (Nov. 1713)
20 HMC Portland VII
21 HMC Portland V
22 Macpherson: *Original Papers* II, 512
23 Brown: op. cit., 403
24 HMC Bath I (22 Dec. 1713)
25 Hamilton: *Diary*, f 60
26 Coke: op. cit., II, 462
27 HMC XIV, App. 3, 225
28 HMC Portland V
29 Ibid
30 Boyer *History*, 655
31 Coke: op. cit., 463
32 Hamilton: *Diary*, f 61
33 HMC Buccleuch I, 361
34 & 35 BM Add. mss 49970
36 Bolingbroke: *Letter to Sir William Wyndham*, 26
37 Wickham Legg: *Jacobite Corresp.* (EHR XXX, 501–18)
38 Churchill: op. cit., II, 1001
39 *Flying Post* No. 3462 (11 March 1714)
40 HMC XV, App. 7, 22
41 Boyer *History*
42 Wickham Legg: op. cit., 516

43 HMC Portland V, 400
44 BM Loan 29/10/10
45 HMC Portland V, 403
46 Ibid, 405
47 Boyer *History*
48 BM Stowe mss 242, f 73

CHAPTER FIFTEEN – THE NICE AND TENDER THREAD

1 Boyer *History*
2 HMC Portland V, 416–7
3 BM Stowe mss 242, ff 94–7
4 HMC Portland V, App.
5 Blenheim E 43
6 BM Loan 29/10/9
7 Hamilton: *Diary*, f 54
8 HMC Portland V, 412
9 BM Loan 29/10/8
10 PRO Baschet Transcript 31/3/202
11 Wickham Legg: op. cit., 517
12 HMC Portland V
13 Ibid
14 Hamilton: *Diary*, f 62
15 Ward: *The Electress Sophia*, 422
16 BM Stowe mss 242, f 130
17 Ibid, ff 115–7
18 Hamilton: *Diary* f 63
19 BM Stowe mss 242, ff 145–6
20 HMC Portland V (8 May 1714)
21 Boyer *History*
22 PRO Baschet Transcript 31/3/202
23 HMC Portland V, 460
24 Pope: *The Rape of the Lock*
25 PRO Baschet Transcript 31/3/203
26 Wentworth Papers, 387
27 BM Stowe mss 242, f 120
28 Michael: op. cit., 40
29 Boyer *History*. See also PRO SP 44/114
30 Hamilton: *Diary*, f 65
31 BM Loan 29/10/8
32 Swift: *Letters*
33 BM Loan 29/10/8

34 Churchill: op. cit., II, 1008
35 PRO SP 44/116
36 Hamilton: *Diary* f 67
37 Ibid ff 67–8
38 Swift: *Letters* (Lewis to Swift, 27 July 1714)
39 Defoe: *The Secret History of the White Staff*
40 Hamilton: *Diary* f 68
41 Boyer *History*
42 Swift: *Letters*
43 Defoe: op. cit. (*White Staff*)
44 Bolingbroke: *Letter to Sir William Wyndham*, 28
45 HMC Portland V, 477
46 Wentworth Papers, 406–8
47 Swift: *Letters*
48 Trevelyan: op. cit. (*The Peace*), 326
49 Swift: *Works* (ed. Scott) XVI, 174
50 Wentworth Papers 408–9
51 Swift: *Letters*
52 Wentworth Papers 416
53 PRO SP 44/116
54 Michael: op. cit., 62
55 Hamilton: *Diary* ff 69–70

EPILOGUE

1 HMC XIV, App. 3, 457
2 PRO Baschet Transcript 31/3/203
3 HMC XII, App. 7, 66
4 PRO Cal. Treasury Books XXIX, 1, 197–203
5 PRO SP XXXV, I, 24
6 Sarah Marlborough: *Corresp.* II, 146
7 Swift: *Letters* II, 221–2
8 HMC XI, App. 4, 244
9 Defoe: *White Staff* II, 38
10 PRO Baschet Transcript 31/3/203
11 BM Add. mss 49970
12 Churchill: op. cit., II, 1021–3
13 Plumb: *The Growth of Political Stability*, 159
14 Sichel: *Bolingbroke*, 520
15 Johnson: *Works* VI, 4–9
16 Michael: op. cit., 60
17 Brown: op. cit., 232

Acknowledgments

This biography, which marks the culmination of some twenty years' research at Blenheim, is gratefully dedicated to the Duke of Marlborough. For unrestricted access to his muniment room I have already, in my books on Blenheim, on Wise and Gibbons and more recently on Sarah Duchess of Marlborough, attempted to express my thanks. With Queen Anne the case has been a little different; because not only did this call for extensive quotation from her unpublished letters at Blenheim, but also for the loan of printed works from the Duke's private library. It meant, for example, daily access over a period of months to the 165 volumes published by the Historical Manuscripts Commission. Far from telephones and from the invigilators who still, in some London research-rooms marked SILENCE, use them, one was able in the Long Library to concentrate on, say, Bath I or Portland IV. This was a privilege indeed and I am most grateful for it.

To Mr Geoffrey Holmes I owe a double debt. With his definitive *British Politics in the Age of Anne* he has not only written the standard work on that complex subject, but has made it unnecessary for a biographer of Anne to probe afresh into those issues which he has already researched in depth and clarified. My second debt to Mr Holmes is yet larger, for he it was who drew my attention to Sir David Hamilton's diary, now lodged in the Hertfordshire Record Office: a 70-page manuscript which reasonably could, on its own merits, be taken to warrant a re-assessment of Anne.

At Longleat – a delightful place to work in – I am grateful to the Marquess of Bath, to Mr Tiffen and to Colonel Ingles.

At the British Museum my thanks are due to the Keeper of Manuscripts Mr T. C. Skeat and his staff; at the Public Record Office to Mr Noel Blakiston, who brought to my notice the invaluable Baschet transcripts of papers in the Paris archives; at the National Register of Archives to Mr Murray Baillie; at the Bodleian Library to the Keeper of Western Manuscripts and his assistants, notably Mrs Roger Green; and at the London Library to the Librarian and his staff.

For permission to quote from Sir David Hamilton's diary I am grateful to Lady Salmond and to the County Archivist Mr Peter Walne at the Hertfordshire County Record Office.

Q.A.

Outstanding among the printed works I have constantly needed to refer to have of course been *The Letters of Queen Anne* edited by Beatrice Curtis Brown, to whom I am greatly indebted; Sarah Marlborough's *Conduct*, Trevelyan's *England Under Queen Anne* and Sir Winston Churchill's *Marlborough His Life & Times*. For allowing me to quote freely from this last I am extremely grateful to the publishers George G. Harrap & Company.

For expert help in specialised fields I have had to resort to teams of experts; for example, in the matter of Anne's health and death (See Appendix I). On this topic alone I have frequently plagued my own doctor, Frank Bevan, and have written to others including Drs Ida Macalpine and Richard Hunter, Professor Chassar Moir, Professor Abe Goldberg and, in Rhodesia, Mr Barton Gilbert. For enlightenment on contemporary portraiture I have turned to Miss Margaret Toynbee and have not been disappointed. Her detective work in dating Anne's letters has seemed to me uncannily shrewd.

For permission to reproduce paintings I am indebted to Her Majesty the Queen, to Mr Oliver Millar, to Dr Roy Strong and Mr Donald Rex, to the Warden of All Souls, to the Duke of Marlborough, to Earl Spencer and, at the British Museum Print Room, to Mr Edward Croft-Murray. Dr Alexander de Rahm has been to untold trouble in the photographing of vast portraits and paintings.

But indeed I cannot hope to name all those who have helped me – about customs, about medicines, about what they ate and drank and read and talked about; but I would like specially to thank Miss Elizabeth Burton, who knows all those things and more and has been generous in sharing her knowledge. And at Blenheim, again, my thanks to Lord Blandford, to Mr W. L. Murdock, to Miss K. M. Gell and to Mr A. M. Illingworth. I would like to remember too Miss Anne Whiteman, who has lent me a small library of books and constantly advised me, Mr Howard Colvin, Mr Richard Ollard, Mr Richard Simon, Mr J. P. Kenyon, Mr Charles Parker, Miss Audrey Russell and Mrs Leslie Brammall.

As this book goes to press I find myself still further in debt to Mr Holmes, who has most generously agreed to read it in proof.

Index